Key Issues

THE ORIGIN OF LANGUAGE

Key Issues

THE ORIGIN OF LANGUAGE

Edited and Introduced by
ROY HARRIS
University of Oxford

Series Editor
Andrew Pyle
University of Bristol

THOEMMES PRESS

© Thoemmes Press 1996

Published in 1996 by
Thoemmes Press
11 Great George Street
Bristol BS1 5RR
England

ISBN
Paper: 1 85506 437 5
Cloth: 1 85506 438 3

The Origin of Language
Key Issues No. 7

British Library Cataloguing-in-Publication Data

A catalogue record of this title is available from the British Library

All rights reserved. No part of this publication may be reproduced, stored in a retrieval system, or transmitted in any way or by any means, electronic, mechanical, photocopying, recording or otherwise, without the written permission of the publisher.

Printed in Great Britain by Antony Rowe Ltd., Chippenham

CONTENTS

INTRODUCTION
by Roy Harris vii

1. INTRODUCTORY LECTURE (extracts)
   From *On the Study of Words* (1851), chap. 1
   by R. C. Trench 1

2. THE THEORETICAL STAGE, AND THE ORIGIN OF LANGUAGE
   From *Lectures on the Science of Language* (1861), Lecture 9
   by Friedrich Max Müller 7

3. ON LANGUAGE
   From *Language and Languages* (1865), chaps. 1–4
   by F. W. Farrar 42

4. ON THE ORIGIN OF LANGUAGE
   From *Fortnightly Review*, vol. 4 (1866)
   by Edward B. Tylor 81

5. THE ORIGIN OF LANGUAGE
   From *Westminster Review*, vol. 30 ns (1866)
   Anonymous 100

6. MENTAL POWERS
   From *Descent of Man* (1871), chap. 2
   by Charles Darwin 140

7. LECTURES ON MR. DARWIN'S PHILOSOPHY OF LANGUAGE
   From *Fraser's Magazine*, vols. 7 and 8 ns (1873)
   by Friedrich Max Müller 147

8. THE ORIGIN OF LANGUAGE
   From *Westminster Review*, vol. 102 (1874)
   Anonymous 234

9. PROFESSOR WHITNEY ON THE ORIGIN OF LANGUAGE
   From *Contemporary Review*, vol. 24 (1874)
   by *George H. Darwin* 277

10. NATURE AND ORIGIN OF LANGUAGE
    From *The Life and Growth of Language* (1875), chap. xiv
    by *W. D. Whitney* 291

11. THE SIMIAN TONGUE
    From *New Review*, vol. 4 (1891–2)
    by *R. L. Garner* 314

The pieces reprinted in this book have been taken from original copies and the different grammatical and stylistic arrangement of each has been preserved.

INTRODUCTION

Linguists of the present century have tended to be rather dismissive of the efforts of their predecessors to tackle the problem of the origin of language, and have treated the subject with scarcely veiled contempt. J. R. Firth, for example, gave the following derisive summary in his book *The Tongues of Men* (1937):

> There are many other theories of the origin of speech in the early history of man as man, but they are all guesswork or highly speculative. One theory is the *bow-wow* or *cuckoo* theory, which suggests that our first words were attempts to make noises similar to non-human noises on the air, and hence *quack-quack*, *tick-tack* and such bird names as *cuckoo* and *kittiwake*. The *pooh-pooh* theory is based on emotional interjections and exclamations evoked by events or caused by pain or pleasure. Hence *oo-er!*, *oh!*, *ah!*, *ssh!* Max Müller's theory was called the *ding-dong* theory, based on the view that language relates us closely to the whole of sentient nature by the harmony of sound and sense. 'Feel not for thyself alone but let thy feeling resound' (Herder, 1722). By means of the hissing sibilants, the murmuring *m*'s, the fluent liquids, the sudden plosives, men *ding-donged* phonetically to their environment. The *yo-he-ho* theory scorns primitive onomatopoeia and echoism, and suggests that strong or difficult muscular effort, and particularly rhythmical efforts, are usually accompanied by the intermittent valvular action of the glottis, tongue, lips or soft palate – that is, by alternately holding the breath and letting it go, sometimes vibrating the cords and producing voice. This theory is much more social, and emphasizes noises that would accompany mating, feeding, fighting, flight, and festal occasions. Here come the *heave, back, yum-yum, yo-he-ho,* and *ta-ra-ra-boom-de-ay* words.

More recently another form of gesture theory has been advanced by Sir Richard Paget. According to this *ta-ta* theory, the tongue makes the same gesture while saying *ta-ta* as would be made by the hand with similar intention; but you need not wag your hand, your friend hears you wag your tongue to the same effect.

Most of these theories are much too narrow to be in any way satisfying, and, even if we add them all together, the sum total falls so far short of any acceptable theory of a thorough-going social and practical character that we must leave them behind.[1]

What is also left behind, unfortunately, in dismissive accounts of this kind is any chance of understanding the important issues. How exactly was the question of the origin of language understood by those who debated it? What was the relevant intellectual context? Why was the range of answers on offer so narrow? In ignoring these questions, Firth and others have been guilty of reducing an interesting chapter in the history of ideas to the level of parody.

Although the question of the origin of language had been discussed for centuries in the Western tradition, at no time did the debate become more passionate than during the nineteenth century. It raged to such an extent that in 1866 the Société de linguistique de Paris instituted a regulation refusing to accept any paper on that subject for presentation or discussion. Ostensibly the reason for this rejection could be explained by reference to the speculative nature of the topic. But the reason for the passion aroused by this speculation was different. What was at stake was the most crucial social, religious, academic and political issue of the day: the credibility of the Biblical account of creation, as opposed to the Darwinian theory of evolution.

The two key passages in the Bible which touch on questions of language are both in the Book of Genesis.

> And out of the ground the Lord God formed every beast of the field, and every fowl of the air; and brought them unto Adam to see what he would call them: and whatsoever Adam called every living creature, that was the name thereof.

---

[1] J. R. Firth, *The Tongues of Men* and *Speech*, London: Oxford University Press, 1964, pp. 25–6.

> And Adam gave names to all cattle, and to the fowl of the air, and to every beast of the field.
>
> (Genesis 2, 19–20)

It is interesting to note that this story offers no explanation of why Adam chose the names he did, but it does by implication offer a primitive theory of lexical meaning. It suggests that the basic semantic process is one in which words have the function of designating things already given in advance of their being named.

The second passage from Genesis relates to a later phase of human history, after the expulsion from the Garden of Eden and the Flood. Here we have a story which supplements the first by offering an explanation of the diversity of human speech.

> And the whole earth was of one language, and of one speech.
>
> And it came to pass, as they journeyed from the east, that they found a plain in the land of Shinar; and they dwelt there.
>
> And they said, one to another, Go to, let us make brick, and burn them thoroughly. And they had brick for stone, and slime had they for morter.
>
> And they said, Go to, let us build us a city and a tower, whose top may reach unto heaven; and let us make us a name, lest we be scattered abroad upon the face of the whole earth.
>
> And the Lord came down to see the city and the tower, which the children of men builded.
>
> And the Lord said, Behold, the people is one, and they have all one language; and this they begin to do: and now nothing will be restrained from them, which they have imagined to do.
>
> Go to, let us go down, and there confound their language, that they may not understand one another's speech.
>
> So the Lord scattered them abroad from thence upon the face of all the earth: and they left off to build the city.
>
> Therefore is the name of it called Babel; because the Lord did there confound the language of all the earth: and from thence did the Lord scatter them abroad upon the face of all the earth.
>
> (Genesis 11, 1–9)

In both these passages, the Biblical narrative invokes divine intervention to supply an answer to an otherwise puzzling linguistic question. But the first point to note is that the account provided is one which leaves so many gaps that it can hardly stand as a theory of the origin of *language*. However plausible an inventory of names for animals and birds may be as a prototype of one part of speech, a communication system with just one part of speech would hardly count as a language.

The significance of this has been ignored by later commentators. The reason why nineteenth-century speculations can easily be ridiculed as trying to conjure language out of primitive calls, grunts and ejaculations is the obvious gap which separates these from grammatically structured sentences. But the combat between those who supported and those who rejected the Biblical account was not fought out on the field of syntax (concerning which the Bible said nothing). The more fundamental question was whether it was possible to explain 'by natural causes' what the Bible explained as a divinely prompted intellectual feat of nomenclature. And here the force of invoking such factors as vocal imitation and expression of emotion was precisely that these, unlike the invention of names, were not unique to *homo sapiens*. In short, the strategy of those who did not accept the story in Genesis 2 was to push back the initial question one stage further and ask what preceded the first names.

What the Bible tells us invites a conflation between what are actually two distinct questions: (i) how our earliest ancestors developed a form of vocal communication, and (ii) what the original language of mankind was. These two questions were still often confused in the nineteenth century. A further distinction also blurred was that between the origin of language and the origin of speech: again, it is significant that the Bible assumes these to be one and the same. Finally, the Biblical scenario can be seen as the source of what Hensleigh Wedgwood called 'the German paradox'. As stated by Humboldt, it ran as follows: 'Man is only man through speech, but in order to discover speech he must already be man.' Specifically, according to the Bible, Adam already spoke before there was any *social* necessity for so doing (for at that stage he was the sole human being). Many concluded that this meant there was no time in pre-history when man lacked speech. This was the view accepted, for instance, by Müller, who regarded any attempt to explain how human beings emerged from an original 'state of mutism' as a complete misconception of the problem.

The historical validity of the Biblical account had been called in question since the eighteenth century, both in Britain and on the Continent. The obvious alternative to the story of Adam's exploits in nomenclature was to suppose that language had gradually emerged in response to human communicational needs. Adam Smith had written *Considerations concerning the First Formation of Languages and the Different Genius of Original and Compounded Languages*, an essay supplementing his *Theory of Moral Sentiments* (1759), in which he endeavoured to show that it was possible to account for the birth of language rationally, without treating it as a mysterious divine gift or appealing to any special innate language faculty. In 1773, Monboddo had brought out his controversial *Origin and Progress of Language*, which represented mankind as emerging gradually from conditions of existence and a state of intelligence not far removed from those of apes. So the ground was in certain respects already prepared for a Darwinian view of the continuity between animal communication and human language well in advance of Darwin.

However, the argument was not all on one side. Defenders of the Bible were not slow to appeal to the evidence supplied by the newly established 'science of language'. In his *Lectures on the Connexion between Science and Revealed Religion* (1836), Nicolas Wiseman argued that the recent discoveries of linguists supported in all essentials the Biblical version of events. As the basis for his case, Wiseman pointed out, in the first place, that comparative philology had now demonstrated the common origin of languages which might otherwise have seemed unconnected. But, at the same time, he found it significant that the application of the comparative method conspicuously failed to explain the divergence between the linguistic archetypes at the origin of the various language families thus identified. He argued from this that it was reasonable to hypothesize a 'violent and sudden cause' for the diversity of languages – a conclusion eminently compatible with the story of Babel.

The most controversial contribution to the debate before the intervention of Darwin was the appearance in 1844 of an anonymous work entitled *Vestiges of the Natural History of*

Creation. Its author (later revealed to be Robert Chambers) used linguistic evidence to support an argument based mainly on astronomical and geological considerations. He concluded that language was a human invention and that the difference between animal communication and human communication was one of degree rather than of kind.

For Darwin himself, the question of the origin of language was of marginal rather than central importance, and his views on the subject are stated simply, concisely and modestly. It is evident from what he writes in *The Descent of Man* (1871) that his main concern was not to attack the Biblical account of glottogenesis as such, nor even to solve the puzzle of the origin of language, but rather to establish that the possession by man of the faculty of language was not in itself counterevidence to 'the belief that man has developed from some lower form'.

Apart from Darwin, notable academic participants in the discussion included Friedrich Max Müller (1823–1900), who held the Chair of Comparative Philology at Oxford, William Dwight Whitney (1827–1894), who was Professor of Sanskrit at Yale, and Edward Burnett Tylor (1832–1917), who became Oxford's first Professor of Anthropology in 1895.

As the contributions selected for this volume demonstrate, the glottogenetic debate continued throughout the nineteenth century. It remains unresolved today, although its focus has shifted away from the Bible. But the underlying issue is still the one which Darwin brought to the fore: whether language is, as Müller once put it, the Rubicon which separates the human race from other species. R. L. Garner's claims in the 1890s to have discovered that apes could use 'words' foreshadow the controversies which surround twentieth-century attempts to demonstrate that they can be taught the rudiments of human language.

Roy Harris
Professor Emeritus, University of Oxford, 1996

EXTRACT FROM 'INTRODUCTORY LECTURE'
R. C. Trench

But the truer answer to the inquiry how language arose, is this, that God gave man language, just as He gave him reason, and just because He gave him reason (for what is man's word but his reason coming forth, so that it may behold itself?) that He gave it to him, because he could not be man, that is, a social being, without it. Yet this must not be taken to affirm that man started at the first furnished with a full-formed vocabulary of words, and as it were with his first dictionary and first grammar ready-made to his hands. He did not thus begin the world *with names*, but *with the power of naming*: for man is not a mere speaking machine; God did not teach him words, as one of us teaches a parrot, from without; but gave him a capacity, and then evoked the capacity which He gave. Here, as in everything else that concerns the primitive constitution, the great original institutes of humanity, our best and truest lights are to be gotten from the study of the three first chapters of Genesis; and you will observe that there it is not God who imposed the first names on the creatures, but Adam – Adam, however, at the direct suggestion of his Creator. *He* brought them all, we are told, to Adam, 'to see what he would call them, and whatsoever Adam called every living creature, that was the name thereof.' (Gen. ii. 19.) Here we have the clearest intimation of the origin, at once divine and human, of speech; while yet neither is so brought forward as to exclude or obscure the other.

And so far we may concede a limited amount of right to those who have held a progressive acquisition, on man's part, of the power of embodying thought in words. I believe that we should conceive the actual case most truly, if we conceived this power of naming things and expressing their relations, as one laid up in the depths of man's being, one of the divine capacities with which he was created: but one, (and in this differing from those which have produced in various people

2 The Origin of Language

various arts of life,) which could not remain dormant in him, for man could be only man through its exercise; which therefore did rapidly bud and blossom out from within him at every solicitation from the world without, or from his fellow-man; as each object to be named appeared before his eyes, each relation of things to one another arose before his mind. It was not merely the possible, but the necessary, emanation of the spirit with which he had been endowed. Man makes his own language, but he makes it as the bee makes its cells, as the bird its nest.

How this latent power evolved itself first, how this spontaneous generation of language came to pass, is a mystery, even as every act of creation is of necessity such; and as a mystery all the deepest inquirers into the subject are content to leave it. Yet we may perhaps a little help ourselves to the realizing of what the process was, and what it was not, if we liken it to the growth of a tree springing out of, and unfolding itself from, a root, and according to a necessary law – that root being the divine capacity of language with which man was created, that law being the law of highest reason with which he was endowed: if we liken it to this rather than to the rearing of an house, which a man should slowly and painfully fashion for himself with dead timbers combined after his own fancy and caprice; and which little by little improved in shape, material and size, being first but a log-house, answering his barest needs, and only after centuries of toil and pain growing for his sons' sons into a stately palace for pleasure and delight.

Were it otherwise, were the savage the primitive man, we should then find savage tribes furnished, scantily enough, it might be, with the elements of speech, yet at the same time with its fruitful beginnings, its vigorous and healthful germs. But what does their language on close inspection prove? In every case what they are themselves, the remnant and ruin of a better and a nobler past. Fearful indeed is the impress of degradation which is stamped on the language of the savage, more fearful perhaps even than that which is stamped upon his form. When wholly letting go the truth, when long and greatly sinning against light and conscience, a people has thus gone the downward way, has been scattered off by some violent revolution from that portion of the world which is the seat of advance and progress, and driven to its remote isles and further corners, then as one nobler thought, one spiritual idea after another has perished from it, the words also that expressed these have perished too. As one habit of civilization has been let go after another, the words which those habits demanded have dropped as well, first out of use, and then out of memory, and thus after awhile have been wholly lost.

Moffat, in his *Missionary Labours and Scenes in South Africa*, gives us a very remarkable example of the disappearing of one of the most significant words from the language of a tribe sinking ever deeper in savagery; and with the disappearing of the word, of course, the disappearing as well of the great spiritual fact and truth whereof that word was at once the vehicle and the guardian. The Bechuanas, a Caffre tribe, employed formerly the word 'Morimo,' to designate 'Him that is above,' or 'Him that is in heaven,' and attached to the word the notion of a supreme Divine Being. This word, with the spiritual idea corresponding to it, Moffat found to have vanished from the language of the present generation, although here and there he could meet with an old man, scarcely one or two in a thousand, who remembered in his youth to have heard speak of 'Morimo;' and this word, once so deeply significant, only survived now in the spells and charms of the so-called rainmakers and sorcerers, who misused it to designate a fabulous ghost, of whom they told the absurdest and most contradictory things.

And as there is no such witness to the degradation of the savage as the brutal poverty of his language, so is there nothing that so effectually tends to keep him in the depths to which he has fallen. You cannot impart to any man more than the words which he understands either now contain, or can be made, intelligibly to him, to contain. Language is as truly on one side the limit and restraint of thought, as on the other side that which feeds and unfolds thought. Thus it is the ever-repeated complaint of the missionary that the very terms are well nigh or wholly wanting in the dialect of the savage whereby to impart to him heavenly truths, or indeed even the nobler emotions of the human heart. Dobrizhoffer, the Jesuit missionary, in his curious *History of the Abipones*, tells us that neither these nor the Guarinies, two of the principal native tribes of Brazil, possessed any word in the least corresponding to our 'thanks.' But what wonder, if the feeling of gratitude was entirely absent from their hearts, that they should not have possessed the corresponding word in their vocabularies? Nay, how should they have had it there? And that this is the true explanation is plain from a fact which the same writer records, that although inveterate askers, they never showed the slightest sense of obligation or of gratitude, when they obtained what they sought; never saying more than, 'This will be useful to me,' or, 'This is what I wanted.'

Nor is it only in what they have forfeited and lost, but also in what they have retained or invented, that these languages proclaim their degradation and debasement, and how deeply they and those that speak them have fallen. Thus I have read of a tribe in New Holland, which has no word to signify God, but has one to designate a process by which an unborn child may be destroyed in the bosom of its mother. And I have been informed, on the authority of one excellently capable of knowing, an English scholar long resident in Van Diemen's Land, that in the native language of that island there are four words to express the taking of human life – one to express a father's killing of a son, another a son's killing of a father, with other varieties of murder; and that in no one of these lies the slightest moral reprobation, or sense of the deep-lying distinction between to 'kill' and to 'murder;' while at the same time, of that language so richly and so fearfully provided with expressions for this extreme utterance of hate, he also reports that any word for 'love' is wanting in it altogether.

Yet with all this, ever and anon in the midst of this wreck and ruin there is that in the language of the savage, some subtle distinction, some curious allusion to a perished civilization, now utterly unintelligible to the speaker; or some other note which proclaims his language to be the remains of a dissipated inheritance, the rags and remnants of a robe which was a royal one once. The fragments of a broken sceptre are in his hand, a sceptre wherewith once he held dominion (he, that is, in his progenitors) over large kingdoms of thought, which now have escaped wholly from his sway.

But while it is thus with him, while this is the downward course of all those that have chosen the downward path, while with every impoverishing and debasing of personal or national life there goes hand in hand a corresponding impoverishment and debasement of language, so on the contrary, where there is advance and progress, where a divine idea is in any measure realizing itself in a people, where they are learning more accurately to define and distinguish, more truly to know, where they are ruling, as men ought to rule, over nature, and making her to give up her secrets to them, where new thoughts are rising up over the horizon of a nation's mind, new feelings are stirring at a nation's heart, new facts coming within the sphere of its knowledge, there will language be growing and advancing too. It cannot lag behind; for man feels that nothing is properly his own, that he has not secured any new thought, or entered upon any new spiritual inheritance, till he has fixed it in language, till he can contemplate it, not as himself, but as his word; he is conscious that he must express truth, if he is to preserve it, and still more if he would propagate it among others. 'Names,' as it has been excellently said, 'are impressions of sense, and as such take the strongest hold upon the mind, and of all other impressions can be most easily recalled and retained in view. They therefore serve to give a point of attachment to all the more volatile objects of thought and feeling. Impressions that when past might be dissipated for ever, are by their connexion with language always within reach. Thoughts, of themselves, are perpetually slipping out of the field of immediate mental vision; but the name abides with us, and the utterance of it restores them in a moment.' And on the necessity of names for the propagation of the truth it has been well observed: 'Hardly any original thoughts on mental or social subjects ever make their way among mankind, or assume their proper importance in the minds even of their inventors, until aptly selected words or phrases have as it were nailed them down and held them fast.'

Nor does what has here been said of the manner in which language enriches itself contradict a prior assertion that man starts with language as God's perfect gift, which he only impairs and forfeits by sloth and sin, according to the same law which holds good in respect of each other of the gifts of heaven. For it was not meant, as indeed was then observed, that men would possess words to set forth feelings which were not yet stirring in them, combinations which they had not yet made, objects which they had not yet seen, relations of which they were not yet conscious; but that up to his needs, (those needs including not merely his animal wants, but all his higher spiritual cravings,) he would find utterance freely. The great logical, or grammatical, framework of language, (for grammar is the logic of speech, even as logic is the grammar of reason,) he would possess, he knew not how; and certainly not as the final result of gradual acquisitions, but as that rather which alone had made those acquisitions possible; as that according to which he unconsciously worked, filling in this framework by degrees with these later acquisitions of thought, feeling, and experience, as one by one they arrayed themselves in the garment and vesture of words.

Here then is the explanation of the fact that language should be thus instructive for us, that it should yield us so much, when we come to analyse and probe it; and yield us the more, the more deeply and accurately we do so. It is full of instruction, because it is the embodiment, the incarnation, if I may so speak, of the feelings and thoughts and experiences of a nation, yea, often of many nations, and of all which through long centuries they have attained to and won. It stands like the pillars of Hercules, to mark how far the moral and intellectual conquests of mankind have advanced, only not like those pillars, fixed and immovable, but ever itself advancing with the progress of these. The mighty moral instincts which have been working in the popular mind have found therein their unconscious voice; and the single kinglier spirits that have looked deeper into the heart of things, have oftentimes gathered up all they have seen into some one word, which they have launched upon the world, and with which they have enriched it for ever – making in that new word a new region of thought to be henceforward in some sort the common heritage of all. Language is the amber in which a thousand precious and subtle thoughts have been safely embedded and preserved. It has arrested ten thousand lightning flashes of genius, which, unless thus fixed and arrested, might have been as bright, but would have also been as quickly passing and perishing, as the lightning. 'Words convey the mental treasures of one period to the generations that follow; and laden with this, their previous freight, they sail safely across gulfs of time in which empires have suffered shipwreck, and the languages of common life have sunk into oblivion.' And for all these reasons far more and mightier in every way is a language than any one of the works which may have been composed in it. For that work, great as it may be, is but the embodying of the mind of a single man, this of a nation. *The Iliad* is great, yet not so great in strength or power or beauty as the Greek language. *Paradise Lost* is a noble possession for a people to have inherited, but the English tongue is a nobler heritage yet.

THE THEORETICAL STAGE, AND THE ORIGIN OF LANGUAGE
F. M. Müller

'In examining the history of mankind, as well as in examining the phenomena of the material world, when we cannot trace the process by which an event *has been* produced, it is often of importance to be able to show how it *may have been* produced by natural causes. Thus, although it is impossible to determine with certainty what the steps were by which any particular language was formed, yet if we can show, from the known principles of human nature, how all its various parts *might* gradually have arisen, the mind is not only to a certain degree satisfied, but a check is given to that indolent philosophy which refers to a miracle whatever appearances, both in the natural and moral worlds, it is unable to explain.'[1]

This quotation from an eminent Scotch philosopher contains the best advice that could be given to the student of the science of language, when he approaches the problem which we have to examine today, namely, the origin of language. Though we have stripped that problem of the perplexing and mysterious aspect which it presented to the philosophers of old, yet, even in its simplest form, it seems to be almost beyond the reach of the human understanding.

If we were asked the riddle how images of the eye and all the sensations of our senses could be represented by sounds, nay, could be so embodied in sounds as to express thought and excite thought, we should probably give it up as the question of a madman, who, mixing up the most heterogeneous subjects, attempted to change colour into sound and sound into thought.[2] Yet this is the riddle which we have now to solve.

---

[1] Dugald Stewart, vol. iii. p. 35.
[2] Herder, as quoted by Steinthal, 'Ursprung der Sprache,' s. 39.

It is quite clear that we have no means of solving the problem of the origin of language *historically*, or of explaining it as a matter of fact which happened once in a certain locality and at a certain time. History does not begin till long after mankind had acquired the power of language, and even the most ancient traditions are silent as to the manner in which man came in possession of his earliest thoughts and words. Nothing, no doubt, would be more interesting than to know from historical documents the exact process by which the first man began to lisp his first words, and thus to be rid for ever of all the theories on the origin of speech. But this knowledge is denied us; and, if it had been otherwise, we should probably be quite unable to understand those primitive events in the history of the human mind. We are told that the first man was the son of God, that God created him in His own image, formed him of the dust of the ground, and breathed into his nostrils the breath of life. These are simple facts, and to be accepted as such; if we begin to reason on them, the edge of the human understanding glances off. Our mind is so constituted that it cannot apprehend the absolute beginning or the absolute end of any thing. If we tried to conceive the first man created as a child, and gradually unfolding his physical and mental powers, we could not understand his living for *one* day without supernatural aid. If, on the contrary, we tried to conceive the first man created full-grown in body and mind, the conception of an effect without a cause, of a full-grown mind without a previous growth, would equally transcend our reasoning powers. It is the same with the first beginnings of language. Theologians who claim for language a divine origin drift into the most dangerous anthropomorphism, when they enter into any details as to the manner in which they suppose the Deity to have compiled a dictionary and grammar in order to teach them to the first man, as a schoolmaster teaches the deaf and dumb. And they do not see that, even if all their premises were granted, they would have explained no more than how the first man might have learnt a language, if there was a language ready made for him. How that languaage was made would remain as great a mystery as ever. Philosophers, on the contrary, who imagine that the first man, though left to himself, would gradually have emerged from a state of mutism and have invented words for every new conception that arose in his mind, forget that man could not by his own power have acquired *the faculty* of speech which is the distinctive character of mankind,[3] unattained and unattainable by the mute creation. It shows a want of appreciation as to the real bearings of our problem, if philosophers appeal to the fact that children are born without language, and gradually emerge from mutism to the full command of articulate speech. We want no explanation how birds learn to fly, created as they are with organs adapted to that purpose. Nor do we wish to inquire how children learn to use the various faculties with which the human body and soul are endowed. We want to gain, if possible, an insight into the original faculty of speech; and for that purpose I fear it is as useless to watch the first stammerings of children, as it would be to repeat the experiment of the Egyptian king who intrusted two new-born infants to a shepherd, with the injunction to let them suck a goat's milk, and to speak no word in their presence, but to observe what word they would first utter.[4] The same experiment is said to have been repeated by the Swabian emperor, Frederic II., by James IV. of Scotland, and by one of the Mogul emperors of India. But, whether for the purpose of finding out which was the primitive language of mankind, or of discovering how far language was natural to man, the experiments failed to throw any light on the problem before us. Children, in learning to speak, do not invent language. Language is there ready made for them. It has been there for thousands of years. They acquire the use of a language, and, as they grow up, they may acquire the use of a second and a third. It is useless to inquire whether infants, left to themselves, would invent a language. It would be impossible, unnatural, and illegal to try the experiment, and, without repeated experiments, the assertions of those who

[3] 'Der Mensch ist nur Mensch durch Sprache; um aber die Sprache zu erfinden, müsste er schon Mensch sein.' – W. *von Humboldt, Sämmtliche Werke*, b. iii. s. 252. The same argument is ridden to death by Süssmilch, 'Versuch eines Beweises dass die erste Sprache ihren Ursprung nicht vom Menschen, sondern allein vom Schöpher erhalten habe.' Berlin, 1766.

[4] Farar, Origin of Language, p. 10; Grimm, Ursprung der Sprache, s. 32. The word βεκός, which these children are reported to have uttered, and which, in the Phrygian language, meant bread, thus proving, it was supposed, that the Phrygian was the primitive language of mankind, is derived from the same root which exists in the English, to bake. How these unfortunate children came by the idea of baked bread, involving the ideas of corn, mill, oven, fire, &c., seems never to have struck the ancient sages of Egypt.

believe and those who disbelieve the possibility of children inventing a language of their own, are equally valueless. All we know for certain is, that an English child, if left to itself, would never begin to speak English, and that history supplies no instance of any language having thus been invented.

If we want to gain an insight into the faculty of flying, which is a characteristic feature of birds, all we can do is, first, to compare the structure of birds with that of other animals which are devoid of that faculty, and secondly, to examine the conditions under which the act of flying becomes possible. It is the same with speech. Speech is a specific faculty of man. It distinguishes man from all other creatures; and if we wish to acquire more definite ideas as to the real nature of human speech, all we can do is to compare man with those animals that seem to come nearest to him, and thus to try to discover what he shares in common with these animals, and what is peculiar to him and to him alone. After we have discovered this, we may proceed to inquire into the conditions under which speech becomes possible, and we shall then have done all that we can do, considering that the instruments of our knowledge, wonderful as they are, are yet far too weak to carry us into all the regions to which we may soar on the wings of our imagination.

In comparing man with the other animals, we need not enter here into the physiological questions whether the difference between the body of an ape and the body of a man is one of degree or of kind. However that question is settled by physiologists we need not be afraid. If the structure of a mere worm is such as to fill the human mind with awe, if a single glimpse which we catch of the infinite wisdom displayed in the organs of the lowest creature gives us an intimation of the wisdom of its Divine Creator far transcending the powers of our conception, who are we to criticise and disparage the most highly organised creatures of His creation, creatures as wonderfully made as we ourselves? Are there not many creatures on many points more perfect even than man? Do we not envy the lion's strength, the eagle's eye, the wings of every bird? If there existed animals altogether as perfect as man in their physical structure, nay, even more perfect, no thoughtful man would ever be uneasy. His true superiority rests on different grounds. 'I confess,' Sydney Smith writes, 'I feel myself so much at ease about the superiority of mankind – I have such a marked and decided contempt for the understanding of every baboon I have ever seen – I feel so sure that the blue ape without a tail will never rival us in poetry, painting, and music, that I see no reason whatever that justice may not be done to the few fragments of soul and tatters of understanding which they may really possess.' The playfulness of Sydney Smith in handling serious and sacred subjects has of late been found fault with by many: but humour is a safer sign of strong convictions and perfect safety than guarded solemnity.

With regard to our own problem, no one can doubt that certain animals possess all the physical requirements for articulate speech. There is no letter of the alphabet which a parrot will not learn to pronounce.[5] The fact, therefore, that the parrot is without a language of his own, must be explained by a difference between the *mental*, not between the *physical*, faculties of the animal and man; and it is by a comparison of the mental faculties alone, such as we find them in man and brutes, that we may hope to discover what constitutes the indispensable qualification for language, a qualification to be found in man alone, and in no other creature on earth.

I say *mental faculties*, and I mean to claim a large share of what we call our mental faculties for the higher animals. These animals have *sensation, perception, memory, will,* and *intellect*, only we must restrict intellect to the comparing or interlacing of single perceptions. All these points can be proved by irrefragable evidence, and that evidence has never, I believe, been summed up with greater lucidity and power than in one of the last publications of M. P. Flourens, 'De la Raison, du Génie, et de la Folie:' Paris, 1861. There are no doubt many people who are as much frightened at the idea that brutes have souls and are able to think, as by 'the blue ape without a tail.' But

---

[5] 'L'usage de la main, la marche à deux pieds, la ressemblance, quoique grossière, de la face, tous les actes qui peuvent résulter de cette conformité d'organisation, ont fait donner aux singe le nom d'*homme sauvage*, par des hommes à la vérité qui l'étaient à demi, et qui ne savaient comparer que les rapports extérieurs. Que serait-ce, si, par une combinaison de nature aussi possible que toute autre, le singe eût eu la voix du perroquet, et, comme lui, la faculté de la parole? Le singe parlant eût rendu muette d'étonnement l'espèce humaine entière, et l'aurait séduite au point que le philosophe aurait eu grand' peine à démontrer qu'avec tous ces beaux attributs humains le singe n'en était pas moins une bête. Il est donc heureux, pour notre intelligence, que la nature ait séparé et placé, dans deux espèces tres-différentes, l'imitation de la parole et celle de nos gestes.'
– *Buffon*, as quoted by Flourens, p. 77.

their fright is entirely of their own making. If people will use such words as soul or thought without making it clear to themselves and others what they mean by them, these words will slip away under their feet, and the result must be painful. If we once ask the question, Have brutes a soul? we shall never arrive at any conclusion; for *soul* has been so many times defined by philosophers from Aristotle down to Hegel, that it means everything and nothing. Such has been the confusion caused by the promiscuous employment of the ill-defined terms of mental philosophy that we find Descartes representing brutes as living machines, whereas Leibniz claims for them not only souls, but immortal souls. 'Next to the error of those who deny the existence of God,' says Descartes, 'there is none so apt to lead weak minds from the right path of virtue, as to think that the soul of brutes is of the same nature as our own; and, consequently, that we have nothing to fear or to hope after this life, any more than flies or ants; whereas, if we know how much they differ, we understand much better that *our* soul is quite independent of the body, and consequently not subject to die with the body.'

The spirit of these remarks is excellent, but the argument is extremely weak. It does not follow that brutes have no souls because they have no human souls. It does not follow that the souls of men are not immortal, because the souls of brutes are not immortal; nor has the *major premiss* ever been proved by any philosopher, namely, that the souls of brutes must necessarily be destroyed and annihilated by death. Leibniz, who has defended the immortality of the human soul with stronger arguments than even Descartes, writes: – 'I found at last how the souls of brutes and their sensations do not at all interfere with the immortality of human souls; on the contrary, nothing serves better to establish our natural immortality than to believe that all souls are imperishable.'

Instead of entering into these perplexities, which are chiefly due to the loose employment of ill-defined terms, let us simply look at the facts. Every unprejudiced observer will admit that –

1. Brutes see, hear, taste, smell, and feel; that is to say, they have five senses, just like ourselves, neither more nor less. They have both sensation and perception, a point which has been illustrated by M. Flourens by the most interesting experiments. If the roots of the optic nerve are removed, the retina

in the eye of a bird ceases to be excitable, the iris is no longer movable; the animal is blind, because it has lost the organ of *sensation*. If, on the contrary, the cerebral lobes are removed, the eye remains pure and sound, the retina excitable, the iris movable. The eye is preserved, yet the animal cannot see, because it has lost the organs of *perception*.

2. Brutes have sensations of pleasure and pain. A dog that is beaten behaves exactly like a child that is chastised, and a dog that is fed and fondled exhibits the same signs of satisfaction as a boy under the same circumstances. We can only judge from these signs, and if they are to be trusted in the case of children, they must be trusted likewise in the case of brutes.

3. Brutes do not forget, or as philosophers would say, brutes have memory. They know their masters, they know their home; they evince joy on recognising those who have been kind to them, and they bear malice for years to those by whom they have been insulted or ill-treated. Who does not recollect the dog Argos in the Odyssey, who, after so many years' absence, was the first to recognise Ulysses?[6]

4. Brutes are able to compare and to distinguish. A parrot will take up a nut, and throw it down again, without attempting to crack it. He has found that it is light; this he could discover only by comparing the weight of the good nuts with that of the bad: and he has found that it has no kernel; this he could discover only by what philosophers would dignify with the grand title of syllogism, namely, 'all light nuts are hollow; this is a light nut, therefore this nut is hollow.'

5. Brutes have a will of their own. I appeal to any one who has ever ridden a restive horse.

6. Brutes show signs of shame and pride. Here again any one who has had to deal with dogs, who has watched a retriever with sparkling eyes placing a partridge at his master's feet, or a hound slinking away with his tail between his legs from the huntsman's call, will agree that these signs admit of but one interpretation. The difficulty begins when we use philosophical language, when we claim for brutes a moral sense, a conscience, a power of distinguishing good and evil; and, as we gain nothing by these scholastic terms, it is better to avoid them altogether.

---

[6] Odyssey, xvii. 300.

7. Brutes show signs of love and hatred. There are well-authenticated stories of dogs following their masters to the grave, and refusing food from any one. Nor is there any doubt that brutes will watch their opportunity till they revenge themselves on those whom they dislike.

If, with all these facts before us, we deny that brutes have sensation, perception, memory, will, and intellect, we ought to bring forward powerful arguments for interpreting the signs which we observe in brutes so differently from those which we observe in men.

Some philosophers imagine they have explained everything, if they ascribe to brutes *instinct* instead of *intellect*. But, if we take these two words in their usual acceptations, they surely do not exclude each other.[7] There are instincts in man as well as in brutes. A child takes his mother's breast by instinct; the spider weaves its net by instinct; the bee builds her cell by instinct. No one would ascribe to the child a knowledge of physiology because it employs the exact muscles which are required for sucking; nor shall we claim for the spider a knowledge of mechanics, or for the bee an acquaintance with geometry, because *we* could not do what they do without a study of these sciences. But what if we tear a spider's web, and see the spider examining the mischief that is done, and either giving up his work in despair, or endeavouring to mend it as well as may be?[8] Surely here we have the instinct of weaving controlled by observation, by comparison, by reflection, by judgment. Instinct, whether mechanical or moral, is more prominent in brutes than in man; but it exists in both, as much as intellect is shared by both.

Where, then, is the difference between brute and man? What is it that man can do, and of which we find no signs, no rudiments, in the whole brute world? I answer without hesitation: the one great barrier between the brute and man is *Language*. Man speaks, and no brute has ever uttered a word. Language is our Rubicon, and no brute will dare to cross it. This is our matter of fact answer to those who speak of development, who think they discover the rudiments at

---

[7] 'The evident marks of reasoning in the other animals, – of reasoning which I cannot but think as unquestionable as the instincts that mingle with it.' – *Brown, Works*, vol. i. p. 446.

[8] Flourens, De la Raison, p. 51.

least of all human faculties in apes, and who would fain keep open the possibility that man is only a more favoured beast, the triumphant conqueror in the primeval struggle for life. Language is something more palpable than a fold of the brain, or an angle of the skull. It admits of no cavilling, and no process of natural selection will ever distil significant words out of the notes of birds or the cries of beasts.

Language, however, is only the outward sign. We may point to it in our arguments, we may challenge our opponent to produce anything approaching to it from the whole brute world. But if this were all, if the art of employing articulate sounds for the purpose of communicating our impressions were the only thing by which we could assert our superiority over the brute creation, we might not unreasonably feel somewhat uneasy at having the gorilla so close on our heels.

It cannot be denied that brutes, though they do not use articulate sounds for that purpose, have nevertheless means of their own for communicating with each other. When a whale is struck, the whole shoal, though widely dispersed, are instantly made aware of the presence of an enemy; and when the grave-digger beetle finds the carcass of a mole, he hastens to communicate the discovery to his fellows, and soon returns with his *four* confederates.[9] It is evident too, that dogs, though they do not speak, possess the power of understanding much that is said to them, their names and the calls of their master; and other animals, such as the parrot, can pronounce every articulate sound. Hence, although for the purpose of philosophical warfare, articulate language would still form an impregnable position, yet it is but natural that for our own satisfaction we should try to find out in what the strength of our position really consists; or, in other words, that we should try to discover that inward power of which language is the outward sign and manifestation.

For this purpose it will be best to examine the opinions of those who approached our problem from another point; who, instead of looking for outward and palpable signs of difference between brute and man, inquired into the inward mental faculties, and tried to determine the point where man transcends the barriers of the brute intellect. That point, if truly determined, ought to coincide with the starting-point of language:

---

[9] Conscience, Boek der Natuer, vi., quoted by Marsh, p. 32.

and, if so, that coincidence ought to explain the problem which occupies us at present.

I shall read an extract from Locke's Essay concerning Human Understanding.

After having explained how universal ideas are made, how the mind, having observed the same colour in chalk, and snow, and milk, comprehends these single perceptions under the general conception of whiteness, Locke continues:[10] 'If it may be doubted, whether beasts compound and enlarge their ideas that way to any degree: this, I think, I may be positive in, that the power of abstracting is not at all in them; and that the having of general ideas is that which puts a perfect distinction betwixt man and brutes, and is an excellency which the faculties of brutes do by no means attain to.'

If Locke is right in considering the having general ideas as the distinguishing feature between man and brutes, and, if we ourselves are right in pointing to language as the one palpable distinction between the two, it would seem to follow that language is the outward sign and realisation of that inward faculty which is called the faculty of abstraction, but which is better known to us by the homely name of Reason.

Let us now look back to the result of our former Lectures. It was this. After we had explained everything in the growth of language that can be explained, there remained in the end, as the only inexplicable residuum, what we called *roots*. These roots formed the constituent elements of all languages. This discovery has simplified the problem of the origin of language immensely. It has taken away all excuse for those rapturous descriptions of language which invariably preceded the argument that language must have a divine origin. We shall hear no more of that wonderful instrument which can express all we see, and hear, and taste, and touch, and smell; which is the breathing image of the whole world; which gives form to the airy feelings of our souls, and body to the loftiest dreams of our imagination; which can arrange in accurate perspective the past, the present, and the future, and throw over everything the varying hues of certainty, of doubt, of contingency. All this is perfectly true, but it is no longer wonderful, at least not in the Arabian Nights sense of that word. 'The speculative mind,' as Dr. Ferguson says, 'in comparing the first and last

---

[10] Book ii. chapter xi. § 10.

steps of the progress of language, feels the same sort of amazement with a traveller, who, after rising insensibly on the slope of a hill, comes to look from a precipice of an almost unfathomable depth to the summit of which he scarcely believes himself to have ascended without supernatural aid.' To certain minds it is a disappointment to be led down again by the hand of history from that high summit. They prefer the unintelligible which they can admire, to the intelligible which they can only understand. But to a mature mind reality is more attractive than fiction, and simplicity more wonderful than complication. Roots may seem dry things as compared with the poetry of Goethe. Yet there is something more truly wonderful in a root than in all the lyrics of the world.

What, then, are these roots? In our modern languages roots can only be discovered by scientific analysis, and, even as far back as Sanskrit, we may say that no root was ever used as a noun or as a verb. But originally roots were thus used, and in Chinese we have fortunately preserved to us a representative of that primitive radical stage which, like the granite, underlies all other strata of human speech. The Aryan root DÂ, to give, appears in Sanskrit *dâ–nam, donum*, gift, as a substantive; in *do*, Sanskrit *dadá–mi*, Greek *di-dō–mi*, I give, as a verb; but the root DÂ can never be used by itself. In Chinese, on the contrary, the root TA, as such, is used in the sense of a noun, greatness; of a verb, to be great; of an adverb, greatly or much. Roots therefore are not, as is commonly maintained, merely scientific abstractions, but they were used originally as real words. What we want to find out is this, What inward mental phase is it that corresponds to these roots, as the germs of human speech?

Two theories have been started to solve this problem, which, for shortness' sake, I shall call the *Bow-wow theory* and the *Pooh-pooh theory.*

According to the first, roots are imitations of sounds, according to the second, they are involuntary interjections. The first theory was very popular among the philosophers of the eighteenth century, and, as it is still held by many distinguished scholars and philosophers, we must examine it more carefully. It is supposed then that man, being as yet mute, heard the voices of birds and dogs and cows, the thunder of the clouds, the roaring of the sea, the rustling of the forest, the murmurs of the brook, and the whisper of the breeze. He tried to imitate these sounds, and finding his mimicking cries useful as signs of the objects from which they proceeded, he followed up the idea and elaborated language. This view was most ably defended by Herder.[11] 'Man,' he says, 'shows conscious reflection when his soul acts so freely that it may separate, in the ocean of sensations which rush into it through the senses, one single wave, arrest it, regard it, being conscious all the time of regarding this one single wave. Man proves his conscious reflection when, out of the dream of images that float past his senses, he can gather himself up and wake for a moment, dwelling intently on one image, fixing it with a bright and tranquil glance, and discovering for himself those signs by which he knows that *this* is *this* image and no other. Man proves his conscious reflection when he not only perceives vividly and distinctly all the features of an object, but is able to separate and recognise one or more of them as its distinguishing features.' For instance, 'Man sees a lamb. He does not see it like the ravenous wolf. He is not disturbed by any uncontrollable instinct. He wants to know it, but he is neither drawn towards it nor repelled from it by his senses. The lamb stands before him, as represented by his senses, white, soft, woolly. The conscious and reflecting soul of man looks for a distinguishing mark; – the lamb bleats! – the mark is found. The bleating which made the strongest impression, which stood apart from all other impressions of sight or touch, remains in the soul. The lamb returns – white, soft, woolly. The soul sees, touches, reflects, looks for a mark. The lamb bleats, and now the soul has recognised it. "Ah, thou art the bleating animal," the soul says within herself; and the sound of bleating, perceived as the distinguishing mark of the lamb, becomes the name of the lamb. It was the comprehended mark, the word. And what is the whole of our language but a collection of such words?'

Our answer is, that though there are names in every language formed by mere imitation of sound, yet these constitute a very small proportion of our dictionary. They are the playthings, not the tools, of language, and any attempt to reduce the most common and necessary words to imitative roots ends in

[11] A fuller account of the views of Herder and other philosophers on the origin of language may be found in Steinthal's useful little work, 'Der Ursprung der Sprache': Berlin, 1858.

complete failure. Herder himself, after having most strenuously defended this theory of Onomatopoieia, as it is called, and having gained a prize which the Berlin Academy had offered for the best essay on the origin of language, renounced it openly towards the latter years of his life, and threw himself in despair into the arms of those who looked upon languages as miraculously revealed. We cannot deny the possibility that *a* language might have been formed on the principle of imitation; all we say is, that as yet no language has been discovered that was so formed. An Englishman in China,[12] seeing a dish placed before him about which he felt suspicious, and wishing to know whether it was a duck, said, with an interrogative accent,

Quack quack?

He received the clear and straightforward answer,

Bow-wow!

This, no doubt, was as good as the most eloquent conversation on the same subject between an Englishman and a French waiter. But I doubt whether it deserves the name of language. We do not speak of a *bow-wow*, but of a dog. We speak of a cow, not of a *moo*. Of a lamb, not of a *baa*. It is the same in more ancient languages, such as Greek, Latin, and Sanskrit. If this principle of Onomatopoieia is applicable anywhere, it would be in the formation of the names of animals. Yet we listen in vain for any similarity between goose and cackling, hen and clucking, duck and quacking, sparrow and chirping, dove and cooing, hog and grunting, cat and mewing, between dog and barking, yelping, snarling, or growling.

There are of course some names, such as *cuckoo*, which are clearly formed by an imitation of sound. But words of this kind are, like artificial flowers, without a root. They are sterile, and are unfit to express anything beyond the one object which they imitate. If you remember the variety of derivatives that could be formed from the root *spac*, to see, you will at once perceive the difference between the fabrication of such a word as *cuckoo*, and the true natural growth of words.

Let us compare two words such as *cuckoo* and *raven*. *Cuckoo* in English is clearly a mere imitation of the cry of that

---

[12] Farrar, p. 74.

bird, even more so than the corresponding terms in Greek, Sanskrit, and Latin. In these languages the imitative element has received the support of a derivative suffix; we have *kokila* in Sanskrit, and *kokkyx* in Greek, *cuculus* in Latin.[13] *Cuckoo* is, in fact, a modern word, which has taken the place of the Anglo-Saxon *geac*, the German *Gauch*, and, being purely onomatopoëtic, it is of course not liable to the changes of Grimm's Law. As the word *cuckoo* predicates nothing but the sound of a particular bird, it could never be applied for expressing any general quality in which other animals might share; and the only derivatives to which it might give rise are words expressive of a metaphorical likeness with the bird. The same applies to *cock*, the Sanskrit *kukkuta*. Here, too, Grimm's Law does not apply, for both words were intended to convey merely the cackling sound of the bird; and, as this intention continued to be felt, phonetic change was less likely to set in. The Sanskrit *kukkuta* is not derived from any root, it simply repeats the cry of the bird, and the only derivatives to which it gives rise are metaphorical expressions, such as the French *coquet*, originally strutting about like a cock; *coquetterie; cocart*, conceited; *cocarde*, a cockade; *coquelicot*, originally a cock's comb, the wild red poppy, likewise so called from its similarity with a cock's comb.

Let us now examine the word *raven*. It might seem at first, as if this also was merely onomatopoëtic. Some people imagine they perceive a kind of similarity between the word *raven* and the cry of that bird. This seems still more so if we compare the Anglo-Saxon *hrafn*, the German *Rabe*, Old High-German *hraban*. The Sanskrit *kârava* also, the Latin *corvus*, and the Greek *korōnē*, all are supposed to show some similarity with the unmelodious sound of *Maître Corbeau*. But as soon as we analyse the word we find that it is of a different structure from *cuckoo* or *cock*. It is derived from a root which has a general predicative power. The root *ru* or *kru* is not a mere imitation of the cry of the raven; it embraces many cries, from the harshest to the softest, and it might have been applied to the nightingale as well as to the raven. In Sanskrit this root exists as *ru*, a verb which is applied to the murmuring sound of rivers as well as to the barking of dogs and the mooing of cows. From it are derived numerous words in Sanskrit. In

---

[13] Pott, Etymologische Forschungen, i. 87; Zeitschrift, iii. 43.

Latin we find *raucus*, hoarse; *rumor*, a whisper; in German *rûnen*, to speak low, and *runa*, mystery. The Latin *lamentum* stands for an original *ravimentum* or *cravimentum*. This root *ru* has several secondary forms, such as the Sanskrit *rud*, to cry; the Latin *rug* in *rugire*, to howl; the Greek *kru* or *klu*, in *klaiō*, *klausomai*; the Sanskrit *kru's*, to shout; the Gothic *hrukjan*, to crow, and *hropjan* to cry; the German *rufen*. Even the common Aryan word for hearing is closely allied to this root. It is *'sru* in Sanskrit, *klyō* in Greek, *cluo* in Latin; and before it took the recognised meaning of hearing, it meant to sound, to ring. When a noise was to be heard in a far distance, the man who first perceived it might well have said I ring, for his ears were sounding and ringing; and the same verb, if once used as transitive, expressed exactly what we mean by I hear a noise.

You will have perceived thus that the process which led to the formation of the word *kârava* in Sanskrit is quite distinct from that which produced *cuckoo*. *Kârava*[14] means a shouter, a caller, a crier. It might have been applied to many birds; but it became the traditional and recognised name for the crow. Cuckoo could never mean anything but the cuckoo, and while a word like *raven* has ever so many relations from a *rumor* down to *a row*, cuckoo stands by itself like a stick in a living hedge.

It is curious to observe how apt we are to deceive ourselves when we once adopt this system of Onomatopoieia. Who does not imagine that he hears in the word 'thunder,' an imitation of the rolling and rumbling noise which the old Germans ascribed to their God Thor playing at nine-pins? Yet *thunder* is clearly the same word as the Latin *tonitru*. The root is *tan*, to stretch. From this root *tan*, we have in Greek *tonos*, our tone, *tone* being produced by the stretching and vibrating of cords. In Sanskrit the sound thunder is expressed by the same root *tan*, but in the derivatives *tanyu*, *tanyatu*, and *tanayitnu*, thundering, we perceive no trace of the rumbling noise which we imagined we perceived in the Latin *tonitru* and the English *thunder*. The very same root *tan*, to stretch, yields some deriva-

---

[14] *Kârava*, explained in Sanskrit by *ku-rava*, having a bad voice, is supposed to be a mere dialectical corruption of *kravar* or *karva*. Κορώνη presupposes κοροων = κοροϜον = h(a)raban. The Sanskrit *kârava* may, however, be derived from *kâru*, singer; but in that case *kâru* must not be derived from *kṛi*.

tives which are anything but rough and noisy. The English *tender*, the French *tendre*, the Latin *tener*, are derived from it. Like *tenuis*, the Sanskrit *tanu*, the English *thin*, *tener* meant originally what was extended over a larger surface, then *thin*, then *delicate*. The relationship betwixt *tender*, *thin*, and *thunder* would be hard to establish if the original conception of thunder had really been its rumbling noise.

Who does not imagine that he hears something sweet in the French *sucre, sucré*? Yet sugar came from India, and it is there called *śarkhara*, which is anything but sweet sounding. This *śarkhara* is the same word as *sugar*; it was called in Latin *saccharum*, and we still speak of *saccharine* juice, which is sugar juice.

In *squirrel* again some people imagine they hear something of the rustling and whirling of the little animal. But we have only to trace the name back to Greek, and there we find that *skiouros* is composed of two distinct words, the one meaning shade, the other tail; the animal being called shade-tail by the Greeks.

Thus the word *cat*, the German *katze*, is supposed to be an imitation of the sound made by a cat spitting. But if the spitting were expressed by the sibilant, that sibilant does not exist in the Latin *catus*, nor in *cat*, or *kitten*, nor in the German *kater*.[15] The Sanskrit *mârjâra*, cat, might seem to imitate the purring of the cat; but it is derived from the root *mrij*, to clean, *mârjâra* meaning the animal that always cleans itself.

Many more instances might be given to show how easily we are deceived by the constant connection of certain sounds and certain meanings in the words of our own language, and how readily we imagine that there is something in the sound to tell us the meaning of the words. 'The sound must seem an echo to the sense.'

Most of these Onomatopoieias vanish as soon as we trace our own names back to Anglo-Saxon and Gothic, or compare them with their cognates in Greek, Latin, or Sanskrit. The number of names which are really formed by an imitation of sound dwindle down to a very small quotum if cross-examined by the comparative philologist, and we are left in the end with the conviction that though *a* language might have been made out of the roaring, fizzing, hissing, gobbling, twittering, crack-

---

[15] See Pietet, Aryas Primitifs, p. 381.

ing, banging, slamming, and rattling sounds of nature, the tongues with which *we* are acquainted point to a different origin.[16]

And so we find many philosophers, and among them Condillac, protesting against a theory which would place man even below the animal. Why should man be supposed, they say, to have taken a lesson from birds and beasts? Does he not utter cries, and sobs, and shouts himself, according as he is affected by fear, pain, or joy? These cries or interjections were represented as the natural and real beginnings of human speech. Everything else was supposed to have been elaborated after their model. This is what I call the Interjectional, or Poohpooh, Theory.

Our answer to this theory is the same as to the former. There are no doubt in every language interjections, and some of them may become traditional, and enter into the composition of words. But these interjections are only the outskirts of real language. Language begins where interjections end. There is as much difference between a real word, such as 'to laugh,' and the interjection ha, ha! between 'I suffer,' and oh! as there is between the involuntary act and noise of sneezing, and the verb 'to sneeze.' We sneeze, and cough, and scream, and laugh in the same manner as animals, but if Democritus tells us that we speak in the same manner as dogs bark, moved

---

[16] In Chinese the number of imitative sounds is very considerable. They are mostly written phonetically, and followed by the determinative sign 'mouth.' We give a few, together with the corresponding sounds in Mandshu. The difference between the two will show how differently the same sounds strike different ears, and how differently they are rendered into articulate language:–

The cock crows	kiao kiao in Chinese	dehor dehor in Mandshu.
The wild goose cries	kao kao in Chinese	kôr kor in Mandhsu.
The wind and rain sound	siao siao in Chinese	chor chor in Mandshu.
Waggons sound	lin lin in Chinese	koungour koungour in Mandshu.
Dogs coupled together	ling-ling in Chinese	kalang kalang in Mandshu.
Chains	tsiang-tsiang in Chinese	kiling kiling in Mandshu.
Bells	tsiang-tsiang in Chinese	tang tang in Mandshu.
Drums	kan kan in Chinese	tung tung in Mandshu.

24 The Origin of Language

by nature,[17] our own experience will tell us that this is not the case.

An excellent answer to the interjectional theory has been given by Horne Tooke.

'The dominion of speech,' he says,[18] 'is erected upon the downfall of interjections. Without the artful contrivances of language, mankind would have had nothing but interjections with which to communicate, orally, any of their feelings. The neighing of a horse, the lowing of a cow, the barking of a dog, the purring of a cat, sneezing, coughing, groaning, shrieking, and every other involuntary convulsion with oral sound, have almost as good a title to be called parts of speech, as interjections have. Voluntary interjections are only employed where the suddenness and vehemence of some affection or passion returns men to their natural state; and makes them for a moment forget the use of speech; or when, from some circumstance, the shortness of time will not permit them to exercise it.'

As in the case of Onomatopoieia, it cannot be denied that with interjections, too, some kind of language might have been formed; but not a language like that which we find in numerous varieties among all the races of men. One short interjection may be more powerful, more to the point, more eloquent than a long speech. In fact, interjections, together with gestures, the movements of the muscles of the mouth, and the eye, would be quite sufficient for all purposes which language answers with the majority of mankind. Lucian, in his treatise on dancing, mentions a king whose dominions bordered on the Euxine. He happened to be at Rome in the reign of Nero, and, having seen a pantomime perform, begged him of the emperor as a present, in order that he might employ him as an interpreter among the nations in his neighbourhood with whom he could hold no intercourse on account of the diversity of language. A pantomime meant a person who could mimic everything, and there is hardly anything which cannot be thus expressed. We, having language at our command, have neglected the art of speaking without words; but in the south of Europe that art

---

[17] Ὁ γὰρ Ἐπίκουρος ἔλεγεμ, ὅτι οὐχὶ ἐπιστημόνως οὗτοι ἔθεντο τὰ ὀνόματα, ἀλλὰ φνσικῶς κινούμενοι, ὡς οἱ βήσσοντες καὶ πταίροντες καὶ μνκώμενοι καὶ ὑλακτοῦντες καὶ στενάζοντες. – Lersch, Sprachphilosophie der Alten, i. 40. The statement is taken from Proklus, and I doubt whether he represented Epicurus rightly.

[18] Diversions of Purley, p. 32.

is still preserved. If it be true that one look may speak volumes, it is clear that we might save ourselves much of the trouble entailed by the use of discursive speech. Yet we must not forget that *hum! ugh! tut! pooh!* are as little to be called words as the expressive gestures which usually accompany these exclamations.

As to the attempts at deriving some of our words etymologically from mere interjections, they are apt to fail from the same kind of misconception which leads us to imagine that there is something expressive in the sounds of words. Thus it is said 'that the idea of disgust takes its rise in the senses of smell and taste, in the first instance probably in smell alone; that in defending ourselves from a bad smell we are instinctively impelled to screw up the nose, and to expire strongly through the compressed and protruded lips, giving rise to a sound represented by the interjections faugh! foh! fie! From this interjection it is proposed to derive not only such words as *foul* and *filth*, but, by transferring it from natural to moral aversion, the English *fiend*, the German *Feind*.' If this were true, we should suppose that the expression of contempt was chiefly conveyed by the aspirate *f*, by the strong emission of the breathing with half-opened lips. But *fiend* is a participle from a root *fian*, to hate; in Gothic *fijan*; and as a Gothic aspirate always corresponds to a tenuis in Sanskrit, the same root in Sanskrit would at once lose its expressive power. It exists in fact in Sanskrit as *pîy*, to hate, to destroy; just as *friend* is derived from a root which in Sanskrit is *prî*, to delight.[19]

There is one more remark which I have to make about the

---

[19] The following list of Chinese interjections may be of interest:–

    hu, to express surprise.
    fu, the same.
    tsai, to express admiration and approbation.
    i, to express distress.
    tsie, vocative particle.
    tsie tsie, exhortative particle.
    a'i, to express contempt.
    û-hu, to express pain.
    shin-î, ah, indeed.
    pŭ sin, alas!
    ngo, stop!

In many cases interjections were originally words, just as the French *hélas* is derived from *lassus*, tired, miserable. Diez, Lexicon Etymologicum, s. v. *lasso*.

Interjectional and the Onomatopoëtic theories, namely this: If the constituent elements of human speech were either mere cries, or the mimicking of the cries of nature, it would be difficult to understand why brutes should be without language. There is not only the parrot, but the mockingbird and others, which can imitate most successfully both articulate and inarticulate sounds; and there is hardly an animal without the faculty of uttering interjections, such as huff, hiss, baa, &c. It is clear also that if what puts a perfect distinction betwixt man and brutes is the having of general ideas, language which arises from interjections and from the imitation of the cries of animals could not claim to be the outward sign of that distinctive faculty of man. All words, in the beginning at least (and this is the only point which interests us), would have been the signs of individual impressions and individual perceptions, and would only gradually have been adapted to the expression of general ideas.

The theory which is suggested to us by an analysis of language carried out according to the principles of comparative philology is the very opposite. We arrive in the end at roots, and every one of these expresses a general, not an individual, idea. Every name, if we analyse it, contains a predicate by which the object to which the name applies was known.

There is an old controversy among philosophers, whether language originated in general appellations, or in proper names.[20] It is the question of the *primum cognitum*, and its consideration will help us perhaps in discovering the true nature of the root, or the *primum appellatum*.

Some philosophers, among whom I may mention Locke, Condillac, Adam Smith, Dr. Brown, and with some qualification Dugald Stewart, maintain that all terms, as at first employed, are expressive of individual objects. I quote from Adam Smith. 'The assignation,' he says, 'of particular names to denote particular objects, that is, the institution of nouns substantive, would probably be one of the first steps towards the formation of language. Two savages who had never been taught to speak, but had been bred up remote from the societies of men, would naturally begin to form that language by which they would endeavour to make their mutual wants intelligible to each other by uttering certain sounds whenever they

---

[20] Sir W. Hamilton's Lectures, ii. p. 319.

meant to denote certain objects. Those objects only which were most familiar to them, and which they had most frequent occasion to mention, would have particular names assigned to them. The particular cave whose covering sheltered them from the weather, the particular tree whose fruit relieved their hunger, the particular fountain whose water allayed their thirst, would first be denominated by the words *cave, tree, fountain*, or by whatever other appellations they might think proper in that primitive jargon, to mark them. Afterwards, when the more enlarged experience of these savages had led them to observe, and their necessary occasions obliged them to make mention of, other caves, and other trees, and other fountains, they would naturally bestow upon each of those new objects the same name by which they had been accustomed to express the similar object they were first acquainted with. The new objects had none of them any name of its own, but each of them exactly resembled another object which had such an appellation. It was impossible that those savages could behold the new objects without recollecting the old ones; and the name of the old ones, to which the new bore so close a resemblance. When they had occasion, therefore, to mention or to point out to each other any of the new objects, they would naturally utter the name of the correspondent old one, of which the idea could not fail, at that instant, to present itself to their memory in the strongest and liveliest manner. And thus those words, which were originally the proper names of individuals, became the common name of a multitude. A child that is just learning to speak calls every person who comes to the house its papa or its mamma; and thus bestows upon the whole species those names which it had been taught to apply to two individuals. I have known a clown who did not know the proper name of the river which ran by his own door. It was *the river*, he said, and he never heard any other name for it. His experience, it seems, had not led him to observe any other river. The general word *river* therefore was, it is evident, in his acceptance of it, a proper name signifying an individual object. If this person had been carried to another river, would he not readily have called it *a river*? Could we suppose any person living on the banks of the Thames so ignorant as not to know the general word *river*, but to be acquainted only with the particular word *Thames*, if he were brought to any other river, would he not readily call it a *Thames*? This, in reality, is no more than what they, who are well acquainted with the general word are very apt to do. An Englishman, describing any great river which he may have seen in some foreign country, naturally says that it is another Thames. . . . It is this application of the name of an individual to a great multitude of objects, whose resemblance naturally recalls the idea of that individual, and of the name which expresses it, that seems originally to have given occasion to the formation of those classes and assortments which, in the schools, are called *genera* and *species*.'

This extract from Adam Smith will give a clear idea of one view of the formation of thought and language. I shall now read another extract, representing the diametrically opposite view. It is taken from Leibniz,[21] who maintains that general terms are necessary for the essential constitution of languages. He likewise appeals to children. 'Children,' he says, 'and those who know but little of the language which they attempt to speak, or little of the subject on which they would employ it, make use of general terms, as *thing, plant, animal,* instead of using proper names, of which they are destitute. And it is certain that all proper or individual names have been originally appellative or general.' And again: 'Thus I would make bold to affirm that almost all words have been originally general terms, because it would happen very rarely that man would invent a name, expressly and without a reason, to denote this or that individual. We may, therefore, assert that the names of individual things were names of species, which were given *par excellence*, or otherwise, to some individual; as the name *Great Head* to him of the whole town who had the largest, or who was the man of the most consideration of the great heads known.'

It might seem presumptuous to attempt to arbitrate between such men as Leibniz and Adam Smith, particularly when both speak so positively as they do on this subject. But there are two ways of judging of former philosophers. One is to put aside their opinions as simply erroneous where they differ from our own. This is the least satisfactory way of studying ancient philosophy. Another way is to try to enter fully into the opinions of those from whom we differ, to make them, for a time at least, our own, till at last we discover the point of view

---

[21] Nouveaux Essais, lib. iii. c. i. p. 297 (Erdmann); Sir W. Hamilton, Lectures, ii. 324.

from which each philosopher looked at the facts before him, and catch the light in which he regarded them. We shall then find that there is much less of downright error in the history of philosophy than is commonly supposed; nay, we shall find nothing so conducive to a right appreciation of truth as a right appreciation of the error by which it is surrounded.

Now, in the case before us, Adam Smith is no doubt right, when he says that the first individual cave which is called cave gave the name to all other caves. In the same manner the first *town*, though a mere enclosure, gave the name to all other towns; the first imperial residence on the Palatine hill gave the name to all palaces. Slight differences between caves, towns, or palaces are readily passed by, and the first name becomes more and more general with every new individual to which it is applied. So far Adam Smith is right, and the history of almost every substantive might be cited in support of his view. But Leibniz is equally right when, in looking beyond the first emergence of such names as cave or town or palace, he asks how such names could have arisen. Let us take the Latin names of cave. A cave in Latin is called *antrum, cavea, spelunca*. Now *antrum* means really the same as *internum*. *Antar* in Sanskrit means *between* and *within*.[22] *Antrum*, therefore, meant originally what is within or inside the earth or anything else. It is clear, therefore, that such a name could not have been given to any individual cave, unless the general idea of being within, or inwardness, had been present in the mind. This general idea once formed, and once expressed by the pronominal root *an* or *antar*, and the process of naming is clear and intelligible. The place where the savage could live safe from rain and from the sudden attacks of wild beasts, a natural hollow in the rock, he would call his *within*, his *antrum*; and afterwards similar places, whether dug in the earth or cut in a tree, would be designated by the same name. The same general idea, however, would likewise supply other names, and thus we find that the *entrails* were called *antra* (neuter) in Sanskrit, *enteron* in Greek, originally things within.

Let us take another word for cave which his *căvea* or *căverna*. Here again Adam Smith would be perfectly right in maintaining that this name, when first given, was applied to one particular cave, and was afterwards extended to other caves. But

---

[22] Pott, Etymologische Forschungen, p. 324, *seq*.

Leibniz would be equally right in maintaining that in order to call even the first hollow *cavea*, it was necessary that the general idea of *hollow* should have been formed in the mind, and should have received its vocal expression *cav*. Nay we may go a step beyond, for *cavus*, or hollow, is a secondary, not a primary, idea. Before a cave was called *cavea*, a hollow thing, many things hollow had passed before the eyes of men. Why then was a hollow thing, or a hole, called by the root *cav*? Because what had been hollowed out was intended at first as a place of safety and protection, as a cover; and it was called therefore by the root *ku* or *sku*, which conveyed the idea of to cover.[23] Hence the general idea of covering existed in the mind before it was applied to hiding-places in rocks or trees, and it was not till an expression had thus been framed for things hollow or safe in general, that caves in particular could be designated by the name of *cavea* or hollows.

Another form for *cavus* was *koilos*, hollow. The conception was originally the same; a hole was called *koilon* because it served as a cover. But once so used *koilon* came to mean a cave, a vaulted cave, a vault, and thus the heaven was called *cœlum*, the modern *ciel*, because it was looked upon as a vault or cover for the earth.

It is the same with all nouns. They all express originally one out of the many attributes of a thing, and that attribute, whether it be a quality or an action, is necessarily a general idea. The word thus formed was in the first instance intended for one object only, though of course it was almost immediately extended to the whole class to which this object seemed to belong. When a word such as *rivus*, river, was first formed, no doubt it was intended for a certain river, and that river was called *rivus*, from a root *ru* or *sru*, to run, because of its running water. In many instances a word meaning river or runner remained the proper name of one river, without ever rising to the dignity of an appellative. Thus *Rhenus*, the Rhine, means river or runner, but it clung to one river, and could not be used as an appellative for others. The Ganges is the Sanskrit *Gangâ*, literally the Go-go; a word very well adapted for any majestic river, but in Sanskrit restricted to the one sacred stream. The Indus again is the Sanskrit *Sindhu*, and means

---

[23] Benfey, Griech. Wurzel Lex. p. 611. From *sku* or *ku*, ακυτος, skin; *cŭtis*, haut.

the irrigator, from *syand*, to sprinkle. In this case, however, the proper name was not checked in its growth, but was used likewise as an appellative for any great stream.

We have thus seen how the controversy about the *primum cognitum* assumes a new and perfectly clear aspect. The first thing really known is the general. It is through it that we know and name afterwards individual objects of which any general idea can be predicated, and it is only in the third stage that these individual objects, thus known and named, become again the representatives of whole classes, and their names or proper names are raised into appellatives.

There is a petrified philosophy in language, and if we examine the most ancient word for name we find it is *nâman* in Sanskrit, *nomen* in Latin, *namo* in Gothic. This *nâman* stands for *gnâman*, which is preserved in the Latin *co-gnomen*. The g is dropped as in *natus*, son, for *gnatus*. *Nâman*, therefore, or name, meant originally that by which we know a thing.

And how do we know things? We perceive things by our senses, but our senses convey to us information about single things only. But to *know* is more than to feel, than to perceive, more than to remember, more than to compare. No doubt words are much abused. We speak of a dog *knowing* his master, of an infant *knowing* his mother. In such expressions, to know means to recognise. But to know a thing, means more than to recognise it. We know a thing if we are able to bring it, and any part of it, under more general ideas. We then say, not that we have a perception, but a conception, or that we have a general idea of a thing. The facts of nature are perceived by our senses; the thoughts of nature, to borrow an expression of Oersted's, can be conceived by our reason only.[24] Now the first step towards this real knowledge, a step which, however small in appearance, separates man for ever from all other animals,

---

[24] 'We receive the impression of the falling of a large mass of water, descending always from the same height and with the same difficulty. The scattering of the drops of water, the formation of froth, the sound of the fall by the roaring and by the froth, are constantly produced by the same causes, and, consequently, are always the same. The impression which all this produces on us is no doubt at first felt as multiform, but it soon forms a whole, or, in other terms, we feel all the diversity of the isolated impressions as the work of a great physical activity which results from the particular nature of the spot. We may, perhaps, till we are better informed, call all that is fixed in the phenomenon, *the thoughts of nature*.'
– Oersted, *Esprit dans la Nature*, p. 152.

is the *naming of a thing*, or the making a thing knowable. All naming is classification, bringing the individual under the general; and whatever we know, whether empirically or scientifically, we know it only by means of our general ideas. Other animals have sensation, perception, memory, and, in a certain sense, intellect; but all these, in the animal, are conversant with single objects only. Man has sensation, perception, memory, intellect, and reason, and his reason is conversant with general ideas only.[25]

Through reason we not only stand a step above the brute creation: we belong to a different world. We look down on our merely animal experience, on our sensations, perceptions, our memory, and our intellect, as something belonging to us, but not as constituting our most inward and eternal self. Our senses, our memory, our intellect, are like the lenses of a telescope. But there is an eye that looks through them at the realities of the outer world, our own rational and self-conscious soul; a power as distinct from our perceptive faculties as the sun is from the earth which it fills with light, and warmth, and life.

At the very point where man parts company with the brute world, at the first flash of reason as the manifestation of the light within us, there we see the true genesis of language. Analyse any word you like, and you will find that it expresses a general idea peculiar to the individual to which the name belongs. What is the meaning of moon? – the measurer. What is the meaning of sun? – the begetter. What is the meaning of earth? – the ploughed. The old name given to animals, such as cows and sheep, was *paśu*, the Latin *pecus*, which means *feeders*. *Animal* itself is a later name, and derived from *anima*, soul. This *anima* again meant originally blowing or breathing, like spirit from *spirare*, and was derived from a root, *an*, to blow, which gives us *anila*, wind, in Sanskrit, and *anemos*, wind, in Greek. *Ghost*, the German *Geist*, is based on the same conception. It is connected with *gust*, with *yeast*, and even with the hissing and boiling *geysers* of Iceland. *Soul* is the Gothic *saivala*, and this is clearly related to another Gothic

---

[25] 'Ce qui trompe l'homme, c'est qu'il voit faire aux bêtes plusieurs des choses qu'il fait, et qu'il ne voit pas que, dans ces choses-là même, les bêtes ne mettent qu'une intelligence grossière, bornée, et qu'il met, lui, une intelligence *doublée d'esprit*.' – Flourens, *De la Raison*, p. 73.

word, *saivs*,[26] which means the sea. The sea was called *saivs* from a root *si* or *siv*, the Greek *seiō*, to shake; it meant the tossed-about water, in contradistinction to stagnant or running water. The soul being called *saivala*, we see that it was originally conceived by the Teutonic nations as a sea within, heaving up and down with every breath, and reflecting heaven and earth on the mirror of the deep.

The Sanskrit name for love is *smara*; it is derived from *smar*, to recollect; and the same root has supplied the German *schmerz*, pain, and the English *smart*.

If the serpent is called in Sanskrit *sarpa*, it is because it was conceived under the general idea of creeping, an idea expressed by the word *sṛip*. But the serpent was also called *ahi* in Sanskrit, in Greek *echis* or *echidna*, in Latin *anguis*. This name is derived from quite a different root and idea. The root is *ah* in Sanskrit, or *anh*, which means to press together, to choke, to throttle. Here the distinguishing mark from which the serpent was named was his throttling, and *ahi* meant serpent, as expressing the general idea of throttler. It is a curious root this *anh*, and it still lives in several modern words. In Latin it appears as *ango, anxi, anctum*, to strangle, in *angina*, the quinsy, in *angor*, quinsy. But *angor* meant not only quinsy or compression of the neck; it assumed a moral import and signifies anguish or anxiety. The two adjectives *angustus*, narrow, and *anxius*, uneasy, both come from the same source. In Greek the root retained its natural and material meaning; in *eggys*, near, and *echis*, serpent, throttler. But in Sanskrit it was chosen with great truth as the proper name of sin. Evil no doubt presented itself under various aspects to the human mind, and its names are many; but none so expressive as those derived from our root, *anh*, to throttle. *Anhas* in Sanskrit means sin, but it does so only because it meant originally throttling, – the consciousness of sin being like the grasp of the assassin on the throat of his victim. All who have seen and contemplated the statue of Laokoon and his sons, with the serpent coiled round them from head to foot, may realise what those ancients felt and saw when they called sin *anhas*, or the throttler. This *anhas* is the same word as the Greek ἄγος, sin. In Gothic the same root has produced *agis*, in the sense of *fear*, and from the same source we have *awe*, in awful, *i.e.* fearful, and *ug*, in *ugly*.

---

[26] See Heyse, System der Sprachwissenschaft, s. 97.

The English *anguish* is from the French *angoisse*, the Italian *angoscia*, a corruption of the Latin *angustíœ*, a strait.

And how did those early thinkers and framers of language distinguish between man and the other animals? What general idea did they connect with the first conception of themselves? The Latin word *homo*, the French *l'homme*, which has been reduced to *on* in *on dit*, is derived from the same root which we have in *humus*, the soil, *humilis*, humble. *Homo*, therefore, would express the idea of a being made of the dust of the earth.[27]

Another ancient word for man was the Sanskrit *marta*,[28] the Greek *brotos*, the Latin *mortalis* (a secondary derivative), our own *mortal*. *Marta* means 'he who dies,' and it is remarkable that where everything else was changing, fading, and dying, this should have been chosen as the distinguishing name for man. Those early poets would hardly have called themselves mortals unless they had believed in other beings as immortal.

There is a third name for man which means simply the thinker, and this, the true title of our race, still lives in the name of *man*. *Mâ* in Sanskrit means to measure, from which, you remember we had the name of moon. *Man*, a derivative root, means to think. From this we have the Sanskrit *manu*, originally thinker, then man. In the later Sanskrit we find derivatives, such as *mânava, mânusha, manushya*, all expressing man. In Gothic we find both *man*, and *mannisks*, the modern German *mann* and *mensch*.

There were many more names for man, as there were many names for all things in ancient languages. Any feature that struck the observing mind as peculiarly characteristic could be made to furnish a new name. The sun might be called the bright, the warm, the golden, the preserver, the destroyer, the wolf, the lion, the heavenly eye, the father of light and life. Hence that superabundance of synonymes in ancient dialects, and hence that *struggle for life* carried on among these words, which led to the destruction of the less strong, the less happy, the less fertile words, and ended in the triumph of *one*, as the recognised and proper name for every object in every language. On a very small scale this process of *natural selection*, or, as

---

[27] Greek χαμαί, Zend *zem*, Lithuanian *zeme*, and *zmenes, homines*. See Bopp, Glossarium Sanscritum, s. v.
[28] See Windischmann, Fortschritt der Sprachenkunde, p. 23.

it would better be called *elimination*, may still be watched even in modern languages, that is to say, even in languages so old and full of years as English and French. What it was at the first burst of dialects we can only gather from such isolated cases as when Von Hammer counts 5744 words relating to the camel.[29]

The fact that every word is originally a predicate, that names, though signs of individual conceptions, are all, without exception, derived from general ideas, is one of the most important discoveries in the science of language. It was known before that language is the distinguishing characteristic of man; it was known also that the having of general ideas is that which puts a perfect distinction betwixt man and brutes; but that these two were only different expressions of the same fact was not known till the theory of roots had been established as preferable to the theories both of Onomatopoieia and of Interjections. But, though our modern philosophy did not know it, the ancient poets and framers of language must have known it. For in Greek language is *logos*, but *logos* means also reason, and *alogon* was chosen as the name, and the most proper name, for brute. No animal thinks, and no animal speaks, except man. Language and thought are inseparable. Words without thought are dead sounds; thoughts without words are nothing. To think is to speak low; to speak is to think aloud. The word is the thought incarnate.

And now I am afraid I have but a few minutes left to explain the last question of all in our science, namely – How can sound express thought? How did roots become the signs of general ideas? How was the abstract idea of measuring expressed by *mâ*, the idea of thinking by *man*? How did *gâ* come to mean going, *sthâ* standing, *sad* sitting, *dâ* giving, *mar* dying, *char* walking, *kar* doing?

I shall try to answer as briefly as possible. The 400 or 500 roots which remain as the constituent elements in different families of language are not interjections, nor are they imitations. They are *phonetic types* produced by a power inherent in human nature. They exist, as Plato would say, by nature; though with Plato we should add that, when we say by nature, we mean by the hand of God.[30] There is a law which

---

[29] Farrar, Origin of Language, p. 85.
[30] Θήσω τὰ μὲν φύσει λεγόμενα ποιεῖσθαι θείᾳ τέχνῃ.

runs through nearly the whole of nature, that everything which is struck rings. Each substance has its peculiar ring. We can tell the more or less perfect structure of metals by their vibrations, by the answer which they give. Gold rings differently from tin, wood rings differently from stone; and different sounds are produced according to the nature of each percussion. It was the same with man, the most highly organised of nature's works.[31] Man, in his primitive and perfect state, was endowed not only, like the brute, with the power of expressing his sensations by interjections, and his perceptions by onomatopoieia. He possessed likewise the faculty of giving more articulate expression to the rational conceptions of his mind. That faculty was not of his own making. It was an instinct, an instinct of the mind as irresistible as any other instinct. So far as language is the production of that instinct, it belongs to the realm of nature. Man loses his instincts as he ceases to want them. His senses become fainter when, as in the case of scent, they become useless. Thus the creative faculty which gave to each conception, as it thrilled for the first time through the brain, a phonetic expression, became extinct when its object was fulfilled. The number of these *phonetic types* must have been almost infinite in the beginning, and it was only through the same process of *natural elimination* which we observed in the early history of words, that clusters of roots, more or less synonymous, were gradually reduced to one definite type. Instead of deriving language from nine roots, like Dr. Murray,[32] or from *one* root, a feat actually accomplished by a Dr. Schmidt,[33] we must suppose that the first settlement of the radical elements of language was preceded by

---

[31] This view was propounded many years ago by Professor Heyse in the lectures which he gave at Berlin, and which have been very carefully published since his death by one of his pupils, Dr. Steinthal. The fact that wood, metals, cords, &c., if struck vibrate and ring, can, of course, be used as an illustration only, and not as an explanation. The faculty peculiar to man, in his primitive state, by which every impression from without received its vocal expression from within, must be accepted as a fact. That faculty must have existed in man, because its effects continue to exist. Analogies from the inanimate world, however, are useful, and deserve further examination.

[32] Dr. Murray's primitive roots were, ag, bag, dwag, cwag, lag, mag, nag, rag, swag.

[33] Curtius, Griechische Etymologie, p. 13. Dr. Schmidt derives all Greek words from the root *e*, and all Latin words from the arch-radical *hi*.

a period of unrestrained growth, – the spring of speech – to be followed by many an autumn.

With the process of elimination, or natural selection, the historical element enters into the science of language. However primitive the Chinese may be as compared with terminational and inflectional languages, its roots or words have clearly passed through a long process of mutual attrition. There are many things of a merely traditional character even in Chinese. The rule that in a simple sentence the first word is the subject, the second the verb, the third the object, is a traditional rule. It is by tradition only that *ngŏ ğin*, in Chinese, means a bad man, whereas *ğin ngŏ* signifies man is bad. The Chinese themselves distinguish between *full* and *empty* roots,[34] the former being predicative, the latter corresponding to our particles which modify the meaning of full roots and determine their relation to each other. It is only by tradition that roots become empty. All roots were originally full whether predicative or demonstrative, and the fact that empty roots in Chinese cannot always be traced back to their full prototypes shows that even the most ancient Chinese had passed through successive periods of growth. Chinese grammarians admit that all empty words were originally full words, just as Sanskrit grammarians maintain that all that is found in grammar was originally substantial. But we must be satisfied with but partial proofs of this general principle, and must be prepared to find as many fanciful derivations in Chinese as in Sanskrit. The fact, again, that all roots in Chinese are no longer capable of being employed at pleasure, either as substantives, or verbs, or adjectives, is another proof that, even in this most primitive stage, language points back to a previous growth. *Fu* is father, *mu* is mother; *fu mu* parents; but neither *fu* nor *mu* is used as a root in its original predicative sense. The amplest proof, however, of the various stages through which even so simple a language as Chinese must have passed is to be found in the comparatively small number of roots, and in the definite meanings attached to each; a result which could only have been obtained by that constant struggle which has been so well described in natural history as the struggle for life.

But although this sifting of roots, and still more the subsequent combination of roots, cannot be ascribed to the mere

---

[34] Endlicher, Chinesische Grammatik, p. 163.

working of nature or natural instincts, it is still less, as we saw in a former Lecture, the effect of deliberate or premeditated art, in the sense in which, for instance, a picture of Raphael or a symphony of Beethoven are. Given a root to express flying, or bird, and another to express heap, then the joining together of the two to express many birds, or birds in the plural, is the natural effect of the synthetic power of the human mind, or, to use more homely language, of the power of putting two and two together. Some philosophers maintain indeed that this explains nothing, and that the real mystery to be solved is how the mind can form a synthesis, or conceive many things as one. Into those depths we cannot follow. Other philosophers imagine that the combination of roots to form agglutinative and inflectional language is, like the first formation of roots, the result of a natural instinct. Thus Professor Heyse[35] maintained that 'the various forms of development in language must be explained by the philosophers as *necessary* evolutions, founded in the very essence of human speech.' This is not the case. We can watch the growth of language, and we can understand and explain all that is the result of that growth. But we cannot undertake to prove that all that is in language is so by necessity, and could not have been otherwise. When we have, as in Chinese, two such words as *kiai* and *tu*, both expressing a heap, an assembly, a quantity, then we may perfectly understand why either the one or the other should have been used to form the plural. But if one of the two becomes fixed and traditional, while the other becomes obsolete, then we can register the fact as historical, but no philosophy on earth will explain its absolute necessity. We can perfectly understand how, with two such roots as *kŭŏ*, empire, and *ćung*, middle, the Chinese should have formed what we call a locative, *kŭŏ ćung*, in the empire. But to say that this was the only way to express this conception is an assertion contradicted both by fact and reason. We saw the various ways in which the future can be formed. They are all equally intelligible and equally possible, but not one of them is inevitable. In Chinese *ẏaó* means to will, *ngò* is I; hence *ngò ẏaó*, I will. The same root *ẏaó*, added to *kiú*, to go, gives us *ngò ẏaó kiú*, I will go, the first germ of our futures. To say that *ngò ẏaó kiú* was the necessary form of the future in Chinese would introduce a

---

[35] System der Sprachwissenschaft, p. 16.

fatalism into language which rests on no authority whatever. The building up of language is not like the building of the cells in a beehive, nor is it like the building of St. Peter's by Michael Angelo. It is the result of innumerable agencies, working each according to certain laws, and leaving in the end the result of their combined efforts freed from all that proved superfluous or useless. From the first combination of two such words as *ğin*, man, *kiai*, many, to form the plural *ğin kiai*, to the perfect grammar of Sanskrit and Greek, everything is intelligible as the result of the two principles of growth which we considered in our second Lecture. What lies beyond the production of roots is the work of nature; what follows after is the work of man, not in his individual and free, but in his collective and moderating, capacity.

I do not say that every form in Greek or Sanskrit has as yet been analysed and explained. There are formations in Greek and Latin and English which have hitherto baffled all tests; and there are certain contrivances, such as the augment in Greek, the change of vowels in Hebrew, the Umlaut and Ablaut in the Teutonic dialects, where we might feel inclined to suppose that language admitted distinctions purely musical or phonetic, corresponding to very palpable and material distinctions of thought. Such a supposition, however, is not founded on any safe induction. It may seem inexplicable to us why *bruder* in German should form its plural as *brüder*; or *brother, brethren*. But what is inexplicable and apparently artificial in our modern languages becomes intelligible in their more ancient phases. The change of *u* into *ü*, as in *bruder, brüder*, was not intentional; least of all was it introduced to express plurality. The change is merely phonetic, and due to the influence of an *i* or *j*,[36] which existed originally in the last syllable, and which reacted regularly on the vowel of the preceding syllable; nay, which leaves its effect behind, even after it has itself disappeared. By a false analogy such a change, perfectly justifiable in a certain class of words, may be applied to other words where no such change was called for; and it may then appear as if an arbitrary change of vowels was intended to convey a grammatical change. But even into these recesses the comparative philologist can follow language, thus discovering a reason even for what in reality was irrational and wrong. It seems

---

[36] See Schleicher, Deutsche Sprache, p. 144.

difficult to believe that the augment in Greek should originally have had an independent substantial existence, yet all analogy is in favour of such a view. Suppose English had never been written down before Wycliffe's time, we should then find that in some instances the perfect was formed by the mere addition of a short *a*. Wycliffe spoke and wrote:[37] *I knowlech to a felid and seid us*; i. e. I acknowledge to have felt and said thus. In a similar way we read: *it should a fallen*; instead of 'it should have fallen;' and in some parts of England common people still say very much the same: *I should a done it*. Now in some old English books this *a* actually coalesces with the verb, at least they are printed together; so that a grammar founded on them would give us 'to fall' as the infinitive of the present, *to afallen* as the infinitive of the past. I do not wish for a moment to be understood as if there was any connection between this *a*, a contraction of *have* in English, and the Greek augment which is placed before past tenses. All I mean is, that, if the origin of the augment has not yet been satisfactorily explained, we are not therefore to despair, or to admit an arbitrary addition of a consonant or vowel, used as it were algebraically or by mutual agreement, to distinguish a past from a present tense.

If inductive reasoning is worth anything, we are justified in believing that what has been proved to be true on so large a scale, and in cases where it was least expected, is true with regard to language in general. We require no supernatural interference, nor any conclave of ancient sages, to explain the realities of human speech. All that is formal in language is the result of rational combination; all that is material, the result of a mental instinct. The first natural and instinctive utterances, if sifted differently by different clans, would fully account both for the first origin and for the first divergence of human speech. We can understand not only the origin of language, but likewise the necessary breaking up of one language into many; and we perceive that no amount of variety in the material or the formal elements of speech is incompatible with the admission of one common source.

The Science of Language thus leads us up to that highest summit from whence we see into the very dawn of man's life on earth; and where the words which we have heard so often

[37] Marsh, p. 388.

from the days of our childhood – 'And the whole earth was of one language and of one speech' – assume a meaning more natural, more intelligible, more convincing, than they ever had before.

ON LANGUAGE
F. W. Farrar

Chapter I
Language, a Human Discovery

Πάντα θεῖα καὶ ἀνθρώπινα πάντα. – Hippokrates.

God, who, in the words of Lactantius,[1] was 'the artificer alike of the intelligence, of the voice, and of the tongue,' gave to man, with those three gifts, the power of constructing a language for himself. Now we are entitled to conclude from the widest possible observation of God's dealings with the human race, that He never bestows *directly* what man can obtain for himself by the patient and faithful use of intrusted powers. Science, for instance, by which we mean the sum total of all that has been discovered respecting the laws of nature, has furnished the human race with blessings of inestimable value; and yet its secrets were never[2] revealed by a voice from heaven, and, although within the reach of human industry, were absolutely unknown to the ancient Hebrews. The living oracles intrusted to *their* charge spoke much of the nature of God, and revealed to the world that which, of himself, man could but dimly and most partially discover or understand – his relation to his Creator, the scheme of the divine government, and the means appointed for the purification and deliverance of the soul. The high majesty and grandeur of this revelation, its sacred origin and unspeakable importance, must not blind us to the fact that there are *other*[3] revelations also, which unveil to us in all their marvellous magnificence the

---

[1] 'Deus et mentis, et vocis, et linguæ artifex.' – Lactant, *Instt.* vi. 21.
[2] 'The Scriptures have *never yet revealed a single scientific truth.*' – Hugh Miller, *Testimony of the Rocks*, p. 265.
[3] 'Deus naturâ cognoscendus, dein doctrinâ recognoscendus.' – Tertullian.
'*Duo* sunt quæ in cognitionem Dei ducant, *Creatio et Scriptura*.' Aug.

works of God, and which yet were never accorded to Psalmist, or Priest, or Prophet, but to those great benefactors of their race who from time to time have been inspired to devote lives of ardent and devout study to the observation of the laws which God has imposed on His created Universe. It is hardly possible to exaggerate the blessings which science, by thus deciphering the divine records of Creation, has conferred upon mankind; yet her lessons have never been whispered by angel or law-giver, but, if we may borrow a poet's simile, they have been unclenched by sheer labour from the granite hand of nature; they have ever been not immediate but mediate; not revealed to the idle, but discovered by the patient; not direct from God, but granted indirectly through the use of appointed means. Men have attained to them, not by gliding down the lazy stream of dogmatic inference, but by

Springing from crystal step to crystal step

of that bright ascent which leads to the serene heights of knowledge. 'And because all those scattered rays of beauty and loveliness which we behold spread up and down all the world over, are only the emanations of that inexhaustible light which is above, they have climbed up always by those sunbeams to the Eternal Father of Light.' God *never* lavishes gratuitously that which man can earn by faithful industry: this is an axiom which may be confidently claimed, a truth which may be broadly asserted, of every discovery which was *possible* to the intelligence of man.

That language *is* such a discovery – that it *is* possible for man to have arrived at speech from a condition originally mute, merely by using the faculties which God had implanted – has been proved repeatedly, and will, we hope, be further illustrated in the following pages. Even those who cling with tenacity to a belief in the revelation of language are compelled to admit the[4] *possibility* of its invention. How, indeed, can this be denied when it has been a matter of constant observation that deaf and dumb children, *before they have been taught*, can and do elaborate for themselves an intelligible language of natural and conventional signs? If, then, the invention of a *voiceless* language, addressed to the eye instead of the ear, – a language so much

---

[4] Chastel, *De la Raison*, pp. 283, 295. Dug. Stewart, *Phil. of the mind*, iii, 1. Comp. Horne Tooke, *Divers of Purley*, i. 2.

more cumbrous and difficult than articulate speech, and one in which the learner can receive little or no assistance from the multitudinous echoes of external nature, – be thus easily within the range of human capabilities so unusually limited, we must conclude that a *spoken* language of which man must at once have perceived the analogon among the living creatures with which he was surrounded, and which required for its ample commencement *no achievement more difficult than the acceptance of sounds as the signs either of sounds or of the things which the sounds naturally recall*, was one which man, by the aid of the divine instincts within him, would spontaneously and easily invent, with nature as his beneficient instructress, and all the world before him as the school wherein to learn. We may therefore conclude, as Dante[5] did five centuries ago,

> That man speaks
> Is Nature's prompting, whether thus or thus
> She leaves to you as ye do most affect it;

'Entia non sunt multiplicanda, præter necessitatem,' said William of Occam; 'frustra fit per plura quod fieri potest per pauciora.' It is astonishing how much spurious philosophy and spurious theology is cut away by this razor of the Nominalists. Those theologians who, by the liberal intrusion of unrecorded and purely imaginary miracles into every lacuna of their air-built theories, do their best to render science impossible, have earned thereby the merited suspicion of scientific men. Nevertheless, all *but* the most obstinate and the most prejudiced even of theologians ought to admit that if man *could* have invented language, we may safely conclude that he[6] *did*; for the wasteful prodigality of direct interposition and miraculous power which plays the chief part in the idle and anti-scriptural exegesis of many churchmen finds no place in the divine economy of God's dealings displayed to us either in nature, in history, or in the inspired Word itself. This single consideration ought to be sufficient for any mind philosophically trained; but as too many engines cannot be employed against the invincible bastions of prejudice, let us proceed to further and yet more conclusive arguments. I have stated elsewhere[7] the *positive*

---

[5] Carey's Dante, *Parad.* xxvi, 128.
[6] Zobel, *Urspr. d. Sprache*, ad f.
[7] *Origin of Lang.*, pp. 23–29.

reasons which are adequate to disprove the revelation of language. The whole character of human speech, its indirect and imperfect methods, its distant metaphoric approximations, its traceable growth and decay, the recorded stages of historic development and decadence through which it passes, and the psychological and phonetic laws which rule these organic changes, furnish us at once with a decisive criterion of its human origin. An invention which, in spite of all its power and beauty, is essentially imperfect, could not have come direct from God. The single fact that the spiritual and abstract signification of roots is *never* the original one, but always arises from some incomplete and often wholly erroneous application or metaphor, is of itself adequate to confirm an *à priori* probability. The vast multitude[8] of human languages – certainly not fewer than 750 in number – differing from each other in words, in structure, and in sound, points inevitably, as we shall see hereafter to the same conclusion.

Speech, moreover, is the correlative of the understanding.[9] It can express nothing which has not been developed by intelligence and thought. It can have no existence independent of, or separate from our conception of things. It may be *unable to keep pace with* the advancing power of abstraction, but it can never by any possibility anticipate or outstrip it. A language without corresponding conceptions would be a babble of unintelligible sounds; 'for words,' says[10] Bacon, 'are but the image of matter; and, except they have life of reason and invention, to fall in love with them is all one as to fall in love with a picture.' If then a language were dictated, or in any

---

[8] The number is very uncertain. Pott reckons about a thousand, *Die Ungleichheit d. Menschl. Rassen.* 230–244. Adrian Babli reckons 860, *Atlas Ethnogr. Dissert. Prélim.* lxxv. sqq. Crawfurd, *Ethnol. Trans.* i. 335. 1863.

[9] Heyse, *Syst. d. Sprachwissenschaft*, p. 51. We do not deny to language a certain *maieutic* power which enables us to bring our conceptions into clearer light, by reducing them into shape, and by enabling us to reason respecting them; but when Hamann calls speech the '*Dei-para* unserer Vernunft', it is easy to see that the expression can with at least equal truth be *reversed*.

[10] *Advancement of Learning*, p. 100; compare the dictum of the Buddhist philosopher: 'Le nom et la forme ont pour cause l'intelligence; et l'intelligence a pour cause le nom et le forme.' – Burnouf, *Le Lotus de la bonne Foi*, p. 550. 'Wie der Mensch eine Einheit von Geist und Leib, so ist das Wort die Einheit von Begriff und Laut.' – Becker, *Organism d. Sprache*, § 1, 2, 4. Hermann, *Das Problem d. Sprache*, p. 1.

other manner directly revealed to the earliest men, the comprehension[11] of ideas must necessarily have been inspired with the signs which expressed them; in other words, the full-grown understanding must have been created together with the language, since the only difference between the imitative vocal faculty of children and some animals consists in the fact that with animals the sound in most instances remains a sound, while the understanding of man teaches him the conceptions *pari passu* with the sounds, so that the *sounds* become *signs*. But to assert in this sense the *creation* of the human understanding, is, after the manner of certain ignorant divines, to force upon us as an article of faith, that which is nothing more than an arbitrary[12] and anti-philosophic hypothesis. For to suppose the creation of a full-grown understanding contradicts the very nature of the understanding as 'the[13] faculty of relations or comparisons.' An understanding can no more exist without having passed through the very processes which constitute its activity, than a tree can show its thousand layers of wood without having passed through as many seasons of growth and change. The impulse to self-development, and the capacity for it, are indeed innate in the higher races of man; but to assert that the *results*[14] of this impulse were revealed, is to contradict both History and the order of nature. For nothing is more certain, even as an historical fact, than that man did not come into the world with his abstract ideas ready made; nothing is more certain than that the *growth* of abstract ideas can be distinctly traced, and that, to be primitive, a word[15] *must* express some material image.

For all reasoners, except that portion of the clergy who in all ages have been found among the bitterest enemies[16] of scientific discovery, these considerations have been conclusive. But, strange to say, here, as in so many other instances, this self-styled orthodoxy, more orthodox than the Bible itself, *directly*

[11] Maine de Biran, *Orig. de Lang.* Œuvres inéd. iii. 239.
[12] Maine de Biran, *ubi supr.* p. 233.
[13] Sir W. Hamilton, *Discussions*, p. 4, note.
[14] Heyse, *l, c.*
[15] Benloew, *Sur l'Origine des Noms de Nombre*, pp. ix. 7.
[16] Witness the lives of Vigilius, of Giordano Bruno, of Vanini, of Galileo, of Kepler, of Descartes, of La Peyrère, of Dr. Morton, of the early geologists, and of hundreds more. There is hardly a single nascent science against which theological dogmatism has not injuriously paraded its menacing array of misinterpreted or inapplicable texts.

contradicts the very Scriptures which it professes to explain, and, by sheer misinterpretation, succeeds in producing a needless and deplorable collision between the statements of Scripture and those other mighty and certain truths which have been revealed to Science and to Humanity as their glory and reward. *On the human origin of language, the voice of the Bible coincides perfectly with the voice of reason and of science.* In the passage which deals directly with the origin of language, the Bible implies, as distinctly as it is possible to imply, that language[17] resulted from the working of human faculties, and was *not* a direct gift from God to man.

We shall consider the chief passage in Genesis immediately: but before doing so it is necessary to clear away a preliminary misconception. We find repeatedly, in the earlier chapters of the Bible, the expression 'God said;' and as this is used before the mention of Adam's gift of speech, it is at once inferred that language was revealed. Surely, such a method of interpretation, stupidly and slavishly literal, and wholly incapable of rising above the simplest anthropomorphism, shows that the vail which was upon the hearts of men when Moses was read in their synagogues some 1800 years ago, is by no means as yet removed! Luther far more advanced, and far more liberal than many modern theologians, could enforce the explanation that 'God said' had nothing to do with the voice or articulations of human language; Bishop Patrick could write 'wherever in the history of the creation these words are used, *God said*, it must be understood to mean 'He[18] willed;' nay, more, St. Gregory of Nyssa could vigorously and eloquently denounce the hypothesis of a revealed language as[19] 'Jewish nonsense and folly' (φγυαρία καὶ ματαιότης Ἰουδαϊκη), and St. Augustine could unhesitatingly write '*Vidit (ratio) imponenda esse rebus vocabula, id est significantes quosdam sonos;*' yet some modern writers, essentially aggressive and essentially retogressive, – doctors of that school which

---

[17] Any one who wishes to support by authorities the Revelation of language has on his side Mohammed and some of the Rabbis! See Kircher, *Tur. Bab.* iii. 4, p. 147. Michaeler, *De Orig. Ling.* Vien. 1738. Everything that *can* be said on the question is to be found in M. de Bonald, Ladevi-Roche, and Süssmilch, *Versuch eines Beweisses dass die erste Sprache ihren Ursprung vom Schöpfer erhalten habe.* – Berl. 1766.

[18] As indeed it is rendered in the Arabic version.

[19] *Contra Eunomium Or.* xii., Aug. *de Ordine*, ii, 12. Cf. St. Basil, *Orat.* ii., and Severianus, *De Mundi Creat.* (Bibl. Patr. xii, 119).

learns nothing, and forgets nothing, and whom eighteen centuries have only pushed back behind the earliest Fathers in tolerance and liberality, – can only see in the certainty of a language discovered by mankind 'a materialist,[20] and deistic hypothesis!' Before being guilty of an inference so groundless as the supposed revelation of language from the obiter dictum of an 'auctoris aliud agentis' – an inference which contradicts the express assertion of the Jehovist when he is treating *directly* of the subject – might they not have observed that the same expression is used by the Elohist of God's laws *respecting animals?* 'And God blessed them (*i.e.* great whales, and every winged fowl, &c.), *saying*, Be fruitful, and multiply, and fill the waters in the seas, and let fowl multiply in the earth' (Gen. i, 22). Are we then to infer from this that God also revealed a language to animals,[21] and invented a dialect for birds and whales, or rather are we to open our purblind eyes to the fact that *the letter killeth*, and the spirit giveth life?

But, as I have said already, the assertors of revealed language distinctly contradict the very book to which, in their desire to usurp the keys of all knowledge, they groundlessly appeal as a scientific authority. For what does the Jehovist say? 'And out of the ground the Lord God formed every beast of the field, and every fowl of the air; and brought them unto Adam to *see*[22] what

---

[20] M. Ladevi-Roche, who in his treatise, *De l'Origine du Langage* (p. 7, 1860, Bordeaux), undertakes to resuscitate the moribund reasonings of M. de Bonald. Such arguments in this day are an anachronism, and they are not worth the trouble of refuting. There is nothing of the slightest value in his little treatise, and Science can afford to despise the declamatory anathemas hurled by the most ignorant of men at all her votaries, from Thales and Anaxagoras down to Darwin and Lyell. 'Cette opinion semblait abandonnée, quand elle a été relevée de nos jours par une école *d'un zèle fougueux et plus orthodoxe que la Bible*, et qui semble avoir pris à tâche de réaliser le fameux *Credo quia absurdum.*' – Baudry, *De la Science du Langage*, p. 32.

[21] Cf. Steinthal *Gesch. de Sprachwissenchaft*, § 15. Charma, *Ess. sur le Langage*, p. 247.

[22] לִרְאוֹת = to try. In the Arabic version it is wrongly rendered '*to teach,*' '*ut ostenderet ei quod vocaret.*' – Walton's *Polyglot*. On the other hand the Chaldee version renders 'man became a living animal,' (לְכְפֵשׁ חַיָּא) by 'a speaking spirit' (לרוח ממללא). If these versions were correct, it is obvious that the texts would contradict each other as much as they do in M. Ladevi-Roche's inference from Gen. ii. 19. 'Ce que signifie que l'homme avait été créé pensant et parlant' (p. 9). One of the rabbis explains 'that was the name thereof,' to mean its name in the thought of God before Adam uttered it. Hamann, Herder's friend, approves this explanation, and illustrates it by 'the Word was God.' – John i. 1. For a

he would call them: and whatsoever Adam called every living creature, that was the name thereof. And Adam gave names to all cattle, and to the fowl of the air, and to every beast of the field' (Gen. ii. 19, 20). When we remember the invariable tendency of the Semitic intellect to overlook in every instance all secondary causes, and to attribute every result *directly* to the agency of superior beings, it is clear that by no possibility could the writer have given more unmistakeable expression to his view that language was the product of the human intelligence, and had no origin more divine than that which is divine in man.

Nature with its infinity of sweet and varied sounds was ringing in the ears of primal man. 'Heavens!' exclaims Herder, 'what a schoolroom of ideas and of speech! Bring no Mercury or Apollo as a *Deus ex machina* from the clouds to earth. The whole many-sounding godlike nature is man's language-teacher and Muse. She leads all her creatures before him; each carries its name upon its tongue, and declares itself vassal and servant to this veiled yet visible god! It delivers to him its markword into the book of his sovereignty, like a tribute, in order that he may by this name remember it, and in the future use and call it. I ask whether this truth, viz., that the understanding, whereby man is lord of nature, was the source of a living speech which he drew for himself from the sounds of creatures, as tokens whereby to distinguish them, – I ask whether this dry truth could in Oriental fashion be more nobly or beautifully expressed than by saying that God led the animals to him to see what he would name them, and the name that he would give them, that should be the name thereof? How, in Oriental poetic fashion, can it be more distinctly stated that man discovered speech for himself out of the tones of living Nature, as a sign of his ruling intelligence? and that is the point which I am proving?[23]

---

mass of idle learning (?) on the subject of Adam's ὀνομοθεσία, see Clem. Alex. *Strom.* i. 335; Jos. *Antt.* 1, 2; Fabricius, *Cod. Pseudep.* v. 6; Buddæus, *Hist. V. T. i.* 93; Heidegger, *Hist. Patr.* i. 148; Witsius, § 3, 162; Carpzov. *Apparat. Crit.* p. 113; Otho, *Lex. Rab.* s. v. Adam; Hottinger, *Hist. Or.* 22, &c. After diligent examination of these passages, and many more on the same topic, I may safely say that more really valuable exegesis may be found in a sentence or two of Steinthal, *Urspr. d. Sprache.* p. 23; *Gesch. d. Sprachwissensch.* p. 12, 15.

[23] *Abhandlung über den Urspr. d. Sprache*, p. 77. This is one of the most eloquent and delightful essays ever written. That Herder should have lived to retract it, and retrograde into the orthodox mysticism of Hamann is truly astonishing. He gave us his own invincible arguments to acquiesce

There are other meanings of the passage in Genesis, full of profundity and moral value. This is not the place to dwell upon them, although they have almost universally been overlooked; but what we *may* at once conclude from the passage is this – that in this case, as in so many others, those who oppose science and try to sweep back with their petty human schemes of interpretation its mighty advancing tide, are usually as much at variance with the true meaning of Scripture, as they are in direct antagonism to reason and truth. 'The expressions of Moses,' says one[24] whose orthodoxy none will call in question – the late Archbishop Sumner in his 'Records of Creation' – 'are evidently adapted to the first and familiar notions derived from the sensible appearances of the earth and heavens; and *the absurdity of supposing that the literal interpretation of terms in Scripture ought to interfere with the advancement of philosophical inquiry* would have been as generally forgotten as renounced, if the oppressors of Galileo had not found a place in history.'

Chapter II
The Experiment of Psammetichus

Καὶ ἐσίοντι τὰ παιδία ἀμφότερα προσπίπτοντα ΒΕΚΟΣ ἐφώνεον. – Herod., ii. 2.

Let us try for a moment to pass back in imagination to the dawn of humanity. Let us try to conceive – not as an idle exercise of the fancy, but in accordance with inductive observations and psychological facts – the processes by which the earliest human beings were led to invent designations for the immense and varied *non-ego* of the universe around them.

The analogy between the childhood of our race and the childhood of every human being has been instinctively observed, and has been used for the purpose of linguistic experiments. Whether Frederic II (of Germany) or James IV

---

in an opinion which had been contemptuously rejected by Plato two thousand years before him, and which had even been refuted by a Father of the Church – Gregory of Nyssa – when it had been supported by Eunomius, the Arian Bishop of Cyzicus.

[24] Abp. Sumner, *Records of Creation*, i. 270.

(of Scotland)[25] ever shut up children in an island or elsewhere, with no attendants, or only such as were dumb, may not be certain; but after due deliberation, I strongly incline to accept as a fact the famous story which Herodotus received from the Egyptian priests, that a similar attempt to discover the original language was made by Psammetichus, king of Egypt. I am not aware that a single valid argument has been adduced against its authenticity. Not only does the story carry with it, in its delicious *naïveté*, the air of truth, but also it is quite certain that a nation, so intoxicated with vanity on the subject of their transcendent age as the Egyptians were, would never have *invented* a story which unjustly conceded to the Phrygians a precedence in antiquity. Accepting the story, therefore, we disagree from Professor Max Müller[26] in despising all such experiments, and, on the contrary, regard this fragment of practical philology as one of extreme value, and all the more valuable because, as he justly observes, all such experiments would now be 'impossible, illegal, and unnatural.' For the story, if it be true, establishes three most important conclusions, which are in themselves highly probable – viz., 1. That children *would* learn for themselves to exercise the faculty of speech; 2. That the first things which the young Egyptian children named were animals; and 3. That they named the goats, the only animals with which they were familiar, *by an onomatopœia;* for that Bekos, the word uttered by the children, is simply an imitation of the bleating of goats[27] is evident. It is to us a strong internal

---

[25] See *Origin of Lang.* p. 9 and p. 14, where I have given some reasons for not rejecting the story about Psammetichus, as is done by Sir G. Wilkinson (Rawlinson's *Herod*. i. 251) on very insufficient grounds.

[26] *Lectures, First Series*, p. 333. He is so far right that the experiment would be inconclusive; but why? because to make it valuable we should require *an indefinite number of children and an indefinite length of time.* But our assertion of the human origin and gradual discovery of language rests on quite other grounds.

[27] 'Bekos' is (if we regard ος as a mere Greek termination added by Herodotus) the exact and natural onomatopœia for the bleat of a goat, as has been noticed by English children; and it is in fact so used in the chorus of more than one popular song, and in the French *becqueter*. The fact that *no suspicion of such an explanation of the sound* occurred to Psammetichus, or any of those who heard the story, is an additional confirmation of the truth it is strange that no Greek was ingenious enough to hit on this explanation, although they had the onomatopœia βήξ, βήσσω, βηχία &c. Compare the French name for a goat *bouc*, Germ. *boc*, Ital. *becco*, &c.

evidence of the truthfulness of the story that it furnishes us with conclusions so exactly in accordance with those at which we arrive from a number of quite different data. The radii of inference from many other sources all converge to the common centre of a similar hypothesis. And be it observed that the fact, so far from being invented in confirmation of any such hypothesis, were interpreted by the Egyptian philosophers in a totally different, and indeed in a most ludicrous manner. The confirmation ought to remain unsuspected, because it is wholly unintentional.

(i.) As regards the first of these conclusions – that children left to themselves would evolve the rudiments of a language – Max Müller says that it 'shows a want of appreciation of the bearings of the problem, if philosophers appeal to the fact that children are born without language, and gradually emerge from mutism to a full command of articulate speech. We want no explanation how birds learn to fly, created as they are with organs adapted to the purpose.' The illustration appears to be unfortunate in many respects, and wholly beside the mark. Every bird flies at once and instinctively when its organs are full-grown – the action is as instinctive to them as sucking is to every infant mammalian; but the exercise of speech is an action infinitely complex, and innumerable accidents have proved that a *single* child growing up in savage loneliness would have *no* articulate language. But is it by any means certain that this would be the case with a *colony* of infants, isolated and kept alive by some casualty which prevented them from learning any existing dialect? The question cannot be answered with *certainty*, though it seems probable that as our knowledge advances we may be able to affirm that such must and would be the case. It is a well-known fact that the neglected children in some of the Canadian and Indian villages,[28] who are often left alone for days, can and do invent for themselves a sort of *lingua franca*, partially or wholly unintelligible to all except themselves. And if it be objected to this illustration that these children have already heard articulate speech, which, on the theory of a human invention of language, would not have been the case with the earliest men, we again appeal to the acknowledged fact that deaf-mutes have an instinctive power

---

[28] Mr R Moffat testifies to a similar phenomenon in the villages of S. Africa, *Mission. Travels.*

to develope for themselves a language of signs – a power which continues in them *until* they have been taught some artificial system, and which then only ceases because it is useful no longer – just as in the animal kingdom an organ decays, and becomes rudimentary when its exercise ceases to be of any importance to the possessor.

(ii.) Our second observation from the story of Herodotus was that the first things which the children named were animals; and this too is precisely in accordance with every-day facts. Even a young infant learns very soon to distinguish practically between the animate and the inanimate creation; and few things excite its astonishment and pleasure more than the various animals around it. Careful observations of the progress of children in the power of using speech will soon convince any one that they learn to name the dog, the cow, the sheep, and the horse among their earliest words, and indeed soon after they have learnt to attach significance to those natural sounds by which all nations express the relationships of father[29] and mother. Thus, in representing the *animals* as the first existing things which received their names from the earliest man, the Jehovist of the Book of Genesis wrote with a profound insight into the nature of language and the germs out of which it is instinctively developed.

(iii.) But, thirdly, from the fact that the only sound used by the Egyptian children was an imitation of the sounds made by the only living things with which they were familiar, we saw another indication of the fact that onomatopœia (which is only a form of the many imitative[30] tendencies which characterize the highest animals) is the most natural and fruitful source out of which the faculty of speech was instinctively evolved; – the first stepping-stone in the stream which separates sound from sense, matter from intelligence, thought from speech; – the keystone of that mighty bridge which divides the δύναμις from the ἔργον, the faculty from the fact. In this point also our inference is curiously confirmed by a variety of observed phenomena.

What, for instance, *are* the names by which, in the present day, children first learn to distinguish animals? *Are they not*

---

[29] See Buschman, *Ueber d. Naturlaut.*
[30] The cause of this particular development of the imitative instinct will be explained hereafter.

invariably onomatopoetic?[31] Is any one acquainted with any child, ordinarily trained, which first learned to a call a dog, a cow, or a sheep by their names, without having learnt, by means of the nursery onomatopœias, that a sound may stand for a thing? *This* is the most difficult lesson of all language; and when, by the use of a few words, the child has once learnt it, – when it has once succeeded in catching this elementary conception, – the rest follows with astonishing rapidity. Hence, *very few* onomatopœias, and these borrowed from the commonest and simplest objects, are sufficient for the purpose. What the child has to learn is, that a modification of the ambient medium by a motion of the tongue can be accepted as a representation of the objects which are mirrored upon his retina – in other words, that the objects of sight may be recalled and identified by articulated sounds. But how is he to learn this marvellous lesson? Only by observing instinctively that since certain things give forth certain sounds, the repetition of the sound, by an inevitable working of the law of association, recalls the object which emits it. Nor is it the slightest objection to this to say that the child does not learn the onomatopœia for itself, but learns it from its nurse. Supposing that we grant this, what does it prove? Simply the fact that every nurse and every mother is guided by the swift, beautiful, and unerring beneficence of instinct to follow the very same process which the great mother, Nature, adopted when man was her infant child – or let us say, in language more reverent, and not less true, that such a process is in instinctive unconscious accord-

---

[31] A horse does not *frequently* neigh; and this is probably the reason that in so many dialects the childish onomatopœia for it is derived, not from the sound it makes, but from the sounds (Lautgeberden) addressed to it, e.g. in English *gee-gee*; in parts of Germany, on the other hand, *hottepärd*; in Finland *humma*, &c. See Wedgwood, *Etym, Dict.* s. v. Hobby, ii. 246. (That *horse* is itself an onomatopœia seems probable from the cognate form *hross*, Germ. *Ross.*) The fact, then, that a young child names a horse from the sounds used in urging horses on, only shows how *widely various are the points which may suggest the onomatopoetic designation.* Similarly in Spain a mule-driver is called *arriero* from his cry *arri*, and in the French argot an omnibus is *aie aie*. The whole observation illustrates the active, living power of speech, which is no mere dead matter that can be handed over from father to son. See Heyse, *Syst. d. Sprachwissenschaft*, § 47. Even a watch is to a child invariably a *tick-tick*, and the very same onomatopœia is used in the Lingua Franca of Vancouver's island, and in which we also find 'hehe', 'liplip', 'tamwater.' &c. for 'laugh', 'boil', 'cataract', &c.

ance with the great method of the Creator. For the whole *idea of language*, – the conception that those impressions which the brain mainly receives through the sense of sight may be combined and expressed by means of the sense of hearing, influenced through the organs of sound, – the discovery, in fact, of a common principle, by virtue of which unity and coherence may be given to every external impression, – all lies in the discovery, by a child, that a rude ideal imitation of the bark of a dog may serve as a sign or mark for the dog itself. Hence, although Professor Max Müller's designation of the onomatopoetic theory of language as the 'bow-wow theory,'[32] was accepted by all flippant minds as a piece of crushing and convincing wit, it is really nothing but an undignified way of expression that which is, as we shall see *by his own admission*, a great linguistic probability, and which at any rate deserves respectful consideration because it has been deliberately accepted by some of the greatest thinkers and the greatest philologists of the century.

Plutarch tells us the commonly-accepted Egyptian legend that Thoth was the first inventor of language; and he adds the curious tradition that, previous to his time, men *had no other mode of expression than the cries of animals.* That such may well have been the case is illustrated by the fact that it has been found to be so among wild children lost in the woods and there caught long afterwards. Thus we are told of Clemens, one of the wild boys received in the asylum at Overdyke (an asylum rendered necessary by the number of children left destitute and uncared for in Germany after Napoleon's desolating wars), that 'his knowledge of birds and their habits was extraordinary,' and that 'to every bird he had given a distinctive and often very appropriate name of his own, which they appeared to recognise as he whistled after them;'[33] a sentence which can only mean that his onomatopœias were of the most

---

[32] We are glad to find an expression of half-regret for this unfortunate term in later editions of Prof. Müller's lectures; to abandon it finally would be but a graceful concession to the many eminent men who have held the view.

[33] See an interesting paper on *Wild Men and Beast Children*, by Mr. E. Burnet Tylor, *Anthropol. Rev.* i. p. 22; and Ladevi-Roche, *De l'Orig. du Lang.* p. 55. H-t. *Hist. d'une jeune Fille sauvage*, Paris, 1775. Tulpius, *Obs. Med.* p. 298. Camerarius, *Hor. Subsec.* Cent 1. Francf. 1602. *Dict. des Merveilles de la Nature*, § v. Sauvage. Virey, *Hist. du Genre Hum.* i. 88 and ad f. &c.

objective and simply-imitative kind. Here, then, in historical times, is a surprising, unquestionable, and most unexpected confirmation of the inferences which we felt ourselves entitled to draw from the story of Psammetichus. Without dwelling on the arguments adduced in a previous[34] work, or attaching too much importance to the fact that the aborigines of Malacca 'lisp their words, the sound of which is like the noise of birds,' or that the vocabulary of the Yamparicos is 'like the growling of a dog, eked out by a copious vocabulary of signs,' we may find a very strong indication of the reasonableness of our belief in the certainty that the more savage (*i.e.* the more natural and primitive) any language is, the more invariably does it abound in onomatopœias, and the more certain we are to find that the large majority of animals has an onomatopoetic designation.

Chapter III
The Naming of Animals

'Fingere . . . Græcis magis concessum est, qui sonis etiam quibusdam et affectibus non dubitaverunt nomina aptare; *non aliâ libertate, quam quâ illi primi homines* rebus appellationes dederunt.'

QUINCTILIAN, *Instt. Or.* viii. 3

Every fact which as yet we have passed in review would lead us to the conclusion that the first men, in *first* exercising the faculty of speech, gave names to the animals around them, and that those names were onomatopoetic.[35] It is hardly too much to say that *they could not have been otherwise*. For unless we agree with the ancient Analogists, and see a divine and mysterious connection, a natural and inexplicable harmony between words and things, by virtue of which each word necessarily expresses the inmost nature of the thing which it designates; or unless we are Anomalists, and attribute the connection of

---

[34] *Origin of Lang.* p. 75 seqq.
[35] The word 'onomatopœia' is now universally understood to mean a word invented on the basis of a sound-imitation. It may be worth a passing notice that Campbell's use of it in his Rhetoric (ii. 194), to signify the transformation of a *name* into a word, as when we call a rich man a Crœsus, or as in the line 'Sternhold himself shall be *out-Sternholded*' – is, so far as we are aware, wholly unauthorised.

words with things to the purest accident, and the most haphazard and arbitrary conventions; – unless we declare ourselves unreservedly the champions of one or other of these equally exploded views, or accept in their place some mystical or inexplicable theory of 'roots', we must be prepared with some other explanation which shall exclude from language alike the miraculous and the accidental. What this explanation is will appear hereafter; but at present we may say that, having disproved the *revelation* of language, we cannot suppose its development possible without *some* connection between sounds and objects. Now, as we have seen already, no connection is so easy and obvious, so self-suggesting and so absolutely satisfactory, as the acceptation of a sound to represent a sound, which in its turn at once recalls the creature by which the sound is uttered. If we consider the natural instinct[36] which leads to the reproduction of sounds, the brute imitations of wild-men and savage children, the onomatopoetic stepping-stones to speech adopted by *all* children, and the *à priori* presumption just explained, little or no doubt upon this point can remain in any candid mind.

But we can go yet further by examining the *actual* nomenclature of animals in existing languages.

If we consider any number of names for animals in any modern language, we shall find that they fall into various classes, viz.: 1. Those for which no certain derivation can be suggested; 2. Those derived from some analogy, or characteristic, or combination of characteristics which the animal presents; 3. Those which are distinctly onomatopoetic in origin or in form.

The first class of words cannot of course furnish us with any linguistic inferences, and may here be left out of the question;[37]

---

[36] This *imitativeness* (in which lies the tendency to onomatopœia) is found even in animals. I once possessed a young canary which never sang until it had heard a child's squeaking doll. It immediately caught up and imitated this sound, *which it never afterwards lost*. It is well-known that nest-birds, if hatched by a bird of another species, will reproduce, or attempt to reproduce, its notes. There are good reasons for believing (since wild dogs do not bark) that the bark of the domestic dog is the result of hearing the human voice. See *Rev. des Deux Mondes*, Feb. 1861.

[37] We assume, however, that every word *has* a reasonable derivation if we only knew what it was; just as we know that no *place* in the world ever received a name which could not be accounted for, though there are hundreds of such names of which we can *now* give no explanation.

under the second and third clases fall *all names of recent origin; and if, as the Bible asserts, and as has been shown to be independently probable, animals were the first objects to receive names, they* MUST *have received names belonging to the third class (viz.: onomatopœias), because no previous words would have existed wherewith to designate or combine their observed qualities.*

But the imitative origin of animal names is not only *à priori* most probable, but reasoning *à posteriori* we see it to be generally the fact. If we would discover any analogies for the speech of primitive man, we must look for them in the languages of those savage nations who approach most nearly to the condition in which man must have appeared upon the earth. Yet if we examine the vocabulary of almost any savage nation for this purpose, what are we certain to discover? *That almost every name for an animal is a striking and obvious onomatopœia.*

Take, for instance, the following names of some of the few birds and animals found in Australia:-

> *Ke-a-ra-pai.* The white cockatoo.
> *Waì-la.* The black cockatoo.
> *Ka-rong-ka-rong.* A pelican.
> *Ki-ra-ki-ra.* The cock king-parrot.
> *Kun-ne-ta.* The hen king-parrot.
> *Mo-a-ne.* The kangaroo.
> *Nga-ü-wo.* The seagull.

These are chosen almost at random from 'Threlkeld's Australian Grammar,' and in other cases the author himself calls marked attention to the similar origin of others, as follows:-

'*Kong-ko-rong.* The emu, *from the noise it makes.*' p. 87.
'*Pip-pi-ta.*[38] A small hawk, *so called from its cry.*' p. 91.
'*Kong-kung.* Frogs, *so called from the noise they make.*' p. 87.
'*Kun-bul.* The black swan, *from its note.*' p. 87.

Or again, let us take some specimens from a North American[39] dialect – the Algonquin. *Shi-sheeb*, duck; *Chee-chish-koo-wan*,

---

[38] Compare the English name *Pippit;* the Latin *Pipilare*, &c.
[39] The highly euphonic character of the *New Zealand* language renders it unsuitable for illustrating the point before us; otherwise one can hardly avoid seeing onomatopœias in *Ti-oi-oi, Aki-aki, Akoa-akoa*, the names of different birds, *Pipipi*, the *turkey*, &c. See the *Ch. Miss. Soc.'s New Zealand Gram.* Lond. 1820.

kos-kos-koo-oo, owl; *oo-oo-me-see*, screech owl; *mai-mai*, redcrested woodpecker; *pau-pau-say*, common woodpecker; *shi-shi-gwa*, rattle-snake; *pah-pah-ah-qwau*, cock.[40]

In Chinese, too, a language which is generally believed to retain more of the characteristics of primitive speech than any other, 'the number of imitative sounds is very considerable.' A few may be seen quoted by Professor Müller in the first series of his Lectures (p. 252); but in point of fact they constitute a whole class. The sixth class of Chinese characters is called Hyai-Shing 'meaning and sound'. 'These,' says Marshman,[41] in his Chinese Grammar, 'are formed by adding to a character which denotes the genus, *another which denotes the imagined sound of the species*, or the individual signified. They adduce by way of example *kyang*, which, by adding to *shooi* water, the character *kong*, forms a character which denotes a rapid stream, from an allusion to the sound of its water when rushing down with violence. And also *ho*, the generic name of rivers, which is formed by adding to *shooi*, water, *ho* the supposed sound of a river in its course.' These, with the signs Chwán-chyn, are about 3,000 in number.

Savage languages are, as we have already observed, the best to show us what *must* have been the primitive procedure; but we can trace the same necessary elements of words in languages far more advanced. In Sanskrit, for instance, is not gô, the original of our cow[42] (Germ. *kuh*; comp. the words *bos*, βοῦς, βοάω, γοάω), a direct imitation of the sound which the English child imitates by *moo* (comp. *mugire*)? Is not *bukka* a goat (comp. *bukkana* barking, *bukhâra* the lion's roar, βύσσω, βύκτης, bucca, buccina, buck, butt) a very obvious onomatopœia? Is not *çukara*[43] a pig (cf. σῦς, sus, Irish *suig*, Welsh *hwch*, Russian *cushka*) as transparently onomatopoetic as *krakara* a partridge, *hiṅkâra* a tiger? Can we see any other origin for *çvâna*, *bhashaka*, and *rudatha*, names for the dog, from *kvan* to sound, *bhash* to bark, and *rud* to cry? In *hañsa* a goose (Lithuan. 'Zâsis, Thibet. *ngangba*), and in the Persian *gígranah*,

---

[40] I have borrowed these Algonquin words from a suggestive chapter in Dr. Daniel Wilson's *Prehistoric Man*, i. 74.

[41] Marshman, *Chinese Gram.* p. 24. It must be admitted that his explanation is not particularly lucid.

[42] Gô, in Sanscrit, also means a *voice;* almost all the derivatives from it adduced by Pictet are evident onomatopœias. Even in Chinese the animal is called *ngow, gü*, &c.

[43] These words mean the animal which makes the sound, çû, kra, hin.

60 *The Origin of Language*

a crane, the same principleis indubitably at work, and in all these instances the onomatopœia, as it is indeed *incontestible*, is frankly admitted by M. Pictet,[44] the highest of authorities in everything which concerns the primitive Aryans, although he never admits such an explanation unless it is absolutely necessitated by the facts. Yet in the following cases also, where the Sanskrit root runs through the whole Aryan family of languages, he cannot avoid referring the names to simple imitation; nor can any candid reader avoid agreeing with him as a glance will show.

Bhêda. Ram; compare the Danish *beede*, &c.
Vasta. Calf; from *vad* and *sar*, giving a voice, *i.e.* lowing.
Menâda. He-goat, 'dont le cri est mê' (cf. μηκάς and the Phrygian μᾶ a sheep).
Makshika. Fly; from maç, to sound (musso).
Bha, Bhramara (cf. φρμάω, fremo, &c.). The bee.
Bambhara (cf. βόμβος, &c.). The bee; like our childish word bumble-bee.
Indindira. Great bee (cf. τιθρήνη).
Druna (probablement aussi une onomatopée). A drone.

Katurava., Frog (cri rauque); and Bhêka, frog; 'sans doute une onomatopée.'
Bhîruka (root bhr, cf. Pers. *bîr*, thunder). A bear.
Kurara and *Kharaçabda.* Eagle.
Kukkuta. A cock.
Grdhra. Vulture.
Krâgha (Pers.). Hawk (cf. *karaghah*, crow).
Krkavâku. Fowl in general; from krka, and vaç, to sound.
Uhîka, âlu, ghûka, gharghara, &c. Owls of different kinds.
Karaka. Crow. Kâka (cf. chough, &c.), 'évidemment une pure onomatopée.'
Kukûka. Cuckoo.
Koka. Swan; 'imitatif du cri kouk! kouk!'
Karatu. Crane.

---

[44] See Pictet, *Les Origines Indo-Européennes, ou les Aryas Primitifs*, i. pp. 330–535. We should certainly feel inclined to add many other words (e.g. sârispra, serpent, &c.), in spite of the often-strained and unlikely derivations suggested for them. If they were not originally onomatopœias, they have at least *become* so; and instances of this reflex tendency are hardly less important, as throwing light upon our inquiries, than names indubitably imitative in their *origin*.

Tittiri. Partridge.
Varvaka. Quail.
Pika. Woodpecker; 'cette racine n'est sans doute qu'une onomatopée.'

The list might be indefinitely multiplied; but let us now turn to the Hebrew, and see what analogous facts it offers. For the sake of English readers we will represent the Hebrew words in English characters also, that they may judge for themselves. Take, for instance, such distinctive imitative words as—

שְׁרַקְרְקָא *Scherakreka.* A pye; the Greek καράκαξα. Bochart, *Hieroz.* ii. p. 298.

זַרזִיר *Zarzîr.* A starling. *Id.* p. 353.

שְׁפִיפוֹן *Schephîphoun.* The horned snake. Gesen. *Thes.* iii. p. 146.

אַרְיֵה *Aryêh.* The lion. The supposed derivations are very doubtful.

אִיִּים *Iyîm.* Lynxes. Nomen ὀνοματοποιητικόν. Bochart, *Id.* i. 845.

גּוּר *Gûr.* A whelp.

שַׁחַל *Shâchal.* The roarer. From an Arabic root, rugitus.

דּוּכִיפַת *Dûkîphath.* Lapwing (rather Hoopoe. cf. Copt. kukupha); Lat. Upupa.[45] Bochart, *Hieroz,* ii. p. 347.

צִיִּים *Tziîm.* Wild cats, &c.

לָבִיא *Lâbhîa.* A lioness; 'rugiendi sonum imitans.' Gesen. *Thes.* s. v.

סִיס *Sîs.* A swallow; compare Ital. zizila, Lat. zinzulare, & Bochart, *Hieroz.* vol. ii. p. 62.

תּוֹר *Tôr.* A turtle-dove (*turtur,* &c.).

צְלָצַל *Tsilâtzâl.* A locust, from its shrill noise.

Again, if we take the ancient Egyptian language[46] we find such words as *mouee,* a lion; *hippep,* an ibis; *ehe,* a cow; *hepepep,* hoopoe; *croor,* frog; *rurr,* pig; *chaoo,* cat; *phin,* mouse.

We see then that, alike in the Semitic and in the Aryan families, onomatopœia supplies a *certain* and satisfactory etymology for the names of many animals; and if we add doubtful cases, where the suggested derivations are awkward and far-fetched, we might say, without exaggeration, of *most* animals.

---

[45] Hence, the Greek legend about its cry, – that it was the transformed Tereus crying Ποῦ, ποῦ.
[46] *Prehistoric Man,* i. 71.

We have seen similar onomatopœias in the ancient Egyptian, which is supposed to have affinities with both; and we have found them immensely prevalent in various sporadic families, which some would call Turanian – a name which we may on some future occasion see very good reason to reject. In fact, in these Allophylian savage dialects, and the more so in proportion to the primitive character of the people who speak them, onomatopœia appears to be the rule, and terms derived from other relations or properties the rare exception. Without going any further, is it possible to doubt what *must* have been the *tendency* of animal nomenclature among the earliest men?

It has often happened in modern times that the extension of travel and commerce has thrown nations into connection with lands in which the flora and fauna are wholly different from their own. The instinctive procedure which they adopt to name these new objects will add new strength to our position. For here again one of these four processes takes place; either 1. They adopt the existing or aboriginal term, which they find already in use; or 2. They use a compound, expressive of some quality or resemblance, as in cat-bird, snow-bird, mocking-bird, blue-bird, &c; 3. They *misapply* some previous name of the animal most nearly resembling the one to be named; or 4. If they invent a new and original (indecomposible) term, *it is invariably an onomatopœia.*

1. The first procedure requires no illustration, as it offers nothing curious or instructive beyond the fact that the shorter and easier a native name is, the more readily is it adopted. The only reason why this practice is not more common is the inordinate length of the delicate imitative appellations in primitive languages.

2. The second process is not so common, and is only interesting as illustrating the *variety* of observed characteristics by which a name may be suggested. For instance, the elephant has been called by names meaning 'the twice-drinking animal (*dvipa*), or the two-tusked (*dvirada*), or the creature that uses its hand (*hastin*); yet these different conceptions all represent one and the same object. Similarly the serpent is called in Sanskrit by names meaning 'going on the breast,'[47] or 'wind-

---

[47] *Les Orig. Indo-Eur.* i. 383. It is perhaps more common in the Zincali language than any other. Biondelli *Studii Linguistici*, p. 114, and in many argots, e.g. in the German Rothwelsch, goose is Plattfusz, hare = Langfusz, ass = Langohr, &c. – *Id.* 113.

eating'. Pictet furnishes us with many similar instances of this method of nomenclature, which is illustrated by the name duck-billed platypus, or 'beast with a bill', for the ornithorhynchus of New Zealand, and the Dutch aardvark, or 'earth-pig', for the Orycteropus capensis. 'Of everything in nature,' says Bopp, 'of every animal, of every plant, speech can seize only one property to express the whole by it.'

3. The third process deserves passing notice, because we shall see hereafter its importance. 'In the slow migrations of the human family,' says Dr. Daniel Wilson, 'from its great central hives, language imperceptibly adapted itself to the novel requirements of man. But with the discovery of America a new era began in the history of migration... In its novel scenes language was at fault. It seemed as if language had its work to do anew as when first framed amid the life of Eden. The same has been the experience of every new band of invading colonists, and it can scarce fail to strike the European naturalist, on his first arrival in the New World, that its English settlers, after occupying the continent for upwards of three centuries, instead of inventing root-words wherewith to designate plants and animals, as new to them as the nameless living creatures were to Adam in Paradise, apply in an irregular and unscientific manner the names of British and European flora and fauna. Thus the name of the English partridge is applied to one American tetranoid (Tetrao umbellus), the pheasant to another (Tetrao cupido); and that of our familiar British warbler, the robin, to the Turdus migratorius, or totally different American[48] thrush.'

Mr. E. J. Eyre remarks that when an Australian sees any object unknown to him, he does not *invent* a name for it, but immediately gives it a name drawn from its resemblance to some known object. This is very true, but it is strange that he should have considered it as peculiar to Australians.[49] On the contrary, the fact has been observed from the earliest times, and is noticed by authors so ancient as Epicurus,[50] Aristotle,[51]

---

[48] *Prehistoric Man*, i. 62.
[49] Der Mensch stellt beständig Vergleichungen an zwischen dem Neuen was ihm vorkommt, mit Alten was er schon kennt.' – Pott. *Etym. Forsch.* ii. 139.
[50] Ὅθεν καὶ περὶ τῶν ἀδήλων ἀπὸ τῶν φαινομένων χρὴ σημειοῦσθαι. – Epic. ap. Diog. Laert. x. 32.
[51] Φύσικα. i. 1.

64 The Origin of Language

and Varro. The latter[52] observes that in Latin the names of fish are usually borrowed from the land creatures whch most resemble them, as *anguilla* (eel) from *anguis* (snake). Several similar instances occur among the Romans. The elephant, for instance, they called the Lucanian *ox*, not being at first familiar with its name, and knowing of no animal larger[53] than the ox; the giraffe they styled *camelopardus*, from its points of resemblance to the camel and the leopard, and *ovis fera*[54] (or foreign sheep), from the mildness of its disposition; and they knew the black lion by the synonym of 'Libyan bear.' The Dakotas, we are told, call the horse *sungka-wakang*,[55] or spirit-dog, and Mr. Darwin[56] tells us that in 1817, 'as soon as a horse reached the shore, the whole population took to flight, and tried to hide themselves from *"the man carrying pig"* as they christened it.' Some American nations call the lion 'the great[57] and mischievous cat.' In the Fiji Islands man's flesh is known as 'long pig.' When first they saw a white paper kite[58] they called it *'manumanu'* (a *bird*), having never seen such a thing before; and money from the same cause they called *'ai Lavo,'* from its resemblance to the flat round seeds of the Mimosa scandens. The Dutch could find no better name than Bosjesbok, bush-*goat*, for the graceful African antelope; and in the Spanish name alligator we see that they regarded that unknown river-monster as a large lizard.[59] The New Zealanders called the first horses they saw 'large dogs,' as the Highlanders are said to have called the first donkey which they brought to their mountains 'a large hare.' The Kaffirs called the first *parasol*[60] to which they were introduced 'a cloud.' To this day the Malays have no better name for rat

[52] 'Vocabula piscium pleraque translata a terrestribus ex aliquâ parte similibus rebus, ut anguilla.' – Varro, *De Ling. Lat.* v. 77 (Comp. ε"χις, ἔγχελος). Compare Amos ix. 3, where 'snake' is used for a sea-creature. By a very natural transference *anguilla* in later Latin means a thong for punishing boys – the Scotch 'tawse.' – Du Cange. s.v.
[53] It is very doubtful whether in some Aryan languages there has not been a confusion between the names for *elephant* and *camel*. See Pictet s. v. *Le Chameau*.
[54] See Plin. viii. 17. Fera = peregrina.
[55] *Prehist. Man*, i. 72.
[56] *Voyage of the Beagle*, p. 408.
[57] Michaelis, *De l'Influence des Opinions sur le Langage*.
[58] Seeman, *Mission to Viti*, pp. 45, 377.
[59] El lagarto, the lizard. See Farrar, *Origin of Lang.* p. 119.
[60] Charma, *Or. du Lang.* p. 277, who refers to Condillac, *Gram.* ch. v.

than[61] 'a large mouse.' This, then, is an important principle to notice in all theories respecting language.

4. If, however, *none* of these processes furnish a convenient name for animals hitherto unfamiliar to new colonists, – if the native name be too uncouth or difficult for adoption, and the animal offer neither a ready analogy, nor any very salient property, to provide itself with a new title, – then a new name *must* be invented; and in this case we venture to assert that there is not to be found in any country *a single instance of a name so invented which is not an onomatopœia*. Such names as whip-poor-will, pee-whee (*Muscicapa rapax*), towhee (*Emberiza erythroptera*), kittawake (*Larus tridactylus*), &c., may be profusely paralleled; and in some cases the onomatopoetic instinct is so strong that it asserts itself *side by side* with the adoption of a name; thus (as in the childish words moo-cow, bumble-bee) the North American Indian will speak of a gun as an *Ut-to-tah́-*gun, or a *Paush-ske-zi-*gun. It has often been asserted that man has lost the power of inventing language, and this present inability is urged as a ground for believing that language could not have been a human invention. We have elsewhere[62] given reasons for disputing the assertion, and even if it were true, it would be beside the mark, seeing that the absence of all necessity of exercise for a faculty is the certain cause of its all-but-irretrievable decay. From the fact, however, that when men *do* invent new words they are almost invariably onomatopœias, *we see an index pointing us back with unerring certainty to the only possible origin of articulate speech*. For whatever may be true of abstract 'roots,' it is demonstrable, and will be shown hereafter, that roots which by their onomatopoetic power are the only ones capable of *explaining and justifying themselves*, so far from being the sterile playthings which Professor M. Müller represents them to be, have in them a fertility and a power of growth which can only be represented by the analogy of vegetable life, and which is as sufficient to account for the fullgrown languages of even the Aryan family as the germinative properties of an acorn are sufficient to account for the stateliest oak that ever waved its arms over British soil.

[61] Crawfurd, *Malay Gram.* i. 68.
[62] *Origin of Lang.* p. 68 sqq. A very few instances of invented words, with some remarks upon them, may be found, *Id.*, pp. 60, 61.

The history of colonisation, then, by reproducing some of the conditions of primitive man, enables us to see his linguistic instincts in *actual operation*, and those instincts undeniably confirm our theory by displaying themselves in the very directions which we have been pointing out. But we can offer yet another proof of the reasonableness of our view in certain languages of modern invention, to which we shall again allude. I mean the various Argots of the dangerous classes throughout Europe. These languages have to fulfil the opposite conditions of being distinct to those who use them, and unintelligible to the rest of the world. And how do they effect this? Partly indeed by generalising the special, and specialising the general; partly by seizing on some one very distinct attribute and describing it, if necessary, by periphrases; but also in great measure by *the obvious resource of direct sound-imitation*. Thus the German thief, no less than the English, calls a watch a *tick*, the French thief calls it *tocquante*; the Italian thief speaks of a pig as *grugnante*, the German as *grunnickel*, the English 'the grunting,' the French as *grondin*, &c. These languages must, from their very nature, remain uncultivated, and the consequence is that they abound in onomatopœia. In the English slang, a pulpit is a *hum*-box; carriages and horses are *rattlers* and *prads*. In the French argot the heart is *battant*; a sheep is *bêlant*; a grimace is *bobine*; a marionette is *bouis-bouis*; to die is *claquer*; a liar is *craquelin*; to drink a health is *cric-croc*; a skeleton-key is *frou-frou*; a glutton is *licheur*; a shoe is *paffe*; a soldier, by an onomatopœia which it would take too long to explain, is *piou-piou*; a little chimney-sweeper is *raclette*; a cab is *roulant*; a dog *tambour*; a noisy child *turabate*; and gendarmes, from the songs which soldiers like, is called *tourlouru*. These are but a few instances out of many, and it is impossible to deny that they establish the necessity of having recourse to onamatopœia when new words have to be invented. They therefore furnish a fresh support to the views here advocated.

When by strict etymological laws we have traced back a word through all its various changes, instructive and valuable as the process is sure to have been, we have done nothing to *explain* its origin or to account for its earliest history, *unless* we can point to its ultimate germ in some onomatopoetic or interjectional root; and perhaps in the *majority* of cases this can be done with a fair amount of probability; for the number of roots required for the formation of a language is extremely small; and that small number is amply supplied by the imitation of natural sounds, and by the instinctive utterances which all violent impressions produce alike in animals and in men. The reason why new words, except of an imitative kind, are *not* invented is because every word involves a long history from its sensational origin to its final meaning, and the result without the process is felt to be a contradiction and an impossibility. This is why all attempts to frame an artificial language have been a failure, and the ponderous schemes of Kircher, and Becker[63] and Dalgarno, and Wilkins and Faignet, and Letellier can only move us to a smile, because they are based on a conventional theory of language which is utterly mistaken. This, too, is the reason why language is stronger than emperors, and Tiberius[64] could neither give the citizenship to a word, nor Claudius[65] procure acceptance even for a useful letter. A radically *new* word to have any chance of obtaining currency must of necessity be of an imitative character. It is a curious fact that some of the tribes[66] on the coast of New Guinea derive *even the names which they give to their children* from direct imitations of the first sounds or cries which they utter.

We are surely entitled then to draw secure inferences from the facts hitherto observed, and those inferences may be summed up in the observation that animals were among the first objects to receive names, and that, in the absence of any previous words, they *could* not have been named except by onomatopoetic designations. This we have endeavoured to render strong and secure by many proofs, drawn both *à priori* from the nature of the case, and from the analogies presented by the methods in use among children and among savages; and *à posteriori* from the phenomena which have invariably recurred when, in the course of history, a condition of circum-

---

[63] For an account of their systems see Du Ponceau, *Mém. sur le Syst. Gram. de quelques Nations Indiennes*, pp. 26–31, 320. Hallam, *Lit. Eur.* iii. 362; and Letellier, *Établissement immédiat de la Langue Universelle*.

[64] Tu enim Cæsar civitatem potes dare hominibus, verbis non potes,' said Capito to Tiberius. – Sueton. *De Illustr. Gram.*

[65] Claudius vainly tried to introduce into the Roman alphabet an antisigma ↃC, with the value Ps. 'pro qua Claudius Cæsar Antisigma ↃC hac figurâ scribi voluit, sed nulli ausi sunt antiquam scripturam mutare. – Priscian, i. *De Literarum Numero et Affinitate*.

[66] Salverte, *Hist. of Names*, i. 62. Engl. Transl.

stances has been reproduced which in any way resembles that which must have existed in the case of primal man.

Chapter IV.
The Infancy of Humanity

Ἦν χρόνος ὅτ᾽ ἦν ἄτακτος ἀνθρώπῳ βίος,
Καὶ θηριώδης, ἰσχύος θ᾽ ὑπηρέτης.
.... τηνικαῦτά μοι δοκεῖ
Πυκνός τις ἄλλος καὶ σοφὸς γνώμην ἀνὴρ
Γεγονέναι, ὅς ...
.... τὸ θεῖον εἰσηγήσατο.

IGNOT. *ap*. SEXT. EMPIRIC.

As we have here arrived at a sort of landing-place, we may devote a separate chapter to consider the full bearing of the conclusions thus formed. In so doing, we are not digressing from the main point, but rather we are removing a groundless prepossession which would lie in the road of all further advance, and we are at the same time calling attention to one of those important facts which it is the object of philology to illustrate or discover.

For, obviously, if language was a human invention, and was due to a gradual development, there must have been a time in man's history when he was possessed of nothing but the merest rudiments of articulate speech; in which, therefore, he must have occupied a lower grade than almost any existing human tribe. This is a conclusion which cuts at the root of many preconceived theories. Thus, Lessing[67] remarks that God is too good to have withheld from his poor children, perhaps for centuries, a gift like speech; and M. de Bonald asks how we can suppose 'that a Good Being could create a social animal without remembering that he ought also from the first moment of his existence to inspire him with the knowledge necessary to his individual, social, physical, and moral life.' Such reasoners, therefore, reject the doctrine of the human origin of language as alike an injustice to God and an indignity to man.

In answer to such 'high priori' reasonings, it might be sufficient to say that we are content, for our part, humbly to

---

[67] *Sämmtl. Schriften*, Bd. x.

observe and record what God *has* done, rather than to argue what He *ought* to do or ought not to do, incompetent as we are in our absolute ignorance 'to measure the arm of God with the finger of man.' Claiming for ourselves the character of observers only, and desirous to accept the results to which our enquiries directly lead, without any regard to system or prejudice, we might easily repudiate assumptions which rest on the mere sandy basis of systematic prejudice. It is childish arrogance in us to argue what plans are consonant to, and what are derogatory of God's Divine Power and Infinite Wisdom. Seeing that we have not the capacity for understanding that which *is*, it is preposterous in us to argue on any general principles as to what *must* have been. Perfect humility and perfect faith, – a faith in Truth which seems to have the least power in many of the loudest champions of a supposed orthodoxy, – are the first elements of scientific success. The problems and mysteries which encumber all our enquiries, – the adamantine wall against which we dash ourselves in vain whenever we seek to penetrate the secrets of the Deity, – should at least prevent us from following Lessing and M. de Bonald in laying down rules of our own, in accordance with which we fancy that God MUST inevitably have worked.

Moreover, if language was a Revelation and not an Invention, at what *period* in man's life was it revealed? If, indeed, man was, according to the Chaldee paraphrast, *created* 'a speaking intelligence' (see p. 10), we get over this difficulty, though it is only at the expense of an absurdity, and by making the Bible contradict itself. But if not, there must have been a time, on any supposition, when man wandered in the woods a dumb animal, till God bethought Him of inspiring language. Surely such a view is even less pious than that of Lucretius himself. 'Any one,' says Steinthal,[68] 'who thinks of man without a Language' [or, he should have added, the *capacity for evolving* a language] 'thinks of him as one of the Brutes; so that any one who calls down the Deity as his teacher of Language, gives Him only an animal as a scholar.' In other words, unless man was *born* speaking, – (and it is apparent in Scripture that language was *subsequent* to creation), – then, even on this theory, man must have *once* been destitute of a language, and must, therefore, on this theory also, have emerged from a

[68] *Urspr. d. Sprache*, p. 40.

condition of mutism. Why then should a similar belief be held an insuperable objection to a theory so certain as the human discovery of language? It is forsooth an insult to the dignity of man and a slur on the beneficence of God to suppose that man appeared on this earth in a low and barbarous condition! But WHY is it? Do those who use such reasonings consider that they are thereby arraigning and impugning before the bar of their own feeble criticisms the *actual* dealings of God? If it be indeed irreconcileable with God's goodness to suppose that He would have created man in a savage state, is it *more* easy to believe that He would *now* suffer, as He *does* suffer, the existence of thousands who are doomed throughout life to a helpless and hopeless imbecility, and that for no fault of their own? – thousands in which the light of reason has been utterly quenched; thousands in whom it never existed, and who pass in helpless idiocy from the cradle to the grave, as irresponsible as the brutes who perish, without language, without religion, without knowledge, without hope? Facts like these ought to silence us for ever when we attempt beforehand to assign limits to the possible workings of God's Providence. We *know* that He is infinitely good and gracious, but we *cannot* know how His Providence will work.

If for many ages millions of the human race have been, and still are, born into a low and barbarous condition, why may they not have been originally so created? We know from history and from ordinary reasoning that existing savage races could not have *sunk*[69] into this condition, and there seems every ground for believing that they are morally, mentally, and physically incapable of rising out of it, since they melt away before the advance of civilisation like the line of snow before the sunlight. 'God,' says M. Jules Simon,[70] 'who suffers millions of savages to exist in three quarters of the globe, may well be supposed to have permitted in the beginning that which he permits at the present day.' What shall we say, for instance, of the tallow-coloured Bosjesman,[71] who lives for the most part

---

[69] Archbp. Whately (*Preliminary Dissert.* iii. in the *Encycl. Britannica*) argues that savages can never, *of themselves*, rise out of degradation; it is as easy to show that they can never *sink* into such a condition. We do not believe that the primeval savages were in any way direct ancestors of the two nobles races – the Aryan and the Semitic.
[70] *Rev. des Deux Mondes*, 1841, p. 536.
[71] Caldwell, *Unity of the Human Race*, p. 75.

on beetles, worms, and pismires, and is glad enough to squabble with the hyæna for the putrid carcass of the buffalo or the antelope? Of the leather-skinned Hottentot,[72] 'whose hair grows in short tufts, like a worn-down shoe brush, with spaces of bare scalp between,' and who is described as a creature 'with passions, feelings, and appetites as the only principles of his constitution'? Of the Yamparico, 'who speaks a sort of gibberish like the growling of a dog,' and who 'lives on roots, crickets, and several bug-like insects of different species'?[73] Of the aboriginies of Victoria,[74] among whom newborn babes are killed and eaten by their parents and brothers, and who have no numerals beyond three? Of the Puris[75] of Brazil, who have to eke out their scanty language by a large use of signs, and who have no words for even such simple conceptions as 'to-morrow' and 'yesterday'? Of the naked, houseless, mischievous, vindictive Andamaner,[76] with a skull hung ornamentally round his neck? Of the Fuegians,[77] 'whose language is an inarticulate clucking,' and who kill and eat their old women before their dogs, because, as a Fuegian boy naïvely and candidly expressed it, 'Doggies catch otters, old women no'? Of the Banaks,[78] who wear lumps of fat meat, artistically suspended in the cartilage of the nose? Of the negroes of New Guinea,[79] who were seen springing from branch to branch of the trees like monkeys, gesticulating, screaming, and laughing? Of the Alforese[80] of Ceram, who live in trees, 'each family in a state of perpetual hostility with all around'? Of the forest-tribes of Malacca,[81] 'who lisp their words, whose sound is like the noise of birds?' Of the wild people of Borneo,[82] whom the

[72] *Personal Adventures in S. Africa*, by Rev. G. Brown (a missionary), p. 7.
[73] Capt. Mayne Reid, *Odd Races*, p. 330 sqq.
[74] W. Stainbridge on the *Aborigines of Victoria*. – *Trans. of Ethn. Soc.* 1861, p. 289. Fern-roots, grubs, mushrooms, and frogs are their main diet; that of some other savages is too disgustful for utterance. – Greenwood, *Curiosities of Savage Life*, p. 15.
[75] Mad. Ida Pfeiffer, *Voyage around the World*.
[76] Mouatt's *Andamaners*, p. 328.
[77] Darwin, *Voyage of a Naturalist*, p. 214. The boy who gave the philosophic defence of cannibalism, imitated, as a great joke, the screams of the poor old women, while being choked in the smoke.
[78] Hutchinson, *Ten years' Wanderings*, p. 245.
[79] Crawfurd, *Malay Gram.* i. clxi.
[80] Pickering, *Races of Man*, p. 304 sqq.
[81] *Id.*
[82] *Id.*

Dyaks hunt as if they were monkeys? Of the cannibal Fans[83] of equatorial Africa, who bury their corpses before eating them? Of the pigmy Dokos,[84] south of Abyssinia, 'whose nails are allowed to grow long like the talons of vultures, in order to dig up ants and tear in pieces the flesh of serpents, which they devour raw'? Of the wild Veddahs[85] of Ceylon, who have gutturals and grimaces instead of language; 'who have no God; no idea of time and distance; no name for hours, days, or years; and who cannot count beyond five on their fingers'? Of the Miautsee,[86] or aborigines of China, whose name means 'children of the soil,' and who, like the Malagassy, the Thibetans, and many African tribes, attribute their origin not to gods and demigods, not even to lions (as do the Sahos), or to goats (as do the Dagalis), but, with unblushing unanimity, to the ape? Of the Negrilloes of Aramanga, the Battas of Sumatra, the wild people of Borneo, the hairy Ainos of Jesso, the Hyglaus of the White Nile, the Kukies and other aborigines of India, even the Cagots and other Races Maudites of France and Spain? These beings, we presume no one will deny, are men with ordinary human souls. If then God can tolerate for unknown generations the perpetuation of such a state of existence as this, – the perpetuation of people with squalid habits, mean and deformed heads, hideous aspect, and protuberant jaws, – what possible ground is there for denying that he may also have suffered men at the Creation to live in what is called a state of nature, which is the name given to a state of squalor and ignorance, of savagery and degradation? Considering these facts, and believing with Schlegel that savage nations are savage by nature, and must ever remain so, some (and among them Neibuhr) have been Polygenists precisely *because* they thought it was more consonant with God's attributes to have created men in different grades of elevation than to have suffered them to degenerate in so many regions from

---

[83] Du Chaillu's *Equatorial Africa*. This has been denied.
[84] Prichard, *Nat. Hist.* i. 306. Norris's Note. Dr. Davy, *Researches*, ii. 177.
[85] Sir J. Emerson Tennent, *Ceylon*.
[86] Authorities for the facts mentioned in these two sentences will be found in Ritter, *Erdkunde, Asien*, ii. 273, 431 sqq; Hope, *Ess. on the Origin of Man*; Virey, *Hist. Nat. du Genre Humain*, ii. 12; i. 190. Pickering, *Races of Man*, 175–179, 302–308; *Journ. Asiat, Soc. of Bengal*, xxiv. 206; Prichard, *Nat. Hist. of Man*, i. 250–274 (ed. Norris). Pouchet, *Des Races*, p. 59; Perty, *Anthropol, Vorträge*, p. 41; Michel, *Hist. des Races maudites*, &c.

a condition originally exalted.[87] The argument in this case may be as worthless as in the other; but what is the value of a method of reasoning from which two conclusions so opposite can be drawn!

It would be an error to suppose that 'the state of nature,' with its imperfect language, its animal life, its few natural wants, its utter ignorance, is necessarily a state so low as to render existence a misfortune or a curse. Nature, in all probability, provided as bountifully for her first-born as she does for many of his descendants; and if not, she at any rate 'makes habit omnipotent and its effects hereditary.' Even the Fuegian, in his land of cold and rain, – crawling from the lair in which he lies, unsheltered, coiled up like an animal on the wet ground, to gather at all hours, from morn till midnight, the mussels and berries, which are his only food, – does not decrease in numbers, and must, therefore, as Mr. Darwin observes,[88] be supposed 'to enjoy a sufficient share of happiness (of whatever kind it may be) to render life worth having.' It is hard to say how little is 'necessary' for man; and it is certain, both from Scripture and history, that not only the luxuries and ornaments of life, but even those things which we regard as indispensable, were the gradual inventions, or long-delayed discoveries, of a race which had received from God certain faculties in order that they might at once be exercised and rewarded by a perpetual progress in dignity and self-improvement. There can be no question that the systems of those Rabbis and Fathers,[89] and their modern imitators, who make Adam a being of stupendous knowledge and superhuman wisdom, are more improbable, as well as more unscriptural, than those of writers who, like Theophilus of Antioch among the Fathers, and Joseph Ben Gorion among the Jews, make his original condition a weak and inferior one. Philosophy, the arts, the sciences, the observations of the simplest natural facts, the elucidation of the simplest natural laws, required centuries to elaborate. We do not even hear of the first *kingdom* till some thousands of years

---

[87] Pouchet, *Plural. des Races*, p. 105.
[88] Darwin, *Voy. of a Naturalist*, p. 216.
[89] Clem. Alex. *Strom.* iv. 25, § 173; 23, § 152. Buddæus, *Philos. Hebr.* 383–388, where he gives the Rabbinic fancies about Adam Kadmon. Suidas *s. v.* 'Αδάμ. South, *State of Man before the Fall*, &c. On the other side see Clem. Alex. *Strom.* vi. 12, § 96; Greg Naz. *Orat.* xxxviii. 12; and even Irenæus, *Adv. Hæres.* iv. 38.

after the first man. It is but as yesterday that man has wrung from the patient silence of Nature some of her most important, and apparently her most open secrets.

It is forsooth a degradation to suppose that man originated in an ignorant and barbarous condition! People prefer the poets' fancies: –

> One man alone, the father of mankind,
> Drew not his life from woman; never gazed
> With mute unconsciousness of what he saw
> On all around him; learned not by degrees:
> Nor owed articulation to his ear;
> But, moulded by his Maker into man,
> At once upstood intelligent, surveyed
> All creatures; with precision understood
> Their purport, uses, properties; assigned
> To each his place significant; and filled
> With love and wisdom, rendered back to Heaven
> In praise harmonious the first air he drew.
> He was excused the penalties of dull
> Minority. . . . History, not wanted yet,
> Leaned on her elbow, watching Time, whose course
> Eventful should supply her with a theme.[90]

Fascinating and poetical, no doubt; the primal man, regarded as a being beautiful of body, gracious in soul,[91] filled in heart with virgin purity and sweetness, and discovering everything with exquisite and lightning-like spontaneity! Nevertheless, 'Science[92] banishes amongst myths and chimeras the fancy of a primitive man, burning with youth and beauty, to show us upon icy shores I know not what abject being, more hideous than the Australian, more savage than the Patagonian, a fierce animal struggling against the animals with which he disputes his miserable existence.' What support is there for the poetic

---

[90] Cowper, *The Task*.
[91] The Bible tells us nothing of this kind; but it would take us too long here to examine fully the Biblical data. I believe that when fairly and thoroughly considered, they *sanction* the view here expressed. For a picture of frightfully degraded aboriginal races, see Job xxx. 1–8; Ewald, *Gesch. d. Volkes Israel*, i. 27; De Gobineau, i. 486.
[92] Aug. Laugel, *Rev. des Deux Mondes*, May 1, 1863; cf. De Gobineau, *De l' Inégalité des Races*, i. 228; Link, *Die Urwelt*, i. 84; Lyell, *Princ. of Geol.* i. 178; Laugel, *Science et Philosophie*, p. 270.

hypotheses of those who love their own assumptions better than they love the truths which science reveals? In a handful of rude and bizarre traditions, in a few skulls of the very meanest and most[93] degraded type, in here and there a gnawed fragment of human bones, in a few coarse and pitiable implements of bone and flint, what traces have we of that radiant and ideal protoplast whom men have delighted to invest with purely imaginary attributes, and to contemplate as the common ancestor of their race? But man, in his futile and baseless arrogance, must exalt the earliest representatives of his kind, though he cannot deny the inifinite debasement of his contemporary brethren. He refuses to see in his far-off ancestors what he *must* see in his living congeners, a miserable[94] population maintaining an inglorious struggle with the powers of nature, wrestling with naked bodies against the forest animals, and forced to dispute their cave-dwellings with the hyæna and the wolf.

Years pass before the infant can realise and express his own individuality; ages may have rolled away before those ancestors of man, who lived in the dim and misty dawn of human[95] existence, could in any way understand their own position in the yet untamed chaos of the ancient world. The recognition of the long and feeble periods of animalism and ignorance is no more degrading to humanity than the remembrance of the time when he was rocked, and swaddled, and dandled in a nurse's arms is a degradation to any individual man. Disbelieving, on the scientific ground of the Fixity of Type,[96] the Darwinian hypothesis, we should yet consider it disgraceful and

[93] It has even been suspected (most likely on insufficient ground), from the position of the *foramen magnum,* that the head was not vertical on the neck. See *Ethnol. Trans.* p. 269, 1863.

[94] It is agreed on all hands that Gen. i. 26, has no bearing on this question, since it refers to the moral and intellectual nature of man – reason, liberty, immortality. 'Non secundum formam corporis factus est ad imaginem Dei, sed secundum rationalem mentem.' – Aug. *de Trin.* xii. 7. Obviously, if all men – even Mundrucus and Ostiaks – are created in the 'image of God,' then the first men were so, however low their grade.

[95] It is a remarkable fact that native legends betray a reminiscence of the Elk, Mastodon, Megalonyx, Deinotherium, &c. Hamilton Smith, *Nat. Hist. of Human Spec.* pp. 104–106; Maury, *Des Ossements humains (Mém. de la Soc. des Antiq.* i. 287), &c.

[96] I may perhaps be allowed to refer to my paper on this subject read before the British Association in 1865, and now in the Ethnolog. Soc.'s *Transactions.*

humiliating to try to shake it by an *ad captandum* argument, or a claptrap platform appeal to the unfathomable ignorance and unlimited arrogance of a prejudiced assembly. We should blush to meet it with an anathema or a sneer; and in doing so we should be very far from the assumption 'that we were on the side of the angels!'

Is it not indisputable that man's body – 'all but an inappreciable fragment of its substance' – is composed of the very same materials, the same protein and fats, and salines, and water, which constitute the inorganic world – which may unquestionably have served long ago as the dead material which was vivified and utilised in the bodies of extinct creatures – and which may serve in endless metensomatosis[97] for we know not what organisms yet to come? Was there, or was there not, a time in the embryonic dawn of individual life, when every one of us drew the breath of life by means not of lungs but of a species of gills? Is this fact any disgrace to us, or will any pseudo-theologian have the dogmatic hardihood to deny it? Are we, in our gross and haughty ignorance, to assume that, because by God's grace we carry in ourselves the destinies of so grand a future, a deep and impassable gulf of separation must therefore divide even the material particles of our frame from those of all other creatures which find their development in so poor a life? What sanction have we for this assumption? Is it to be found in the future fate of the elements of our body – destined, as we know they are, to be swept along by the magic[98] eddy of nature, to be transmuted by her potent alchemy into nameless transformations, and subjected by her pitiless economy to what we should blindly consider as nameless dishonour? or, looking backwards as well as forwards, is it to be found in the fact that there are stages in the earlier development of the human embryo, during which the most powerful microscope, and the most delicate analysis, can neither detect nor demonstrate the slightest difference between the[99] three living germs of which one is destined to be a wolf, the second a horse, and the third a man? If the question *is* to be degraded from scientific decision into a matter for tea-table æsthetics

---

[97] If the word, which has the authority of Clemens Alexandrinus, and which is now imperiously demanded by the wants of science, may be pardoned on the score of its necessity.
[98] Coleridge, *Aids to Reflection*; Huxley, *Lect.* pp. 15–19; *Hamlet*, v. 1.
[99] Karl Snell, *Die Schöpfung des Menschen*, p. 130.

and ignorant prepossessions, is this certain embryonic degradation of immaturity *less* oppressive than the admission of a bare possibility that, myriads of centuries ago, there may have been a near genetic connection between the highest of the animals and the lowest of the human race? It is not yet proved that there was; we believe that there was *not*; but nevertheless, the hypothesis is neither irreverent nor absurd. Let those who love truth only consider what *are* the certain facts about our mortal bodies, and be still; – awaiting the gradual revelation of His own past workings which the All-wise Creator may yet vouchsafe, not assuredly to the clamorous, the idle, and the ignorantly denunciative, but to humble and studious enquirers – to those loftier and less self-complacent souls, whom He has endowed with the desire, the wisdom, and the ability to search out the pathless mystery of His ways, through long years of noble and self-sacrificing toil.

It has, indeed, been asserted that the languages of some barbarous nations – for instance, the Greenlanders and the North American Indians – are of so rich, so perfect, and so artistic a structure, that they could not possibly have been achieved by them in their present condition, and furnish a proof that they have sunk into savagery from a state of higher culture. Du Ponceau[100] speaks in the most glowing terms of the genius displayed in the infinite variety and perfect regularity of those languages. Charlevoix calls attention to the beautiful union of energy and nobleness in the Huron, where, as in the Turkish, 'tout se conjugue.' Dr. James says that there are seven or eight thousand possible forms of the verb in Chippeway. Appleyard[101] tells us that 'the South African languages, though spoken by tribes confessedly uncivilised and illiterate, are highly systematic and truly philosophical;' that in Kafir there are a hundred different forms for the pronoun 'its,'[102] and that 'the system of alliteration maintained throughout its grammatical forms is one of the most curious and ingenious ever known.' Threlkeld[103] tells us similar facts about the Australian dialects; and Caldwell,[104] in his 'Comparative Grammar of the Dravid-

---

[100] Ét. du Ponceau, *Mém. sur le Syst. Gram. de quelques Nations indiennes*, passim. A most valuable and brilliant work.
[101] *Kafir Grammar*, pref.
[102] *Id*. p. 66; p. 6, note, &c.
[103] Threlkeld, *Australian Gram.* p. 8.
[104] *Dravidian Grammar*, pp. 126–138.

ian Languages,' occupies many pages with the laws of euphonic permutation of consonants and harmonic sequence of vowels, which exist both in those and in the Scythian languages. Instances of similar exuberance and complexity in savage languages might be indefinitely multiplied:[105] and the argument that they imply an intellectual power superior to what we now find in these races, and that they therefore prove a condition previously exalted, is so plausible that in a former[106] work I regarded it as convincing. Further examination has entirely removed this belief. For this apparent wealth of synonyms and grammatical forms is chiefly due *to the hopeless poverty of the power of abstraction*. It would be not only no advantage, but even an impossible incumbrance to a language required for literary purposes. The 'transnormal' character of these tongues only proves that they are the work of minds incapable of all subtle analysis, and following in one single direction an erroneous and partial line of development. When the mind has nothing else to work upon, it will expend its energy in a lumbering and bizarre multiplicity of linguistic expedients, and by richness of expression will try to make up for poverty of thought. Many of these vaunted languages (*e.g.* the American and Polynesian) – these languages which have countless forms of conjugation, and separate words for the minutest shades of specific meaning – these holophrastic languages, with their 'jewels fourteen syllables long,' to express the commonest and most familiar objects – so far from proving a once elevated intellectual condition of the people who speak them, have not even yet arrived at the very simple abstraction[107] required to express the verb 'to be,' which Condillac assumed to be the earliest of invented verbs! The state of these languages, so far from proving any retrogression from previous culture, is an additional proof of primordial and unbroken barbarism. The

---

[105] Appleyard, p. 69; Du Ponceau, p. 95; Howse, *Cree Gram.* p. 7; Pott, *Die Ungleichheit d. menschl. Raçen*, p. 253; Steinthal, *Charakteristik*, p. 176; Maury, *La Terre et l'Homme*, p. 463.
[106] *Origin of Lang.* p. 28. See, too, Vater, *Mithrid.* iii. 328.
[107] In American and Polynesian languages there are forms for 'I am well,' 'I am here,' &c., but not for 'I am.' In Elliot's Indian Bible 'I am that I am,' is rendered 'I do, I do' (compare the French idiom 'il *fait* nuit,' & c.) More than this, savage nations cannot even adopt the verb 'to be.' A negro says, 'Your hat no *lib* that place you put him in.' 'My mother done *lib* for devilly' (=is dead). – Hutchinson, *Ten Years' Wanderings*, p. 32.

triumph of civilisation is not complexity but simplicity: and unless an elaborate Polytheism be more intellectual than Monotheism – unless the Chinese ideography, with its almost indefinite number of signs, be a proof of greater progress than our alphabet – then neither is mere Polysynthetism and exuberance of synonyms a proof of actual culture in the past, or possible progress in the future. If language proves anything, it proves that these savages must have lived continuously in a savage condition.[108]

I will here quote two high and unbiassed authorities in support of the same conclusion:–

'It has already been observed,' says Mr. Garnett,[109] 'that very exaggerated and erroneous ideas have been advanced respecting the structure of the class of languages of which we have been treating in the present paper. They have been represented as the products of deep philosophical contrivance, and totally different in organisation from those of every part of the known world. The author of "Mithridates" regards it as an astonishing phenomenon that a people like the Greenlanders, struggling for subsistence among perpetual ice and snow, would have found the means of constructing such a complex and artificial system. It is conceived that there cannot be a greater mistake than to suppose that a complicated language is like a chronometer, or a locomotive engine, a product of deep calculation, and preconceived adaptation of its several parts to each other. The compound parts are rather formed like crystals, by the natural affinity of the component elements; and whether the forms are more or less complex, the principle of aggregation is the same.'

'In those which abound most in inflections,' says Mr. Albert Gallatin,[110] 'nothing more has been done than to effect, by a most complex process, and with a cumbersome and unnecessary machinery, that which, in almost every other language, has been as well, if not better performed by the most simple means. Those transitions, in their complexness, and in the still visible amalgamation of the abbreviated pronouns with the verb, bear, in fact, the impress of primitive and unpolished languages.'

---

[108] See among many other authorities Pott, *Die Ungl. der menschl Raçen*, p. 86; Due Ponceau, *Transl. of Zeisberger's Lenni-Lenape Gram.* p. 14; Crawfurd, *Malay Gram.* i. 68; Adelung, *Mithrid.* iii. 6, 205.
[109] *Philological Essays*, p. 321.
[110] *Archæologia Americana*, ii. p. 203, quoted by Mr. Garnett.

Language, then, from whatever point of view we regard it, seems to confirm instead of weakening the inference to which we are irresistibly led by Geology, History, and Archæology – that Man,

> The heir of all the ages in the foremost files of Time,

is a very much nobler and exalted animal than the shivering and naked savage whose squalid and ghastly relics are exhumed from Danish kjökken-möddings, and glacial deposits, and the stalactite flooring of freshly-opened caves. These primeval lords of the untamed creation, so far from being the splendid and angelic beings of the poet's fancy, appear to have resembled far more closely the Tasmanian, the Fuegian, the Greenlander, and the lowest inhabitants of Pelagian caverns or Hottentot kraals. We believe that in Scripture itself there are indications that they appeared upon the surface of the globe many ages before those simple and noble-minded shepherds from whose loins have sprung the Aryans and Semites – those two great races to whom all the world's progress in knowledge and civilisation has been solely due.

ON THE ORIGIN OF LANGUAGE
Edward B. Tylor

Source: *Fortnightly Review*, vol. 4, April 1866

When we study the pictures and gestures by which savages and the deaf and dumb express their minds, we can mostly trace the relation between the outward sign and the inward thought which it makes manifest. Seeing the idea of 'sleep' shown in gesture by the head with shut eyes, leant heavily against the open hand; or the idea of 'running' by the attitude of the runner, with chest forward, mouth half open, elbows and shoulders well back; or 'candle' by the straight forefinger held up, and, as it were, blown out; or 'salt' by the imitated act of sprinkling it with thumb and finger, – we so far understand the nature of this means of human utterance, that we can see how we should of ourselves express our thoughts by like methods, so that others, seeing our signs, should thereby perceive our meaning. And, again, the figures of the child's picture-book, the sleeper and the runner, the candle and the salt-cellar, show their purport by the same sort of evident relation between thought and sign. What St. Thomas Aquinas said of language, that the names of things ought to agree with their natures (*nomina debent naturis rerum congruere*), is not only true, but obviously true, of the Gesture-Language and Picture-Writing. But if, encouraged by our ready success in making out the nature and mode of action of these ruder methods, we turn to the higher art of Speech, and ask how such and such words have come to express such and such thoughts, we find ourselves face to face with a problem of which it is as yet only possible to offer a solution of some small parts, large enough indeed to inspirit us to push forward the research, but only covering, as it were, a corner here and there of a vast and elsewhere unknown field.

When I speak of solutions of this problem of the Origin of Language, I mean positive and definite solutions, not metaphysical or abstract ones. Of these latter there is, indeed, no lack. Some have held that language was revealed to man by supernatural interference; others, that he spoke naturally and instinctively as a bird sings; others, that language was contrived artificially by men who settled in conclave what arbitrary meaning each sound should bear; others, that the roots of language were sounds having an inherent suitability to express certain ideas, and so on. But however much of truth may be contained in such theories as these, they all have this fatal defect, that to us they stand none the better for being true, and none the worse for being false. Like the stories of strange monsters dwelling in the outer regions of the world, they may place themselves on an equal ground of assertion until the time when real knowledge shall come to divide the true from the false. The one-eyed Arimaspi who rob the guardian griffins of their treasures in the gold fields of the far North, and the Antipodes who walk, feet up and head down, on the under side of the earth, like flies upon a ceiling, the headless men of Africa and the noseless men of Asia, have to stand side by side in books of geography till travellers prove which are fabulous, and which are altogether or at least colourably true. So our business in studying the great problem of language is not, with the metaphysician, to map out imaginary roads through an ideal land, but rather, with the patient student of detail, to follow up tracks which really lead somewhere, though it be but a very little way, and to seek out the openings to new ones.

Of words which have their meaning, not by inheritance from parents or adoption from foreigners, but by being taken up directly from the world of sound into the world of sense, there are three kinds at present known. The first two, Interjectional Words and Imitative or Onomatopoetic Words, have grown familiar to us by long and even popular discussion. When a philosopher has in his hands a morsel of solid truth, he is apt enough to stretch it further than it will bear. The magic umbrella must spread and spread till it becomes a tent wide enough to shelter the king's army. No wonder that students' who found in nature real and direct sources of articulate speech, in interjectional sounds like *ah! ugh! h'm! sh!* and in imitative sounds like *cuckoo, tomtom, purr, whiz*, should have fancied that the whole secret of language lay within their grasp, and that they had but to fit the keys thus found into one hole after another in order to open every lock. These are the theories which, stretched as they often have been from reasonable argument into mere fanciful dogmatism, were laid open by Max Müller in one of his most caustic passages as the 'Pooh-pooh theory' and the 'Bow-wow theory.' But it must be borne in mind that what criticism touches in these opinions is their exaggeration, not their reality. That interjections and imitative words are really taken up to some extent, be it small or large, into the very body and structure of language, no one denies. Such a denial, if any one offered it, the advocates of the disputed theories might dispose of in the single phrase, that they would neither be *pooh-poohed* nor *hooted* down. The question is only one of extent; – some say such words are few and of little importance; others, such as Wedgewood, Farrar, and Wilson, that they are many and of a great deal. Dispassionate inquirers, who are advocates of neither theory, will follow both, trusting them, as the saying is, just so far as they can see them. The third or Symbolic class of words shades gradually into the Imitative class. To discuss, with the aid of some new materials, the characters of these three classes of direct words, as they may be called, the Interjectional, the Imitative, and the Symbolic, is the object of the present essay.

'The brutish inarticulate *Interjection*,' as Horne Tooke called it, has long been set down by the grammarians as a natural sound, used to express some passion or emotion of the mind. Such a definition may not teach us much about what purpose interjections really serve, and how, but it goes far toward explaining something else, namely, why we know so little about them. For of all means of stifling rational inquiry nothing equals this – to get the opinion firmly held that any phenomenon is 'natural.' The reason little girls give to an embarrassing 'Why is so-and-so?' – 'Because it is,' is somewhat too crude; but put it, 'Because it is naturally so,' and the philosophic mind rests and is thankful that a new problem has been solved, and thus the secret of other whys and wherefores underlying this 'naturally' is kept by that most effectual of means, the concealment of there being anything to conceal. The unlucky interjections, too, have fared badly in another way. Alphabetic writing is far too incomplete and clumsy an instrument to render their peculiar and variously modulated sounds, for which a few conventionally written words do duty poorly enough, while in reading aloud, and sometimes even in the talk of those who have learnt rather from books than from the living world, we hear these awkward copies, *ahem! hein! tush! tut! pshaw*! now carrying the unquestioned authority of words printed in a book, and reproduced, letter for letter, with an accuracy worthy of all praise.

Written letters can indeed do little more than suggest the real sounds of interjections proper. From these must of course be distinguished the many sense-words which, often in a mutilated or old-fashioned guise, come close to them both in outward appearance and in use. Such a word is *hail*! that is, whole, hale, prosperous, originally, as the Gothic Bible shows, an adjective used vocatively like *bravo! brava*! Again, when the East African negro cries out in fear or wonder *mámá! mámá*! he might be thought to be uttering a real interjection, 'a word used to express some passion or emotion of the mind,' as Lindley Murray has it, but in fact he is simply calling, like the great grown-up baby that he is, for his mother. Other exclamations consist of a pure interjection combined with a pronoun, as *οἴμοι, oimè! ah me*! or with an adjective, as *alas! hélas* (ah weary!). The calls to domestic animals are interjectional cries, whose history is mostly very hard to make out. Not only is *dill* a recognised call to ducks in England, 'Dilly, dilly, dilly, come and be killed!' but *dlidli* is set down as used for the like purpose in Bohemia. A cockney might very well take for a pure interjection the *coop! coop*! which calls cows, which is only 'come up! come up!'

> 'Come uppe, Whitefoot, come uppe, Lightfoot,
> Come uppe, Jetty, rise and follow,
> Jetty, to the milking shed.'

Sometimes the call seems to be merely the creature's name. The Bohemian peasant calls to his dog, *ps', ps'*, but when *pes* means 'dog.' The Hindu child calls *mun! mun*! to the cat, but then its name in Hindustani is *mano*. The English child calls *puss! puss*! and in the call keeps up an old Celtic name for the cat, Irish *pus*, Erse *pusag*, one of those words which, like *basket* and *piggin*, remain in English to mark the presence of the Celt in the country of the invading Saxon.

When the ground has been cleared of obscure or mutilated sense-words, a residue of real sound-words, or pure interjections, remains behind. Among these, in the first place, there appears a class which I think any one conversant with the gesture-signs of savages and deaf-mutes would admit, when the case was properly put before him, to be themselves gesture-signs of the same nature as those he is accustomed to, though made with the assistance of vocal sound. The sound *m'm*, *m'n*, made with the lips closed, is the sign of the man who tries to speak, but cannot. Even the deaf-and-dumb child, though he cannot hear what he is saying, makes this noise to show that he is dumb, that he is *mu mu*, as the Vei Negroes of West Africa would say. To the speaking man the articulation which we write *mum*! says plainly enough 'hold your tongue!' 'mum's the word.'[1] The gesture of blowing is a familiar expression of contempt and disgust, and when vocalised gives the labial interjections which are written *pah! bah! pugh! pooh!* in Welch *pw*! in low Latin *puppup*! and which correspond to a number of imitative words, which in very various languages describe the action of *puffing* or blowing. Laura Bridgman was not only deaf-and-dumb, but also blind, yet when she did not like to be touched, she would vocalise the sign of her disgust and say, *f*! In like manner the gesture of spitting gives the dental interjection *t't't'*, which is written *tut*! That this is no fancy, imitative words like Tahitian *tutua*, 'to spit,' may serve to show.[2]

Such vocalised gesture-signs as these of mumbling, blowing, and spitting, which express their meanings by a kind of symbol or metaphor, should be kept apart from other interjectional sounds, which answer their end in a more direct way. The laugh is sounded (when it is sounded, which is not at all necessary) as *ha ha! hi hi! ho ho! χa χa! χi χi! ka ka! ki ki!* and so forth, according as it is a laugh proper, a chuckle, a giggle, or a snigger. And other interjections common to races speaking the most widely various languages may be set down in a rough way as representing the signs, groans, moans, cries, shrieks, and growls by which man gives utterance to various of his feelings. Such are some of the many sounds for which *ah! oh! ahi! aïe!* are written, the sigh which is put down in English as *heigho*! and in the Wolof language of Africa as *hhihhe*, and the kind of groan which is represented by *weh*!

---

[1] Tah. *mamu*, Fij. *nomo*, Chil. *nomn*, 'to be silent.'
[2] Skr. *t'hût'hú*, 'the sound of spitting;' *t'hûtkrita*, 'noisy spitting,' *i.e.* *t'hût*-making; Persian *t'hu kerdan*, 'to spit,' *i.e.* to make *t'hu*; Galla *twu*; Yoruba *tu*.

ouais! o'vai! vae! Coptic *ouae!* Galla *wayo!* Ossetic *voy!* There is more propriety in calling such sounds as these 'natural,' than such symbolic sounds as *pooh!* or *mum!* Of course there is a reason why it comes to pass that we laugh when joyful or amused, and sigh when sorrowful or weary, though for the explanation of this reason, whatever it may be, we must look to the physiologist, not to the philologist, – every man to his trade. Yet before giving over the problem to be treated physiologically, we may carry its examination a step further.

In a note in the famous 'Diversions of Purley,' mention is made of 'The industrious and exact Cinonio, who does not appear ever to have had a single glimpse of reason.' Horne Tooke's method of treating any one who stood in the way of his argument was, to say the least, rough, somewhat like that of the American lady who was heard to remark to her friend, as they crushed into the Sistine chapel on Easter Eve, that she always did well in a crowd, for when she didn't get right along she just kicked. The offence of the grammarian who is 'just kicked' as above, was simply his having said that one interjection, *ah!* could express, when pronounced in different ways, more than twenty ideas, such as outcry, pain, and so forth. The thing is indeed such commonplace matter of fact, that Horne Tooke's most effective way to answer the grammarian who said it, was to abuse him. But how does it come to be true that *ah!* and *oh!* and *ugh!* and other such sounds, should be able to express, as they do, such varied and complex feelings? Without professing to go into the full question of the effect of tone and emphasis on the mind, an observation may be made as to the nature of these interjections which has escaped at all events general notice, and perhaps any notice at all, possibly by reason of its extreme obviousness, like, to borrow Edgar Poe's comparison, the names of the continents printed in great staring capitals right across the map. Every one recognises the fact that certain expressions of face, as well as certain interjectional sounds, correspond to certain feelings, but it is not thus generally recognised that there is a real connection or dependence between the expression of the face and the sound which comes out from it. The human body is among other things an instrument for producing vocal sounds, and the different attitudes of mouth, cheeks, &c., which belong to different feelings of the mind modify the position of the vocal organs, and thereby the sounds uttered. The laugh made with a solemn, contemptuous, or sarcastic face, is quite different from that which comes from a joyous one; the *ah! oh! ho! hey*! and so on, change their modulations to match the expression of the countenance, which expression may even be known in the dark by hearing the sound it produces, while the forced character given by the attempt to bring out a sound not matching even the outward play of the features can hardly be hidden by the most expert ventriloquist, and in such forcing the sound perceptibly drags the face into the attitude which fits with it. The change of tone which accompanies such change of feature is in great measure due to alteration of the musical quality or 'colour' of the vowels, which, as Helmholtz's beautiful researches have shown, is affected by changing the dimensions of the cavity of the mouth. This hollow acts as a resonator or sounding-box, and is, in any particular position, in time to a particular note. Now; a vowel being a sound compounded of a fundamental note and a long series of upper tones, the cavity of the mouth brings out strongly such of these tones as are most nearly correspondent to it, and damps the rest. By this means the effect of change of feature changing the interior shape of the mouth is to alter the upper tones of the vowel, and thereby its musical quality. Now, why should a particular tone of voice convey to the mind the feeling of joy, surprise, or disgust? There is considerable reason to suppose that the character of such tone is in great part caused by the expression of the features, for on the one hand, the sound can hardly be made without the appropriate expression of face; while, on the other hand, this expression is constantly put on with no view of uttering any sound, even by the deaf and dumb, who have clearly nothing to do with sound in the matter. So far, then, as the tone of an interjection is modified by expression of feature, its action on the mind of the hearer may be explained by association of ideas, without assuming the existence of a direct relation between certain sounds and certain emotions. Knowing that a particular state of feeling brings on a particular expression of face, and that this again gives out a particular interjectional sound, we may explain the effect of an interjection on the mind by making one and the same action account for the expression of the face and that of the sound which it utters. On this view the association of each tone with its proper meaning would be due to experience. A child would learn the meaning of an interjectional tone partly by making it when the feelings have brought the face to a proper attitude for producing it. Of the expression of its own features a child has hardly any means of judging, and it may come to connect the sound directly with the feeling without taking any thought of the intermediate process of change of face. Besides this, it learns by a series of observations the relations of its own feelings and tones and the expressions of face and voice in others. Children of three or four may be seen in the act of learning by repeated observation to do this; they will turn and look at the speaker's face to make sure of the meaning of his tone, and then, and not till then, they will act on what he says. Among the blind the process is of course more restricted; they take no account of expression of face either in themselves or others, and only connect their own tones and feelings with the tones of others and the accompanying words and acts. Yet they, like the rest of mankind, have to go through the process of putting the appropriate expression upon their faces in order to produce the tone it belongs to. The same conditions affect the expression given to ordinary words by the tone of their utterance, which puts into them the interjectional quality over and above the mere combination of rigidly defined ideas. Indeed, the deadness and want of emotional power in ordinary reading aloud is in a considerable measure due to the restraint which the reader puts upon his features, to prevent their following the feeling of the subject, and which thus necessarily robs his voice of the power to give to each words its lifelike modulation.

A number of other interjectional forms, about whose origin it is more difficult to speak with any confidence, I pass by here without remark. But taking pure interjections as a class, how far do they pass into the kind of words which go to form the propositions of logical language, the verb, noun, adjective, &c.? Such transition has not been proved to exist to any very great extent, but it goes far enough to give the interjection its right to claim a share, though it may prove but a small one, in the Origin of Language. Thus, in the language of the Gallas (south of Abyssinia), *o*! is the usual answer to a call, and also a cry to drive cattle, whence, with the addition of ordinary verbal terminations, *oada* becomes a verb, meaning 'to answer,' and *ofa* another, meaning 'to drive cattle.' So *birefado*, 'to be afraid,' is simply 'to make *brr*!' The Arab gurgles to his camel *ikh! ikh*! till it kneels down, and thus to *nakh* a camel, that is, to make it kneel, to *ikh! ikh!* it, has been plausibly explained as derived from this interjection. The exclamation *io!* which the German adds to the cry of 'Fire!' 'Murder!' *Feurio! Mordio!* remains as mere an interjection as the *o!* in our street cries of 'Pease-*o*!' 'Dust-*o*!' but the Iroquois of North America makes a fuller use of his materials, and carries his *io!* of admiration into the very formation of compound words, adding it to a noun to say that it is beautiful – thus, *Oh-io* is 'the beautiful river,' and *Ontario* is formed in a like way. In Ceylon, a *hoo*, the sound of a shout, becomes, like the 'far cry to Loch Awe,' a measure of distance, 'as far as one can hear a shout.' The interjection *weh! ouais! vae!* passes into a term for pain, suffering, woe, in Indo-European languages – German, *weh*; Anglo-Saxon, *wa, wea*; Scotch, *wae*; and just as plainly among the Turanian Esths, Lapps, and Finns, *waiw, waiwa, waja*. These are the first suitable instances which occur to me of interjections passing into the main body of language; it is not my object to draw up a long list, but only enough cases to show that such sense-words, derived from mere sound-words, may exist in reasonable numbers in different parts of the world. Yet it must be acknowledged, that our liability to devise fanciful origins for words which may, after all, have sprung from ordinary sense-roots, is very destructive to confidence in a method of explanation so apt to be abused.

To turn now to the class of Imitative or Onomatopoetic words. That words imitated from the cries of animals, the notes of musical instruments, and various other kinds of sound or noise, really are made, and form part of human language, is a thing which everybody admits in principle. There is, indeed, no denying the fact; the difficulty lies in settling the details of such action, and the limits it extends to. Flies *buzz*, bees *hum*, snakes *hiss*, a cracker or a bottle of ginger-beer *pops*, a cannon or a bittern *booms—*

'Where by the marishes
Boometh the bittern,'

as Mr. Sebastian Evans has it, and so on. The names of the *cuckoo*, the *ai-ai* sloth, the *kaka* parrot, the Eastern *tomtom*, which is a drum; the African *ulule*, which is a flute, the Siamese *khong-bong*, which is a wooden harmonicon, – are mere imitations of sounds, like a host of other words. But when a philologist, holding truly enough that he has caught a glimpse of a great principle, sets to work right and left to explain language by its means, he is apt presently to catch up some word which is really, or may be only in his fancy, like some appropriate sound, but which, in fact, has an etymology of its own. Then the first etymologist who meets with the unlucky theoriser falls upon him and crushes him to splinters. Let us take am imaginary case: '*Fiddle*,' says the advocate of the Imitative or Bow-wow theory, 'is a word imitated from the sound of that instrument, as may be more fully seen in *fiddle-de-dee*, which imitates its meaningless scraping, like *tweedle-dum* and *tweedle-dee*, which imitate the descending and ascending scale. In the hands of Mr. Robert Browning it gets an extra scrape, and becomes *fiddle-diddle-dee*.' 'Nonsense,' says the etymologist, 'the name of the fiddle has nothing in the world to do with its sound, it is nothing but Latin – *fidicula*, a lyre, a diminutive of *fidis*.' In discussions like these we have the elements of the prettiest of all quarrels, that in which there is a dash of right on both sides. For, no doubt, though *fiddle* is not a sound-word, *fiddle-de-dee* does really imitate its scraping. For language, being (as it is, indeed, the main object of this essay to bring prominently into view) not the mere mechanical working out of a uniform plan, but a highly artificial system, in which every shift and contrivance which suggests itself to the word-maker is pressed into the service of making sound available to utter sense, he combines in the most varying way the making of words for the sake of their sound, with the taking of them for the sake of the sense he has learnt from others to attach to them. So ready-made sense-words, if suitable, are taken in hand and added to, modified, so to speak, coloured, by mere sound. Thus such a combination as *fiddle-de-dee* comes to be made; nor, I think, would a prudent man even assert that *tweedle-dum* and *tweedle-dee*, obvious imitations as they are, have not a sense-word at the bottom of them. When a philologist, led on by finding undoubted imitative words in a language, sets himself of malice prepense to hear articulate sounds, in the cries of animals, for instance, there is no knowing how far his imagination may carry him. The Coptic has several good imitative words, *eeio*, an ass, *krour*, a frog, *moui*, a lion; but beyond such as these, I have seen *ehe*, a cow, claimed as an imitation. Who ever heard a cow say *ehe*? Such speculations are indeed on the high road to the language of the wood-pigeons. A certain Welshman, says the story, was put upon his trial for stealing two cows. 'I never stole them,' he said, 'they were given me.' 'Given you, who gave them you?' 'Why, as I was going along the lane, I came to the field where the cows were, and there was a little gentleman sitting in a tree, and saying in a nice soft voice, "Take-two-oo-coos-Taffy – take-two-oo-coo-oos," and as he was so pressing, I did just take two.'

The advocate of the Imitative theory, when he goes in among the root-words of known language, and begins to explain meaning by sound, has indeed taken in hand a perilous task, if he trusts his own powers of discernment. For in fact, of all judges of the question at issue, he has nourished and trained himself up to become the very worst. His imagination is ever suggesting to him what his judgement would like to be true; like a witness answering the leading questions of the counsel on his own side, he answers in good faith, but with what bias we all know. What is then to be done? Fortunately for the study of his problem, the student may in great measure rid himself of the task he executes so ill. It so happens that a number of unprejudiced witnesses have long ago put their evidence on record: these witnesses are the various languages of the world, living and dead.

If several languages which we cannot class as distinctly of the same family, unite in expressing a notion by a word which may fairly claim to be a more imitation of sound, their combined testimony will go far to prove the claim a just one. For if it be objected that such words may have come into both from a common source, of which the trace is for the most part lost, it may be answered by the question, why there is not a proportionate agreement between the languages in question throughout the far larger mass of words which cannot claim to be direct sound-words. If several languages have independently chosen like words to express like sounds, then we may reasonably suppose we are not deluding ourselves in thinking that such words are highly appropriate to their purpose. Thus we have such forms as *pu, puf, bu, buf*, recurring in the most remote and different languages with the meaning of blowing or *puffing*.[3]

The way in which one savage race after another have named the European musket, when they saw it, by the sound *pu*,

---

[3] Tongan *buhi*, Maori *pupui*, Zulu *pu*, Hebrew *puach* &c.

describing as it seems not the report, but the *puff* of smoke issuing from the muzzle, is very curious. The South Sea Islanders supposed at first that the white men blew through the barrel of the gun, and they called it accordingly *pupuhi*, form the verb *puhi*, 'to blow,' very much as the Indians of Yucatan call the blow-tube of their bird-hunters a *pub*. The Ama-Zosa of South Africa call a gun a *umpu*, for *pu*, 'to blow.' The Indians of British Columbia described how, when the white man pointed his gun at a bird, a violent *poo* went forth, and the bird fell down dead. When Dampier was on the coast of Australia in 1699, he fired his muskets to put the natives in awe of him, but when this had happened several times and they saw that nobody was hurt, they began to mock at them, and when a gun was let off threw up their hands and cried *pooh! pooh!* When a European, then, uses the word *puff* to denote the discharge of a gun, or the explosion of gunpowder, he is merely using the same imitative word for blowing which does duty as a *puff* of wind, or even a powder-*puff* or a *puff*-ball, to describe the action which we quite consistently call 'blowing up.' The prudent wholesale grocer in 'Soll und Haben' objects to the help of Anton's brace of *puffers* in getting back his merchandise from the Poles, and calmly lets them off out of the carriage windows. A piece of Gallic Dog-Latin, of which I remember only the fag end, thus described a woeful catastrophe, of whom or what I cannot say:— 'Tunc de branca in brancam degringo- lavit, atque in terram cadens detonavit, et fecit *pouf*!'

The claim of the Eastern *tomtom* to have its name from a mere imitation of its sound seems an indisputable one; but when we notice in what different languages the beating of a resounding object is expressed by something like *tum, tumb, tump, tup*, it becomes evident that the admission involves a good deal more than at first sight appears. Thus in the Galla language *tuma* is 'to beat,'[4] whence *tmtu*, a workman, especially one who beats a smith. With the aid of another imitative word, *bufa*, 'to blow,' is made a complete imitative sentence, *tumtum bufa bufti*, 'the workman blows the bellows,' as an English child might say, 'the *tumtum puffs* the *puffer*.' There is indeed another side to this question, but the advocate of the Imitative Theory could hardly be expected to keep his

---

[4] Malay *timpa, tampa*, to beat out, hammer, forge; Javan *tumbuk*, Coptic *tuino* pound in a mortar; etc.

hands off the sacred precincts of the Sanskrit very-roots, for *tup, tump*, has in Greek the meaning of to beat, to *thump*, producing, for instance, τύπανον, a drum or *tomtom*. Again, the verb to *crack* has become in modern English as thorough a root-word as the language possess; we speak of a cracked cup or a cracked reputation without a thought of any imitation of sound, but the word appears in other European languages not yet developed in meaning to this extent, but remaining in its earlier imitative stage, *krachen* or *craquer*, for instance.[5] These few examples may serve to illustrate the way in which words may be formed by direct imitation of sound, and afterwards developed into ordinary sense-roots, claiming to associate on equal terms with other roots whose pretentions to be creatures of a higher order may rest simply on their first origin and meaning being undiscovered.

Something has been already said of the propensity of language to expand, modify, or 'colour' words with imitative or symbolic sound. Thus by the side of the words in which sound merely imitates sound there grows a vast class of symbolic words, in which sound comes in to express length or shortness of time, strength or weakness of action, then passes into a further stage to describe greatness or smallness of size or of distance, and thence makes its way into the widest fields of metaphorical expression. Thus, the Bachupin of Africa call any one with the cry *héla*, but according as he is far or further off, the sound of the *he - —la, hé - —la*, is lengthened out. Wilhelm von Humboldt notices the habit of a South American tribe, of dwelling a more or less time on the suffix of the perfect tense *yma y - ma*, to indicate how long ago the action happened. In the Gaboon, the strength with which such as *mpolu* (great) is uttered, serves to show whether it is great, very great, very very great. In Malagasy *ratchi* means 'bad,' but *râtchi* is 'very bad.' Writing, even with the aid of italics and capitals, ignores much of this symbolism in spoken language, but every child understands the use and meaning of such processes, in spite of the efforts of book-learning and school teaching to set aside whatever their imperfect symbols

---

[5] Dahoman *kra-kra*, a watchman's rattle; Sanskrit *kra-kara, kra-kacha* (i.e. *kra*-maker, *kra*-crier), a saw; Malay *graji*, a saw, *karat*, to gnash the teeth, *karot*, to make a grating noise; Coptic *khrij*, to gnash the teeth, *khrajrej*, to grate.

cannot express, nor their narrow rules control. Again, how imitative words while preserving, so to speak, the same skeleton, will follow the variation of sound, of force, of duration, of size, a single imitative group may show, *crick, creak, crack, crash, crush, crunch, craunch, scrunch, scraunch.* Not imitative words alone, but the most thorough sense-words, formed from a verb-root for their meaning and not for their sound, are taken up and receive their colouring from sound in the same way. Thus to *stamp* with the foot, which has been claimed as an imitation of sound, is only a coloured word. The root *sta*, 'to stand,' Sanskrit, *sthâ*, forms a causative *stap*, Sanskrit *sthâpay*, 'to make to stand,' English to *stop*, and a foot-*step* is when the foot comes to a stand, a foot-*stop*. Thus we have Anglo-Saxon, *stapan, stœpan, steppan*, English to *step*, varying to express its meaning by sound in to *staup*, to *stamp*, to stump, and to *stomp*, contrasting in their violence or clumsy weight with the foot on the cottage sill,

> 'Where love do seek the maiden's evenèn vloor,
> Wi' stip-step light, and tip-tap slight
>
> Agean the door.'

One of the most interesting and important developments of symbolism in language, is the device of making the vowels into a graduated scale, and thus using them to convey different ideas of distances. Some thirty years ago Baron Wilhelm von Humboldt, in his great work on the Kawi language, referred to an account of the Javan demonstrative pronouns by Mr. Crawfurd, from whose late Malay dictionary I take their spelling. A group of three is formed by *iki*, this (close by); *ika*, that (at some distance); *iku*, that (farther off). Similar groups have since been noticed by Pott and Max Müller, such as Canarese *ivanu*, this; *avanu*, that; with an intermediate form *uvanu*, not now used, to complete the set. The list of such forms, which I give at the foot of the page, is partly quoted and partly from my own observation, and will show the immense geographical range over which this ingenious contrivance has come into use; always similar in the main principle, though varying a good deal in the details of its action.[6] The great philological import-

---

[6] Malagasy: *ao*, there (at a short distance); *eo*, there (at a shorter distance); *io*, there (close at hand); *atsy*, there (not far off); *etsy*, there (nearer); *itsy*, this or these. Magyar: *ez*, this; *az*, that. Abchasian: *abri*, this; *ubri*, that. Japanese; *ko*, here; *ka*, there; *korera*, these; *karera*, they. Ossetic: *am*,

ance of these words lies in the fact that they enable us for the first time to trace not mere derivation, but actual creation by the direct transfer of sound to sense, into the very stronghold of language, among the pronouns and local adverbs which are held even more specifically to characterise particular families of language than even the verbal roots. It may be convenient to give to sets of words like these, in which a ground-word is thus symbolically modified or differenced, the name of 'differential words.'

How the differencing of words by change of vowels may be used to distinguish between the sexes may be well shown by quoting further from the passage of Max Müller's lately referred to. 'The distinction of gender.... is sometimes expressed in such a manner that we can only explain it by ascribing an expressive power to the more or less obscure sound of vowels. *Ukko* in Finnic, is an old man; *akka*, an old woman.... In Mangu, *chacha* is masc......*cheche*, fem. Again, *ama*, in Mangu, is father, *eme*, mother, *amcha*, father-in-law, *emche*, mother-in-law.'

This contrivance of distinguishing the male from the female by a difference of vowels is, however, but a small part of the process of formation of language which it is possible to trace among such words as those for father and mother. Their consideration leads into a very important and curious philological region, that of 'Children's Language.' If we take a few of the pairs of words which stand for father and mother in different and distant languages, *papa* and *mama*, Welsh *tad* (*dad*) and *mam*, Hungarian *atya* and *anya*, Ibu, *nna* and *nne*, Mandingo, *fa* and *ba*, the principle on which they are differenced is seen to act more on consonants than vowels. Words of the class of *papa* and *mama*, occurring in remote parts of the world, were once used freely as evidence of a common origin of the languages in which they were found, but Buschmann's paper on

---

here; *um*, there. Zulu: *apa*, here; *apo*, there. Tumal: *re*, this; *ri*, that; *ngi*, I; *ngo*, thou; *ngu*, he. Greenlandish: *uv*, hero, there (where one points to); *iv*, there up there [found in composition]. Sahaptin: *kina*, here; *kuna*, there. Tarahumara: *ibe*, here; *abe*, there. Chilian: *tva*, this; *tvey*, that; *vachi*, this; *veychi*, that. (See Humboldt, 'Kawi-Spr.,' vol. ii. p. 36; Max Müller, 'Turanian Languages,' in Bunsen, 'Philosophy of Universal History,' vol. i. p. 329; and especially Pott: 'Doppelung,'' an invaluable collection of facts and arguments, which I have used repeatedly in the present essay.)

96 The Origin of Language

'Nature-Sound,' published in the Berlin Transactions for 1853, finally settled the view that their appearance was largely to be set down to independent invention, often repeating itself in exact detail. It was clearly no use to say that Carib and English were allied because the word *papa*, father, belongs to both, or Hottentot and English because both use *mama* for mother, seeing that these first childish articulations might be used just as well in the opposite way, the Chilian word for mother being *papa*, and the Georgian for father being *mama*, and so on.[7]

The immense list of names collected by Buschmann shows the types *pa* and *ta*, with the similar forms *ap* and *at*, to preponderate as names for father, while *ma*, and *na, am* and *an*, preponderate as names for mother. His explanation of this state of things, as caused by direct symbolism choosing the stronger and harder sound for the father's name and the softer and gentler for the mother's, seems to have much truth in it, though it must not be pushed too far; it can hardly be, for instance, the same principle of symbolism which leads the Welshman to say *tad* for father and *mam* for mother, and the Georgian to say *mama* for father and *deda* for mother.

The names for parents must not be studied as thought they stood alone in language. They are, in fact, only important members of a great class of words belonging to all times and all countries within our experience, and forming a 'children's language,' whose common character is due to its concerning itself with the limited set of ideas in which little children are interested, and expressing these ideas by the limited set of articulations suited to the child's first attempt to talk. Such words are continually coming fresh into existence, and the law of natural selection determines their fate. The great mass of the *nana's* and *dada's* of the nursery die out almost as soon as made. Some few take more root, and spread over large districts as accepted nursery words, and now and then a curious philologist makes a collection of them. Of such, part are obvious mutilations of longer words, as French faire *dodo*, 'to sleep' (*dormir*), Brandenburg *wiwi* a common cradle lullaby (*wiegen*, to rock); but others, whatever their real origin, are brought

---

[7] Such words may not be quote worthless as evidence of connection of languages: the English and Scotch use of *dad* for father may possibly be derived from the Celtic population of the country. There are, however, similar forms, *dadi*, &c., in German dialects.

through the small variety of articulations out of which they must be chosen, into a curiously indiscriminate and unmeaning mass, as Swiss *bobo*, 'a scratch,' *bambam*, 'all gone!' Italian *bobò*, 'something to drink!' *gògò*, 'little boy,' far *dede*, 'to play.' These are words quoted by Pott, and for English examples *nana*, 'nurse,' and *tata*, 'good-bye,' may serve. But all baby words do not stop short even at this stage. A small proportion of them establish themselves in the ordinary talk of grown-up men and women, and when they have once made good their place as constituents of general language they may pass on by inheritance from age to age. Such examples as have been quoted of mere nursery words not only give a clue to the origin of a mass of names for father, mother, grandmother, aunt, baby, breast, toy, doll, &c., but they explain the indifference with which, out of the small stock of available materials, the same sound does duty for the most different ideas; why *mama* means here mother, there father, there uncle, *maman* here mother, there father-in-law, *dada* here father, there breast, *tata* here father, there son.

A single group of words may serve to show the character of this peculiar region of language:—Blackfoot Indian *ninnah*, 'father;' Greek νέννος, 'uncle,' νέννα, (aunt;' Sangir *nina*, Malagasy *nini*, 'mother;' Vayu *nini*, 'paternal aunt;' Darien Indian *ninah*, 'daughter;' Spanish *niño, niña*, 'child;' Italian *ninna*, 'little girl;' Milanese *ninin*, Italian *nanna*, 'bed,' *ninnare*, 'to rock the cradle,' &c. &c. That this process of sorting out a dozen child's articulations among a dozen child's ideas has not only given a number of words to ordinary language, but has even contributed somewhat to its stock of roots, I am disposed to believe, but cannot here discuss the necessary evidence.

Such are some of the ways (and probably there are many more) in which vocal sounds seem to have commended themselves to the mind of the word-maker as suited to express his meaning, and to have been used accordingly. In concluding this brief survey of them, some general considerations suggest themselves as to the nature and first beginnings of language. When we study the higher departments of speech, where words already existing are turned to account to express new meanings and shade off new distinctions, we find these ends attained not by anything like a philosophical system, but by an endless series of contrivances, varying from extreme dexterity down to utter clumsiness. The great method of giving new meaning to old sound is metaphor, which transfers ideas from hearing to seeing, from touching to thinking, from the concrete of one kind to the abstract of another, and which is capable of making almost anything in the world help to describe or suggest anything else. What the German philosopher described as the relation of a cow to a comet is sufficient, and more than sufficient, to the language-maker: both have tails. Modern habits have so far superseded the original meaning of the *pipe (pipa)*, an imitative word clearly belonging to the sound of the musical instrument, as to justify the rustic in the story in answering the inquiry, 'Shepherd, where is your pipe?' by the matter-of-fact explanation that was out out of 'baccy. The word *chagrin*, again, is only a metaphor of gnawing care, taken from the sharp rasping 'shagreen;' and books of etymology are full of cases compared with which these are plain and straightforward. Indeed, the processes by which words have really come into existence may often enough remind us of the game of 'What is my thought like?' When one knows the answer it is easy to see what *junketting* or cathedral *canons* have to do with reeds; but who would guess, who did not know the intermediate links? Yet there is about the process of derivation a thoroughly human character. When we know the whole facts of any case, we can generally understand it at once, and see that we might have done the same ourselves had it come in our way. Wilhelm von Humboldt's view that language is an 'organism,' has been considered a great step in philological speculation; but, so far as I can see, it has caused an increase of vague thinking and talking, and thereby no small darkening of counsel. If it were meant to say that human thought language, and action generally, are organic in their nature, and work under fixed laws, this might be a very different matter; but this is distinctly not what is meant, and the very object of calling language an organism is to keep it apart from other human arts and contrivances. It was a hateful thing to Humboldt's mind to 'bring down speech to a mere operation of the understanding.' 'Man,' he says, 'does not so much form languages, as discern with a kind of joyous wonder its developments, coming forth as of themselves.' Yet, if the practical shifts by which words are shaped or applied to fit new meanings are not devised by an operation of the understanding, we ought consistently to carry the stratagems of the soldier in the field, or the contrivances of the workman at his bench, back into the dark regions of instinct and involuntary action. As for the ways in which, so far as our very scanty knowledge extends, sounds are in the first instance chosen and arranged to express ideas, they are as simple and practical as need be. A child of five years old could catch the meaning of imitative sounds, interjectional words, symbolism of sex or distance by contrast of vowels; and just as no one is likely to enter into the real nature of mythology who has not the keenest appreciation of nursery tales, so the spirit in which we guess riddles and play at children's games is needed to appreciate the lower phases of language. So far as we can see, the processes by which words are made and adapted in their early stages have less to do with systematic arrangement and scientific classification than with mere rough and ready ingenuity and the great rule of thumb.

Attempts to solve as much as may be of the fundamental nature of speech by tracing out in detail such processes as have here been described, are likely to increase our knowledge by sure and steady steps wherever imagination does not get the better of sober comparison of facts. But there is one side of this problem of the Origin of Language on which such studies have by no means an encouraging effect. Much of the popular interest in such matters is centred in the question whether the known languages of the world have their source in one or many primæval tongues. On this subject the opinions of the philologists who have compared the greatest number of languages are utterly at variance, nor has any one brought forward a body of philological evidence strong and direct enough to make anything beyond mere opinion possible. Such actions as to the growth of imitative or symbolic words from a part, be it small or large, of the Origin of Language, but they are by no means restricted to any particular place or period, and are, indeed, more or less in activity now. So far as such causes have acted, their tendency has been to make it practically of less and less consequence to a language what its original stock of words may have been at starting, and the philologist's extension of his knowledge of such ways of direct formation must compel him to strip off more and more of any language, as being possibly of later growth, before he can act upon such a residuum as may have come by direct inheritance from times of primæval speech.

THE ORIGIN OF LANGUAGE
Anonymous

Source: Westminster Review, vol. 30ns, July, 1866

1. *Max Müller. Lectures on Language.* 1st and 2nd Series.
2. *Chapters on Language.* By Rev. F. FARRAR.

The Science of Language possesses at the present day strong and peculiar claims on the attention of the student. Beyond that interest which intrinsically belongs to it, that interest which every thinker would be likely to claim in a pre-eminent degree for the especial study which had engaged his attention, and to err only thereby in underrating its sister sciences, not in over-rating itself; Philology presents to the present generation the further attraction of a particular science just attained to that stage of development which best illustrates the progress of all science, in contemplating which the learner may draw inferences not bearing only on the special phenomena which it professes to explain, but on principles which are common to all hypotheses of the natural world. Philology, in short, is at this day interesting, not only to the philologist, but to the philosopher. In inviting the attention of the reader to this subject, we are proposing to him to investigate the structure, not merely of language, but of science; and he who cares little for etymologies, or the ethnological theories with which they are connected, may well spare a portion of his time and thought to considerations which bear on that ultimate intellectual region where the laws of nature and the laws of thought are seen in their closest combination. It is exclusively with this reference that the subject of Language is treated in the following pages. The endeavour made in them is not to estimate the evidence for or against a particular view of philology, but to prepare the way for its unprejudiced discussion by pointing out the fallacies which obstruct its progress, and exemplifying them from other sources – to test a particular hypothesis, not by the particular argument on which it rests, but by its accordance with analogous truth, and its influences on conceptions which are not logically affected by it. Such considerations form a large part of the evidence on which we receive or reject any theory. They do not indeed constitute even the most important portion of this evidence; but, on the other hand, they form a natural prelude to the rest; the point of view in which they present the subject is the most accessible to an ordinary thinker, as it lies nearest to surrounding regions of inquiry; and finally, it is the part of the discussion that has been least dwelt upon. For these reasons it is to this portion of the subject that the present article is confined.

The division made by Comte, of the theological, the metaphysical, and the positive phase of thought, as indicating the successive stages of what is ultimately scientific development, is now well known to readers who know nothing of its author, and the first obvious and superficial replies are well known too. The epithet 'theological,' for instance, is far more applicable to the present time than to that which preceded the French Revolution, while, if we ascend to the fountain-head of all speculation, the fragments left us of the first Greek thinkers, we shall find much that is metaphysical and hardly anything that is theological. But this division is not one to be tested by chronology. As a tropical mountain reaching the limits of eternal snow presents under one meridian specimens of every season, so the inhabited world at any moment affords us examples of every age of civilization and development of thought. We may even find these different stages exhibited by a single mind, according to the subject on which it is exercised. Take an average country clergyman – any one, in fact, who would defend the prayers for fair weather; his opinions on the movements of the heavenly bodies afford us an example of the positive or the theological stage of thought according as he considers their annual movements, or the circumstances which modify their influence on our globe from day to day. He would of course say that it was the will of God that we should have winter, just as much as that winter should be severe. But he would allow, if he were consistent, that the reference to God's will was an answer in the one case in a totally different sense to what it was in the other. His astronomy is already positive, while his meteorology is theological.

Nevertheless, these phases are really consecutive; they mark out different regions, of which, in the search after truth, one naturally succeeds the other, though our journeyings in that path are too fitful and complicated to reveal their sequence until the goal is nearly won. On a broad view of our progress in natural knowledge, each view will be seen as an advance upon the other, indicating the wider horizon that is gained by a higher point of view. The first phase of thought is, however, long since left behind by anything that calls itself a science. Indeed, till it was understood that to refer a phenomenon to the will of any supernatural being was not to explain its place in nature, there was no possibility of physical science. The reader will recall the well-known passage in the 'Phædo,' where Socrates is made to express his disappointment in the teaching of Anaxagoras, because, after having learnt from him that *Nous*, or Mind, is the ruler of all things, he finds him proceed to explain the various phenomena of nature on physical grounds, instead of deducing them from a regard to the fitness of things, such as is characteristic of mind. We see at once that Socrates is here expressing his disappointment that Anaxagoras aimed at physical science at all. Although the theological stage of natural science may even co-exist with the positive in such a mind as we have imagined, as an epoch of national thought it has passed away for ever.

Comte's law appears to us capable of translation into a nomenclature that shall commend itself as true to every thinker. Speculation starts from the supernatural; it refers all change to an arbitrary volition, it knows nothing of law. It arrives at the natural – at the conception of an unbroken change of cause and effect, linking all that shall be to all that has been. Between these two stages intervenes a third, partaking in some degree of the character of both, for which the metaphysical is not on the whole a bad epithet. The supernatural stage is crystallised in mythology; but it survives still in every view which links events to the will of God as a series of separate acts of volition – in such a manner, that is to say, that they are dislocated from the chain of cause and effect. Some relic of it lingers in every prayer for a physical event, in every expectation implied in such a prayer that some single link in this chain will be touched by creative will, apart from all that has gone before. Now when we reconsider how few there are who would consistently retain either view – who would hope, for instance, that some mighty effort of prayer should affect any operation of nature the causes of which are perfectly known – as for instance the course of the seasons, – or who would renounce the belief that such an effect might affect these operations of which the causes are imperfectly known – as for instance the temperature of the seasons – we shall understand how strong is the fascination of that intermediate stage of speculation which unites to some extent the qualities of the two extremes. We shall find instances of this fascination in the history of some of the most severely scientific minds. The example which first occurs is afforded us by the speculations of Newton on the cause of gravity. At one time of his life he seems to have thought that the fact of gravity might receive its explanation from some facts connected with the ether; these facts themselves, and their truth or falsehood, being entirely irrelevant to the present question. It is curious to trace in the mind of a man like Newton the fancy that in dealing with the ether he was getting any nearer a spiritual entity than in dealing with the solid earth. Of course if these facts could have been substantiated they would have been a valuable contribution to our knowledge; but we should just as much have needed to have their cause as we now need to know the cause of gravitation. Evidently he thought that we should not. He seems to have fancied there would be something more ultimate in a doctrine about the ether than in a doctrine about the earth. The link of association which connects *gas* and *geist* was what he was leaning upon in this belief. The ether was in his mind playing that part which is assigned to the 'animal spirits' in our older writers; neither he nor they perceive that in using these phrases they have got out of the region of things into the region of names – that their subtle fluids are either a diluted form of matter just as far removed from spirit as lead is, or they are a mere unknown x, representing a particular cause, and not the explanation of that cause. We have given this instance because it appears to illustrate in a very remarkable degree the attraction of these metaphysical entities for scientific minds. Of course we do not mean that the ether is a metaphysical entity. But it was on this ground that Newton was contemplating it in these speculations. It was as cause of something which could have no cause so simple as itself, which must therefore, by being explained, make our general scheme of belief more complicated than it was before, that he regarded this subtle fluid, which was to pervade all space, and which took to his mind under that point of view almost the aspect of a universal soul. Less apposite, perhaps, but still not without its bearing on the strife between metaphysical and positive conceptions as the origin of true science, is the theory of phlogiston. The idea of a material of fire, possessing the quality of positive lightness – a substance which, being disengaged from any substance, left that substance heavier – a substance whose expression was in light and heat – comes so very near to the conception of a soul, that in entertaining it we feel ourselves almost treading on mythological ground, we are as near to the φλὸξ 'Ηφαίστοιο as to the modern theory of combustion. We feel that all such theories as these are indeed the residuum of a complete impersonation of the operative powers of nature, and that though Science takes its rise here, it is not science in its strictest sense till this region is left behind. It is, however, never evaded. When people begin to see that to make a particular result the operation of the will of God is not in any scientific sense an explanation of that result, they do not pass immediately from this personal agency of a Divine being to a physical law. The mind halts at an intermediate stage: it surrenders the personality of the cause, but keeps its spirituality, and the result is a metaphysical entity, which, though a mere empty abstraction, satisfies the mind with a convenient formulized statement of ignorance which it mistakes for cause, till some stimulus from without shall rouse it to the discovery that words are not things. This is the turning point of science; this also is the stage reached by philology in our day. On this ground, therefore, we claim the interest of the reader; we invite his attention to a struggle between the metaphysical theory of language, now almost in sole possession of the field, and its positive rival – a rival for whom the victory is no less certain than for a body of well-disciplined troops engaged against savages. The disproportion of the forces may be immense, the issue of the contest at present most unfavourable; but the result is not even doubtful; for the contest lies between a positive cause and a metaphysical abstraction – between a principle of acknowledged operation to some extent, and a figment of the mere indolent understanding, a product of the *'intellectus sibi permissus'* – the unquestioned, undisciplined prejudice of mankind.

This is the fact we are trying to point out. Our object is not here the sifting of evidence, the cross-examination of witnesses.

This is an important part of the process by which any theory of the Origin of Language must be established; but it has been well fulfilled in the work of Mr. Farrar, mentioned at the head of this Article, and it does not appear to us to lie within the function of a review. Moreover, we are inclined to protest at the very outset at the importance which has been assigned to the amount of evidence for the mimetic theory of the Origin of Language, which we here assert as the sole *vera causa* yet suggested for it. The question is not only, 'What is the evidence for it?' but, 'Is there any evidence against it?' We have not to ask ourselves, 'Which is true of two theories of the subject?' but, 'Is there really more than one theory about it at all?' We have, in fact, to choose between a hypothesis, allowed by its bitterest enemies to possess some plausible evidence in its favour, and a statement which investigation will prove to be a mere fine name for our ignorance. For this purpose we shall not touch any contested evidence, frivolous as are the grounds on which much of this is rejected. We start from the admission of our adversaries.

Before proceeding, however, to examine what is implied in these admissions, let us put before our readers, in definite language, the statements which, in answer to the question, How did language originate? supply respectively illustrations of the theological, the metaphysical, and the positive stages of the linguistic science. The first of these theories supposes, that as children now learn to speak from their parents, the first man learnt to speak from God. It is a curious instance of our dull apprehension of the meaning conveyed in familiar words, that something of this kind is supposed to be implied in the first chapter of Genesis. As M. Renan has well pointed out in his 'Essay on the Origin of Language,' the only words which are there capable of bearing on the subject have a directly opposite force. We have no intention of discussing the question on this ground, but any candid person who refers to Gen. ii. 19, will at once acknowledge that, if the authority of the Bible is to have any weight, it tends distinctly to establish the human origin of language. The sole statement[1] which the Old Testament can be made to yield as a contribution to our investigations is compatible either with the metaphysical or the

---

[1] Gen, xi. 7, has no bearing on this question at all. What is treated there is the origin of the diversity of languages, and not of language.

positive theories of language, but it is directly at issue with the theological. But there is now no need to insist upon this. Indeed, the theological, or, as we should prefer to call it, supernatural view on this subject is distinctly unscientific, and can never be illustrated from any work that aims at science; we must be satisfied, therefore, in order to indicate our meaning of the epithet, with referring to the indistinct prejudices which would emerge in the minds of most religious and half-educated people in answer to the question. How did language originate?

The metaphysical theory of language was enunciated more than two thousand years ago by Plato, and repeated in a modern lecture-room the other day by Professor Müller. Before we go on to inquire into the foundation for this theory, to investigate the exact meaning of some such absolute connection between sound and sense as is implied by it, let us bring before our minds the peculiar temptations which the study of language offers to the belief in such a theory. Every one will agree that, from whatever cause, there is a certain graduation in the senses with regard to the degree in which they appear to put us in connexion with the outward world. Of the causes of this gradation there are[2] endless controversies, but with these we have nothing to do. The feeling of being more or less directly in contact with something external may be instinctive; it may be the subtly-hidden trace of experience, it may even be erroneous; all we argue is that it exists. Some one asks, 'When will this din of bells stop?' and hears quite calmly that it is only a ringing in his ears. If he had believed himself to *see* the bell, he would not so quietly have learnt that the sense gave no information of anything without him. As a matter of fact, the one allusion would have indicated very much greater physical disorder than the other. Facts like these establish the position that hearing has a larger subjective element than some other senses, so that if we compare the five senses to five windows from which each of us contemplates the world around him, we should represent hearing by a coloured window, while sight would at all events be much nearer to colourless glass; this medium being perhaps most closely approached by touch. Touch connects us at once with the *without*; sight, rather less directly and positively; hearing, again, still less directly and

---

[2] See Turgot's allusion to this difference in his observations on Maupertuis's 'Essay on the Origin of Language.'

positively. It seems to keep us more within ourselves, to belong less to nature and more to the mind. As a consequence of this it is, far more than the sense of vision, associated with emotion and thought; it is the channel of far more overwhelming association, it bears the perfume of keener joy and keener pain. Something of this is, perhaps, due to the fact, that we are always seeing and are not always hearing, and that an intermittent sense can absorb an amount of association which one that is exercised at every moment has no energy to retain; but this, so far as it is the case, is again an argument on the side we are urging – that hearing is a sense that seems, as it were, to lie less than halfway between the mind and the thing. Sound, therefore, being a material peculiarly plastic to imagination, peculiarly sensitive to the touch of memory, and liable to be saturated with associations of joy or pain, is it not exactly that impression on the senses in which the mind is likely to feign that link between the spiritual and material world which it is impelled by so strong a fascination to seek? What can be seen, or what can be ascertained in some way through the sense of touch, is, under the light of modern science, stubborn against the spiritualizing process. We see that, let us attenuate our gas as finely as we will, we are not even approaching a region halfway between matter and spirit. But we only half see this (for, after all, people would not seriously entertain the absolute theory at the present day when it is put distinctly before them) with regard to sound. We do not at once perceive that to suppose an inherent fitness in a particular sound to express a particular thing is just as much a jumble of physical and metaphysical ideas as nature's abhorrence of a vacuum.

Such considerations as these may, perhaps, do something to explain the amount of authority by which this theory is supported, and the length of time during which it has been prevalent. A theory entertained by such men as Plato and Lucretius (one of the very few, probably, which we could quote as a common element in the belief of the two most diverse of great thinkers), a theory supported both by the earliest and the latest dissertation on the subject of language, and upheld (so far as we can understand them) by the writers of that nation who have made the subject their especial study, must be able to make out a very good case for itself. But this may be said of every view which enlists upon its side the prejudices and the vague beliefs generated by association, which, to the generality of mankind, look like the strongest arguments. A circumstance which also tells in its favour is, that it may be stated in very different language; it may, in fact, be clothed in a phraseology which altogether disguises its characteristic features, and approximates it to the positive theory, to which it is nevertheless essentially opposed; such, for instance, is the statement in the Platonic dialogue. Let the reader judge from our condensed translation of the apposite passage.

> Answer me, Hermogenes – says Socrates, addressing the vanquished upholder of the conventional theory – if we had neither tongue nor voice, and wished to point out anything, should we not imitate it as well as we could with our gestures? Thus, for instance, if we wished to indicate anything either elevated or light, we should indicate it by raising our hand upwards, and *vice versá*; while the attempt to describe any animal would be made by as near an approach to imitation as was possible in our own person.
>
> H. That seems to me unquestionable.
>
> S. Now, since we have organs of speech to point out objects with do we not point out any object by their means whenever we imitate anything with them?
>
> H. Certainly.
>
> S. The name of any object, then, is a vocal imitation of that object.
>
> H. So it seems to me.
>
> S. By Jupiter, that wont do, though, my dear fellow!
>
> H. Why not?
>
> S. We should have to say, if that were the case, that whoever mimicked the cry of a sheep, or of a cock, named the animal in question. Does that seem to you sound doctrine?
>
> H. Not at all. But what sort of imitation is the name, then?
>
> S. Not of the same kind, nor of the same objects, as the imitation effected in music, though the voice is used in both. To explain myself – have not objects shape and sound, and most of them colour?
>
> H. Certainly.
>
> S. Now, imitations of these qualities belong to the art of the musician and the painter, and have nothing to do with our subject. But has not every object an *essence*, besides those qualities of which we have spoken? Nay, have not

colour, sound, and shape themselves an essence, as well as whatever is worthy of the name of being at all?

H. I think so.

S. And if any one could represent this essence with letters and syllables, would he not then show the true nature of the thing represented?

H. Of course.

S. And as we called the former kind of imitation music and painting, what should we call this?

H. Just what we have been seeking all this time – the linguistic art (ὁ ὀνομαστικός).

S. If this is so, we must examine the words you were asking about, to see if they represent the essence of the things they apply to or not.

H. Very good.

S. Well, then, the best way is, like the students of rhythm, to begin by distinguishing the powers of different letters; after which we must proceed to examine names [or things, the passage is obscure and possibly corrupt], and apply each name to a thing according to the resemblance we find in it. I dare say it sounds very absurd to talk of representations of things by means of mimetic words and syllables. However, there is no choice in the matter, we have no better means of explaining the elementary words, unless we follow the example of the tragic writers who bring down a *Deus ex machiná* to get them out of a difficulty (the theological hypothesis is already past); and in this way let ourselves off with the assertion that the first names are imposed by the gods, and are right on this account. Or shall we try this explanation, that we have received them from the barbarians? (for there are barbarians of a more ancient date than our own) – or that through their great antiquity it is impossible to investigate them? These are all very pretty excuses for any one who wishes to escape the discussion of this fitness of the elementary words; but it is clear that whoever makes use of these excuses must not pretend to explain any of the compounds. [This strange assertion, put forth as a self-evident fact, is a good specimen of that in this philosophy which had to be unlearnt before any scientific treatment of the subject was possible.]

H. I entirely agree with you.

S. My own notions respecting the elementary words seem

to me absurd and audacious. However, I will share them with you, *i.e.*, if you like, and if you have anything better to suggest, I shall be glad to receive it in return. First of all, the letter R seems to me the appropriate instrument to express every kind of movement, as containing a certain mobility in itself. Its power of imitation is seen in such words as rush, tremble, rough, break, &c. [the Greek words are fairly represented in sound as well as sense by the equivalents we have given], in all which words the imitation is contained in the R. I suppose that the first originator of language found that the tongue was most active and vibrates with the greatest rapidity in producing this sound. (Here the reader will observe Socrates glides into the mimetic theory, which, however, he has distinctly described and rejected.) The letter I, on the other hand, expresses what is fine and subtle, and fitted to penetrate through all things, it is therefore used to imitate the action of going. [We cannot illustrate this by any English equivalent for ἰέναι.] φ, ψ, σ, and ζ, are all letters which express the idea of blowing, and hence are used in such words as ψυχρον, ζεον, σειεσθαι, &c. D and T produce a compression of the tongue, in which the author of language saw the imitation of every kind of bond (δεσμος) (he is again mimetic); while as he observed that in the letter L the tongue glides most smoothly, he used this letter for the imitation of whatever is smooth and gliding (λιπαρον, κολλωδες, &c.) The G, having the power of arresting this gliding movement of the tongue, he made use of, imitating whatever is viscous or sweet (γλισχρον, γλυκυ, γλοιωδες, gluey). Perceiving that N kept the voice inwards, he used this letter for the word in, α and η were used for μεγαλα and μηλος, as being both large sounds. In this way the author of language has applied, by means of letters and syllables, its own proper symbol to every individual object. Such, Hermogenes, is the natural fitness of language from my point of view, unless Cratylus can give me a better one.

Such is the earliest exposition of this theory, which, but for its distinct exclusion of the positive doctrine, we might rather quote as an early anticipation of that hypothesis. Let us now turn to the latest, which is consistently separated from what we hold the truth.

'The 400 or 500 roots,' says Professor Müller, 'which remain as the constituent elements in different families of language are not interjections, neither are they imitations, they are phonetic types produced by a power inherent in human nature. They exist, as Plato would say, by nature; though with Plato we should add that when we say by nature we mean by the hand of God. There is a law which runs through nearly the whole of nature, that everything which is struck rings. Each substance has its peculiar ring; we can tell the more or less perfect structure of metals by their vibrations, by the answer which they give. Gold rings differently from tin, wood rings differently from stone; and different sounds are produced according to the nature of each percussion. It was the same with man, the most highly organized of Nature's works. The fact that wood, metals, cords, &c., if struck, vibrate and ring, can of course be used as an illustration only, and not as an explanation. The faculty peculiar to man, in his primitive state, by which every impression from without received its vocal expression from within, must be accepted as an ultimate fact that faculty must have existed in man, because its effects continue to exist. Analogies from the inanimate world, however, are useful, and deserve further examination. Man, in his primitive and perfect state, was not only endowed, like the brute, with the power of expressing his sensations by interjections, and his perceptions by onomatopœia; he possessed likewise the faculty of giving more articulate expression to the rational conceptions of his mind. That faculty was not of his own rational conceptions of his mind. That faculty was not of his own making, it was an instinct – an instinct of the mind as irresistible as any other instinct: so far as language is the production of that instinct, it belongs to the realm of nature. Man loses his instincts as he ceases to want them; his senses become fainter when, as in the case of scent, they become useless. Thus the creative faculty which gave to each conception, as it thrilled for the first time through the brain, a phonetic expression, became extinct when its object was fulfilled.'

We comment on this passage with reluctance. It is an ungracious task to criticise that portion of an able and valuable work which is written with the left hand. If the progress of philology in general interest in the last few years has been mainly due to the eloquence and genius of the writer – to borrow Mr. Farrar's graceful tribute to his opponent – it seems hardly in accordance with our gratitude to him to single out for comment a small fragment of his work which bears no impress of his mind, and might be detached from the whole without leaving a scar, which seems, in short, the addition of a commentator to the work of a scholar anxious to round off the work of his master into a completeness which that master had wisely refrained from seeking. If, as Bacon has quoted, 'truth is less remote from error than from confusion,' the man who has quickened general interest in philology has certainly done more to advance true opinions concerning it than he can have done to hinder these by any amount of false theory. In this respect we look upon the Professor as a second Horne Tooke. Philologists may spend their lives in confuting his errors, and owe to him the first gleam of interest which ultimately led to a detection of those errors. Still, as he has enshrined them in his peculiarly lucid and brilliant style (a style which those who study the writings of his countrymen will often remember with a sigh), he cannot complain that those who combat a particular doctrine should avail themselves of a statement which best discovers its intrinsic weakness by exhibiting it in a form which is free from any other.

Our quotation is taken from Professor Müller's first series of lectures on languages – the second series appears to indicate some change of view, and a disposition to leave the question of origin open. He has a perfect right to take this course. Any one may investigate the laws which regulate the changes and varieties of language without committing himself to any hypothesis as to the source from which it originates, and as life is short and art – and still more we may say science – is long, it is quite possible that he may achieve the first aim all the more effectually, if he rigidly excludes the second. Only let it be taken distinctly and consistently, let one who avows it see that he remains neutral with regard to *the* question of language. Let him allow that Mr. Farrar is in the right when he says that—

> 'If, for instance, a large class of words belong to the root "ach," and another large class have the root "dhu" and if the former be an interjection, and the latter an onomatopœia, we have got the final facts which give a new meaning and

interest to the history of the derivations from these roots; but if we are told that a large family of words come from these roots, and that of these roots nothing more can be said, then, what have we learnt?'

Well – perhaps not quite nothing, but nothing that throws any light on the origin of language.

The foregoing theory, we have said, represents the metaphysical phase of the science of language. It does not require many words to justify this assertion. The question which this theory attempts to answer is this: How did the first man learn to speak? The answer is, 'There is an instinct in man which, in his primitive and perfect state, led him to connect certain sounds and certain ideas.' This instinct is something of which we have no evidence but the fact which it professes to explain. It is not an actual existence, which, whether or not a particular function be assigned to it with justice, remains in unquestioned reality before our mental eye; it is something called into ideal operation to satisfy a need of the intellect. Nobody would assert that any principle is now operating through which 'every impression from without receives its vocal expression from within' – the proof of its existence is that 'its effects continue to exist.' We do not encounter it under any other aspect but as the cause of these particular effects. We are not, for instance, the least helped by it where we should expect to find it tested – in our study of a new language. We receive an impression of an animal with four legs and a woolly coat, and the vocal impression with which it is associated in the mind of a foreigner is not suggested to us by anything but the experience of that association in the past. The phonetic types explain the origin of language, and they do nothing else. They intervene to fill a gap in the chain of cause and effect, and we know no more of them. Their operation is confined to strictly metaphysical ground.

We now come to the positive hypothesis of the origin of language – a hypothesis that demands no withering of our primitive instincts, no chasm in the progress of the race, no exceptional agency at work during any part of its existence. It is a hypothesis that is perplexing from its very simplicity: it asserts that language originated long ago, just as language would originate to-day, if any person were isolated among the speakers of a tongue unknown to him. Any one who, under such circumstances, wished to designate a sheep, would certainly not seek for the vocal expression corresponding to the impression of a woolly quadruped of small size; he would imitate its baaing sound. Those who adopt this theory assert that such is the origin of the Greek μῆλον. Their opponents may question the latter assertion, they must agree with the former. They must allow, that is, that the question is of the limits of operation of a particular principle, not of the fact of its existence. Whether the Greek μῆλον preserves for us the traces of a time when animals were represented by an endeavour to imitate their cries may be matter of question. Whether any one who had now to invent some name, not significant, for an animal with any cry that admitted of imitation, would take this course, surely can be a question to no rational man. Some language, it is conceded, might be framed upon this principle, but not all. Nay, it is allowed that some language *is* framed on this principle. 'There are some recognised Aryan root-words,' says an article in the *Quarterly Review*, which may be adopted as the most convenient compendium of the arguments of this school, 'such as *pat*, fall; *lih*, lick, which may be claimed with some colour of right as imitative sounds.' Now, take the first of these roots, which Liddell and Scott – no partial authority – would connect with the English *path*, the only obvious English representative of this root, and we have a noun, surely not specially suggestive of sound, connected with a mimetic root. No one can say that there is anything exceptional in this word. It is surely a fair average specimen of language. If this word springs from a mimetic root, why should not all others do the like?

That really seems to us the only argument to urge or to answer. Of course, as a matter of fact, it is important to determine the soundness of particular etymologies which connect particular words with a mimetic root. Whether fusee be derived from fizz, for instance, or from the Latin fusus, is in itself an interesting question. But it does not appear to us that the advocates of the mimetic theory are under any necessity to investigate such cases, or to produce a long list of unquestioned instances of mimetic origin. The question is simply this – Is the explicable portion of language an exceptional one? Is there anything but imitation to explain language? When we are comparing two theories which relate to actual entities the amount of evidence is an element of consideration – if there is anything but imitation to explain language, let us weigh the evidence on each side. But where, as in the present case, the rival cause is one which is only known *as* a cause, the very lightest amount of positive evidence is enough to weigh down the opposite scale. It is as if we found in two different accounts of the same transaction, two different persons designed as the author of some particular action, one of whom was well known to us from other quarters as living at the time when it took place, while of the other, we could find out nothing but the simple mention which we were seeking to justify. Surely the amount of external evidence needed to authenticate the first of these agents would be very trifling.

The question has been confused by Professor Müller's baseless division of the mimetic view into the pooh-pooh, and bow-wow theory. The pooh-pooh theory *is* the bow-wow theory. The theory which would select the interjection Pooh! as a typical illustration of language, is one with that theory which would do the same by the words Bow-wow. The mimetic theory asserts that the first men originated language, as our contemporaries would originate it now, by means of some vocal representation of particular sounds, or objects in which some analogy could be traced to sounds. Thus would arise onomatopœia, or imitations of sounds not due to vocal utterance, thus also would arise interjections, or imitations of sounds which are due to vocal utterance. A cry of pain is not language, any more than the mooing of a cow is language. Whether we imitate the first sound, and produce the interjection Ah! or whether we imitate the second sound, and produce (in German) the noun *Kuh*, we are in both cases using language and in both cases illustrating the same theory. In both alike the matter is supplied by sound, the form by imitation. What pretence is there for finding a different principle here at work?

This is a part of the subject which needs to be insisted upon at some length, it is so frequently misunderstood. The most thoughtful and learned men of the present day repeat Horne Tooke's fallacy, which has been so much harped upon in the late controversy, that we might as well reckon a cry of pain among the parts of speech as the interjection. The fact is, that the interjection can only be denied its place among the parts of speech, because it is speech in a wider sense than any of these. It is, in fact, a condensed sentence. It is speech in its earlier stage – speech not yet broken up into parts – speech unresolved into verbs, and pronouns, and the other elements of language. But it is certainly not less than any of these, true language. Mr. Farrar, the writer whose work may be used as the best popular summary of the argument on the mimetic side – seems to us to go much too far in his concessions when he says, 'We do not assert that a mere interjectional cry has attained to the dignity of language, but that *like the imitation of natural sounds*, it was a stepping-stone to true language.'[3] We have italicised the words which appear to us to render the whole passage unsatisfactory. They seem to indicate a confusion between 'the mere interjectional cry' and the interjection. The interjectional cry is the natural sound, the interjection is the imitation. It sets the whole idea wrong to compare *the cry* to an imitation. We notice this mistake merely as an instance of what appears to us a too anxious candour in Mr. Farrar, leading him to find more sense and meaning in the argument he is combating that it really contains, for the chapter from which this quotation is taken is an attempt to prove the identity of the two theories which this inconsistent admission would tend to separate. Yet he seems here to allow that an interjection is, as Horne Tooke says in the now almost classical quotation, 'only employed when the suddenness and vehemence of some affection or passion returns men to their natural state, and makes them for a moment forget the use of speech.' Surely even the artificial eighteenth century never gave birth to a more curious theory on the natural state of man! How many times in his life did Horne Tooke say Oh no, without the slightest tinge of this vehemence or passion which could make him forget the use of speech? Of those two words, the first is language in exactly the same sense as the last, it is definite sound used to convey meaning, which is all that we can see in language on any theory of its origin. We might paraphrase the word by such expressions as 'certainly,' 'to be sure,' 'of course.' These might all be implied in the Oh, they are meant by the speaker, and understood by the hearer; the interjection condenses, as it were absorbs them – is it therefore less language than they are? Of course it sometimes happens that 'some affections return men to their natural state, and make them forget the use of language,' but then they do not use interjections. They may give utterance to inarticulate cries, and

[3] Chapters on Language, p. 93.

these are no more language than a sob or a laugh. But the Oh or Ah which represents these cries has nothing irrepressible or unconscious about it. It is used, just like any other word, to convey a definite meaning to another mind, only that the meaning here is wider than in any other single word that can be used, for it contains an undeveloped sentence.

The want of a clearer and stronger assertion of the identity of the bow-wow and pooh-pooh theories, is one of the few faults we have to find with Mr. Farrar's instructive essay. He does indeed make this assertion, 'both the interjectional and onomatopœitic theories might,' he says,[4] 'without impropriety, be classed under the same name,' but his conclusion to the sentence, 'the impulsive instinct to reproduce a sound is precisely analogous to that which gives vent to a sensation by an interjection,' carries us back into the error already noticed, that the impulsive cry, and not the imitation of that impulsive cry, is the interjection. The mistake is repeated on the next page, where he says that interjections may be divided into two kinds, 'those which are caused by some inward sensation,' which are 'perfectly vague, both as to the form they assume, and the source from which they arise;' – and, 'those which are evoked by some external impression,' which 'do not like imitations, express the external character of the thing perceived, but the inward excitement of the soul in consequence of the perception.' Again, we repeat it, Mr. Farrar has dropped a link. It seems to us a contradiction to say that sounds which are perfectly vague both as to the form which they assume and the source from which they arise, are language. And surely we have not two kinds of cry for pain which is caused from without, and pain which is caused from within. Mr. Farrar has made two classes of language out of the raw materials for language and language itself. The vague cries due to any emotion or sensation are the materials for the words which express that sensation or emotion, the formative element being supplied by imitation. We are not consciously imitating a vocal cry when we say, Ah me! but we are using an imitation, first suggested by an unconscious cry, now, just like any other word, conventionally associated with a particular feeling. A person who is under irrepressible anguish says neither Oh nor Ah. There is the same kind of translation, so to speak (not perhaps

[4] P. 88.

the same degree), in repressing the inarticulate cry by these vowels, as there is by representing the cry of the cock by Cock-a-doodle-doo.

It is quite true that the instinctive character of imitation has hardly been sufficiently recognised, and Mr. Farrar's observations on this particular have much value. There is an instinct which leads us to imitation quite apart from any meaning to be conveyed by it. From this instinct we laugh or yawn in the company of those who do the like; from this instinct, too, we often make signs which our words render perfectly unnecessary. And no doubt all words which are due to interjections represent the more impulsive elements of thought. But the principle on which they are formed is precisely that on which we name the Cuckoo. A particular sound is in each case associated with a particular idea, and we imitate it to recall that idea; such is the statement of the mimetic theory of language, and it may be applied to interjections or onomatopœia indifferently.

We repeat, therefore, that interjections, just as much as onomatopœia, are an illustration and proof of the mimetic theory. To split this up into the bow-wow and pooh-pooh theories is as rational an arrangement as it would be to insist on finding some other word than sculpture to express that art, as it might be exercised on some material different from marble. If it were a mere question of nomenclature, or of convenient arrangement, this argument would have been urged at a length disproportionate to its importance, but in fact to make one see that the mimetic theory of language includes both the interjectional and the onomatopœitic theories, or rather that these are two different names for the former – is almost to make him see that the mimetic theory is true. For the supposed fact of there being two theories to consider entirely disguises from the mind the true nature of the argument. If there were two different suggestions of a *vera causa* to consider, the question would be one of conflicting evidence, and we should have to investigate every etymology capable of bearing on the question before we could answer it. But the case is different when we have to choose not between two rival theories, but between a theory, and a fine name for our ignorance. The metaphysical theory is, as we have shown, nothing more than a fine name for our ignorance. It is not by any means a useless name. It groups together cognate facts, it indicates their connection, it suggests, to some more advanced observer, the direction in which to seek their cause. Take for instance that despised axiom already quoted, 'Nature abhors a vacuum.' Here is a metaphysical theory on physical ground, and as such of course it is false, if we may not rather call it unmeaning. Yet as Mr. Grove has well remarked in his work on the Correlation of Force,[5] 'this aphorism contains in a terse, though somewhat metaphorical form of expression, a comprehensive truth, and evinces a large extent of observation in those who first generalized by this sentence the facts of which they became cognisant.' And all this we might say of the phonetic types. As stated in Professor Müller's pages, it is true, they seem to us valueless, because they are distinctly opposed to that hypothesis which otherwise they might have suggested. In upholding them he is in the position of a person who finds the theory of Nature's abhorrence of a vacuum more tenable as an explanation of certain facts than the pressure of the atmosphere. But this view taken in its earlier form, as it appears in the pages of Plato, just throws the facts of language into such groups as are most convenient for the discovery of the law that rules them. The letter I has no more inherent connection with what is fine and subtle, than Nature has any abhorrence of a vacuum. In both cases where the contrary is asserted it is sought to bridge that chasm which separates the physical and the spiritual world, and in all cases such an effort is vain. But the spirit of overstrained metaphor which leads to such an effort is the fostermother, till it becomes the enemy, of science. At a certain stage it is no doubt the enemy of science. The idea of any absolute connection between sound and sense appears to us quite incompatible with any scientific view of language at the present day, but some such idea was the indispensable preliminary to a scientific investigation of the subject. We need theories to arrange facts, these facts may ultimately prove the falsity of the theories which grouped and retained them in the memory (as in the instance of Nature's abhorrence of a vacuum), but a theory of some kind is the almost indispensable condition of any coherent observation at all. Bewildered by the multitude of phenomena in the physical world, overwhelmed by the complexity and entanglement of the chain of cause and effect which runs through it, man would never have arrived at any

[5] Correlation of Physical Forces, p. 146.

large physical law, if he had not simplified the problem at starting by those metaphysical assumptions which, in lending Nature his own impulses, arrange its infinite variety on a definite plan. In a word, science would never have arrived at the positive stage, if it had not passed through the metaphysic. And yet it is not truly science, in the severe modern sense of the word, till it has left the metaphysic stage behind. These metaphors are useful props, but when the plant has grown strong and vigorous, they check its growth if they are not removed. The idea that the vowel I has some absolute fitness to express what is fine and subtle is a good preparation for the idea that this vowel has a mimetic force in representing to the ear the effect of something small, – a fact perfectly explicable on physiological grounds. But it is only good as a preparation for this last conception, held against this, it becomes false. When Professor Müller tells us that 'the faculty by which every impression from without receives its vocal impression from within, must be received as an ultimate fact,' he is taking his stand just on that portion of the theory which is simply false. He ensconces himself in the portico, and refuses to enter the building. Or rather he pulls up the plant to make way for the trellis which supported it.

A metaphysical explanation of a physical fact, then, is never anything more than a name for our ignorance. It is sometimes a very useful thing to have a name for a thing, and to suppose that our having a particular word to denote a particular fact explains the cause of that fact. Such a name weighs nothing against a positive cause. We need not calculate evidence between the two, it is not a case of evidence. Be the rival cause as light as it may, it will weigh down the scale when that opposed to it is empty. Now the mimetic school proves such a cause of language to exist. They assert, and no one denies, that we should have recourse to imitation if *we* had to invent language. They assert, and no one denies, that some portion of language is directly due to imitation. They deny, and no one asserts, that any other hypothesis suggests any rational explanation of the connection of sound and sense. Of course, declaring that this connection is absolute is only another way of saying it is incomprehensible. If it must be accepted as an ultimate fact, we cannot expect a reason for it. But if a reason is to be given, one has been suggested, and only one. There is a certain amount of evidence for this hypothesis, which philologists will estimate very differently. But the true question for them to consider is not so much, 'What is the evidence for this theory?' as 'What is the alternative if it is rejected?' If articulate sound did not arise in an imitation of inarticulate, whence did it arise? They may say that they are not obliged to frame any theory on the subject, that they may point out arguments against a particular hypothesis, without being prepared with a substitute. Arguments *against* the hypothesis, yes; but this is what has not been done. All the argument that has been produced on this side is precisely of a piece with the 100 witnesses whom the Irishman was ready to call upon to swear that they did not see him commit the murder, to confute the one who swears that he did see it. Sometimes the witnesses are not even so favourable as this. For instance, what is the value of the objection made by Professor Müller, and repeated by the *Quarterly Review*, that the mimetic school draw their examples from secondary words, not from roots? Let us hear the objection in its latest form.

'That they refuse to conform to this rule' [*i.e.*, to start from the roots] 'is,' says the Quarterly Reviewer, who has not got beyond the fallacy of the two theories, 'the besetting sin of the advocates of the imitative and interjectional theories; and the motives for such refusal are not difficult to see. In developed words, often, as it seems, *modified with an express view of making their sound suitable to their sense*, like 'stamp' or 'waddle,' it is extremely easy to suggest real or fancied analogies of sound as their original derivation; while short-root words, like 'sta' or 'bad,' are by no means so tractable. Yet this is one of the cases where what is wrong is both easy and satisfactory to immediate desire, while what is right is difficult, and offers small profit for the moment. In so far Mr. Farrar's able and learned essay is a vindication of the view that part of the original constituents of language may be traceable to imitation, interjection, and baby language' [again he misses the principle of the mimetic theory, that the original constituents of language may be traced to imitation of baby language, and the interjectional cries from which interjections are formed] – 'it is a valuable combination to philosophy, but in so far as he assails the main principle of the school of Bopp, Pott, and Müller, by ignoring the work of analysis into elementary roots, and treating secondary words off-hand, independently both of structure and development, he only shows how strong a citadel of sound science this school maintains against the inroads of an undisciplined imagination.'

Now, without stopping to investigate the nature of an argument which rests its whole weight on a certain consecrated canon of writers, which asks of an opponent not whether it bears the stamp of accurate observation and sound logic, but whether it be orthodox according to the school of Bopp, and Pott, and Müller, which in short, seems inclined to adopt the weapons, that honourable men are beginning to discard in theology, without possessing the excuses of theologians for adopting any weapons likely to be efficacious – without criticising the argument itself; are we not perfectly justified in asserting that as given here it tells for us and not against us? If developed words are 'modified to make their sound suitable to their sense,' is not this, as Mr. Farrar has well pointed out, as strong a proof as it is possible to give that the original germs of these words were probably moulded to make their sound suitable to their sense? If, with all the resources of elaborated language, we still find a mimetic principle at work, where it is so nearly superfluous, is not this an argument on the side of those who assert that it was at work when it was *not* superfluous? We are balked by the very obviousness of the principle for which we are contending. It is so much of a truism to assert that if language tends to imitation when it has other resources at its command, still more must it have tended to imitation when it had none – that it is not altogether easy to persuade people it is a truth. Surely to point out that a certain deposit of earth is due to yesterday's shower, is not to disprove that an analogous deposit is of alluvial formation. Yet this seems to us the drift of the argument given above.

The assertors of the mimetic theory are not obliged to give in their adhesion to any doctrine about roots. Just as Professor Müller is prepared to stand neuter to their theory, they may stand neuter to his. There is no prejudice more fatal to the progress of knowledge, than the belief that we ought not to leave open questions behind us, that a particular opinion must stand or fall by a particular inference with which it is linked by any but demonstrative reasoning. Such a method presents double chances of error at every step, the inference may be false in the first place, or irrelevant in the second. Perhaps the labours of Bopp, and Pott, and Müller are not quite free from some admixture of error, perhaps too they are not inconsistent with the mimetic theory of the origin of language. In either case it simplifies the matter to discuss the two things separately, as Professor Müller avows his intention of doing on the one hand, and (if we had sufficient influence over the mimetic school) as they would do on the other. If both views are true, they will certainly be proved not to be inconsistent in the end.

The theory advocated in these pages, that language originated long ago just as it would originate now, is one presenting so much evidence and so little difficulty on purely intellectual ground, that if this were the region on which the battle were fairly fought, it would be over by this time. Let us briefly recapitulate this evidence. First, this is the only hypothesis that joins the present and the past, that does not endow our forefathers with instincts of which their children know nothing; and this one argument, to our thinking, is enough – not indeed to settle the question, but to throw the whole onus of argument on those who deny the theory. Secondly, there is a certain portion of language which is unquestionably due to this principle. Thirdly, there is no portion whatever which is explicable as due to any other. Now, let any one ask himself if these, the admissions of our opponents – and to these the present article has been rigorously confined – would not be enough for the establishment of any theory, if it were not one that was settled on other than intellectual ground; one on which some warping influence intervened between men's knowledge and their opinions? The origin of language is a question on which men's prejudices, right and wrong, have much to say and all they have to say is, we admit, against the view advocated in these pages. An examination of these prejudices – which are of two kinds, those which are and those which are not purely intellectual – will occupy what space remains to us.

The first class is the most important. It influences the smallest set of minds, but then it influences those minds which form and direct general opinion. The number of those who would be biassed by a secret fear of some theological inference from the mimetic theory is greater than the number of those who would be shackled by an intellectual fallacy concerning it, but the opinions of the second would be received with an attention which would be wanting to those of the first. On the fallacies which obstruct the progress of language, therefore, we have something to say; on the prejudices, properly so called, almost nothing.

We have spoken of *fallacies*, but we might have used the word in the singular. The one great obstacle to a true view of the origin of language is the difficulty of conceiving that things which have always been inseparable in our experience are inseparable in their own nature. On this fallacy the metaphysical theory erects its stronghold. The name and the thing are so identified in the mind of every one, that the hypothesis of 'phonetic types,' of 'some faculty peculiar to man, by which every impression from without received its vocal expression from within,' finds a nook ready prepared for it in the general impressions which go so much further in their influence on any opinion than any logical reasoning. Imagination has forged a link between the sign and the thing signified which the intellect, having endeavoured in vain to break, readily accepts as existing in nature.

No other association of two distinct entities is so close as that between thought and language. No human being can recall a time when the particular sound by which we designate a particular image did not recur to the mind as the inseparable companion of that image, and as images of some kind or other pass before our eyes or our fancy during the larger part of our waking and some portion of our sleeping hours, the name and the thing have a mutual affinity for which we seek some deeper source than invariable connexion in time. And if we had to solve the problem of the origin of language, without any help from the diversity of languages, this tendency would, it seems to us, be irresistible. If all over the world, in every variety of climate, civilization, and all the varied circumstances by which nations are distinguished from each other, we still found a member of the human race associated with that sound which we write down as *man*, it seems almost inevitable that we should ascribe to that sound an inherent connexion with its associated idea; or, to translate into the language of Professor Müller, that we should regard it as the phonetic type of humanity. Nor are we driven to mere hypothesis for this inference. Any one who will carefully study the dialogue of Plato from which we have made the above extract will grant that we have much reason on our side when we assert that the whole state of mind there presented is one deeply coloured by the fact that when Socrates talks about language he really means Greek. It would be a deeply interesting discussion, and one by one means irrelevant to the present subject, though exceeding the limits possible for its discussion in this place, to inquire how far the whole tone of Greek speculation was influenced by these thinkers knowing no language but their own; to investigate its relation to the suppressed premiss in almost every argument of Socrates, that language is the undistorted shadow of nature, and that our knowledge of things, therefore, proceeds *pari passu* with our accurate apprehension of the meaning of words. This statement might, no doubt, be contradicted in the words of Socrates himself. In making it we are not forgetting that striking passage (to our perception the only valuable portion of the dialogue) where Socrates, after having established against Hermogenes that language, like every other instrument used by man, must, if it is to be efficacious, conform itself to laws not invented by man, turns round and establishes against Cratylus[6] that the instrument may be perverted to evil uses. Certainly no clearer assertion of the distinctness of words and things could be looked for from Mr. Mill himself. Nevertheless, we believe that the comparison of ancient and modern thought establishes the assertion, that one great instrument for teaching us to separate words and things is the diversity of language which now prevails in the civilized world.

Our modern training, however, has not been altogether directed against this tendency. A great portion of our modern education, indeed, consists in learning foreign languages, but then the language to which we accord the front rank is one which, both from its own perfection and the wealth which is enshrined in it, is best fitted to disguise from us all that the diversity of languages is adapted to teach. Till we look upon all languages with perfect impartiality, ranging side by side the dialect of Plato and of some naked savage, we are in no position to enter on the study of philology. Hence in this direction, as in so many others, the scholar is to some extent at issue with the student. Learning is not always the best friend to science – the two pursuits require attitudes of mind which are

---

[6] Φερε δε, ἐννοησαμεν, ἐι τις ξητων τα πραγματα ἀκολονθοι τοις ὀνομασι, σκοπων οἰον ἐκαστον βονλεται ἐιναι, μη ἐννοεις ὁτι οὐ σμικρὸς κινδυνος ἐjτιν ἐξαπατηθηναι ; &c.

not invariably helpful to each other. We see this exemplified, for instance, in such books as Harris's 'Hermes' – a book which may be read now with a certain interest, as affording us a good specimen of the kind of work produced by a mere scholar, on a subject with which scholarship has very little to do. Everywhere we see predominating the scholar's sense of an aristocracy of languages of a particular group, and an individual tongue to which the term language may be applied in some peculiar and typical sense, which is not shared by the vulgar herd of dialects, whereby men communicate with each other. This is exactly the feeling of Socrates. Those Greek words which he supposes to have been adopted from the barbarians, are for him exceptional words. He has no sarcastic or moral etymology to extract from them – he lays them aside, as in some degree irrelevant to the question of language. There is a close connection between this belief, and the impossibility of seeing that no theory as to the vocal labels by which our conceptions are kept distinct can afford any inference as to those conceptions themselves. Socrates implies, in the Cratylus, that according to our decision as to the origin of language will be our view as to the nature of truth, that the conventional theory advocated by Hermogenes, for instance, ignores the fact that truth is absolute, that the absolute theory advocated by Cratylus ignores the fact that language may be false. No one in our day would repeat exactly this mistake. We use without scruple metaphors founded on the dreams of mythology or astrology, we borrow words from every illusion or delusion which has lasted long enough to leave its stamp upon language, and never feel ourselves thereby committed to any advocacy of the theories of which our words are, as it were, the commemorating medals. We speak, for instance, of a favourable conjunction, and are not astrologists, we criticise a saturnine temperament, and are not astrologists, we criticise a saturnine temperament, and are not pagans. Nevertheless, we, too, confuse the label and the thing labelled. We may suppose etymology to be a mere human work, reflecting all the errors, the hasty inferences, the prejudices, the false metaphors of common thought, but we cling unconsciously to ourselves, to the belief that there is something more than this in *roots* – that they reflect some inherent connexion between sound and sense, lying in a stratum below the reach of human error. We recoil from the belief that the connexion in this case, as well as the other, is no more than some resemblance which the fancy of mankind has detected between the name and the thing.

In short, we have in language, and especially in the great language of antiquity, which has formed the study of the learned world, an instrument the perfection of which disguises from us that it is no more than an instrument. Suppose, to use a metaphor which has been applied to this subject before, that the plough were elaborated to some much more extensive use than at present. Suppose it not only turned up the soil, but scattered and watered the seed, weeded the young drop, and reaped the corn, – suppose, in short, that there were no process of agriculture that was not performed by it, – would not there be a very powerful tendency in the minds of those who knew nothing of the stages by which the instrument had been thus perfected, to believe that it was something more than an expedient for bringing together the two elements of the desired result – the seed and the soil – to believe that it possessed an actual fertilizing power of its own? This is the case with language. It has done its work so well, that we forget that this work is no more than to communicate thoughts, which are seldom, indeed, separated from it in fact, but are perfectly independent of it in essence. We say, that thought and language are *seldom* separated in fact, we deny that this is never the case. As M. Charna has well remarked in his eloquent and discursive essay on the subject, every time any one stops to seek for a word, he has the thought without the name in his mind. We could not carry on a train of reasoning with these vague unlabelled thoughts; thinking certainly is in the minds of human beings invariably a process of words. But, that this is even an unchangeable necessity in the nature of things, and not a mere consequence of human infirmity, a poverty of memory and imagination, demanding the symbol to correct the weakness its hold on the thing symbolized, is what we have no reason whatever to believe. The instrument, for aught we know, may be one which can be well dispensed with by higher natures than ours.

Both the uncultivated and the learned mind, therefore, are specially liable to influences which tend to the confusion of words and thoughts, and inclined, therefore, to the reception of any theory which treats the connexion between the two as absolute. The uncultivated, because, with such a mind the fallacy of invariable association is always strongest, – the learned, because learning, which consists with us in the study of a language which is the shrine of the most valuable legacy of the world's thinkers, tends both to give undue importance to a language in general, and to pick out a particular language as entitled to a certain typical significance which disqualifies the mind for an impartial study of comparative philology. While both these influences are active on that vague composite body of readers and talkers who make up what is called public opinion, we must expect the progress of the truth, to which they are opposed, to be but slow. Nevertheless, it is a perceptible one. 'That interjections and imitative words are really taken up to some extent, be it large or small, into the very body and structure of language, is what no one denies,'[7] is an admission that would not have been made ten years ago.

Before passing on to the consideration of other and deeper-seated prejudices which encumber our way, let us pause to notice one objection to this theory, which certainly would not deserve even the most cursory notice, if it were due to any less-respected authority than Prof. Max Müller. 'If language were nothing more than vocal imitation,' he says, 'it would be hard to understand why animals should be without it.' Like Charles II. and the fish in his bowl of water, we should like to be sure of the fact before we argue about it. Is it easy now, or on any theory, to understand why animals are without language? Those who would answer in the affirmative confuse two very different things: a firm conviction that a particular fact will always continue unchanged and a comprehension of the reason for that fact. We protest against the introduction into the discussion of the question of animals. If, indeed they were distinguished from men in their want of language and in nothing besides – if speech were the *differentia* which separated the species Homo from the genus Animal – then it would be an essential part of every theory on the subject to adapt it to this difference, to explain this negative instance where the causes, which in man produced their full effect, met with counteracting causes by which this effect was neutralized. But is this the case between man and animals? Is the brute man minus speech? is man the brute plus speech? Those who think that he is really include in speech all that speech implies, and so again make the connexion of Thought and Language

[7] Origin of Language. By Edward B. Tylor. 'Fortnightly Review,' April 13th.

absolute. So that the question of animals can never be made apposite to the question except by begging the question. The mental condition of animals is one of these subjects which would appear profoundly mysterious to us if the mere facts of the case were not so familiar. No one, we think, can understand the state of mind in an intelligent dog in the same sense as he understands every shade of intelligence in a human being. We cannot, in imagination, put ourselves into that stage of mental being. We cannot gradually diminish our intellectual light till we reach the twilight of canine intelligence. It is not a mere process of subtraction: if we put ourselves back so far, we shall find ourselves much further. We can much more easily figure to ourselves the mental state of idiots than of animals. The present writer once gave a nut to a monkey at the Zoological Gardens, which he held out in the left hand, clapping down the right upon it until the nut was cracked and returned to him. Can any one imagine himself in the state of mind to make a similar sign, and not to attempt some vocal imitation of sounds he must often have heard? The animal world is a mystery to us on which a theory on the Origin of Language is not bound to thrown any light whatever. Why a creature who can remember, reason, and understand language cannot speak, is a problem left unsolved by any view we take upon the subject of speech. Again we protest against the notion, that any question left open by a particular theory is any objection to that theory; let arguments be confuted on their own ground, and not on that of some inference with which the fancy of men may connect them. The mimetic school undertakes to answer the question 'How did language arise?' With the question 'How did it not arise?' it has nothing to do.

A large part of the opposition encountered by our theory, then, is accounted for by the common intellectual fallacy of supposing invariable association in experience to indicate connexion in nature. Speaking loosely, we should say that the remedy lay in a somewhat lessened idea of the importance of language – in a clear understanding that it is nothing more than a system of elaborate labelling our ideas. We shall learn much in the study of language of the history of human thought; we shall discover much that is valuable concerning the association of ideas and the theories in which they have been arranged; but after all we shall learn nothing about things in studying language, except what our forefathers thought about them. No manipulation of words will teach us anything but the thoughts of their maker; we cannot get anything out of language, but what men have put into it. If this is clearly understood, it will be seen that a name was given just as a child is christened, for some reason that may or may not be a good one. We shall be ready, in short, to enter on an investigation of names with a full assurance that they form no part of the things to which they apply – that whatever may be the reason for that application, it is one that belongs to the mind and not to nature.

But the larger part of that prejudice which prevents such simple and obvious arguments as those by which the mimetic theory is supported from producing their just effect, is not intellectual. It is felt too that this theory on the origin of language indicates a particular view on the origin of humanity, from which the greater number of those who criticise it would shrink with abhorrence. We cannot go back in thought to a period when our ancestors communicated with each other by mimetic cries and gestures without going back a little further, and ask ourselves whether such creatures could, properly speaking, be called human. This, we believe, is the real stumbling block to the mimetic theory. Logic does its work in vain: a mightier adversary holds the passage to belief, and will not confess itself vanquished. Some portion of the objection arising from this source has been answered already as far as it can be answered. Man's place in nature is a question to be decided of his place out of nature. The circumstances which attended the first appearance of our race on this globe may be very unlike what we should have imagined: they may include events which we find very difficult to arrange in harmony with convictions which it is impossible to surrender. But they must stand or fall on their own evidence, and not on their adaptability to those convictions. The past is, in this respect, simply on a level with the present. We actually do reconcile with these convictions – reconcile them, that is, so far as to keep both in our mind together – a hundred unquestionable facts which present precisely that kind of opposition to those convictions on which we reject other facts that but for these difficulties would also be considered unquestionable. We *cannot* weed the present of all circumstance which conflicts with our fundamental belief, and therefore we learn to admit this mutual hostility between different clauses of our creed as a possible fact; but we do not, as we ought, apply this lesson to our judgement on the past. There it is possible to set up our belief on certain subjects as a sieve, and reject all evidence which will not pass through it. What we hear and see we must believe: we even extend this belief to what our contemporaries hear and see. And the results thus admitted to our mind surely ought to teach us that we are not intended to fit into each other the different sections of our knowledge, like a child's dissected map – that we should simply admit every fact that rests on sufficient evidence, and leave it to find its own place. We make a double mistake in this respect. We suppose every fact which does not illustrate a principle (if it be of considerable importance) to conflict with it, and we suppose every fact which does conflict with a principle considered exclusively must be untrue. Both these mistakes are exemplified in popular prejudice on the origin of language. A large part of the objection felt to it arises simply from the first – from a notion of the dignity of humanity, and of language as its characteristic, which is certainly not helped out by the mimetic theory of the origin of language. But then so long as we keep to the subject itself, neither is this preconceived idea at all hindered by it. With inferences, and perfectly sound inferences from the theory, we admit that the case is different; but the value and importance of language itself is not affected by our view of the manner in which it was developed. We may open Liddell and Scott's Greek Dictionary with just the same delight as at a masterly exhibition of a perfect instrument, and yet believe that it has been entirely developed from a few awkward attempts at rendering natural sound. Our admiration for the palace or the temple of a civilized nation is not touched by the belief that it is the expansion of an attempt to imitate the cave, or the tent, or the forest nook, in which man may at first have found shelter, and which have been regarded as each the type of an elaborate and highly organized style of architecture. Neither language nor anything else loses its dignity with its mystery.

We return to the work which we have treated as the best exponent of the mimetic theory, and again in a spirit of dissent. This time, however, it is not an excess of concession with which we would tax Mr. Farrar, but the opposite defect. He dwells upon the fact that the larger part of the world is sunk in barbarism now, as a difficulty quite as great as that of barbarism being the original state of mankind; and on the inference that our incapacity to reject the one is an argument against our finding any obstacle in the other. Any one may, no doubt, hear and see in one week of his life more events which conflict with the idea of the dignity of man and the moral government under which he is placed, than he will find in any theory on the Origin of Language. Still, it is a difficulty of quite another dimension to believe in any degraded state of humanity existing upon the earth now, and to believe in it as the original state of mankind. It is not the mere fact of barbarism that is perplexing. It is the fact, apart from any shadow of human error; it is the assumption of this condition as the starting-point of humanity that is difficult to reconcile with our belief on other subjects. We must believe in degradation, and we can to some degree reconcile ourselves to the belief by connecting this disorder with preceding sin. But the mimetic theory demands a step beyond this: it forces us to accept a condition which we can only describe as degraded as the starting-point of the human race; and there is no question that this difficulty is one of a different order from the former.

If the conception of humanity, however, slowly emerging from a state scarcely distinguished from that of the brutes, conflicts with our belief on other subjects, does it not harmonize with every particle of evidence that can be brought to bear on the subject from other quarters? All evidence on the earlier state of mankind leads us to the conclusion that it was a low one. Whatever leads in the other direction is the legend which embodies the popular feeling we are endeavouring to justify. What a significance is there in the Lake-dwellings, the *débris* of which yields us so much of our evidence as to pre-historic man! What a tale of insecurity, of mutual distrust and terror, is told in the remnants of those uncomfortable water homes! They lead us far away from the Golden Age. We smile at the extravagance of the earlier theologians of the Church of England in their pictures of the primitive state of man – at that state which, as Glanvill says, 'as far exceeded the hyperboles with which fond fancy decorates the objects of her affection as these transcend their dim originals' – at that strange glow which, reflected from classic feeling on the simple narrative in Genesis, turned Adam to a paragon of wisdom, and created a vision of excellence which exceeded anything that we could make the goal of humanity; but we cling to the illusion all the same. In a softened form the Golden Age is still precious to us, and we listen for long in vain to the arguments for any theory which bids us renounce it. Yet they coincide with every other argument drawn from the early history of mankind. Nor is the result to which they point without analogy, surely, in the history of an individual life.

The true theory of language, like that of every other science, would have before it a comparatively short and easy task in the persuasion of mankind, if the state of mind to which it addressed itself were that of conscious ignorance. But the truth is, that conscious ignorance is not the learner's starting point, but a station first attained at an advanced stage of the journey. The state of mind, with regard to the subject-matter of such a science as philology, is not a mere blank. With the mind, as with the soil, a large part of the labour of cultivation consists in what is merely negative, in the weeding out the self-sown seeds of prejudice, and breaking up the hard soil of custom and association. The mind does not lie fallow any more than the earth: with both of these we must eradicate many weeds before we sow one seed, and the lightest thistle-down does not spread more rapidly, or retain its hold with more stubbornness, than the prejudices, and, what Bacon would call, 'prejudicate opinions' (for there is a shade of distinction between the two), which possess the mind of an ordinary man on the subject of anything so familiar as the words he uses at every hour of the day. These prejudicate opinions, various as they are, may all be traced to one seed. With whatever variety, according to the nature of the mind in which they have taken root, they are all due to some form of, or inference from, the notion, that words are something more than the signs of things, – signs which in nature have absolutely no connexion with their object. This is a fallacy of so wide a prevalence, and of an influence so hostile to many different kinds of truth, that we look upon the adoption of the mimetic view of language as a valuable gain to a very much wider region of truth than that which is directly illustrated by it. To us it seems that some among the finest minds of our day waste a large part of their energy through an obstinate adhesion to the belief – from which the varied languages of the modern world seem expressly intended to deliver us – that nomenclature is a part of truth. At all events, those who know anything of controversy will admit that it would be wonderfully shortened and sweetened, if each combatant would renounce the names which they knew their adversary to use in a different sense from themselves. Certainly it would be some step towards this end, if these words were accepted as metaphors, good or bad, derived at first-hand from some imitative sound, whereby the original subject of the metaphor was pointed out. When their slender connexion with the thing was clearly seen, how entirely its whole practical import would be seen to rest on convention. We despise the meagre conventional theory of the eighteenth century, and indeed its absurdity was refuted by Lucretius as completely as is possible to the most advanced linguist of our day. Nevertheless, though the theory is below contempt with reference to the origin of language as a historical event, it seems to us practically to contain a much true view of the *nature* of language than the Platonic extreme. M. Renan's saying that the connexion of the word and the thing is 'never absolute, never arbitrary, always *motivé*,' has been cited with approval among others by Mr. Farrar, and of course it expresses an important truth in pointing out that men must at first have chosen names which actually did suggest their objects, and that with this *will* had nothing to do. We fell, however, with regard to this phrase, much as an able writer in the *Fortnightly Review*[8] does with regard to Humboldt's discovery, that language is an 'organism,' a phrase which seems specially devised, as he truly remarks, to keep language apart from other human arts and contrivances. 'If,' he continues, 'the practical shifts, by which words are shaped or applied to fit new meanings, are not devised by an operation of the understanding, we ought consistently to carry the strategem of the soldier on the field, or the contrivances of the workman at his bench, back into the dark regions of instinct and involuntary action.' How is it with words of which we have actually witnessed the origin? The word *telegram*, for instance, is certainly younger than the youngest of those who use it; it is the latest specimen we can select of that increment to language which is the legacy of each generation to its successor, as it came into use with all the painful association of the Indian Mutiny of 1857. We all remember, amid the agitation and anguish of that time, how cool and deliberate was the discussion as to the name which should be applied to the message that so deeply stirred our hearts. *Arbitrary* is not the word to give our selection, perhaps, for the word was

[8] Mr. E. B. Tylor. April 15th, p. 559.

formed according to analogy, but we made it in just the same spirit that a mother names her infant after his father. We gave a particular name for a particular reason, there was nothing unconscious or instinctive in the proceeding.

The truth is that the analogy of the Cratylus, inconsistently as this is carried out, where language is throughout compared to an instrument, is a very much better one than the analogy more familiar to modern ears, where language is compared to a plant. The very name of the roots which is now of course a part of philology, seems to us in some respects unfortunate. It is not a bad metaphor, but people are apt to forget that it is only a metaphor, and then it becomes false. The opposition to the mimetic theory, for instance, which rests upon the demand that every word shall be traced back to a root before any attempt to discover in it some attempt at imitation, seems to us merely to arise from the fact, that those who make use of it are enslaved by a metaphor. Take, for instance, the reviewer's criticism on Mr. Farrar's analysis of those words which have arisen from the imitation of the infantine sound, ba.

'Mr. Farrar reasonably enough assumes,' says the writer, 'what may be called children's language, such as papa, baby, &c., as having contributed something to the materials of language, yet here too he appears to fall into a pitfall which lay temptingly open before him. He compares, *e.g.*, babbo father, basium kiss; βαβαζω stammer, badare gape, and so on, to show the wonderful fertility of a root ba. Yet 'tis evidently unfair to pick out a mass of words with totally different meaning, and for no other reason than that they being with ba, to refer them to a common root. That there is some reason why certain sounds, such as pa, ma, ba, & c., appear in so many languages as representatives of notions familiar to children is evident enough; but when, for instance, baba appears within the same family of languages in Frisian as father, in Russian as grandmother, while baby is English (and there are hundreds of such cases), it is a misuse of terms to call that a root which conveys no common meaning with its sound, and probably only owes its frequent appearance to the scarcity of articulate sounds suitable for children's use, which would lead to the same being adopted again and again.'

It is then evidently unfair (to turn to the typical example of the reviewer's master) to pick out a couple of words with such a totally different meaning as speculation and spice, and for no other reason than that they both begin with a syllable spic or spec, to trace them to a common root. Is it in this case a misuse of terms to call that a root which conveys no common meaning with its sound? If so, the sacred canon of Bopp, and Pott, and Müller must undergo some modification. If basium kiss, babbo father, badare gape, all originated in the attempt to imitate the sound made in simply opening the lips and emitting the breath, that sound seems to us as more obviously the root of those words than any of Professor Müller's derivatives from a root spac. Those derivations afford as good an example as could be desired, that the offshoots of a common root have very often received no common meaning with their common sound. Such objections seem to arise from overlooking the fact that all that we mean in calling one word the root of another, is that it is some modification of a particular sound to express an object in which a resemblance can be traced to another object suggested by the original sound. But the fact is, that the reviewer is arguing upon an assumption which, if he did but express, he would see was begging the question. It really is a part of his definition of a root, that it shall be significant, the mimetic theory of the Origin of Language is a false one. If the very first words used to point out an object had a meaning of their own previous to that use, then that meaning could not have been derived from imitation. But that is the point to be proved, and not assumed.

Here, no doubt, as in dealing with interjection, Mr. Farrar has weakened his position by supposing these infant cries to originate language otherwise than through imitation. It is not the child saying, mum-mum-mum, that originates the word mamma. It is the mother, adopting these syllables as the imitation of the sounds most easily uttered by her infant, who leads him to associate them with herself. We have dwelt with sufficient length on this flaw in Professor Farrar's interesting and learned work. Could we persuade him to amend it, could we further induce him, by the omission of a certain small portion of the work, to withdraw all countenance to the erroneous theory that any view of the Origin of Language connects itself with any view of metaphysics, we should find little wanting in the work as a popular exhibition of what we hold to be one of the scientific theories of the greatest importance under discussion at the present day. We have spoken chiefly of the defects of this work in the foregoing paper, because our aim has been less to criticise the volume itself than to give a general view of the object which the writer sets before himself in that work, and to suggest to him those alterations by which it might be most successfully carried out. The blemishes in his production are, therefore, dwelt upon in this article at a length quite disproportionate to their real importance – we have, in fact, endeavoured to write a supplement to Mr. Farrar's 'Essay on Language,' and not a criticism upon it.

We have spoken of one or two scientific fancies which appear to us illustrations of the metaphysical stage of thought. The hypothesis, however, which presents us with a conception most completely analogous to the phonetic types is the 'plastic powers' of the older geologists, – that influence of the stars on the materials of mountains, by which the rock was fashioned into the likeness of shells and other organic remains. In both these theories we have a blending of physical and metaphysical ideas such as can only be received into the imagination by being thrown back into the past. 'Where,' asks Leonardo da Vinci, one of the first opponents of these mystical agents, 'are the stars *now* forming in the hills shells of distinct ages and species?' 'Where,' we may repeat, 'are men now discovering vocal expressions corresponding to visual impressions?' The answer from our opponents would be also the answer from Leonardo's, these 'phonetic types' – these 'plastic powers' – must have existed 'because their effects continue to exist.' The last notion only seems more irrational to us than the first, partly because we have not yet got beyond it, and partly because the association of sound with metaphysical ideas is so much closer than is possible in the case of sight. The notion of stars doing the part of artists is only more *obviously* magical than that of sense throwing, as it were, a shadow on sound; in reality the two conceptions imply an equally wide departure from the course of law. And in both cases they disguise from us a precisely analogous truth – or rather the same truth, that the past is uniform with the present, that like causes then produced like effects, and that those results which our imagination summons unknown agents to achieve were due to the mere continuance of those now working under our eyes. Though we must go so far back into the past for an example of the complete metaphysical fallacy in geology, the triumph of the opposite truth is an event of our own day. Precisely analogous to the contempt with which people now receive the hypothesis of the Mimetic School is that which was poured upon the doctrines of Scrope and Lyell when they first began to explain the present condition of the earth's surface on principles now acting under our eyes. Nobody attempted to deny *some* scope to these agencies; an insignificant margin of the whole gigantic work might, it was conceded, be due to their operation; but the assertion that all that was needed to spread this supposed margin over the whole was a simple extension of the time demanded for its production, was received with a smile. The controversy is now exactly repeated on the ground of philology. 'Here and there, it is said, you will no doubt find an imitative word that has crept into true language – a "sound-word," as Mr. Tylor calls it – doing duty for a "sense-word;" but the proportion of this mere fringe of true language to the wide garment that forms the mantle of thought, is too trifling to be taken into account.' It is the illusion of an impatient child who watches for a couple of minutes the progress of some vast building while a single stone, perhaps, is fitted into its place, and would scorn the supposition that these walls and towers were raised by workmen no more powerful or agile than those whose additions to the structure his short interval of watching – not short to him – would fail to detect. Such is the attitude of the half-cultivated mind towards all sciences that deals with the past. The child's interval of curiosity measures a larger fragment of the progress of a building than the observation of a life-time can follow of such changes as those which have fashioned the earth we inhabit, or the mighty instrument we make use of in the communication of thought. Our observation follows too small a portion of the vast curve to detect its deviation from a straight line, and when its goal is pointed out to us we refuse to believe that this can be attained otherwise than by a violent change of direction. But the progress of all physical knowledge converges to the certainty that there is nothing in the past history of this universe that corresponds to such a change of direction. The path which men's fancies have marked out for science would be represented by a zig-zag line, a succession of changes, no one of which suggested that which should follow, or recalled that which should precede. The curve by which we have symbolized that path which all evidence indicates as marked out for it by God is one for which our feeble analysis as yet supplies no formula. We cannot, except to a very trifling extent, generalize from the progress of natural knowledge in our own day, and determine its course in the future; but this much we know, that it forms an unbroken unity. Scientific men would attach little value to the speculations which occupied the earliest European thinkers, their endeavours to find some one principle which should form, as it were, the *mot d'énigme* of the universe seems to our contemporaries puerile; but here, perhaps, as in so many other directions, the truth is less unlike the first instinctive feeling of childhood than the negative criticism of youth, and mature thought, enriched by the knowledge of the ages, may yet return to that simpler view from which it started, and learn, in some sense that is still impossible to us, to recognise the force of the universe as *One*.

MENTAL POWERS
Charles Darwin

Language.—This faculty has justly been considered as one of the chief distinctions between man and the lower animals. But man, as a highly competent judge, Archbishop Whately remarks, 'is not the only animal that can make use of language to express what is passing in his mind, and can understand, more or less, what is so expressed by another.'[1] In Paraguay the *Cebus azaræ* when excited utters at least six distinct sounds, which excite in other monkeys similar emotions.[2] The movements of the features and gestures of monkeys are understood by us, and they partly understand ours, as Rengger and others declare. It is a more remarkable fact that the dog, since being domesticated, has learnt to bark[3] in at least four or five distinct tones. Although barking is a new art, no doubt the wild species, the parents of the dog, expressed their feelings by cries of various kinds. With the domesticated dog we have the bark of eagerness, as in the chase; that of anger; the yelping or howling bark of despair, as when shut up; that of joy, as when starting on a walk with his master; and the very distinct one of demand or supplication, as when wishing for a door or window to be opened.

Articulate language is, however, peculiar to man; but he uses in common with the lower animals inarticulate cries to express his meaning, aided by gestures and the movements of the muscles of the face.[4] This especially holds good with the more simple and vivid feelings, which are but little connected with our higher intelligence. Our cries of pain, fear, surprise, anger, together with their appropriate actions, and the murmur of a

---

[1] Quoted in 'Anthropological Review,' 1864, p. 158.
[2] Rengger, ibid. s 45.
[3] See my 'Variation of Animals and Plants under Domestication,' vol. i. p. 27.
[4] See a discussion on this subject in Mr. E. B. Tylor's very interesting work. 'Researches into the Early History of Mankind,' 1865, chaps. ii to iv.

mother to her beloved child, are more expressive than any words. It is not the mere power of articulation that distinguishes man from other animals, for as every one knows, parrots can talk; but it is his large power of connecting definite sounds with definite ideas; and this obviously depends on the development of the mental faculties.

As Horne Tooke, one of the founders of the noble science of philology, observes, language is an art, like brewing or baking; but writing would have been a much more appropriate simile. It certainly is not a true instinct, as every language has to be learnt. It differs, however, widely from all ordinary arts, for man has an instinctive tendency to speak, as we see in the babble of our young children; whilst no child has an instinctive tendency to brew, bake, or write. Moreover, no philologist now supposes that any language has been deliberately invented; each has been slowly and unconsciously developed by many steps. The sounds uttered by birds offer in several respects the nearest analogy to language, for all the members of the same species utter the same instinctive cries expressive of their emotions; and all the kinds that have the power of singing exert this power instinctively; but the actual song, and even the call-notes, are learnt from their parents or foster-parents. These sounds, as Daines Barrington[5] has proved, 'are no more innate than language is in man.' The first attempts to sing 'may be compared to the imperfect endeavour in a child to babble.' The young males continue practising, or, as the bird-catchers say, recording, for ten or eleven months. Their first essays show hardly a rudiment of the future song; but as they grow older we can perceive what they are aiming at; and at last they are said 'to sing their song round.' Nestlings which have learnt the song of a distinct species, as with the canary-birds educated in the Tyrol, teach and transmit their new song to their offspring. The slight natural differences of song in the same species inhabiting different districts may be appositely compared, as Barrington remarks, 'to provincial dialects;' and the songs of allied, though distinct species may be compared with the languages of distinct races of man. I have given the foregoing

---

[5] Hon. Daines Barrington in 'Philosoph. Transactions,' 1773, p. 262. See also Dureau de la Malle, in 'Ann. des Sc. Nat.' 3rd series, Zoolog. tom. x. p. 119.

details to shew that an instinctive tendency to acquire an art is not a peculiarity confined to man.

With respect to the origin of articulate language, after having read on the one side the highly interesting works of Mr. Hensleigh Wedgwood, the Rev. F. Farrar, and Prof. Schleicher,[6] and the celebrated lectures of Prof. Max Müller on the other side, I cannot doubt that language owes its origin to the imitation and modification, aided by signs and gestures, of various natural sounds, the voices of other animals, and man's own instinctive cries. When we treat of sexual selection we shall see that primeval man, or rather some early progenitor of man, probably used his voice largely, as does one of the gibbon-apes at the present day, in producing true musical cadences, that is in singing; we may conclude from a widely-spread analogy that this power would have been especially exerted during the courtship of the sexes, serving to express various emotions, as love, jealousy, triumph, and serving as a challenge to their rivals. The imitation by articulate sounds of musical cries might have given rise to words expressive of various complex emotions. As bearing on the subject of imitation, the strong tendency in our nearest allies, the monkeys, in microcephalous idiots,[7] and in the barbarous races of mankind, to imitate whatever they hear deserves notice. As monkeys certainly understand much that is said to them by man, and as in a state of nature they utter signal-cries of danger to their fellows,[8] it does not appear altogether incredible, that some unusually wise ape-like animal should have thought of imitating the growl of a beast of prey, so as to indicate to his fellow monkeys the nature of the expected danger. And this would have been a first step in the formation of a language.

As the voice was used more and more, the vocal organs would have been strengthened and perfected through the prin-

---

[6] 'On the Origin of Language,' by H. Wedgwood, 1866. 'Chapters on Language,' by the Rev. F. W. Farrar, 1865. These works are most interesting. See also 'De la Phys. et de Parole,' par Albert Lemoine, 1865, p. 190. The work on this subject, by the late Prof. Aug. Schleicher, has been translated by Dr. Bikkers into English, under the title of 'Darwinism tested by the Science of Language,' 1869.

[7] Vogt, 'Mémoire sur les Microcéphales,' 1867, p. 169. With respect to savages, I have given some facts in my 'Journal of Researches,' &c., 1845, p. 206.

[8] See clear evidence on this head in the two works so often quoted, by Brehm and Rengger.

ciple of the inherited effects of use; and this would have reacted on the power of speech. But the relation between the continued use of language and the development of the brain has no doubt been far more important. The mental powers in some early progenitor of man must have been more highly developed than in any existing ape, before even the most imperfect form of speech could have come into use; but we may confidently believe that the continued use and advancement of this power would have reacted on the mind by enabling and encouraging it to carry on long trains of thought. A long and complex train of thought can no more be carried on without the aid of words, whether spoken or silent, than a long calculation without the use of figures or algebra. It appears, also, that even ordinary trains of thought almost require some form of language, for the dumb, deaf, and blind girl, Laura Bridgman, was observed to use her fingers whilst dreaming.[9] Nevertheless a long succession of vivid and connected ideas, may pass through the mind without the aid of any form of language, as we may infer from the prolonged dreams of dogs. We have, also, seen that retriever-dogs are able to reason to a certain extent; and this they manifestly do without the aid of language. The intimate connection between the brain, as it is now developed in us, and the faculty of speech, is well shewn by those curious cases of brain-disease, in which speech is specially affected, as when the power to remember substantives is lost, whilst other words can be correctly used.[10] There is no more improbability in the effects of the continued use of the vocal and mental organs being inherited, than in the case of handwriting, which depends partly on the structure of the hand and partly on the disposition of the mind; and hand-writing is certainly inherited.[11]

Why the organs now used for speech should have been originally perfected for this purpose, rather than any other organs, it is not difficult to see. Ants have considerable powers of intercommunication by means of their antennæ, as shewn by Huber, who devotes a whole chapter to their language. We might have used our fingers as efficient instruments, for a person with practice can report to a deaf man every word of

[9] See remarks on this head by Dr. Maudsley, 'The Physiology and Pathology of Mind,' 2nd edit. 1868, p. 199.
[10] Many curious cases have been recorded. See, for instance, 'Inquiries Concerning the Intellectual Powers,' by Dr. Abercrombie, 1838, p. 150.
[11] 'The Variation of Animals and Plants Under Domestication,' vol. ii. p. 6.

a speech rapidly delivered at a public meeting; but the loss of our hands, whilst thus employed, would have been a serious inconvenience. As all the higher mammals possess vocal organs constructed on the same general plan with ours, and which are used as a means of communication, it was obviously probable, if the power of communication had to be improved, that these same organs would have been still further developed; and this has been effected by the aid of adjoining and well-adapted parts, namely the tongue and lips.[12] The fact of the higher apes not using their vocal organs for speech, no doubt depends on their intelligence not having been sufficiently advanced. The possession by them of organs, which with long-continued practice might have been used for speech, although not thus used, is paralleled by the case of many birds which possess organs fitted for singing, though they never sing. Thus, the nightingale and crow have vocal organs similarly constructed, these being used by the former for diversified song, and by the latter merely for croaking.[13]

The formation of different languages and of distinct species, and the proofs that both have been developed through a gradual process, are curiously the same.[14] But we can trace the origin of many words further back than in the case of species, for we can perceive how they have actually arisen from the imitation of various sounds. We find in distinct languages striking homologies due to community of descent, and analogies due to a similar process of formation. The manner in which certain letters of sounds change when others change is very like correlated growth. We have in both cases the reduplication of parts, the effects of long-continued use, and so forth. The frequent presence of rudiments, both in languages and in species, is still more remarkable. The letter *m* in the word *am*, means *I*; so that in the expression *I am* a superfluous and

---

[12] See some good remarks to this effect by Dr. Maudsley, 'The Physiology and Pathology of Mind,' 1868, p. 199.

[13] Macgillivray, 'Hist. of British Birds,' vol. ii. 1839, p. 29. An excellent observer, Mr. Blackwall, remarks that the magpie learns to pronounce single words, and even short sentences, more readily than almost any other British bird; yet, as he adds, after long and closely investigating its habits, he has never known it, in a state of nature, display any unusual capacity for imitation. 'Researches in Zoology,' 1834, p. 158.

[14] See the very interesting parallelism between the development of species and languages, given by Sir C. Lyell in 'The Geolog. Evidences of the Antiquity of Man,' 1863, chap. xxiii.

useless rudiment has been retained. In the spelling also of words, letters often remain as the rudiments of ancient forms of pronunciation. Languages, like organic beings, can be classed in groups under groups; and they can be classed either naturally according to descent, or artificially by other characters. Dominant languages and dialects spread widely and lead to the gradual extinction of other tongues. A language, like a species, when once extinct, never, as Sir C. Lyell remarks, reappears. The same language never has two birth-places. Distinct languages may be crossed or blended together.[15] We see variability in every tongue, and new words are continually cropping up; but as there is a limit to the powers of the memory, single words, like whole languages, gradually become extinct. As Max Müller[16] has well remarked:—A struggle for life is constantly going on amongst the words and grammatical forms in each language. The better, the shorter, the easier forms are constantly gaining the upper hand, and they owe their success to their own inherent virtue.' To these more important causes of the survival of certain words, mere novelty may, I think, be added; for there is in the mind of man a strong love for slight changes in all things. The survival or preservation of certain favoured words in the struggle for existence is natural selection.

The perfectly regular and wonderfully complex construction of the languages of many barbarous nations has often been advanced as a proof, either of the divine origin of these languages, or of the high art and former civilisation of their founders. Thus F. von Schlegel writes: 'In those languages which appear to be at the lowest grade of intellectual culture, we frequently observe a very high and elaborate degree of art in their grammatical structure. This is especially the case with the Basque and the Lapponian, and many of the American languages.'[17] But it is assuredly an error to speak of any language as an art in the sense of its having been elaborately and methodically formed. Philologists now admit that conjugations, declensions, &c., originally existed as distinct words, since joined together; and as such words express the most

---

[15] See remarks to this effect by the Rev. F. W. Farraar, in an interesting article, entitled 'Philology and Darwinism' in 'Nature', March 24th, 1870, p. 528.
[16] 'Nature,' Jan. 6th, 1870, p. 257.
[17] Quoted by C. S. Wake, 'Chapters on Man,' 1868, p. 101.

obvious relations between objects and persons, it is not surprising that they should have been used by the men of most races during the earliest ages. With respect to perfection, the following illustration will best shew how easily we may err: a Crinoid sometimes consists of no less than 150,000 pieces of shell,[18] all arranged with perfect symmetry in radiating lines; but a naturalist does not consider an animal of this kind as more perfect than a bilateral one with comparatively few parts, and with none of these alike, excepting on the opposite sides of the body. He justly considers the differentiation and specialisation of organs as the test of perfection. So with languages, the most symmetrical and complex ought not to be ranked above irregular, abbreviated, and bastardised languages, which have borrowed expressive words and useful forms of construction from various conquering, or conquered, or immigrant races.

From these few and imperfect remarks I conclude that the extremely complex and regular construction of many barbarous languages, is no proof that they owe their origin to a special act of creation.[19] Nor, as we have seen, does the faculty of articulate speech in itself offer any insuperable objection to the belief that man has been developed from some lower form.

---

[18] Buckland, 'Bridgewater Treatise,' p. 411.
[19] See some good remarks on the simplification of languages, by Sir J. Lubbock, 'Origin of Civilisation,' 1870, p. 278.

LECTURES ON MR. DARWIN'S PHILOSOPHY OF LANGUAGE
Friedrich Max Müller

Source: *Fraser's Magazine*, vols 7 and 8ns, May, June and July 1873

FIRST LECTURE

Delivered at the Royal Institution, March 22, 1873

Philosophy is not, as is sometimes supposed, a mere intellectual luxury; it is, under varying disguises, the daily bread of the whole world. Though the workers and speakers must always be few, those for whom they work and speak are many; and though the waves run highest in the centres of literary life, the widening circles of philosophic thought reach in the end to the most distant shores. What is thought-out and written down in the study, is soon taught in schools, preached from the pulpits, and discussed at the corners of the streets. There are at the present moment materialists and spiritualists, realists and idealists, positivists and mystics, evolutionists and specialists to be met with in the workshops as well as in the lecture-rooms, and it may safely be asserted that the intellectual vigour and moral health of a nation depend no more on the established religion than on the dominant philosophy of the realm.

No one who at the present moment watches the state of the intellectual atmosphere of Europe, can fail to see that we are on the eve of a storm which will shake the oldest convictions of the world, and upset everything that is not firmly rooted. Whether we look to England, France, or Germany, everywhere we see, in the recent manifestoes of their philosophers, the same thoughts struggling for recognition – thoughts not exactly new, but presented in a new and startling form. There is everywhere the same desire to explain the universe, such as we know it, without the admission of any plan, any object, any superintendence; a desire to remove all specific barriers, not only those which separate man from the animal, and the animal from the plant, but those also which separate organic from inorganic bodies; lastly, a desire to explain life as a mode of chemical action, and thought as a movement of nervous molecules.

It is difficult to find a general name for these philosophic tendencies, particularly as their principal representatives differ widely from each other. It would be unfair to class the coarse materialism of Büchner with the thoughtful realism of Spencer. Nor does it seem right to use the name of Darwinism in that vague and undefined sense in which it has been used so frequently of late, comprehending under that title not only the carefully worded conclusions of that great observer and thinker, but likewise the bold generalisations of his numerous disciples. I shall mention only one, but a most important point, on which so-called Darwinism has evidently gone far beyond Mr. Darwin. It is well known that, according to Mr. Darwin, all animals and plants have descended from about eight or ten progenitors. He is satisfied with this, and declines to follow the deceitful guidance of analogy, which would lead us to the admission of but one prototype. And he adds, that even if he were to infer from analogy that all the organic beings which have ever lived on this earth had descended from some one primordial form, he would hold that life was first breathed into that primordial form by the Creator. Very different from this is the conclusion proclaimed by professor Haeekel, the most distinguished and most strenuous advocate of Mr. Darwin's opinions in Germany. He maintains that in the present state of physiological knowledge, the idea of a Creator, a Maker, a Life-giver, has become unscientific; that the admission of one primordial form is sufficient; and that that first primordial form was a Moneres, produced by self-generation.

I know, indeed, of no name sufficiently comprehensive for this broad stream of philosophic thought, but the name of *'Evolutionary Materialism'* is perhaps the best that can be framed. I am afraid that it will be objected to by those who imagine that materialism is a term of reproach. It is so in a moral sense, but no real student of the history of philosophy would use the word for such a purpose. In the historical evolution of philosophy, materialism has as much right as spiritualism, and it has taught us many lessons for which we ought to be most grateful. To say that materialism degrades mind to the level of matter is a false accusation, because what the materialist means by matter is totally different from what the spiritualist means by it, and from what it means in common parlance. The matter of the materialist contains, at least potentially, the highest attributes that can be assigned to any object of knowledge; the matter of the spiritualist is simply an illusion; while, in common parlance, matter is hardly more than stuff and rubbish. Let each system of philosophy be judged out of its own mouth, and let us not wrangle about words more than we can help. Philosophical progress, like political progress, prospers best under party government, and the history of philosophy would lose half its charm and half it usefulness, if the struggle between the two great parties in the realm of thought, the spiritualist, and the materialist, the idealist, and the realist, were ever to cease. As thunderstorms are wanted in nature to clear the air and give us breath, the human mind, too, stands in need of its tempests, and never does it display greater vigour and freshness than after it has passed through one of the decisive battles in the world of thought.

But though allowing to the materialist philosophers all the honour that is due to a great and powerful party, the spiritualist may hate and detest materialism with the same hatred with which the conservative hates radicalism, or at all events with such a modicum of hatred as a philosopher is capable of; and he has a perfect right to oppose, by all the means at his disposal, the exclusive sway of materialistic opinions. Though from a purely philosophical point of view, we may admit that spiritualism is as one-sided as materialism, that they are both but two faces of the same head, that each can see but one half of the world, yet no one who has worked his way honestly through the problems of materialism and spiritualism would deny that the conclusions of Hume are more disheartening than those of Berkeley, and that the strongest natures only can live under the pressure of such opinions as those which were held by Lametrie or Schopenhauer. To some people, I know, such considerations will seem beside the point. They hold that scientific research, whatever its discoveries may be, is never to be allowed to touch the deeper convictions of our soul. They seem to hold that the world may have been created twice, once according to Moses, and once according to Darwin. I confess I cannot adopt this artificial distinction, and I feel tempted to ask those cold-blooded philosophers the same question which the German peasant asked his bishop, who, as a prince, was amusing himself on week-days, and, as a bishop, praying on Sundays. 'Your Highness, what will become of the bishop, if the Devil comes and takes the prince?' Scientific research is not intended for intellectual exercise and amusement only, and our scientific convictions will not submit to being kept in quarantine. If we once embark on board the *Challenger*, we cannot rest with one foot on dry land. Wherever it leads us, we must follow; wherever it lands us, there we must try to live. Now, it does make a difference whether we live in the atmosphere of Africa or of Europe, and it makes the same difference whether we live in the atmosphere of spiritualism or materialism. The view of the world and of our place in it, as indicated by Mr. Darwin, and more sharply defined by some of his followers, does not touch scientific interests only; it cuts to the very heart, and must become to every man to whom truth, whether you call it scientific or religious, is sacred, a question of life and death, in the deepest and fullest sense of the word.

In the short course of three Lectures which I have undertaken to give this year in this Institution, I do not intend to grapple with the whole problem of Evolutionary Materialism. My object is simply to point out a strange omission, and to call attention to one kind of evidence – I mean the evidence of language – which has been most unaccountably neglected, both in studying the development of the human intellect, and in determining the position which man holds in the system of the world. Is it not extraordinary, for instance, that in the latest work on Psychology, language should hardly ever be mentioned, language without which no thought can exist, or, at all events, without which no thought has ever been realised or expressed? It does not matter what view of language we take; under all circumstances its intimate connection with thought cannot be doubted. Call language a mass of imitative cries, or a heap of conventional signs; let it be the tool or the work of thought; let it be the mere garment or the very embodiment of mind – whatever it is, surely it has something to do with the historical or palæontological, and with the individual or embryological evolution of the human self. It may be very interesting to the psychologist to know the marvellous machinery of the senses, beginning with the first formation of nervous channels, tracing the process in which the reflex action of the molecules of the afferent nerves produces a reaction in the molecules of the efferent nerves, following up the establishment of nervous centres and nervous plexuses, and laying bare the whole network of the telegraphic wires through which messages are flashed from station to station. yet, much of that network and its functions admits, and can admit, of an hypothetical interpretation only; while we have before us another network – I mean language – in its endless variety, where every movement of the mind, from the first tremor to the last calm utterance of our philosophy, may be studied as in a faithful photograph. And while we know the nervous system only such as it is, or, if we adopt the system of evolution, such as it has gradually been brought from the lowest to the highest state of organisation, but are never able to watch the actual historical or palæontological process of its formation, we know language, not only as it is, but can watch it in its constant genesis, and in its historical progress from simplicity to complexity, and again from complexity to simplicity. For let us not forget that language has two aspects. We, the historical races of mankind, use it, we speak and think it, but we do not make it. Though the faculty of language may be congenital, all languages are traditional. The words in which we think are channels of thought which we have not dug ourselves, but which we found ready-made for us. The work of making language belongs to a period in the history of mankind beyond the reach of tradition, and of which we, in our advanced state of mental development, can hardly form a conception. Yet that period must have had an historical reality as much as the period during which small annual deposits formed the strata of the globe on which we live. As during enormous periods of time the Earth was absorbed in producing the abundant carboniferous vegetation which still supplies us with the means of warmth, light, and life, there must have been a period during which the human mind had no other work but that of linguistic vegetation, the produce of which still supplies the stores of our grammars and dictionaries. After the great bulk of language was finished, a new work began, that of arranging and defining it, and of now and then coining a new word for a new thought. And all this we can still see with our own eyes, as it were, in the quarries opened by the Science of Language. No microscope will ever enable us to watch the formation of a new nervous ganglion, while the Science of Language shows us the formation of new mental ganglia in the formation of every new word. Besides, let us not forget that the whole network of the nerves is outside the mind. A state of nervous action may be parallel, but it never is identical with a state of consciousness (*Principles of Psychology*, II. 592), and even the parallelism between nervous states and states of consciousness is, when we come to details, beyond all comprehension (*Ib*. I. 140). Language, on the contrary, is not outside the mind, but is *the* outside of the mind. Language without thought is as impossible as thought without language; and although we may by abstraction distinguish between what the Greeks called inward and outward Logos, yet in reality and full actuality language is one and indivisible – language is very thought. On this more hereafter.

Just at the end of his interesting work on the *Principles of Psychology*, Mr. Herbert Spencer shows, by one remark, that he is well aware of the importance of language for a proper study of psychology.[1] 'Whether it be or be not a true saying,' he writes, 'that mythology is a disease of language, it may be said with truth that metaphysics, in all its anti-realistic developments, is a disease of language.' No doubt it is; but think of the consequences that flow from this view of language for a proper study of psychology! If a disease of language can produce such hallucinations as mythology and metaphysics, what then is the health of language, and what its bearing on the healthy functions of the mind? Is this no problem for the psychologist? Nervous or cerebral disorders occupy a large portion in every work on psychology; yet they are in their nature obscure, and must always remain so. Why a hardening or softening of the brain should interfere with thought will never be explained, beyond the fact that the wires are somehow damaged, and do not properly receive and convey the nervous currents. But what we call a disease of language is perfectly intelligible; nay, it has been proved to be natural, and almost inevitable. In a lecture delivered in this Institution some time ago, I endeavoured to show that mythology, in the widest sense of the word, is the power exercised by language on thought in every possible sphere of mental activity, including metaphysics as well as religion; and I called the whole history of philosophy,

[1] Spencer, *Principles of Psychology*, Vol. II. p. 502.

from Thales down to Hegel, one uninterrupted battle against mythology, a constant protest of thought against language. Not till we understand the real nature of language shall we understand the real nature of the human Self; and those who want to read the true history of the development of the soul of man, must learn to read it in language, the primeval and never-ending autobiography of our race.

In order to show the real bearing of the Philosophy of Language on the problem which occupies us at present, viz. the position of man in the animal world, it is absolutely necessary to go back to Hume and Kant. Nothing seems to me so much to be regretted in the philosophical discussions of our time as the neglect which is shown for the history of former struggles in which the same interests were at stake, and in which the same problems were discussed, not without leaving, one would have thought, something that is still worth remembering. A study of the history of philosophy cannot, at the present moment, be too strongly recommended, when one sees men of the highest eminence in their special spheres of study, approaching the old problems of mankind as if they had never been discussed before, and advancing opinions such as Sokrates would not have dared to place in the mouths of his antagonists. Even if a study of ancient philosophy, and particularly of Oriental philosophy, should appear too heavy a task, it seems at all events indispensable, that those who take an active part in the controversies on the theory of general evolution and development, as opposed to specific variety and a reign of law, should be familiar with the final results of that great debate which, about one hundred years ago, was carried on on very similar, nay, essentially the same topics, by such giants as Berkeley, Hume, and Kant. In the permanent philosophical parliament of the world there is, and there must be, an order of business. The representatives of the highest interests of mankind cannot be discussing all things at all times. At all events, if an old question is to be opened again, let it be opened in that form in which it was left at the end of the last debate.

In order to appreciate the full import of the questions now agitated by positivist and evolutionist philosophers, in order to understand their antecedents, and to do justice to their claims, we must go back to Hume and Kant. The position which Kant took and maintained against the materialist philosophy of Hume and the idealist philosophy of Berkeley, may be attacked afresh, but it cannot be, and it ought not to be, ignored. Kant's answer was not simply the answer of one German professor, it was a vote carried in a full house, and at the time accepted as decisive by the whole world.

The circumstances under which Kant wrote his *Criticism of Pure Reason* show that his success was due, not only to his own qualifications, great as they were, but to the fact that the tide of materialism was on the turn, that a reaction had set in in the minds of independent thinkers, so that, when he wrote his great and decisive work he was but lending the most powerful expression to the silent convictions of the world's growing majority. Unless we keep this in view, the success of Kant's philosophy would be inexplicable. He was a Professor in a small university of Eastern Prussia. He had never been out of his native province, never but once out of his native town. He began to lecture at Königsberg as a *Privat-Docent* in 1755, just a year before the beginning of the Seven Years' War, when other questions rather, and not the certainty of synthetic judgments *à priori*, would seem to have interested the public mind of Germany. Kant worked on for sixteen years as an unpaid University lecturer; in 1766 he took a Librarianship which yielded him about 10*l*. a year, and it was not till he was forty-six years of age (1770) that he succeeded in obtaining a Professorship of Logic and Metaphysics with a salary of about 60*l*. a year. He lectured indefatigably on a great variety of subjects: – on Mathematics, Physics, Logic, Metaphysics, Natural Law, Morals, Natural Religion, Physical Geography, and Anthropology. He enjoyed a high reputation in his own University, but no more than many other professors in the numerous universities of Germany. His fame had certainly never spread beyond the academic circles of his own country, when in the year 1781, at the age of fifty-seven, he published at Riga his *Critik der reinen Vernunft (The Criticism of Pure Reason)*, a work which in the onward stream of philosophic thought has stood, and will stand for ever, like the rocks of Niagara. There is nothing attractive in that book, nothing startling; far from it. It is badly written, in a heavy style, full of repetitions, all grey in grey, with hardly a single ray of light and sunshine from beginning to end. And yet that book soon became known all over Europe, at a time when literary intelligence travelled much more slowly than at present. Lectures were given in London on Kant's new system, even at Paris the philosopher of Königsberg became an authority, and for the first time in the history of human thought the philosophical phraseology of the age became German.

How is this to be explained? I believe simply by the fact that Kant spoke the word which the world had been waiting for. No philosopher, from Thales down to Hegel, has ever told, has ever taken and held his place in the history of philosophy, whose speculations, however abtruse in appearance, however far removed at first sight from the interests of ordinary mortals, have not answered some deep yearning in the hearts of his fellow-men. What makes a philosopher great, or, at all events, what makes him really powerful, is what soldiers would call his feeling for the main body of the army in its advance from truth to truth; his perfect understanding of the human solicitudes of his age, his sympathy with the historical progress of human thought. At the time of Kant's great triumph, the conclusions of Locke and Hume had remained unanswered for a long time, and seemed almost unanswerable. But for that very reason people longed for an answer. The problems which then disquieted not only philosophers, but all to whom their 'Being and Knowing' were matters of real concern, were not new problems. They were the old problems of the world, the questions of the possibility of absolute certainty in the evidence of the senses, of reason, or of faith, the questions of the beginning and end of our existence, the question whether the Infinite is the shadow of a dream, or the substance of all substances. The same problems had exercised the sages of India, the thinkers of Greece, the students of Rome, the dreamers of Alexandria, the divines and scholars of the Middle Ages, the Realists and Nominalists, and against the schools of Descartes and Leibniz, in their conflict with the schools of Locke and Hume. But these old problems had in Kants time, as in our own, assumed a new form and influence. If, in spite of its ever varying aspects, we may characterise the world-wide struggle by one word, as a struggle for the primacy between matter and mind, we can clearly see that in the middle of the last, as again in the middle of our own century, the materialistic view had gained the upper hand over the spiritualistic. Descartes, Malebranche, Leibniz, and Wolf might influence the opinions of hard-working students and independent thinkers, but their language was hardly understood by the busy world outside the lecture rooms; while the writings of Locke, and still more those of Hume and his French followers, penetrated alike into boudoirs and club-rooms. Never, perhaps, in the whole history of philosophy did the pendulum of philosophic thought swing so violently as in the middle of the eighteenth century, from one extreme to the other, from Berkeley to Hume; never did pure spiritualism and pure materialism find such outspoken and uncompromising advocates as in the Bishop of Cloyne, – who considered it the height of absurdity to imagine any object as existing without, or independent of, that which alone will produce an object, viz. the subject,[2] – and the Librarian of the Advocates' Library at Edinburgh, who looked upon the conception of a subjective mind as a mere illusion, founded on nothing but on that succession of sensations to which we wrongly assign a sentient cause. But it is easy to see, in the literature of the age, that of these two solutions of the riddle of mind and matter, that which looked upon matter as the mere outcome of the mind. The former was regarded by the world as clever, the latter almost as silly.

That all-powerful, though most treacherous ally of philosophy, Common Sense, was stoutly opposed to Berkeley's idealism, and the typical representative of Common Sense, Dr. Samuel Johnson, maintained that he had only to strike his foot with characteristic force against a stone in order to convince the world that he had thoroughly refuted Berkeley and all idealists.[3] Voltaire, a less sincere believer in Common Sense, joked about ten thousand cannon balls and ten thousand dead men, being only ten thousand ideas; while Dean Swift is accused of having committed the sorry joke of keeping Bishop Berkeley, on a rainy day, waiting before his door, giving orders not to open it, because, he said, if his philosophy is true, he can as easily enter with the door shut as with the door open. Though at present philosophers are inclined to do more justice to Berkeley, yet they seldom speak of him without a suppressed smile, totally forgetting that the majority of real thinkers, may, I should almost venture to say, the majority of mankind agree with Berkeley in looking upon the phenomenal or so-called real world as a mere mirage, as mere *Māyā*, or illusion of the thinking Self.

---

[2] *Berkeley's Works*, ed. Fraser, Vol. IV. p. 376.
[3] *Berkeley's Works*, Vol. IV. p. 368.

In the last century the current of public opinion – and we know how powerful, how overwhelming that current can be at times – had been decidedly in favour of materialism, when Kant stood forth to stem and to turn the tide. He came so exactly in the nick of time that one almost doubts whether the tide was turning, or whether he turned the tide. But what secures to Kant his position in the history of philosophy is, that he brought the battle back to that point where alone it could be decided, that he took up the threat in the philosophical woof of mankind at the very point where it threatened to ravel and to break. He wrote the whole of his *Criticism of Pure Reason* with constant reference to Berkeley and Hume; and what I blame in modern philosophers is that, if they wish to go back to the position maintained by Hume, they should attempt to do it without taking into account the work achieved by Kant. To do this is to commit a philosophical anachronism, it is tantamount to removing the questions which now occupy us, from that historical stage on which alone they can be authoritatively decided.

It has sometimes been supposed that the rapid success of Kant's philosophy was due to its being a philosophy of compromise, neither spiritualistic, like Berkeley's, nor materialistic, like Hume's. I look upon Kant's philosophy, not as a compromise, but as a reconciliation of spiritualism and materialism, or rather of idealism and realism. But whatever view we may take of Kant, it is quite clear that, at the time when he wrote, neither Berkeley's nor Hume's followers would have accepted his terms. It is true that Kant differed from Berkeley in admitting that the raw material of our sensations and thoughts is given to us, that we accept it from without, not from within. So far the realistic school might claim him as their own. but when Kant demonstrates that we are not merely passive recipients, that the conception of a purely passive recipient involves in fact an absurdity, that what is given us we accept on our own terms, these terms being the forms of *our* sensuous perception, and the categories of *our* mind, then the realist would see that the ground under his feet was no longer safe, and that his new ally was more dangerous than his old enemy.

Kant's chief object in writing the *Criticism of Pure Reason* was to determine, once for all, the organs and the limits of our knowledge; and therefore, instead of criticising, as was then the fashion, the results of our knowledge, whether in religion, or in history, or in science, he boldly went to the root of the matter, and subjected Reason, pure and simple, to his searching analysis. In doing this, he was certainly far more successful against Locke and Hume than against Berkeley. To call the human mind a *tabula rasa* was pure metaphor, it was mythology and nothing else. *Tabula rasa* means a tablet, smoothed and made ready to receive the impressions of the pencil (γραφεῖον). It makes very little difference whether the mind is called a *tabula rasa*, or a mirror, or wax, or anything else that the French call *impressionable*. Nor does it help us much if, instead of impressions, we speak of sensations, or states of consciousness, or manifestations. The question is, how these states of consciousness come to be, whether 'to know' is an active or a passive verb, whether there is a knowing Self, and what it is like. If we begin with states of consciousness as ultimate facts, no doubt Hume and his followers are unassailable. Nothing can be more ingenious than the explanation of the process by which the primary impressions, by mere twisting and turning, develop at last into an intellect, the passive mirror growing into a conscious Self. The sensuous impressions, as they are succeeded by new impressions, are supposed to become fainter, and to settle down into what we call our memory. General ideas are explained as the inevitable result of repeated sensuous impressions. For instance, if we see a *green* leaf, the *green* sea, and a *green* bird, the leaf, the sea, and the bird leave each but one impression, while the impression of the green colour is repeated three times, and becomes therefore deeper, more permanent, more general. Again, if we see the leaf of an oak tree, of a fig tree, of a rose tree, or of any other plant or shrub, the peculiar outline of each individual leaf is more or less obliterated, and there remains, we are told, the general impression of a leaf. In the same manner, out of innumerable impressions of various trees arises the general impression of tree, out of the impressions of trees, shrubs, and herbs, the general impression of plant, of vegetative species, and at last of substance, animate or inanimate. In this manner it was supposed that the whole furniture of the human mind could be explained as the inevitable result of repeated sensuous impressions; and further, as these sensuous impressions, which make up the whole of what is called Mind, *are received by animals as well as by men*, it followed, as a matter of course, that the difference between the two was a difference of degree only, and that it was a mere question of time and circumstances for a man-like ape to develop into an ape-like man.

We have now reached a point where the intimate connection between Hume's philosophy and that of the Evolutionist school will begin to be perceived.

If Mr. Darwin is right, if man is either the lineal or lateral descendant of some lower animal, then all the discussions between Locke and Berkeley, between Hume and Kant, have become useless and antiquated. We all agree that animals receive their knowledge through the senses only; and if man was developed from a lower animal, the human mind, too, must have been developed from a lower animal mind. There would be an end to all further discussions: Kant, and all who follow him, would simply be out of court.

But have the followers of Mr. Darwin no misgivings that possibly Kant's conclusions may be so strong as to resist even the hypothesis of evolution? Do they consider it quite safe in their victorious advance to leave such a fortress as Kant has erected unnoticed in the rear? If no attempt had ever been made at answering Hume, there would be no harm in speaking again of the mind of man and the mind of animals as a *tabula rasa* on which impressions are made which faint, and spontaneously develop into conceptions and general ideas. They might revive the old watchword of Locke's school – though it is really much older than Locke[4] – 'that there is nothing in the intellect that was not before in the senses,' forgetting how it had been silenced by the triumphant answer of Kant's small army, 'that there is nothing in the senses that was not at the same time in the intellect.' But when one has watched these shouts and counter-shouts, when one has seen the splendid feats of arms in the truly historical battles of the world, then to be simply told that all this is *passé*, that we now possess evidence which Berkeley, Locke, and Kant did not possess, and which renders all their lucubrations unnecessary; that, man being the descendant of some lower animal, the development of the human mind out of the mind of animals, or out of no mind, is a mere question of time, is certainly enough to make one feel a little impatient.

---

[4] Locke, 1632–1704. In a letter from Sir T. Bodley to Sir F. Bacon, February 1607, we read: 'It being a maxim of all men's approving, in intellectu nihil est quod non prius fuit in sensu.'

It is not for one moment maintained that, because Kant had proved that sensations are not the only ingredients of our consciousness, the question of the development of the human mind out of mere sensations is never to be opened again. Far from it. Only, if it is to be opened again, it should be done with a full appreciation of the labours of those who have come before us; otherwise philosophy itself will fall back into a state of prehistoric savagery.

What, then, is that *tabula rasa*, which sounds so learned, and yet is mere verbal jugglery? Let us accept the metaphor, that the mind is like a smooth writing tablet with nothing on it or in it, and what can be clearer even then, than that the impressions made on it must be determined by the nature of such a tablet? Impressions made on wax are different from impressions made on the human Self must likewise be determined by the nature of the recipient. We see, therefore, that the conditions under which each recipient is capable of receiving impressions, constitute at the same time the conditions or terms to which all impressions must submit, whether they be made on a *tabula rasa*, or on the human Self, or on anything else.

And here is the place where Kant broke through the phalanx of the sensualistic school. That without which no impressions on the human mind are possible or conceivable, constitutes, he would say, the *transcendental* side of our knowledge. What, according to Kant, is *transcendental* is generally identified with what other philosophers call *à priori* or subjective. But this is true in a very limited sense only. Kant does not mean by transcendental what is merely biographically, i.e. in each individual, or even palæontologically, i.e. in the history of the whole race of man, *à priori*. The *à priori* in these two senses has to be discovered by experimental and historical psychology, and Kant would probably have no objection whatever to any of the conclusions arrived at in this domain of research by the most advanced evolutionist. The *à priori* which Kant tries to discover is that which makes the two other *à priori*'s possible; it is the ontological *à priori*. Let all the irritations of the senses, let all the raw material of our sensuous perceptions be given, the fact of our not simply yielding to these inroads, but resisting them, accepting them, realising them, knowing them, all this shows a reacting and realising power in the Self. If anything is to be seen, or heard, or felt, or known by *us*, such as we are – and, I suppose, we are something – if all is not to end with disturbances of the retina, or vibrations of the tympanum, or ringing of the bells at the receiving stations of the brain, then what is to be perceived by *us*, must submit to the conditions of *our* perceiving, what is to be known by *us*, must accept the conditions of *our* knowing. This point is of so much importance for the solution, or, at all events, for the right apprehension of the problem with which we have to deal, that we must examine Kant's view on the origin and on the conditions of our knowledge a little more carefully.

According to Kant, then, there are, first of all, two fundamental or inevitable conditions of all sensuous manifestations, viz. *Space* and *Time*. They are called by Kant pure intuitions, which means *à priori* forms to which all intuitions, if they are to become *our* intuitions, must submit. By no effort can we do away with these forms of phenomenal existence. If we are to become conscious of anything, whether we call it an impression, or a manifestation, or a phase, we must place all phenomena side by side, or *in space*; and we can accept them only as following each other in succession, or *in time*. If we wanted to make it still clearer, that Time and Space are subjective, or at all events determined by the Self, we might say that there can be no *There* without a *Here*, there can be no *Then* without a *Now*, and both the *Here* and the *Now* depend on us as recipients, as measurers, as perceivers.

Mr. Herbert Spencer brings three arguments against Kant's view, that Space and Time are *à priori* forms of our sensuous intuition. He says it is absolutely impossible to think that these forms of intuition belong to the *ego*, and not to the *non-ego*. Now Kant does not, according to the nature of his system, commit himself to any assertion that some such forms may not belong to the *non-ego*, the *Ding an sich*; he only maintains that we have no means of knowing it. That Kant's view is perfectly thinkable, is proved by Berkeley and most Idealists.

Secondly, Mr. H. Spencer argues that if Space and Time are forms of thought, they can never be thought of, since it is impossible for anything to be at once the form of thought and the mater of thought. Against this argument it must be remarked that Kant never takes Space and Time as forms of thought. He carefully guards against this view, and calls them 'reine Formen sinnlicher Anschauung' (pure forms of sensuous intuition). But even if this distinction between thought and intuition is eliminated by evolution, it remains still to be proved that the forms of thought can never become the matter of thought. The greater part of philosophy makes the forms of thought the matter of thought.

Thirdly, Mr. Spencer maintains that some of our sense-perceptions, and more particularly that of hearing, are not necessarily localised. This objection again seems to me to rest on a misunderstanding. Though it is true that we do not always know the exact place where sounds come from, we always know, even in the case of our ear ringing, that what we perceive is outside, is somewhere, comes towards us; and that is all that Kant requires.

But besides these fundamental forms of sensuous intuition, Space and Time, without which no sensuous perception is possible, Kant, by his analysis of Pure Reason, discovered other conditions of our knowledge, the so-called *Categories of the Intellect*. While the sensualistic school, beginning with the ordinary *à priori* of experience, looked upon these forms of thought as mere abstractions, the residue or shadow of repeated observations, Kant made it clear that without them no experience, not even the lowest, would be possible, and that therefore they could not themselves be acquired by experience. Grant, he would say, that we have, we do not know how, the sensations of colour, sound, taste, smell, or touch. They are given, and we must accept them. But think of the enormous difference between a vibration and a sensation; and again between a succession or agglomeration of the sensations of yellowness, softness, sweetness, and roundness, and what we mean when we speak of an orange! The nerves may vibrate forever – what would that be to us? The sensations might rush in for ever through the different gates of our senses, the afferent nerves might deliver them to one central point, yet even then they would remain but so many excitations of nervous action, so many sensations, coming and going at pleasure, but they would never by themselves alone produce in us the perception of an orange. The common-sense view of the matter is that we perceive all these sensations together as an orange, because the orange, as such, exists without us as something substantial, and the qualities of yellowness, softness, sweetness, and roundness are inherent in it. This is, no doubt, very unphilosophical, and ignores the positive fact that all that we have consists and can consist only of sensations and phases of consciousness, and that nothing can ever carry us beyond. Yet there is this foundation of truth in the common-sense view, that it shows our utter inability of perceiving any sensations without referring them to something substantial which causes them, and is supposed to possess all those qualities which correspond to our sensations. But if we once know that what is given us consists only of phases of sensation, whatever their origin may be, it then becomes clear that it can only be our Self, or whatever else we like to call it, which adds all the rest, and does this, not consciously or deliberately, but of necessity, and, as it were, in the dark.

We cannot receive sensations without at once referring them to a substantial cause. To say that these sensations may have no origin at all, would be to commit an outrage against ourselves. And why? Simply because our mind is so constituted that to doubt whether anything phenomenal had a cause would be a logical suicide. Call it what you like, a law, a necessity, an unconscious instinct, a category of the understanding, it always remains the *fault* of our Self, that it cannot receive sensations without referring them to a substance of which they are supposed to tell us the attributes.[5] And if this is so, we have a clear right to say with Kant, that that without which even the lowest perception of an object is impossible must be given, and cannot have been acquired by repeated perception. The premiss in this argument, viz. that what we mean by cause has no warrant in the Non-ego, is indeed accepted, not only by Kant, but also by Hume; nay, there can be no doubt that on this point Kant owed very much to Hume's scepticism. Kant has nothing to say against Hume's argumentation. That the ideas of *cause* and *effect*, of *substance* and *quality*, in that sense in which we use them, are not found in actual experience. But while Hume proceeded to discard those ideas as mere illusions, Kant, on the contrary, reclaimed them as the inevitable forms to which all phenomena must submit, if they are to be phenomena, if they are to become *our* phenomena, the perceptions of a human Self. He established their truth, or, what with him is the same, their inevitability in all phenomenal knowledge, and by showing their inapplicability to any but phenomenal knowl-

---

[5] Cf. Bacon, *Nov. Org.* I. 41. 'Omnes perceptiones, tam Sensus quam Mentis, sunt ex analogia Hominis, non ex analogia universi. Estque Intellectus humanus instar speculi inaequalis ad radios rerum, qui suam naturam Naturae rerum immiscet, *camque distorquet et inficit.*' – Liebmann, *Kant*, p. 48.

edge, he once for all determined the limits of what is knowable and what is not.

These inevitable forms were reduced by Kant to twelve, and he arranged them systematically in his famous table of Categories:—

(1) *Unity, Plurality, Universality;*
(2) *Affirmation, Negation, Limitation;*
(3) *Substantiality, Causality, Reciprocity;*
(4) *Possibility, Reality, Necessity.*

There is no time, I am afraid, to examine the true character of these categories in detail, or the forms which they take as *schemata*. What applies to one applies to all, viz. that without them no thought is possible. Take the categories of *quantity*, and try to think of anything without thinking of it at the same time as one or many, and you will find it is impossible. Nature does not count for us, we must count ourselves, and the talent of counting cannot have been acquired by counting, any more than a stone acquires the talent of swimming by being thrown into the water.

Put in the shortest way, I should say that the result of Kant's analysis of the Categories of the Understanding is, '*Nihil est in sensu, quod non fuerit in intellectu.*' We cannot perceive any object, except by the aid of the intellect.

It is not easy to give in a few words a true abstract of Kant's philosophy, yet if we wish to gain a clear view of the progressive, or, it may be, retrogressive, movement of human thought from century to century, we must be satisfied with short abstracts, as long as they contain the essence of each system of philosophy. We may spend years in exploring the course of a river, and we may have in our note-books accurate sketches of its borders, of every nook and corner through which it winds. But for practical purposes we want a geographical map, more or less minute, according to the extent of the area which we wish to survey; and here the meandering outline of the river must vanish, and be replaced by a bold line, indicating the general direction of the river from one important point to another, and nothing else. The same is necessary if we draw, either for our own guidance or for the guidance of others, a map of the streams of philosophic thought. Whole pages, nay, whole volumes, must here be represented by one or two lines, and all that is essential is that we should not lose sight of the salient points in each system. It has been said that every system of philosophy lies in a nutshell, and this is particularly true of great and decisive systems. They do not wander about much; they go straight to the point. What is really characteristic in them is the attitude which the philosopher assumes towards the old problems of the world: that attitude once understood, and everything else follows almost by necessity. In the philosophy of Kant two streams of philosophic thought, which had been running in separate beds for ages, meet for the first time, and we can clearly discover in his system the gradual mingling of the colours of Hume and Berkeley. Turning against the one-sided course of Hume's philosophy, Kant shows that there is something in our intellect which could never have been supplied by mere sensations; turning against Berkeley, he shows that there is something in our sensations which could never have been supplied by mere intellect. He maintains that Hume's sensations and Berkeleys intellect exist for each other, depend on each other, presuppose each other, form together a whole that should never have been torn asunder. And he likewise shows that the two factors of our knowledge, the matter of our sensations on one side, and their form on the other, are correlative, and that any attempt at using the forms of our intellect on anything which transcends the limits of our sensations is illegal. Hence his famous saying, *Begriffe ohne Anschauungen sind leer, Auschauungen ohne Begriffe sind blind.* ('Conceptions without Intuitions are empty, Intuitions without Conceptions are blind.') This last protest against the use of the categories with regard to anything not supplied by the senses, is the crowning effort of Kant's philosophy, but, strange to say, it is a protest unheeded by almost all philosophers who follow after Kant. To my mind Kant's general solution of the problem which divided Hume and Berkeley is perfect; and however we may criticise the exact number of the inevitable forms of thought, his Table of Categories as a whole will for ever remain the Magna Charta of true philosophy.

In Germany, although Kant's system has been succeeded by other systems, his reply to Hume has never been challenged by any leading philosopher. It has been strengthened rather than weakened by subsequent systems which, though widely differing from Kant in their metaphysical conceptions, never questioned his success in vindicating certain ingredients of our knowledge as belonging to mind, not to matter; to the subject, not to the object; to the understanding, not to sensation; to the *à priori*, not to experience. They have disregarded Kant's warning that *à priori* laws of thought must not be applied to anything outside the limits of sensuous experience, but they have never questioned the true *à prior* character of those laws themselves.

Nor can it be said that in France the step which Kant had made in advance of Hume has ever been retraced by those who represent in that country that historical progress of philosophy. One French philosopher only, whose position is in many respects anomalous, Auguste Comte, has ventured to propose a system of philosophy in which Kant's position is not indeed refuted, but ignored. Comte did not know Kant's philosophy, and I do not think that it will be ascribed to any national prejudice of mine if I consider that this alone would be sufficient to exclude his name from the historical roll of philosophers. I should say just the same of Kant if he had written in ignorance of Locke and Hume and Berkeley, or of Spinoza if he had ignored the works of Descartes, or of Aristotle if he had ignored the teaching of Plato.

It is different, however, in England. Here a new school of British philosophy has sprung up, not entirely free, perhaps, from the influence of Comte, but supported by far greater learning, and real philosophical power – a school which deliberately denies the correctness of Kant's analysis, and falls back in the main on the position once occupied by Locke or Hume. This same school has lately met with very powerful support in Germany, and it might seem almost as if the work achieved by Kant was at last to be undone in his own country. These modern philosophers do not ignore Kant, but in returning to the stand point of Locke or Hume, they distinctly assert that Kant has not made good his case, whether in his analysis of the two feeders of knowledge, or in his admission of general truths, not attained and not attainable by experience. The law of causality on which the whole question of the *à priori* conditions of knowledge may be said to hinge, is treated again, as it was by Hume, as a mere illusion, produced by the repeated succession of events; and psychological analysis, strengthened by physiological research, is called in to prove that mind is but the transient outcome of matter, that the brain secretes thought as the liver secretes bile. No phosphorus, no thought! is the triumphant war-cry of this school.

In speaking of the general tendencies of this school of thought, I have intentionally avoided mentioning any names, for it is curious to observe that hardly any two representatives of it agree even on the most essential points. No two names, for instance, are so frequently quoted together as representatives of modern English thought, as Mr. Stuart Mill and Mr. Herbert Spencer, yet on the most critical point they are as diametrically opposed as Hume and Kant. Mr. Stuart Mill admits nothing *à priori* in the human mind; he stands on the same point as Locke, nay, if I interpret some of his paragraphs rightly, he goes as far as Hume. Mr. Herbert Spencer, on the contrary, fights against this view of the human intellect with the same sharp weapon that Kant had used against them, and he arrives, like Kant, at the conclusion that there is in the human mind, such as we know it, something *à priori* call it intuitions, categories, innate ideas or congenital dispositions, something at all events that cannot honestly be explained as the result of individual experience. Whether the prehistoric genesis of these congenital dispositions or inherited necessities of thought, as suggested by Mr. Herbert Spencer, be right or wrong, does not signify for the purpose which Kant had in view. In admitting that there is something in our mind, which is not the result of our own *à posteriori* experience, Mr. Herbert Spencer is a thorough Kantian, and we shall see that he is a Kantian in other respects too. If it could be proved that nervous modifications, accumulated from generation to generation, could result in nervous structures that are fixed in proportion as the outer relations to which they answer are fixed, we, as followers of Kant, should only have to put in the place of Kant's intuitions of Space and Time, 'the constant space relations, expressed in definite nervous structures, congenitally framed to act in definite ways, and incapable of acting in any other way.' If Mr. Herbert Spencer had not misunderstood the exact meaning of what Kant calls the intuitions of Space and Time, he would have perceived that, barring his theory of the prehistoric origin of these intuitions, he was quite at one with Kant.

Some of the objections which Mr. Herbert Spencer urges against Kant's theory of innate intuitions of Space and Time were made so soon after the appearance of his work, that Kant himself was still able to reply to them.[6] Thus he explains himself that by intuitions he does not mean anything innate in the form of ready-made ideas or images, but merely passive states or receptivities of the Ego, according to which, if affected in certain ways, it has certain forms in which it represents these affections, and that what is innate is not the representation itself, but simply the first formal cause of its possibility.'

Nor do I think that Kant's view of causality, as one of the most important categories of the understanding, has been correctly apprehended by his English critics. All the arguments that are brought forward by the living followers of Hume, in order to show that the idea of cause is not an innate idea, but the result of repeated observations, and, it may be, a mere illusion, do not touch Kant at all. He moves in quite a different layer of thought. That each individual becomes conscious of causality by experience and education, he knows as well as the most determined follower of Hume; but what he means by the category of causality is something totally different. It is an unconscious process which, from a purely psychological point of view, might truly be called prehistoric. So far from being the result of repeated observations, Kant shows that what he means by the category of causality is the *sine quâ non* of the simplest perception, and that without it we might indeed have states of feeling, but never a sensation of *something*, an intuition of *an object*, or a perception of *a substance*. Were we to accept the theory of evolution which traces the human mind back to the inner life of a mollusc, we should even then be able to remain Kantians, in so far as it would be, even then, the category of causality that works in the mollusc, and makes it extend its tentacles towards the crumb of bread which has touched it, and has evoked in it a reflex action, a grasping after the prey. In this lowest form of animal life, therefore, the category of causality, if we may use such a term, would show itself simply as conscious, or, at all events, as no longer involuntary, reaction; in human life, it shows itself in the first glance of recognition that lights up the infant's vacant stare.

This is what Kant means by the category of causality, and no new discoveries, either in the structure of the organs of sense or in the working of the mental faculties, have in any

---

[6] See *Das Unbewusste*, p. 187, Kant's *Werke*, ed. Rosenkranz, B. I, pp. 445, 446.

way, so far as I can see, invalidated his conclusions that that category, at all events, whatever we may think of the others, is *à priori* in every sense of the word.

Among German philosophers there is none so free from what are called German metaphysical tendencies as Schopenhauer, yet what does he say of Kant's view of causality?

'Sensation,' he says, 'is something essentially subjective, and its changes are brought to our cognisance in the form of the internal sense only, therefore in time, i.e. in succession.[7] The understanding, through a form belonging to it and to it alone, viz. the form of causality, takes hold of the given sensations, *à priori*, previous to all experience (for experience is not yet possible), as effects which, as such, must have a cause; and through another form of the internal sense, viz. that of space, which is likewise pre-established in the intellect, it places that cause outside the organs of sense.' And again: 'As the visible word rises before us with the rising of the sun, the understanding, by its one simple function of referring all effects to a cause, changes with one stroke all dull and unmeaning sensations into intuitions. What is felt by the eye, the ear, the hand, is not intuition, but only the *data* of intuition. Only by the step which the understanding makes from effect to cause, the world is made, as intuition, extended in space, changing in form, permanent in substance; for it is the understanding which combines Space and Time in the conception of matter, that is, of activity or force.'

Professor Helmholtz, again, who has analysed the external apparatus of the senses more minutely than any other philosopher, and who, in England, and, at all events, in this Institution, would not be denied the name of a philosopher, arrives, though starting from a different point, at identically the same result as Schopenhauer.

'It is clear,' he says, 'that starting with the world of our sensations, we could never arrive at the conception of an external world, except by admitting, from the changing of our sensations, the existence of external objects as the causes of change; though it is perfectly true that, after the conception of such objects has once been formed, we are hardly aware how we came to have this conception; because the conclusion is so self-evident that we do not look upon it as the result

[7] Liebmann, *Objectiver Anblick* p. 114.

of a conclusion. We must admit, therefore, that the law of causality, by which from an effect we infer the existence of a cause, is to be recognised as *a law of our intellect, preceding all experience*. We cannot arrive at any experience of natural objects without having the law of causality acting within us; it is impossible, therefore, to admit that this law of causality is derived from experience.'

Strengthened by such support from opposite quarters, we may sum up Kant's argument in favour of the transcendental or *à priori* character of this and the other categories in this short sentence:

'That without which no experience, not even the simplest perception of a stone or a tree, is possible, cannot be the result of repeated perceptions.'

There are those who speak of Kant's philosophy as cloudy German metaphysics, but I doubt whether they have any idea of the real character of his philosophy. No one had dealt such heavy blows to what is meant by German metaphysics as Kant; no one has drawn so sharp a line between the Knowable and the Unknowable; no one, I believe, at the present critical moment, deserves such careful study as Kant. When I watch, as far as I am able, the philosophical controversies in England and Germany, I feel very strongly how much might be gained on both sides by a mere frequent exchange of thought. Philosophy was far more international in the days of Leibniz and Newton, and again in the days of Kant and Hume; and much mental energy seems wasted by this absence of a mutual understanding between the leaders of philosophic thought in England, Germany, France, and Italy. It is painful to read the sweeping condemnation of German metaphysics, and still more to see a man like Kant lectured like a schoolboy. one may differ from Kant, as one differs from Plato or Aristotle, but those who know Kant's writings, and the influence which he has exercised on the history of philosophy, would always speak of him with respect.

The blame, however, does not attach to the English side only. There are many philosophers in Germany who think that, since the days of Hume, there has been no philosophy in England, and who imagine they may safely ignore the great work that has been achieved by the living representatives of British philosophy. I confess that I almost shuddered when in a work by an eminent German professor of Strassburg, I saw the most advanced thinker of England, a mind of the future rather than of the present, spoken of as – *antediluvian*. That antediluvian philosopher is Mr. John Stuart Mill. Antediluvian, however, was meant only for Ante-Kantian, and in that sense Mr. Stuart Mill would probably gladly accept the name.

Yet, such things ought not to be, if nationality must still narrow our sympathies in other spheres of thought, surely philosophy ought to stand on a loftier pinnacle.

SECOND LECTURE

Delivered at the Royal Institution, March 29, 1873

If we want to understand the history of the Norman Conquest, the Reformation, the French Revolution, or any other great crisis in the political, religious, and social state of the world, we know that we must study the history of the times immediately preceding those momentous changes. Nor shall we ever understand the real character of a great philosophical crisis unless we have made ourselves thoroughly familiar with its antecedents. Without going so far as Hegel, who saw in the whole history of philosophy an unbroken dialectic evolution, it is easy to see that there certainly is a greater continuity in the history of philosophic thought than in the history of politics, and it therefore seemed to me essential to dwell in my first Lecture on the exact stage which the philosophical struggle of our century had reached before Mr. Darwin's publications appeared, in order to enable us to appreciate fully his historical position, not only as an eminent physiologist, but as the restorer of that great empire in the world of thought which claims as its founders the glorious names of Locke and Hume. It might indeed be said of Mr. Darwin what was once said of the restorer of another empire, 'Il n'est pas parvenu, il est arrivé.' The philosophical empire of Locke and Hume had fallen under the blows of Kant's *Criticism of Pure Reason*. But the successors of Kant – Fichte, Schelling, and Hegel – disregarding the checks by which Kant had so carefully defined the legitimate exercise of the rights of Pure Reason, indulged in such flights of transcendent fancy, that a reaction became inevitable. First came the violent protest of Schopenhauer, and his exhortation to return to the old fundamental principles of

Kant's philosophy. These, owing to their very violence, passed unheeded. Then followed a complete disorganisation of philosophic though, and this led in the end to a desperate attempt to restore the old dynasty of Locke and Hume. During the years immediately preceding the publication of Darwin's *Origin of Species* (1860) and his *Descent of Man*, the old problems which had been discussed in the days of Berkeley, Hume, and Kant, turned up again in full force. We had to read again that sensuous impressions were the sole constituent elements of the human intellect; that general ideas were all developed spontaneously from single impressions; that the only difference between sensations and ideas was the faintness of the latter; that what we mean by substance is only a collection of particular ideas, united by imagination, and comprehended by a particular name;[1] and that what we are pleased to call our mind, is but a delusion, though who the deluder is and who the deluded, would seem to be a question too indiscreet to ask.

But the principal assault in this struggle came from a new quarter. It was not to be the old battle over again, we were told; but the fight was to be carried on with modern and irresistible weapons. The new philosophy, priding itself, as all philosophics have done, on its positive character, professed to despise the endless argumentations of the schools, and to appeal for evidence to matter of fact only. Our mind, whether consisting of material impressions or intellectual concepts, was not to be submitted to the dissecting knife and the microscope. We were shown the nervous tubes, afferent and efferent, through which the shocks from without pass on to the sensitive and motive cells; the commissural tubes holding these cells together were laid bare before us; the exact place in the brain was pointed out where the messages from without were delivered; and it seemed as if nothing were wanting but a more powerful lens to enable us to see with our own eyes how, in the workshop of the brain, as in a photographic apparatus, the pictures of the senses and the ideas of the intellect were being turned out in endless variety.

And this was not all. The old stories about the reasoning of animals, so powerfully handled in the school of Hume, were brought out again. Innumerable anecdotes that had been told from the time of Aelian to the days of Reimarus, were told once

---

[1] Hume, *Treatise on Human Nature*, book i. see. i. p. 33.

more, in order to show that the intellect of animals did not only match, but that in many cases it transcended the powers of the human intellect. One might have imagined oneself living again in the days of La Mettrie, who, after having published his work, *Man, a Machine*, followed it up by another work, *Brutes, more than Machines*. It is true there were some philosophers who protested energetically against reopening that question, which had been closed by common consent, and which certainly ought not to have been reopened by positive philosophers. For if there is a *terra incognita* which excludes all positive knowledge, it is the mind of animals. We may imagine anything we please about the inner life, the motives, the foresight, the feelings and aspirations of animals – we can *know* absolutely nothing. How little analogy can help us in interpreting their acts is best proved by the fact, that a philosopher like Descartes could bring himself to consider animals as mere machines, while Leibniz was unwilling to deny to them the possession of immortal souls. We need not wonder at such discrepancies, considering the nature of the evidence. What can we know of the inner life of a mollusc? We may imagine that it lives in total darkness, that it is hardly more than a mass of pulp; but we may equally well imagine that, being free from all the disturbances produced by the impressions of the senses, and out of the reach of all those causes of error to which man is liable, it may possess a much truer and deeper insight into the essence of the Absolute, a much fuller apprehension of eternal truths than the human soul. It may be so, or it may not be so, for there is no limit to an anthropomorphic interpretation of the life of animals. But the tacit understanding, or rather the clear compromise, established among the philosophers of the last century, and declaring the old battlefield, on which so much useless ink had been shed over the question of the intellect of animals, to be for ever neutralised, ought hardly to have been disturbed, least of all by those who profess to trust in nothing but positive fact.

Nor do I think that philosophers would have allowed the reopening of the flood-gates of animal anthropomorphism, if it had not been for the simultaneous rise of Mr. Darwin's theories. If it can be proved that man derives his origin genealogically, and, in the widest sense of the word, historically, from some lower animal, it is useless to say another word on the mind of man being different from the mind of animals.

The two are identical, and no argument would be required any longer to support Hume's opinions; they would henceforth rest on positive facts. This shows the immense importance of Mr. Darwin's speculations, in solving, once for all, by evidence that admits of no demurrer, the long-pending questions between man and animal, and, in its further consequences, between mind and matter, between spiritualism and materialism, between Berkeley and Hume; and it shows at the same time that the final verdict on his philosophy must be signed, not by zoologists and physiologists only, but by psychologists also, nay, it may be, by German metaphysicians.

Few men who are not zoologists and physiologists by profession can have read Mr. Darwin's books *On the Origin of Species* and *On the Descent of Man* with deeper interest than I have, and with a more intense admiration of his originality, independence, and honesty of thought. I know of few books so useful to the student of the Science of Language, in teaching him the true method for discovering similarity beneath diversity, the general behind the individual, the essential hidden by the accidental; and helping him to understand the possibility of change by natural means. There may be gaps and flaws in the genealogical pedigree of organic life, as drawn by Mr. Darwin and his followers; there may be or there may not be a possibility of resisting their arguments when, beginning with a group of animals, boldly called 'organisms without organs,'[2] such as the *Bathybius Haeckelii*, they advance step by step to the crown and summit of the animal kingdom, and to the *primus inter primates*, man.

This is a point to be settled by physiologists; and if Carl Vogt may be accepted as their recognised representative and spokesman, the question would seem to be settled, at least so far as the savants of Europe are concerned. 'No one,' he says, 'at least in Europe, dares any longer to maintain the independent and complete creation of species.'[3] The reservation, 'at least in Europe,' is meant, as is well known, for Agassiz in America, who still holds out, and is bold enough to teach, 'that the different species of the animal kingdom furnish an

---

[2] Haeckel, *Natürliche Schöpfungsgeschichte*, p. 165.
[3] 'Personne, en Europe au moins, n'ose plus soutenir la création indépendante et de toutes pièces des espèces.' Quoted by Darwin, in his *Descent of Man*, vol. i. p. 1.

unexpected proof that the whole plan of creation was maturely weighed and fixed, long before it was carried out.'[4] Professor Haeckel, however, the fiery apostle of Darwinism in Germany, speaks more diffidently on the subject. In his last work on *Kalkschwämme* (p. xii), just published, he writes: 'The majority, and among it some famous biologists of the first class, are still of opinion that the problem of the origin of species has only been reopened by Darwin, but by no means solved.'

But, however that may be, and whatever modification Mr. Darwin's system may receive at the hands of professed physiologists, the honour of having cleared the Augean stable of endless species, of having explained many things which formerly seemed to require the interference of direct creation, by the slow action of natural causes, of having made us see the influence exercised by the individual on the family, and by the family on the individual, of having given us, in fact, a few really new and fresh ideas, will always remain his own.

In saying this, however, I do not wish to imply assent to Mr. Darwin's views on the development of all species; I only wish to say that, in the presence of such high authorities, one ought to refrain from expressing an opinion, and be satisfied to wait. I am old enough to remember the equally authoritative statements of the most eminent naturalists with regard to the races of man. When my own researches on language and the intellectual development of man led me to the conclusion that, if we had only sufficient time (some hundreds of thousands of years) allowed us, there would be no difficulty in giving an intelligible account of the common origin of all languages, I was met with the assurance that, even hypothetically, such a view was impossible, because the merest tyro in anatomy knew that the different races of man constituted so many species, that species were the result of independent creative acts, and that the black, brown, red, yellow, and white races could not possibly be conceived as descended from one source. Men like Prichard and Humboldt, who maintained the possibility of a common origin, were accused of being influenced by extraneous motives. I myself was charged with a superstitious belief in the Mosaic ethnology. And why? Simply because, in the Science of Language, I was a Darwinian before

---

[4] *See* Durand, *Origines*, pp. 77, 78.

Darwin; simply because I had protested against scientific as strongly as against theological dogmatism; simply because I wished to see the question of the possibility of a common origin of languages treated, at least, as an open question.[5] And what has happened now? All the arguments about hybridity, infertility, local centres, permanent types, are swept away under the powerful broom of development, and we are told that not only the different varieties of man, but monkeys, horses, cats, and dogs, have all one, or at the utmost four progenitors; nay, that 'no living creature, in Europe at least, dares to affirm the independent creation of species.' Under these circumstances it seems but fair to follow the old Greek rule of abstaining, and to wait whether in the progress of physical research the arguments of the evolutionists will really remain unanswerable and unanswered.

The two points where the system of Mr. Darwin, and more particularly of his followers, seems most vulnerable to the general student, are the beginning and the end. With regard to the beginning of organic life, Mr. Darwin himself has exercised a wise discretion. He does not, as we saw, postulate one primordial form, nor has he ever attempted to explain the first beginnings of organic life. He is not responsible, therefore, for the theories of his disciples, who either try to bridge over the chasm between inorganic and organic bodies by mere 'Who knows?' or who fall back on scientific mythology; for to speak of self-generation is to speak mythologically.

Mr. Herbert Spencer writes thus in answer to Mr. Martineau, who had dwelt on the existence of this chasm between the living and the not-living as a fatal difficulty in the way of the general doctrine of evolution: 'Here, again, our ignorance is employed to play the part of knowledge: the fact that we do not know distinctly how an alleged transition has taken place, is transformed into the fact that no transition has taken place.'

The answer to this is clear. Why allege a transition, if we do not know anything about it? It is in alleging such a transition that we raise our ignorance to the rank of knowledge. We need not say that a transition is impossible, if impossible means

---

[5] See 'The Possibility of a Common Origin of Language,' in my letter to Bunsen 'On the Turanian Languages,' published in Bunsen's *Christianity and Mankind*, 1854.

inconceivable; but we ought not to say either that it is possible, unless we mean by possible no more than conceivable.

Mr. Spencer then continues: 'Merely noting this, however, I go on to remark that scientific discovery is day by day narrowing the chasm. Not many years since it was held as certain that chemical compounds distinguished as organic could not be formed artificially. Now, more than a thousand organic compounds have been formed artificially. Chemists have discovered the art of building them up from the simpler to the more complex; and do not doubt that they will eventually produce the most complex. Moreover, the phenomena attending isomeric change give a clue to those moments which are the only indications we have of life in its lowest forms. In various colloidal substances, including the albumenoid, isomeric change is accompanied by contraction or expansion, and consequent motion; and in such primordial types as the *Protogenes* of Haeckel, which do not differ in appearance from minute portions of albumen, the observed motions are comprehensible as accompanying isomeric changes caused by variations in surrounding physical actions. The probability of this interpretation will be seen on remembering the evidence we have, that in the higher organisms the functions are essentially effected by isomeric changes from one to another of the multitudinous forms which protein assumes.'

This is, no doubt, very able pleading on the part of an advocate, but I doubt whether it would convince Mr. Spencer himself, as a judge. I see no narrowing of the chasm between inorganic and organic bodies, because certain substances, called organic, have lately been built up in the laboratory. These so-called organic substances are not living bodies, but simply the secretions of living bodies. The question was not, whether we can imitate some of the productions turned out of the laboratory of a living body, but whether we can build up a living body.

Secondly, unless Mr. Spencer is prepared to maintain that life is nothing but isomeric change, the mere fact that there is an apparent similarity between the movements of the lowest of living bodies and the expansion and contraction produced in not-living substances by isomeric change, carries no weight. Even though the movements of the *Protogenes Haeckelii* were in appearance the same as those produced in chemical substances by isomeric change, no one knows better than Mr.

Spencer, that life is not merely movement, but that it involves assimilation, oxidation and reproduction, at lest reproduction by fission. No chemist has yet produced albumen, much less a *moneres*; and till that is done we have as much right to protest against the hypothetical admission of a transition from no-life into life as Mr. Spencer would have to protest against the assertion that such a transition is impossible.

By the frequent repetition of such words as *generatio spontanea, autogony, plasmogony, Urzeugung*, and all the rest, we get accustomed to the sound of these words, and at last imagine that they can be translated into thought. But the Science of Language teaches us that it is always dangerous to do violence to words. Self-generation is self-contradictory; for as long as we use generation in its original sense, it is impossible that the object of generation should be the same as the subject. Why, therefore, use the word generation? We should never venture to say that a man was his own father or his own son; and if anyone believes that the production of life is possible by means of purely mechanical combinations, a new word should be coined for this new idea. What is really intended, is a complete reformation of the two concepts of organic and inorganic substance, of lifeless and living bodies. The two are no longer to be considered as mutually exclusive, but as co-ordinate, and both subordinate to some higher concept. Life may hereafter be discovered as the result of a chemical combination[6] of given substances; a peculiar mode of force or being, dependent on ascertainable conditions, and analogous to heat and electricity. Or it may be proved that millions of years ago the chemical state of the earth was different, and that what is impossible now in our laboratories was possible then in the primeval laboratory of nature. But, for the present, it seems to me a violation of the fundamental laws of scientific research, were we to use such an hypothesis as a real explanation of the problem of life, or were we to attempt to use *autogony* as a real word. The origin of life is as unknown to use as it was to Zoroaster, Moses, or Vasish*th*a; and Mr. Darwin shows a truly Kantian spirit in abstaining from any expression of opinion on this old riddle of the world.

But while with regard to the first point, viz. the beginning of life, Mr. Darwin would seem to hold a neutral position,

---

[6] Strauss, p. 171.

we shall see that with regard to the second point, viz. the development of some higher animal into man, Mr. Darwin is responsible himself. He feels convinced that, if not lineally, at all events laterally, man is the descendant of an ape. Much stress has lately been laid on this, as a kind of salve to out wounded pride, that man need not consider himself as the lineal descendant of any living kind of ape.[7] We might, indeed, if we had any feelings of reverence for our ancestors, hope to discover their fossil bones in the tertiary strata of Southern Asia and Africa, but we need not be afraid of ever meeting them face to face, even in a South African congregation. I confess I do not see that this constitutes any real difference, nay, the statement that man is *only* laterally, not lineally, descended from a catarrhine ape, seems to me to rest on a complete confusion of thought.

Supposing the first ancestor of all living beings to have been a *Moneres*, as Haeckel tells us, and that this moneres developed into an *Amœba*, and that the Amœba, after passing through sixteen[8] more stages of animal life, emerged as a *Prosimia*, a half-ape, or tailed ape, then an *Anthropoid* ape, like the gorilla, then a *Pithecanthropus* or an ape-man, till at last the ape-man (a purely mythological being) begat a man; surely, in that case, man is the lineal descendant of an ape, though his first ancestor was the small speck of protoplasm, called a Moneres, that has not yet reached even the dignity of a cell.[9] The admission of hundreds and thousands of intermediate links between the gorilla and man would not make the smallest difference, as long as the genealogical continuity is not broken. Even if we represented to ourselves the genealogical tree of the animal family as a real tree, sending out by gemmation leaves and branches, representing the different species of animals from the amœba to the ape, and developing its leader into man, we should gain nothing; for if the primordial moneres is our common ancestor, all his descendants are brothers; all have, strictly speaking, some molecule of that living substance which existed in the first living individual; all are liable, therefore, to the capricious working of an unsuspected atavism.

---

[7] Haeckel, p. 577.
[8] Ib. p. 578.
[9] Haeckel, p. 168.

Nor do I see any necessity for softening the true aspect of Darwin's theory, or disguising its consequences. The question is not whether the belief that animals so distant as a man, a monkey, an elephant, and a humming bird, a snake, a frog, and a fish could all have sprung from the same parents is monstrous;[10] but simply and solely, whether it is true. If it is true, we shall soon learn to digest it. Appeals to the pride or humility of man, to scientific courage or religious piety, are all equally out of place. If it could be proved that our bodily *habitat* had not been created in all its perfection from the first, but had been allowed to develop for ages before it became fit to hold a human soul, should we have any right to complain? Do we complain of the injustice or indignity of our having individually to be born or to die? of our passing through the different stages of embryonic life, of our being made of dust, that is, of exactly the same chemical materials from which the bodies of animals are built up? Fact against fact, argument against argument, that is the rule of scientific warfare, a warfare in which to confess oneself convinced or vanquished by truth is often far more honourable than victory.

But while protesting against these sentimental outcries, we ought not to allow ourselves to be intimidated by scientific clamour. It seems to me a mere dogmatic assertion to say[11] that it would be unscientific to consider the hand of a man or a monkey, the foot of a horse, the flipper of a seal, the wing of a bat, as having been formed on the same ideal plan! Even if 'their descent from a common progenitor, together with their adaptation to diversified conditions,' were proved by irrefragable evidence, the conception of an ideal plan would remain perfectly legitimate. If this one member could be so modified as to become in course of time a wing, a flipper, a hoof, or a hand, there is nothing unscientific, nothing unphilosophical in the idea that it may from the first have been intended for these later purposes and higher developments. Not every member has become a hand; and why? Three reasons only are admissible; either because there was for the hand a germ which, under all circumstances, would have developed into a hand, and into a hand only; or because there were outward circumstances which would have forced any member

---

[10] Darwin, *Descent*, vol. i. p. 203.
[11] *Descent*, vol. i, p. 32.

into the shape of a hand; or lastly, because there was from the beginning a correlation between that particular member and the circumstances to which it became adapted. I can understand the view of the evolutionist, who looks upon an organ as so much protoplasm, which, according to circumstances, might assume any conceivable form, and who treats all environing circumstances as facts requiring no explanation; but I am not prepared to say that Kant's view is unphilosophical when he says: 'Every change in a substance depends on its connection with and reciprocal action of other substances, and that *reciprocal action* cannot be explained, except through a Divine mind, as the common cause of both.'[12] At all events the conception that all these modifications in the ascending scale of animal life are the result of natural selection, transcends the horizon of our understanding quite as much as the conception that the whole creation was foreseen at once, and that what seems to us the result of adaptation through myriads of years, was seen as a whole from beginning to end by the wisdom and power of a creative Self. Both views are transcendent, both belong to the domain of faith; but if it were possible to measure the wonders of this universe by degrees, I confess that, to my mind, the self-evolution of a cell which contains within itself the power of becoming a man, or the admission of a protoplasm which in a given number of years would develop into a *homunculus* or a Shakespeare – nay, the mere formation of a *nucleus* which would change the moneres into an amœba, would far exceed in marvellousness all the speculations of Plato and the wonders of Genesis. The two extremes of scientific research and mythological speculation seem sometimes on the point of meeting; and when I listen to the language of the most advanced biologists, I almost imagine I am listening to one of the most ancient hymns of the Veda, and that we shall soon have to say again; 'In the beginning there was the golden egg.'

It is easy to understand that the Darwinian school, having brought itself to look upon the diverse forms of living animals as the result of gradual development, should have considered it an act of intellectual cowardice to stop short before man. The gap between man and the higher apes is so very small, whereas the gap between the ape and the moneres is enormous. If, then, the latter could be cleared, how could we hesitate

[12] Zeller, *Geschichte der Deutschen Philosophie*, p. 413.

about the former? Few of those who have read Darwin or Haeckel could fail to feel the force of this appeal; and so far from showing a want of courage, those who resist it require really all the force of intellectual convictions to keep them from leaping with the rest. I cannot follow Mr. Darwin because I hold that this question is not to be decided in an anatomical theatre only. There is to my mind one difficulty which Mr. Darwin has not sufficiently appreciated, and which I certainly do not feel able to remove. There is between the whole animal kingdom on one side, and man, even in his lowest state, on the other, a barrier which no animal has ever crossed, and that barrier is – *Language*. By no effort of the understanding, by no stretch of imagination, can I explain to myself how language could have grown out of anything which animals possess, even if we granted them millions of years for that purpose. If anything has a right to the name of *specific difference*, it is language, as we find it in man, and in man only. Even if we removed the name of specific difference from our philosophic dictionaries, I should still hold that nothing deserves the name of man except what is able to speak. If Mr. Mill[13] maintains that a rational elephant could not be called a man, all depends on what he means by rational. But it may certainly be said with equal, and even greater truth, that a speaking elephant or an elephantine speaker could never be called an elephant. I can bring myself to imagine with evolutionist philosophers that that most wonderful of organs, the eye, has been developed out of a pigmentary spot, and the ear out of a particularly sore place in the skin; that, in fact, an animal without any organs of sense may in time grow into an animal with organs of sense. I say I can imagine it, and I should not feel justified in classing such a theory as utterly inconceivable. But, taking all that is called animal on one side, and man on the other, I must call it inconceivable that any known animal could ever develop language. Professor Schleicher, though an enthusiastic admirer of Darwin, observed once jokingly, but not without a deep meaning, 'If a pig were ever to say to me, "I am a pig," it would *ipso facto* cease to be a pig.' This shows how strongly he felt that language was out of the reach of any animal, and the exclusive or specific property of man. I do not wonder that Mr. Darwin and other philosophers belonging to his school

[13] *Logic*, i. 38.

should not feel the difficulty of language as it was felt by Professor Schleicher, who, though a Darwinian, was also one of our best students of the Science of Language. But those who know best what language is, and, still more, what it presupposes, cannot, however, Darwinian they may be on other points, ignore the *veto* which, as yet, that science enters against the last step in Darwin's philosophy. That philosophy would not be vitiated by admitting an independent beginning for man. For if Mr. Darwin admits, in opposition to the evolutionist *pur et simple*, four or five progenitors for the whole of the animal kingdom, which are most likely intended for the *Radiata, Mollusca, Articulata,* and *Vertebrata,* there would be nothing radically wrong in admitting a fifth progenitor for man. As Mr. Darwin does not admit this, but declares distinctly that man has been developed from some lower animal, we may conclude that *physiologically* and *anatomically* there are no tenable arguments against this view. But if Mr. Darwin goes on to say[14] that in a series of forms graduating *insensibly* from some ape-like creature to man as he now exists, it would be impossible to fix on any definite point where the term 'man' ought to be used, he has left the ground, peculiarly his own, where few would venture to oppose him, and he must expect to be met by those who have studied man, not only as an ape-like creature, which he undoubtedly is, but also as an un-ape-like creature, possessed of language, and of all that language implies.

My objections to the words of Mr. Darwin, which I have just quoted, are twofold: first, as to form; secondly, as to substance.

With regard to the form which Mr. Darwin has given to his argument, it need hardly be pointed out that he takes for granted in the premiss what is to be established in the conclusion. If there existed a series graduating *insensibly* from some ape-like creature to man, then, no doubt, the very fact that the graduation is *insensible* would preclude the possibility of fixing on any definite point where the animal ends and man begins. This, however, may be a mere slip of the pen, and might have been passed by unnoticed, if it were not that the same kind of argument occurs not unfrequently in the works of Mr. Darwin and his followers. Whenever the distance

[14] I. 235.

between two points in the chain of creation seems too great, and there is no chance of finding the missing links, we are told again and again that we have only to imagine a large number of intermediate beings, insensibly sloping up or sloping down, in order to remove all difficulty. Whenever I meet with this line of reasoning, I cannot help thinking of an argument used by Hindu theologians in their endeavours to defend the possibility and the truth of Divine revelation. Their opponents say that between a Divine Being, who they admit is in possession of the truth, and human beings who are to receive the truth, there is a gulf which nothing can bridge over; and they go on to say that, admitting that Divine truth, as revealed, was perfect in the Revealer, yet the same Divine truth, as seen by human beings, must be liable to all the accidents of human frailty and fallibility. The orthodox Brahmans grow very angry at this, and, appealing to their sacred books, they maintain that there was between the Divine and the human a chain of intermediate beings, Rishis or seers, as they call them; that the first generation of these seers was, say, nine-tenths divine and one-tenth human; the second, eight-tenths divine and two-tenths human; the third, seven-tenths divine and three-tenths human; that each of these generations handed down revealed truth, till at last it reached the ninth generation, which was one-tenth divine and nine-tenths human, and by them was preached to ordinary mortals, being ten-tenths, or altogether human. In this way they feel convinced that the gulf between the Divine and the human is safely bridged over; and they might use the very words of Mr. Darwin, that in this series of forms graduating *insensibly* from the Divine to the human, it is impossible to fix on any definite point where the term 'man' ought to be used.

This old fallacy of first imagining a continuous scale, and then pointing out its indivisibility, affects more or less all systems of philosophy which wish to get rid of specific distinctions. That fallacy lurks in the word 'Development', which is now so extensively used, but which requires very careful testing before it should be allowed to become a current coin in philosophical transactions. The admission of this insensible graduation would eliminate, not only the difference between ape and man, but likewise between black and white, hot and cold, a high and a low note in music; in fact, it would do away with the possibility of all exact and definite knowledge, by removing these wonderful lines and laws of nature which change the

Chaos into a Kosmos, the Infinite into the Finite, and which enable us to count, to tell, and to know.

There have always been philosophers who have an eye for the Infinite only, who see All in One, and One in All. One of the greatest sages of antiquity, nay, of the whole world, Herakleitos (460 B.C.), summed up the experience of his life in the famous words, πάντα χωρεῖ καὶ οὐδὲν μένει, 'All is moving, and nothing is fixed,' or as we should say, 'All is growing, all is developing, all is evolving.' But this view of the universe was met, it may be by anticipation, by the followers of Pythagoras. When Pythagoras was asked what was the wisest of all things, he replied, 'Number,' and next to it, 'He who gave names to all things.' How should we translate this enigmatical saying? I believe, in modern philosophical language, it would run like this: 'True knowledge is impossible without definite generalisation or concepts (that is, number), and without definite signs for these concepts (that is, language).'

The Herakleitean view is now again in the ascendant. All is changing, all is developing, all is evolving. Ask any evolutionist philosopher whether he can conceive any two things so heterogeneous that, given a few millions of years and plenty of environment, the one cannot develop into the other, and I believe he will say, No. I do not argue here against this line of thought; on the contrary, I believe that in one sphere of mental aspirations it has its legitimate place. What I protest against is this, that in the sphere of exact knowledge we should allow ourselves to be deceived by inexact language. 'Insensible graduation' is self-contradictory. Translated into English, it means graduation without graduation, degrees without degrees, or something which is at the same time perceptible and imperceptible. Millions of years will never render the distance between two points, however near to each other, imperceptible. If the evolutionist philosopher asks for a few millions of years, the specialist philosopher asks for eyes that will magnify a few million times, and the Bank which supplies the one will readily supply the other. Exact science has nothing to do with insensible graduation. It counts thousands of vibrations that make our imperfect ears hear definite tones; it counts millions of vibrations that make our weak eyes see definite colours. It counts, it tells, it names, and then it knows; though it knows at the same time that beyond the thousands and beyond the millions of vibrations there is that which man can neither count, nor tell, nor name, nor know, the Unknown, the Unknowable – ay, the Divine.

But if we return to Mr. Darwin's argument, and simply leave out the word 'insensibly,' which begs the whole question, we shall then have to meet his statement, that in a series of forms graduating from some ape-like creature to man as he now is, it would be impossible to fix on any definite point where the term 'man' ought to be used. This statement I meet by a simple negative. Even admitting, for argument's sake, the existence of a series of beings intermediate between ape and man – a series which, as Mr. Darwin repeatedly states, does not exist[15] – I maintain that the point where the animal ends and man begins could be determined with absolute precision, for it would be coincident with the beginning of the Radical Period of language, with the first formation of a general idea embodied in the only form in which we find them embodied, viz. in the roots of our language.

Mr. Darwin was, of course, not unprepared for that answer. He remembered the old pun of Hobbes, *Homo animal rationale, quid orationale* (Man is a rational animal, because he is an orational animal), and he makes every effort in order to eliminate language as something unattainable by the animal, as something peculiar to man and beast. In every book on Logic, language is quoted as the specific difference between man and all other beings. Thus we read in Stuart Mill's *Logic*:[16] 'The attribute of being capable of understanding a language is a *proprium* of the species man, since, without being connoted by the word, it follows from an attribute which the word does connote, viz. from the attribute of rationality.'

It is curious to observe how even Mr. Darwin seems, in some places, fully prepared to admit this. Thus he says in one passage,[17] 'Articulate language *is* peculiar to man.' In former days we could not have wished for a fuller admission, for *peculiar* then meant the same as *special*, something that constitutes a species, or something which belongs to a person in exclusion of others. But in a philosophy which looks upon all living beings as developed from four or five primordial cells, there can, in strict logic, exist four or five really and truly

---

[15] *Descent*, i. p. 185.
[16] Vol. i. p. 180.
[17] I. p. 54.

peculiar characters only, and therefore it is clear that peculiar, when used by Mr. Darwin, cannot mean what it would have meant if employed by others.

As if to soften the admission which he had made as to articulate language being peculiar to man, Mr. Darwin continues: 'But man uses, in common with the lower animals, inarticulate cries to express his meaning, aided by gestures, and the movements of the muscles of the face.' No one would deny this. There are many things besides, which man shares in common with animals. In fact, the discovery that man is an animal was not made yesterday, and no one seemed to be disturbed by that discovery. Man, however, was formerly called a *'rational animal,'* and the question is, whether he possesses anything peculiar to himself, or whether he represents only the highest form of perfection to which an animal, under favourable circumstances, may attain. Mr. Darwin dwells more fully on the same point, viz. on that kind of language which man shares in common with animals, when he says, 'This holds good, especially with the more simple and vivid feelings, which are but little connected with out higher intelligence. Our cries of pain, fear, surprise, anger, together with their appropriate actions, and the murmer of a mother to her beloved child, are more expressive than any words.'

No doubt they are. A tear is more expressive than a sigh, a sigh is more expressive than a speech, and silence itself is sometimes more eloquent than words. But all this is not language, in the true sense of the word.

Mr. Darwin himself feels, evidently, that he has not said all; he struggles manfully with the difficulties before him; nay, he really represents the case against himself as strongly as possible. 'It is not the mere power of articulation,' he continues, 'that distinguishes man from other animals, for, as everyone knows, parrots can talk; but it is his large power of connecting *definite sounds with definite ideas.*'

Here, then, we might again imagine that Mr. Darwin admitted all we want, viz. that some kind of language is peculiar to man, and distinguishes man from other animals; that, supposing man to be, up to a certain point, no more than an animal, he perceived that what made man to differ from all other animals was something nowhere to be found except in man, nowhere indicated even in the whole series of living beings, beginning with the *Bathybius Haeckelii*, and ending with the tailless ape. But, no; there follows immediately after, the finishing sentence, extorted rather, it seems to me, than naturally flowing from his pen, 'This obviously depends on the development of the mental faculties.'

What can be the meaning of this sentence? If it refers to the mental faculties of man, then no doubt it may be said to be obvious. But if it is meant to refer to the mental faculties of the gorilla, then, whether it be true or not, it is, at all events, so far from being obvious, that the very opposite might be called so – I mean the fact that no development of mental faculties has ever enabled one single animal to connect one single definite idea with one single definite word.

I confess that after reading again and again what Mr. Darwin has written on the subject of language; I cannot understand how he could bring himself to sum up the subject as follows: 'We have seen that the faculty of articulate speech in itself does not offer any insuperable objection to the belief that man has been developed from some lower animal' (p. 62).

Now the fact is that not a single instance has ever been adduced of any animal trying or learning to speak, nor has it been explained by any scholar or philosopher how that barrier of language, which divides man from all animals, might be effectually crossed. I do not mean to say that there are no arguments which might be urged, either in favour of animals possessing the gift of language, but preferring not to use it,[18] or as tending to show that living beings, to use the words of Demokritos, speak naturally, and in the same manner in which they cough, sneeze, bellow, bark, or sigh. But Mr. Darwin has never told us what he thinks on this point. He refers to certain writers on the origin of language, who consider that the first materials of language are either interjections or imitations; but their writings in no wise support the theory that animals also could, either out of their own barkings and bellowings, or out of the imitative sounds of mocking-birds, have elaborated anything like what we mean by language, even among the lowest savages.

It may be in the recollection of some of my hearers that, in my Lectures on the Science of Language, when speaking of Demokritos and some of his later followers, I called his theory on the origin of language the *Bow-wow* theory, because I felt

---

[18] See Wundt, *Menschen- und Thierseele*, vol. ii. p. 265.

certain that, if this theory were only called by its right name, it would require no further refutation. It might have seemed for a time, to judge from the protests that were raised against that name, as if there had been in the nineteenth century scholars holding this Demokritean theory in all its crudity. But it required but very little mutual explanation before these scholars perceived that there was between them and me but little difference, and that all which the followers of Bopp insist on as a *sine quâ non* of scholarship is the admission of roots, definite in their form, from which to derive, according to strict phonetic laws, every word that admits of etymological analysis, whether in English and Sanskrit, or in Arabic and Hebrew, or in Mongolian and Finnish. For philological purposes it matters little, as I said in 1866, what opinion we hold on the origin of roots so long as we agree that, with the exception of a number of purely mimetic expressions, all words, such as we find them, whether in English or in Sanskrit, encumbered with prefixes and suffixes, and mouldering away under the action of phonetic decay, must, in the last instance, be traced back, by means of definite phonetic laws, to those definite primary forms which we are accustomed to call roots. These roots stand like barriers between the chaos and the kosmos of human speech. Whoever admits the historical character of roots, whatever opinion he may hold on their origin, is not a Demokritean, does not hold that theory which I called the Bow-wow theory, and cannot be quoted in support of Mr. Darwin's opinion that the cries of animals represent the earliest stage of the language of man.

If we speak simply of the materials, not of the elements, of language – and the distinction between these two words is but too often overlooked – then, no doubt, we may not only say that the phonetic materials of the cries of animals and the languages of man are the same, but, following in the footsteps of evolutionist philosophers, we might trace the involuntary exclamations of men back to the inanimate and inorganic world. I quoted formerly the opinion of Professor Heyse, who appealed to the fact that most substances, when struck or otherwise set in motion, show a power of reaction manifested by their various rings, as throwing light on the problem of the origin of language; and I do not think that those who look upon philosophy as a 'knowledge of the highest generalities' should have treated Professor Heyse with so much contempt.

But neither those who traced the material elements of language back to interjections and imitations, nor those who went farther and traced them back to the ring inherent in all vibrating substances, ought to have imagined for one moment that they had thus accounted for the real elements of language. We may account for the materials of many things, without thereby accounting for what they are, or how they came to be what they are. If we take, for instance, a number of flints more or less carefully chipped and shaped and sharpened, and if we were to say that these flints are like other flints found by thousands in fields and quarries, this would be as true as that the materials for forming the words of our language are the same as the cries of animals, or, it may be, the sounds of bells. But would this explain the problem which we wish to explain? Certainly not. If, then, we were to go a step farther, and say that apes had been seen to use flints for throwing at each other,[19] that they could not but have discovered that sharp-edged flints were the most effective, and would therefore have either made a natural selection of them, or tried to imitate them – that is to say, to give to other flints a sharp edge – what would antiquaries say to such heresies? And yet I can assure them that to say that no traces of human workmanship can be discovered in these flints,[20] that they in no wise prove the early existence of man, or that there is no insuperable objection to the belief that these flints were made by apes, cannot sound half so incongruous to them, as to a man who knows what language is made of being told that the first grammatical edge might have been imparted to our words by some lower animals, or that, the materials of language being given, everything else, from the neighing of a horse to the lyric poetry of Goethe, was a mere question of development.

It would not be fair, however, to disguise the fact that in his view that animals possess language, Mr. Darwin has some very powerful allies, and that in quarters where he would least expect to find them. Archbishop Whately writes: 'Man is not the only animal that can make use of language to express what is passing in his mind, and can understand more or less what is so expressed by others.'

But even with bishops and archbishops against me, I do not despair. I believe I have as high an opinion of the faculties of

---

[19] 'The Pavians in Eastern Africa.' See Caspari, *Urgeschichte*, i. p. 244.
[20] See *Whitley's Researches on Flints near Spiennes, in Belgium.*

animals as Mr. Darwin, Archbishop Whately, or any other man – nay, I may perhaps claim some credit for myself for having, in my Lectures delivered in 1862, vindicated for the higher animals more than ever was vindicated for them before.

But after reading the most eloquent eulogies on the intellectual powers and social virtues of animals – of which we have had a great deal of late – I always feel that all this and even much more might be perfectly true, and that it would yet in no way affect the relative position of man and beast.

Let us hear the most recent panegyrist: 'To become man! Who should believe that so many, not only laymen, but students of nature, believe in God becoming man, but consider it incredible that an animal should become man, and that there should be a progressive development from the ape to man? The ancient world, and even now the highest among the Eastern nations, thought and think very differently on this point. The doctrine of metampsychosis connects man and beast, and binds the whole world together by a mysterious cord. Judaism alone, with its hatred of nature deities, and dualistic Christianity, have made this rift between man and beast. It is remarkable how in our own time and among the most civilised nations a deeper sympathy of the animal world has been roused, and has manifested itself in the formation of societies for preventing cruelty towards animals, thus showing that what, on one side, is the result of scientific research, viz. the surrendering of the exclusive position of man in nature, as a spiritual being, is received at the same time as a general sentiment.

'Public opinion, however, and what I may call the old orthodox natural science, persist nevertheless in considering man and beast as two separate worlds which no bridge can ever connect, were it only because man is man in so far only as he from the beginning possesses something which the beast has not and never will have. According to the Mosaic account, God created the beasts, as it were, in a lump; but in the case of man. He first formed his body of the dust of the ground and breathed into his nostrils the breath of life, and man became a living soul. This living soul of the old Jewish writers has afterwards been changed by Christianity into an immortal soul, a being different in kind and dignity from such other common souls as might be allowed to beasts. Or, the soul of man and beast being admitted to be the same, man was endowed in addition with a spirit, as the substantial principle of the higher intellectual and moral faculties by which he is distinguished from the beast.

'Against all this,' the writer continues, 'we have now the fact of natural sciences which can no longer be ignored, viz. that the faculties of beasts differ from those of man in degree only, and not in kind. Voltaire said truly, "Animals have sensation, imagination, memory, also desires and movements, and yet no one thinks of claiming for them an immaterial soul. Why should we, for our small surplus of these faculties and acts, require such a soul?" Now the surplus on the side of man is not indeed so small as Voltaire's rhetoric represents it; on the contrary, it is enormous. But for all that, it is a *plus* only, it is not something new. Even with animals of the lower orders it would take volumes, as Darwin says, to describe the habits and mental powers of an ant. The same with bees. Nay, it is remarkable that the more closely an observer watches the life and work of any class of animals, the more he feels inclined to speak of their understanding. The stories about the memory, the reflection, the faculties of learning and culture in dogs, horses, and elephants are infinite; and even in so-called wild animals similar qualities may be detected. Brehm, speaking of birds of prey, says: "They act after having reflected; they make plans and carry them out." The same writer says of thrushes: "They perceive quickly and judge correctly; they use all means and ways to protect themselves." Those varieties which have grown up in the quiet and undisturbed forests of the North are easily taken in; but experience soon makes them wise, and those who have once been deceived are not easily cheated a second time (therein they certainly differ from man). Even among men, whom they never trust completely, they know well how to distinguish between the dangerous and the harmless; they allow the shepherd to approach more nearly than the hunter. In the same sense Darwin speaks of the incredible degree of acuteness, caution, and cleverness on the part of the furry animals of North America, as being chiefly due to the constant snares and wiles of the hunter.

'Mr. Darwin tries particularly to show in the higher animals the beginnings of moral sentiments also, which he connects with their social instincts. A kind of sense of honour and of conscience can hardly fail to be recognised in nobler and well-bred horses and dogs. And even if the conscience of dogs has not unjustly been traced back to the stick, it may well be asked whether the case is very different with the lower classes of man. Those instincts in animals which refer to the education of their young, to the care, trouble, and sacrifices on their behalf, must be considered as the first germs of higher moral faculties. Here, as Goethe says, we see indicated in the animal the bud of what in man becomes a blossom.'

So far the panegyrist; in reply to whom I can only say that, without doubting any of the extraordinary accounts of the intellect, the understanding, the caution, the judgement, the sagacity, acuteness, cleverness, genius, or even the social virtues of animals, the rules of positive philosophy forbid us to assert anything about their instincts or intellectual faculties. We may allow ourselves to be guided by our own fancies or by analogy, and we may guess and assert very plausibly many things about the inner life of animals; but however strong our own belief may be, the whole subject is transcendent, i.e. beyond the reach of positive knowledge. We all admit that, in many respects, the animal is even superior to man. Who is there but at one time or other has not sighed for the wings of birds? Who can deny that the muscles of the lion are more powerful, those of the cat more pliant, than ours? Who can doubt that the eagle possesses a keener vision, the deer a sharper hearing, the dog a better scent than man? Who has not sometimes envied the bear his fur, or the snail its house? Nay, I am quite prepared to go even farther, and if metaphysicians were to tell me that our senses only serve to distract the natural intuitions of the soul, that our organs of sense are weak, deceptive, limited, and that a mollusc, being able to digest without a stomach and to live without a brain, is a more perfect, certainly a more happy, being than man, I should bow in silence; but I should still appeal to one palpable fact – viz. that whatever animals may do or not do, *no animal has ever spoken.*

I use this expression advisedly, because as soon as we speak of language, we open the door to all kinds of metaphor and poetry. If we want to reason correctly, we must define what we mean by language. Now there are two totally distinct operations which in ordinary parlance go by the same name of language, but which should be distinguished most carefully as *Emotional* and *Rational* language. The power of showing by outward signs what we feel, or, it may be, what we think, is the source of emotional language, and the recognition of such emotional signs, or the understanding of their purport, is no more than the result of memory, a resuscitation of painful or pleasant impressions connected with such signs. *That* emotional language is certainly shared in common by man and animals. If a dog barks, that may be a sign, according to circumstances, of his being angry or pleased or surprised. Every dog speaks that language, every dog understands it, and other animals too, such as cats or sheep, and even children, learn it. A cat that has once been frightened or bitten by a barking dog will easily understand the sound, and run away, like any other so-called rational being. The spitting of a cat, again, is a sign of anger, and a dog that has once had his eyes scratched by a cat would not be slow to understand that feline dialect, whenever he hears it in close proximity. The purring of a cat has a very different meaning, and it may be, as we have been told, like the murmuring of a mother to her beloved child. The subject of the emotional language of animals and man is endless, but we must leave it to the pen of the poet rather than of the philosopher.[21]

What, then, is the difference between *emotional* language and *rational* language? The very name shows the difference. Language, such as we speak, is founded on reason, reason meaning for philosophical purposes the faculty of forming and handling general concepts; and as that power manifests itself outwardly by articulate language only, we, as positive philosophers, have a right to say that animals, being devoid of the only tangible sign of reason which we know, viz. language, may by us be treated as irrational beings – irrational, not in the sense of devoid of observation, shrewdness, calculation, presence of mind, reasoning in the sense of weighing, or even genius, but simply in the sense of devoid of the power of forming and handling general concepts.

The distinction here made between emotional and rational language may seem fanciful and artificial to those who are not acquainted with the history and origin of language, but they have only to consult the worlds of modern physiologists and medical men to convince themselves that this distinction rests on what even they would admit to be a most solid basis. Dr. Hughlings Jackson, in some articles published in the *Medical Times and Gazette* for December 14 and 21, 1867, speaking of the disease of a particular part of the brain, says: 'This

---

[21] See Darwin, *Descent*, vol. i. pp. 53, 54.

disease may induce partial or complete defect of *intellectual* language, and not cause corresponding defect of *emotional* or *interjectional* language. The typical patient in this disease misuses words or cannot use words at all, to express his thoughts; nor can he express his thoughts by writing, or by any signs sufficiently elaborate to serve instead of vocal or written words; nor can he read books for himself. But he can smile, laugh, cry, sing, and employ rudimentary signs of gesticulation. So far as these means of communication serve, therefore, he is able to exhibit his feelings to those around him. He can copy writing placed before him, and, even without the aid of a copy, sign his own name. He understands what is said to him, is capable of being interested in books which are read to him, and remembers incidents and tales. Sometimes he is able to utter a word or words, which he cannot vary, and which he must utter if he speak at all, no matter on what occasion. When excited, he can swear, and even use elaborate formulæ of swearing[22] (as, for example, "God bless my life"), which have come by habit to be of only interjectional value.[23] But he cannot repeat such words and phrases at his own wish or at the desire of others. And as he is able to copy writing, so he can, when circumstances dictate, as it were, to him, give utterance to phrases of more special applicability. Thus, a child being in danger of falling, one speechless patient, a woman, was surprised into exclaiming, "Take care." But in this, as in every other case, the patient remains perfectly incompetent to repeat at pleasure the phrase he has just used so appropriately, and has so distinctly uttered . . . It would seem that the part of the brain affected in such cases is that which is susceptible of education to language, and which has been after the birth of the patient so educated. The effect of the disease, in relation to speech, is to leave the patient as if he had never been educated at all to language, and had been born without the power of being so educated. The disease in question is an affection of but one side, the left side, of the brain.' And again: 'Disease of a particular region of the left cerebral hemisphere is followed by a complete or partial loss of power in the *naming* process, and by consequent inability to speak, even

---

[22] Dr. Gairdner, *The Function of Articulate Speech*, 1866, p. 17.
[23] In another paper Dr. Jackson describes an oath extremely well as 'a phrase which emotion has filched from the intellect.'

when all the machinery of voice and articulation recognised in anatomy remains unchanged.'

The whole of this subject has of late been very fully examined, as may be seen in Dr. Bateman's book on Aphasia; and though one may feel doubtful as to the minute conclusions which Dr. Broca has drawn from his experiments, so much seems to be established: If a certain portion of the brain on the left side of the anterior lobe happens to be affected by disease, the patient becomes unable to use rational language; while, unless some other mental disease is added to aphasia, he retains the faculty of emotional language, and of communicating with others by means of signs and gestures.

In saying this, I shall not be suspected, I hope, of admitting that the brain, or any part of the brain, secretes rational language, as the liver secretes bile. My only object in referring to these medical observations and experiments was to show that the distinction between emotional and rational language is not artificial, or of a purely logical character, but is confirmed by the palpable evidence of the brain in its pathological affections. No man of any philosophic culture will look on the brain, or that portion of the brain which interferes with rational language, as the seat of the faculty of speech, as little as we place the faculty of seeing in the eye, or the faculty of hearing in the ear. That without which anything is impossible is not necessarily that by which it is possible. We cannot see without the eye, nor hear without the ear; perhaps we might say, we cannot speak without the third convolution of the left anterior lobe of the brain; but neither can the eye see without us, the ear hear without us, the third convolution of the left anterior lobe of the brain speak without us. To look for the faculty of speech in the brain would, in fact, be hardly less Homeric than to look for the soul in the midriff.

This distinction between *emotional* and *rational* language, is, however, of great importance, because it enables us to see clearly in what sense man and beast may be said to share the gift of language in common, and in what sense it would be wrong to say so. Interjections, for instance, which constitute a far more important element in conversation than in literary composition, are emotional language, and they are used by beasts as well as by men, particularly by a man in a passion, or on a low scale of civilisation. But there is no language, even among the lowest savages, in which the vast majority of words is not rational. If, therefore, Mr. Darwin (p. 35) says that there are savages who have no *abstract* terms in their language, he has evidently overlooked the real different between rational and emotional language. We do not mean by rational language, a language possessing such abstract terms as whiteness, goodness, to have or to be; but any language in which even the most concrete of words are founded on general concepts, and derived from roots expressive of general ideas.

There is in every language a certain layer of words which may be called purely *emotional*. It is smaller or larger according to the genius and history of each nation, but it is never quite concealed by the alter strata of rational speech. Most interjections, many imitative words, belong to this class. They are perfectly clear in their character and origin, and it could never be maintained that they rest on general concepts. But if we deduct that inorganic stratum, all the rest of language, whether among ourselves or among the lowest barbarians, can be traced back to *roots*, and every one of these roots is the sign of a general concept. This is the most important discovery of the Science of Language.

Take any word you like, trace it back historically to its most primitive form, and you will find that besides the derivative elements, which can easily be separated, it contains a predicative root, and that in this predicative root rests the connotative power of the word. Why is a *stable* called a *stable*? Because it stands. Why is a *saddle* called a *saddle*? Because you sit in it. Why is a *road* called a *road*? Because we ride on it. Why is *heaven* called *heaven*? Because it is heaved on high. In this manner every word, not excluding the commonest terms that must occur in every language, the names for *father, mother, brother, sister, hand* and *foot*, &c., have been traced back historically to definite roots, and every one of these roots expresses a *general concept*. Unless, therefore, Mr. Darwin is prepared to maintain that there are languages which have no names for *father* and *mother*, for *heaven* and *earth*, or only such words for those objects as cannot be derived from predicative roots, his statement that there are languages without abstract terms falls to the ground. Every root is an abstract term, and these roots, in their historical reality, mark a period in the history of the human mind – they mark the beginning of rational speech.

What I wish to put before you as clearly as possible is this, that roots such as *dā*, to give, *sthā*, to stand, *gā*, to sing, the ancestors of an unnumbered progeny, differ from interjectional or imitative sounds in exactly the same manner as general concepts differ from single impressions. Those, therefore, who still think with Hume that general ideas are the same thing as single impressions, only fainter, and who look upon this fainting away of single impressions into general ideas as something that requires no explanation, but can be disposed of by a metaphor, would probably take the same view with regard to the changes of cries and shrieks into roots. Those, on the contrary, who hold that general concepts, even in their lowest form, do not spring spontaneously from a *tabula rasa*, but recognise the admission of a co-operating Self, would look upon the roots of language as irrefragable proof of the presence of human workmanship in the very elements of language, as the earliest manifestation of human intellect, of which no trace has ever been discovered in the animal world.

It will be seen from these remarks that the controversy which has been carried on for more than two thousand years between those who ascribe to language an onomatopœic origin, and those who derive language from roots, has a much deeper significance than a mere question of scholarship. If the words of our language could be derived straight from imitative or interjectional sounds, such as *bow wow* or *pooh pooh*, then I should say that Hume was right against Kant, and that Mr. Darwin was right in representing the change of animal into human language as a mere question of time. If, on the contrary, it is a fact which no scholar would venture to deny, that, after deducting the purely onomatopœic portion of the dictionary, the real bulk of our language is derived from roots, definite in their form and general in their meaning, then that period in the history of language which gave rise to these roots, and which I call the *Radical Period*, forms the frontier – be it broad or narrow – between man and beast.

That period may have been of slow growth, or it may have been an instantaneous evolution: we do not know. Like the beginnings of all things, the first beginnings of language and reason transcend the powers of the human understanding, nay, the limits of human imagination. But after the first step has been made, after the human mind, instead of being simply distracted by the impressions of the senses, has performed the first act of abstraction, were it only by making one and one to be two, everything else in the growth of language becomes as intelligible as the growth of the intellect; nay, more so. We still possess, we still use, the same materials of language which were first fixed and fashioned by the rational ancestors of our race. These roots, which are in reality our oldest title-deeds as rational beings, still supply the living sap of the millions of words scattered over the globe, while no trace of them, or anything corresponding to them, has ever been discovered even amongst the most advanced of catarrhine apes.

The problem that remains to be solved in our last Lecture is the origin of those roots.

THIRD LECTURE

Delivered at the Royal Institution, April 5, 1873

The problem which of late years has most deeply stirred the philosophic mind of Europe is the problem of creation. No doubt that problem is as old as the world, or at least as old as the first questionings of the human mind; and the solutions which it has received, both from poets and philosophers, are innumerable. Out of many solutions one, which best satisfies the enquiring intellect of the time, generally prevails. In ancient times one or the other solution has even been invested with a kind of sacred authority; and, as the subject is one on which real knowledge is impossible, it is hardly to be wondered at, that, with us too, the prevailing conception of creation should have continued, up to the nineteenth century, very much the same as what it was at the time of Moses.

Owing to the great development, however, of the study of nature in this century, and the wide diffusion of physical knowledge among all classes of society, the problem of creation has lately risen to the surface again. Now facts challenge new thoughts, and the mass of new facts, throwing light on the earliest history of the world, has become so large that we need not wonder if philosophers felt inspired with fresh courage, and by elaborating a new theory of creation, which should not outrage the convictions of men and science and friends of truth, tried to wrest a new province from the land of the Unknowable.

The approaches were made from three points. First of all, there were the ancient vestiges of creation discovered in the strata of the earth; secondly, there was the living history of creation to be studied in the minute stages of embryonic development; and thirdly, there was the comparative method of anatomy, laying bare essential coincidences in the structures of living beings, even of such as had never before displayed the slightest traces of relationship.

The zealous and successful pursuit of these three branches of physical study, now generally spoken of as *Palæontology, Embryology*[1], and *Comparative Anatomy*, has produced the same effect with regard to the problem of creation which our own linguistic studies have produced with regard to the problem of the origin of language and thought.

As long as the question of the origin of language was asked in a general and indefinite way, the answers were mostly as general and as unsatisfactory as the questions themselves. In fact, the rude question, How was human language made, or how did it arise? admitted of no scientific answer, and the best that could be said on the subject was, that, like the beginnings of all things, the beginning of language, too, transcends the powers of the human understanding. But, when what we may call palæontological studies had placed before us the earliest vestiges of human speech in the most ancient inscriptions and literatures of the world; when, secondly, a study of living languages had disclosed to us the minute stages of dialectic growth and phonetic decay, through which all languages are constantly passing in their passage from life to death and from death to life; and when, lastly, the comparative method had disclosed to us the essential coincidences in languages, the relationship of which had never been suspected before, then the question of the origin of language started up again, and called for a new and more definite answer.

The analogy between the researches carried on by the students of physical science and by the students of language goes still farther. Whatever the difference of opinion there may be between the different schools of physiologists, this one result seems to be permanently established, that the primary elements

---

[1] It is impossible to use Ontology in the sense of Embryology, for Ontology has its own technical meaning and to use it in a new sense would give rise to endless confusion.

of all living organisms are the simple *cells*, so that the problem of creation has assumed a new form, and has become the problem of the origin and nature of these cells.

The same in the Science of Language. The most important result which has been obtained by a truly scientific study of languages is this, that, after accounting for all that is purely formal as the result of juxtaposition, agglutination, and inflection, there remain in the end certain simple elements of human speech – phonetic *cells* – commonly called roots. In place, therefore, of the old question of the origin of language, we have here, too, to deal with the new question of the origin of roots.

Here, however, the analogy between the two sciences, in their solution of the highest problems, comes to an end. There are, indeed, two schools of physiologists, the *polygenetic* and the *monogenetic*, the former admitting from the beginning a variety of primitive cells, the latter postulating but one cell, as the source of all being. But it is clear, that the monogenetic school is becoming more and more powerful. Mr. Darwin, as we saw, was satisfied with admitting four or five beginnings for plants, and the same number for animals. But his position has become almost untenable, and his most ardent disciple, Professor Haeckel, treats his master's hesitation on this point with ill-disguised contempt. One little cell is all that he wants to explain the Universe, and he boldly claims for his primordial Moneres, the ancestor of plants and animals and men, a self-generating power, the so-called *generatio spontanea* or *æquivoca*.

Professor Haeckel is very anxious to convince his readers that the difference between these two schools, the *monogenetic* and *polygenetic*, is of small importance. The differences, he says, between the various Moneres, whose bodies consist of simple matter without form or structure, and which are in fact no more than a combination of carbon in the form of white of eggs, are of a chemical nature only; and the differences of mixture in the endless varieties of combination of white of eggs are so fine as to be, for the present, beyond the powers of human perception.[2] But if this is so, surely the rule of all scientific research would be, that we should wait before definitely deciding in favour of *one* primordial cell, and thus creating new trammels in the progress of free enquiries. What-

---

[2] Haeckel, *Vorlesungen*, p. 372.

ever the physiologist may say to the contrary, it does make a very great difference to the philosopher, whether the beginning of organic life has happened once, or may be supposed to have happened repeatedly; and though I do not grudge to the *Bathybios* of Haeckel the dignity of a new Adam, I cannot help feeling that in this small speck of slime, dredged up from the bottom of the Atlantic Ocean, there is too much left of the old Adam, too much of what I call mythology, too much of human ignorance, concealed under the veil of positive knowledge.

The students of language have given to the problem of the origin of language a far more exact and scientific form. As long as they deal with what may be called the Biology of language, as long as they simply wish to explain the actual phenomena of spoken dialects all over the world, they are satisfied with treating the variety of living cells, or the significant roots of language, as ultimate facts. These roots are what remains in the crucible after the most careful analysis of human language, and there is nothing to lead us on to search for one primordial root, or for a small number of uniform roots, except the mediæval idea that Nature loves simplicity. There was a time when scholars imagined they could derive a language from nine roots, or even from one; but these attempts were purely ephemeral.[3] At present we know that, though the number of roots is unlimited, the number of those which remain as the actual feeders of each single language amounts to about one thousand.

Some of these roots are no doubt, secondary and tertiary formulations, and may be reduced to a smaller number of primary forms. But here, too, philological research seems to me to show far more deference to the commandments of true philosophy than the prevalent physiological speculations. While the leading physiologists are striving to reduce all variety to uniformity, the student of language, in his treatment of roots, distinguishes where, to all outward appearance, there is no perceptible difference whatsoever. If in the same language, or in the same cluster of languages, there are roots of exactly the same sound, but different in their later development, a separate existence and an independent origin are allowed to each. There is, for instance, in the Aryan family, the well-

---

[3] *Lectures on the Science of Language*, I. p. 44.

known root DA. From it we have Sk. dádāmi, I give; Greek δίδωμι; Lat. *do*; Slavonic, da-mǐ; Lithuanian, dŭ-mi;[4] and an endless variety of derivatives, such as *donum*, a gift; French, *donner*, to give, *pardonner*, to forgive; Latin, *trado*, to give over; Greek, προδίδωμι, to surrender; then Italian, *tradire*; French, *trahir*, *trahison*; English, treason; Latin, *reddo*, to give back; the French, *rendre*, with all its derivatives, extending as far as *rente* and *rentier*. Another derivative of DA, to give, is *dōs, dōtis*, a giver, in which sense it occurs at the end of *sacerdos*; and *dōs, dōtis*, what is given to the bride, the English *dower* (the French *douaire*), which comes from the French *douer*, dotare, to endow; a *dowager* being a widow possessed of a dowry.

I might go on for hours before I could exhaust the list of words derived from this one root, DA, to give. But what I wish to show you is this, that by the side of this root DA there is another root DA, exactly the same in all outward appearance, consisting of D + Ā, and yet totally distinct from the former. While from the former we have, in Sanskrit, *dā'–tram*, a gift, we have from the latter *dā'-tram*, a sickle. The meaning of the second root is to cut, to carve; from it Greek δαίω, and δαίομαι, δαιτρός, a man who carves. The accent remains, in Sanskrit, on the radical syllable in *dā'-tram*, i.e. the cutting (active); whilst it leaves the radical syllable in *dātrám*, i.e. what is given (passive).

There are still other roots, in outward appearance identical with these two, yet totally distinct in their potential character; meaning, neither to give, nor to cut, but to bind (for instance, in διάδημα diadem, what is bound through the hair; δέμα, a band or bundle, κρή–δεμνον (κράς, δέμα) head-dress; and another, meaning to teach, and to know, preserved in διδάσκω, Aor. Pass, ἐ-δά–ην, &c.

We have the root GAR, meaning to swallow, which yields us the Sanskrit *girati*, he swallows, the Greek βιβρώ-σκει, the Latin *rorat*. We have, secondly, a root GAR, meaning to make a noise, to call, which yields us gar-ate in Sanskrit, γαργαρίζειν, βαρβαρίζειν, and βορβορύζειν in Greek, and both *garrire* and *gingrire* in Latin. It is conceivable that these two roots may have been originally one and the same, and that GAR from meaning to swallow may have come to mean the indistinct

---

[4] Pott, *Etymologische Forschungen*, 2nd edit. 1867, p. 105.

and disagreeable noise which even now is called swallowing the letters, in Sanskrit *grāsa*, in German *Verschlucken*. But a third root GAR meaning to wake, the Greek ἐγείρω, perf. γρήγορα, can hardly be traced back to the same source, but has a right to be treated as a legitimate and independent companion of the other root GAR.

Many more instances might be given, more than sufficient to establish the principle, that even in the same language two or more roots may be discovered, identical in all outward appearance, yet totally different from each other in meaning and origin.

Then why, it may be asked, do students of language distinguish, where students of nature do not? Why are physiologists so anxious to establish the existence of cells, uniform from their beginning, yet – I quote from Professor Haeckel – capable of producing by the process of monogony, gemmation, polysporogony, and amphigony?[5] Students of language, too, might say, like the physiologists, that, in such cases as the root DĀ, 'the difference of mixture in the endless varieties of consonants and vowels are so fine as to be, for the present at least, beyond the powers of human perception.' If they do not follow that Siren voice, it is because they hold to a fundamental principle of reasoning, which the evolutionist philosopher abhors, viz., that if two things, be they roots or cells or anything else, which appear to be alike, become different by evolution, their difference need not always be due to outward circumstances (commonly called environment), but may be due to latent dispositions which, in their undeveloped form, are beyond the powers of human perception. If two roots of exactly the same sound produce two totally distinct families of words, we conclude that, though outwardly alike, they are different roots. And if we applied this reasoning to living germs, we should say that, if two germs, though apparently alike, grow, under all circumstances, the one always into a ape, and never beyond, the other always into a man, and never below, then the two germs, though indistinguishable at first, and though following for a time the same line of embryonic development, are different from the beginning, whatever their beginning may have been.

[5] Haeckel, *Natürliche Schöpfungsgeschichte*, achte Vorlesung; Strauss, *Alter und Neuer Glaube*, p. 169.

There is another point of difference between the treatment of cells by physiologists, and the treatment of roots by philologists, which requires careful attention. The physiologist is not satisfied with the admission of his uniform cells, but, by subjecting these organic bodies to a new chemical analysis, he arrives in the end at the ordinary chemical substances (the πρῶτα στοιχεῖα of nature), and looks upon these, not simply as ruins, or as the residue of a violent dissolution, but as the elements out of which everything that exists, whether lifeless or living, was really built up. He maintains, in fact, the possibility of inorganic substances combining, under favourable circumstances, so as to form organic substances, and he sees in the lowest Moneres the living proof of an independent beginning of life.[6]

In the Science of Language we abstain from such experiments, and we do so on principle. We do not expect to discover the origin of living roots by dissolving them into their inorganic or purely phonetic elements; for, although every root may be reduced to at least one consonant and one vowel, these consonants and vowels are simply the *materials*, but not the *elements* of language; they have, in fact, no real independent existence, they are nothing but the invention of grammarians, and their combination would only give rise to meaningless sounds, never the significant roots. While the physiologist still entertains a lingering hope that, with the progress of chemical science, it may be possible to produce a living cell out of given materials, *we know* that roots are simple, that they cannot and should not be decomposed, and that consonants and vowels are lifeless and meaningless materials, out of which no real root ever arose, and out of which certainly, nothing like a root can ever be reconstructed. The root DA, for instance, means, as we saw, to give; dissolve it into D and A, and you have meaningless slag and scum. Recompose D and A, and you

---

[6] A further distinction is made between *Autogony* and *Plasmogony*. The former is the generation of the most simple organic individuals from an inorganic formative fluid, a fluid which contains the requisite elements for the composition of an organism, dissolved in simple and firm combinations, e.g. carbonic acid, ammoniac, binary salts, &c. The latter is the generation of an organism from an organic formative fluid, a fluid which contains the requisite elements dissolved in complicated and loose combination of compounds of carbon, e.g, whites of eggs, fat, &c. (Haeckel, *Vorlesungen*, p. 302.)

have indeed the same sound, but its life and meaning are gone, and no language could, by its own free choice, accept such an artificial compound into its grammar or dictionary.

Such are some of the coincidences and some of the differences between Biology and Philology in their attempts to solve the problems of the origin of life and the origin of language; and the question does now arise, Are we, in the Science of Language, driven to admit that roots, because they yield to no further analysis, are therefore to be accepted as unintelligible in their origin, as miraculously implanted in man, but not in animals; or may we hope to be able to go beyond this limit, and discover something which, while it makes the origin of roots perfectly intelligible in man, explains to us, at the same time, why they should never have arisen in any other animal?

Now I say, without hesitation, that roots, though they must be accepted as ultimate facts in the Science of Language, are not ultimate facts in the Science of Thought. The scholar naturally shrinks from a subject which does not directly concern him, and which, according to its very nature, does not admit of that exact treatment to which he is accustomed; but the philosopher must accept facts as they are, and his interests are with the Chaos as well as with the Kosmos. As the medical man, who has to study the marvellously arranged net-work of the nerves, shrinks instinctively from hypothetical explanations of the first formation of nervous channels, and centres, and ganglia, and plexus, the scholar, too, is frightened by the chaotic proceedings which are inevitable when we come to ask, how roots came to be what they are. But to those who are ready to deal with hypothetical manner, there is nothing mysterious or irrational in the origin of roots. Only let us not forget that roots are not merely sounds, but sounds full of meaning. To take the roots *gā*, to sing, *dā*, to give, *vā*, to blow, and to ask why the three different consonants, g, d, v, should produce such difference of meaning, is absurd, and can never lead to any results. Those consonants, though, when we learn our A B C, they look so very real, are nothing by themselves; they can, therefore, possess no meaning by themselves; or produce by themselves any effect whatsoever. All scholars, from Plato down to Humboldt, who imagine that they can discover certain meanings in certain consonants, have forgotten that neither consonants nor vowels are more than abstractions; and if there is any truth in their observations, as there undoubtedly is, we shall see that this must be explained in a different way. A root, on the contrary, is not, as is sometimes supposed, a mere abstraction or invention of grammarians. We have in many languages to discover them by analysis, no doubt; but no one who has ever disentangled a cluster of words can fail to see that, without granting to roots an independent, and really historical existence, the whole evolution of language would become an impossibility. There are languages, however, such as ancient Chinese, in which almost every word is still a root, and even in so modern a language as Sanskrit, there are still many words which, in outward appearance, are identical with roots.

As roots therefore have two sides, an outside, their sound, and an inside, their meaning, it is quite clear that we shall never arrive at a proper understanding of their nature, unless we pay as much attention to their soul as to their body. We must, before all things, have a clear insight into the mechanism of the human mind, if we want to understand the origin of roots; and by placing before you the simplest outline of the mind in the act of knowing, (without considering what concerns emotion and will), I believe I shall be able to lay bare the exact point where the origin of roots becomes, not only intelligible, but inevitable.

It is difficult, at the present moment, to speak of the human mind in any technical language whatsoever without being called to order by some philosopher or other. According to some, the mind is one and indivisible, and it is the subject-matter only of our consciousness which gives to the acts of the mind the different appearances of feeling, remembering, imagining, knowing, willing, or believing. According to others, mind, as a subject, has no existence whatever, and nothing ought to be spoken of except states of consciousness, some passive, some active, some mixed. I myself have been sharply taken to task for venturing to speak, in this enlightened nineteenth century of ours, of different faculties of the mind, faculties being merely imaginary creations, the illegitimate offspring of mediæval scholasticism.

Now I confess I am amused rather than frightened by such pedantry. Faculty, *facultas*, seems to me so good a word, that, if it did not exist, it ought to be invented, in order to express the different modes of action of what we may still be allowed to call our Mind. It does not commit us to more than if we were to speak of the *facilities* or *agilities* of the mind, and only those who change the forces of nature into gods or demons, would be frightened by the faculties, as green-eyed monsters seated in the dark recesses of our self. I shall, therefore, retain the name of faculty, in spite of its retrogressive appearance; and, in speaking of the act of knowing in the most general, and least technical language, I shall say, that the mind acts in two different ways, or, that its knowledge has two aspects; the one *sensuous* or *intuitional*, sometimes called *precentative*, the other, *rational* or *conceptual*, sometimes called *representative*. I do not mean that the two can be separated or cut asunder, as on a dissecting table, but only that they can be, and ought to be, distinguished.[7]

Although knowledge is impossible, whether for man or beast, without intuitions, the knowledge of man, as soon as he has left the stage of infancy, i.e. speechlessness, is never intuitional only, but always both intuitional and conceptual. Intuition is knowledge too, but it is not knowledge in the technically defined and restricted sense of the word. It is experience concerned with individual objects only, whether external, as supplied by sense, or internal, as supplied by emotion or volition.

True knowledge, even in its lowest form, always consists in the combination of an intuition and a concept. When I say, This is a dog, or, This is a tree, or This is anything else, I must have the concept of a dog or a tree to which I refer this or that intuition, this or that state of consciousness. These concepts are not intuitive. There is no word in the whole of our dictionary, with the exception of proper names, to which anything real or intuitional corresponds. No one ever saw a dog, or a tree; but only this or that dog, a Scotch terrier or a Newfoundland dog; a fire tree, or an oak tree, or an apple tree; and then again, but only a few parts of it, a little of the bark, a few leaves, an apple here and there; and all these again, not as they really are, but one side of them only. Tree, therefore, can never be seen or perceived by the senses, can never acquire phenomenal or intuitional form. We live in two worlds, the world of sight and the world of thought; and, strange as it may sound,

---

[7] Kant, *Prolegomena*, p. 60. 'Die Summe hiervon ist diese: die Sache der Sinne ist anzuschauen, die des Verstandes zu denken. Denken aber ist Vorstellungen in einem Bewusstsein vereinigen.'

nothing that we name, nothing that we find in our dictionary, can ever be seen, or heard, or perceived.

Now our concepts and our words are produced by a faculty, or by a mode of mental action, which is not simply a barrier between man and beast, but which creates a new world in which we live. If all animals were blind, and man alone possessed the faculty of seeing, that would not constitute a barrier between man and beast; it would simply be an increase of that intuitional knowledge which we share in common with the beast.

But the faculty of forming concepts is something, not simply beyond, but altogether beside the world of sense. Concepts are formed by what is called the faculty of abstraction, a very good word, as expressing the act of dissolving sensuous intuitions into their constituent parts, divesting each part of its momentary and purely intuitional character, and thus imparting to it that general capacity which enables is to gain general, conceptual, real knowledge.

There is, no doubt, considerable difference of opinion among psychologists as to the exact process by which concepts are formed; but, for the object which we here have in view, any theory, from Plato down to Hume, will be acceptable. What is important to us is to see clearly that, as long as we have intuitional knowledge only, as long as we only see, hear, or touch this or that, we cannot predicate, we cannot name, we cannot reason, in the true sense of the word. We can do many things intuitively; perhaps the best things we ever do are done intuitively, and as if by instinct; and for the development of animal instincts, for all the clever things that, we are told, animals do, intuitional knowledge is more important than conceptual knowledge. But, in order to say 'This is green,' we must have acquired the concept of green; we must possess what is generally called the idea of green, with its endless shades and varieties; we must, at least, to speak with Berkeley, 'have made the idea of an individual the representative of a class.' Thus only can we predicate green of any single object which pronounces in us, besides other impressions, that impression also which we have gathered up with many others in the concept and the name of 'green.'

The difference between intuitional and conceptional knowledge has been dwelt on by all philosophers; nor do I know of any philosopher of note who has claimed for animals the possession of conceptual knowledge. Even evolutionist philosophers, who admit no difference in kind whatsoever, and who therefore can look upon human reason as a development only of brute reason, seldom venture so far as to claim for animals the actual possession of conceptual knowledge.

Locke, who can certainly not be suspected of idealistic tendencies, says,[8] 'If it may be doubted whether beasts compound and enlarge their ideas that way to any degree, this, I think, I may be positive in, that the power of abstracting is not at all in them; and that the having of general ideas is that which puts a perfect distinction betwixt man and brutes, and is an excellency which the faculties of brutes do by no means attain to. For, it is evident, we observe no footsteps in them of making use of general signs for universal ideas; from which we have reason to imagine that they have not the faculty of abstracting or making general ideas, since they have no use of words or any other general signs.'

Few philosophers have studied animals so closely, and expressed their love for them so openly as Schopenhauer. 'Those,' he says, 'who deny understanding to the higher animals, can have very little themselves.' 'It is true,' he says, in another place, 'animals cannot speak and laugh. But the dog, the only real friend of man, has something analogous, – his own peculiar, expressive, good-natured, and thoroughly honest wagging of the tail. How far better is this natural greeting than the bows and scrapings and grinnings of men! How much does it surpass in sincerity, for the present at least, all other assurances of friendship and devotion? How could we endure the endless deceits, tricks and frauds of men, if there were not dogs into whose honest faces one may look without mistrust.'

The same philosopher assigns to animals both memory and imagination (*Phantasie*). He quotes the case of a puppy, unwilling to jump from a table, as a proof that the category of causality belongs to animals also. But he is too expert a philosopher to allow himself to be carried away by fanciful interpretations of doubtful appearances; and when he explains the formation of general notion as the peculiar work of reason, he states, without any hesitation or qualification, 'that it is this

---

[8] *Lectures on the Science of Language*, I. 405.

function which explains all those facts which distinguish the life of men from the life of animals.'[9]

I have said again and again that according to the strict rules of positive philosophy, we have no right either to assert or to deny anything with reference to the so-called mind of animals. But to those who think that philosophy may trust to anthropomorphic analogies, and that at least no counter arguments can be brought forward against their assertions that animals generalise, form concepts, and use them for the purpose of reasoning, exactly as we do, I may be allowed to propose at least two cases for explanation. They are selected out of a large mass of stories which have lately been collected in illustration of the animal intellect, and they possess at least this advantage, that they are both told by truly scientific observers.

The first is taken from Autenrieth, in his *Ansichten über Natur und Seelenleben*, published in 1836.

'The grub of the *Nachtphauenauge* spins, at the upper end of its case, a double roof of stiff bristles, held together at the end by very fine threads. This roof opens through a very light pressure from within, but offers a strong resistance to any pressure from without. If the grub acted according to judgment and reason, it would, according to human ideas, have had to consider as follows: – That it might possibly become a chrysalis, and be exposed to all sorts of accidents without any chance of escape, unless it took sufficient precautions; that it would rise from the chrysalis as a butterfly, without having the organs and power to break the covering which it had spun as a grub, or without being able, like other butterflies, to emit a liquid capable of dissolving silky threads; that, therefore, unless it had, while a grub, made preparations for an easy exit from its prison, it would suffer in it a premature death. While engaged in building such a prison the grub ought to have perceived clearly that, in order to escape hereafter as a butterfly, it would have to make a roof so constructed that it should protect from without, but open easily from within, and that this could be effected by means of stiff silky bristles, converging in the middle, but otherwise free. It would also have to know beforehand that, for that purpose, the same silky substance had to be used out of which the whole covering was built up, only with greater art. And yet it could not have been instructed in

[9] Frauenstädt, *Schopenhauer-Lexicon*, s.v. *Begriff*.

this by its parents, because they were dead before it escaped from its egg. Nor could it have learnt it by habit and experience, for it performs this work of art only once in its life; nor by imitation, for it does not live in society. Its understanding, too, could be but little cultivated during its grub-life, for it does nothing but creep about on the shrub on which it first saw the light, eat its leaves, cling to it with its feet, so as not to fall to the ground, and hide beneath a leaf, so as not to be wetted by the rain. To shake off by involuntary contortions its old skin, whenever it became uncomfortable, was the whole of its life, the whole of its reasoning, before it began to spin its marvellous shroud.'

The other case is an experiment very ingeniously contrived, with a view of discovering traces of generalisation in the ordinary habits of animals. The experiment was made by Mr. Amtsberg, of Stralsund, and described by Dr. Möbius, Professor of Zoology at Kiel.[10]

'A pike, who swallowed all small fishes which were put into his aquarium, was separated from them by a pane of glass, so that, whenever he tried to pounce on them, he struck his gills against the glass, and sometimes so violently that he remained lying on his back, like dead. He recovered, however, and repeated his onslaughts, till they became rarer and rarer, and at last, after three months, ceased altogether. After having been in solitary confinement for six months, the pane of glass was removed from the aquarium, so that the pike could again roam about freely among the other fishes. He at once swam towards them, but he never touched any one of them, but always halted at a respectful distance of about an inch, and was satisfied to share with the rest the meat that was thrown into the aquarium. He had therefore been trained so as not to attack the other fishes which he knew as inhabitants of the same tank. As soon, however, as a strange fish was thrown into the aquarium, the pike in nowise respected him, but swallowed him at once. After he had done this forty times, all the time respecting the old companions of his imprisonment, he had to be removed from the aquarium on account of his large size.'

'The training of this pike,' as Professor Möbius remarks, 'was not, therefore, based on judgment; it consisted only in

---

[10] *Schriften des Naturwissenschaftlichen Vereins für Schleswig-Holstein.* Separatabdruck. Kiel, 1873.

the establishment of a certain discretion of will, in consequence of uniformly recurrent sensuous impressions. The merciful treatment of the fishes which were familiar to him, or, as some would say, which he knew, shows only that the pike acted without reflection. Their view provoked in him, no doubt, the natural desire to swallow them, but it evoked at the same time the recollection of the pain which he had suffered on their account, and the sad impression that it was impossible to reach the prey which he had so much desired. These impressions acquired a greater power than his voracious instinct, and repressed it at least for a time. The same sensuous impression, proceeding from the same fishes, was always in his soul the beginning of the same series of psychic acts. He could not help repeating this series, like a machine, but like a machine with a soul, which has this advantage over mechanical machines, that it can adapt its work to unforeseen circumstances, while a mechanical machine can not. The pane of glass was to the organism of the pike one of these unforeseen circumstances.'

Truly scientific observations and experiments, like the two here mentioned, will serve at least to show how much can be achieved by purely intuitional knowledge, possessed in common by men and animals, and without the help of that conceptual knowledge which I regard as the exclusive property of man.

With us, every element of knowledge, even the simplest impression of the senses, has been so completely conceptualised, that it is almost impossible for us to imagine intuitional without conceptual knowledge. It is not always remarked that we men have almost entirely left the sphere of purely intuitional knowledge, and that the world in which we live and move and have our being is a world of concepts; a world which we have created ourselves, and which, without us, without the spectators in the theatre, would vanish into nothing.

What do we mean when we say we know a thing? A child which for the first time in his life sees an elephant, may stare at the huge beast, may fix his eyes on its trunk and tusks, may touch its skin, and walk round the monster so as to measure it from every side. While this is going on the child sees the beast, feels it, measures it; but we should never say the first time the child sees an elephant, that he knows it.

When the child sees the same elephant, or another elephant, a second time, and *re*cognises the animal as the same, or *nearly* the same which he saw before, then, for the first time, we say that the child knows the elephant. This is knowledge in its lowest and crudest form. It is no more than a connecting of a present with a past intuition or phantasm; it is, properly speaking, *remembering* only, and not yet *cognition*. The animal intellect, according to the ordinary interpretation, would go as far as this, but no farther.

But now let us take, not exactly a child, but a boy who for the first time sees an elephant. He, too, does not know the elephant, but he knows that what he sees for the first time, is an *animal*. What does that mean? It means that the boy possesses the concept of a living and breathing being, different from man, and that he recognises this general concept in the elephant before him. Here, too, cognition takes place by means of *re*cognition, but what is recognised is not connected with a former intuition, but with a concept, the concept of animal.[11]

Now, an animal, as such, has no actual existence. A boy may have seen dogs, cats, and mice, but never an animal in general. The concept of animal is therefore of man's own making, and its only object is to enable man to know.

But now let us make a further step, and instead of a child or a boy, take a young man who knows the elephant, not only as what he has seen in the Zoological Garden, not only as an animal, but scientifically, we call it, as a vertebrate. What is the difference between his knowledge and that of the boy? Simply this, that he has formed a new concept – that of the vertebrate – comprehending less than the concept of animal, but being more definite, more accurate, and therefore more useful for knowing one class of animals from another. These scientific concepts can be made narrower and narrower, more and more accurate and scientific, till at last, after having classes the elephant as a vertebrate, a mammal, a pachydermatous animal, and a proboscidate, we leave the purely physical metaphysical classification, and branching off into metaphysical language, call the elephant a living object, a material object, an objection general. In this, and in no other way, do we gain knowledge, whether scientific or unscientific; and if we should

---

[11] When the Romans first became acquainted with the elephant, they used the concept of *ox* for the conception of the new animal, and called it *Bos Luca*. In the same manner savage tribes, who had never seen horses, called horses large pigs.

ever meet with an intuition for which we have no concept whatsoever, not even that of material object, then that intuition would be inconceivable, and utterly unknowable; it would transcend the limits of our knowledge.[12] The whole of what we call the human intellect consists of these concepts, a kind of net for catching intuitional knowledge, which becomes larger and stronger with every draught that is brought to land. Wonderful as the human intellect may appear, when we look upon it as a whole, its nature is extremely simple. It separates and combines, it destroys and builds up, it throws together at haphazard or classifies with the minutest care, the materials it intermixes, or interlaces, or interlinks, that it was called the *Inter-lect*, softened into *Intellect*. The more concepts we possess, the larger is our knowledge; the more carefully we handle or interlink our concepts, the more closely do we reason; and the more freely we can tumble out the contents of these pigeon-holes, and throw them together, the more startling is our power of imagination.

We now come to the next point, How is this work of the human intellect, the forming and handling of concepts, carried on? Are concepts possible, or, at least, are concepts ever realised without some outward form or body? I say decidedly, No. If the Science of Language has proved anything, it has proved that conceptual or discursive thought can be carried on in words only. *There is no thought without words, as little as there are words without thought*. We can, by abstraction, distinguish between words and thought, as the Greeks did, when they spoke of inward ($\dot{\varepsilon}\nu\delta\iota\acute{\alpha}\theta\varepsilon\tau o\varsigma$) and outward ($\pi\rho o\phi o\rho\iota\kappa\acute{o}\varsigma$) Logos, but we can never separate the two without destroying both. If I may explain my meaning by a homely illustration, it is like peeling an orange. We can peel an orange, and put the skin on one side and the flesh on the other; and we can peel language, and put the words on one side and the thought or meanings on the other. But we never find in nature an orange without peel, nor peel without an orange; nor do we ever find in nature thought without words, or words without thought.

It is curious, however, to observe how determinately this conclusion has been resisted. It is considered humiliating that

---

[12] See the whole of this subject treated most excellently by Mr. Herbert Spencer, *First Principles*, p. 79.

what is most spiritual in us, our thoughts, should be dependent on such miserable crutches as words are supposed to be. But words are by no means such miserable crutches. They are the very limbs, aye, they are the very wings of thought. We do not complain that we cannot move without legs. Why then should we consider it humiliating that we cannot think without words?

The most ordinary objection to this view of thought and language is, that if thought were dependent on words, the deaf and dumb would be without conceptual thought altogether. But, according to those who have best studied this subject, it is perfectly true[13] that deaf and dumb persons, if left entirely to themselves, have no concepts, except such as can be expressed by less perfect symbols – and that it is only by being taught that they acquire some kind of conceptual thought and language. Were this otherwise, language, we, at all events, could know nothing of their concepts, except through some kind of language, intelligible both to them and to ourselves, while, according to the premiss, the deaf and dumb are supposed to be without language altogether.

Another and more powerful objection is, that the invention of language involves the previous existence of concepts, because we can only feel impelled to express what already exists in our mind. This objection, however, has been met by showing that in the usual sense of that word language was never invented, and that here, as in all other cases, though we may say that, logically, the function is the antecedent of the organ, yet in reality organ and function always presuppose each other, and cannot exist the one without the other.

A third objection is, that language, in the usual sense of the word, is not the only organ of conceptual thought. Now this is perfectly true, and has never been questioned. Besides the phonetic symbols of language, there are other less perfect symbols of thought, which are rightly called *ideographic*. We can form the concept of '*three*' without any spoken word, by simply holding up three fingers. In the same manner the hand might stand for *five*, both hands for *ten*, hands and feet for *twenty*. This is how people who possessed no organs of speech, would speak; this is how the deaf and dumb *do* speak.[14] Three

---

[13] *Lectures on the Science of Language*, II. 74, note.
[14] See some excellent remarks on gesture-language by Mr. E. B. Tylor, in the *Fortnightly Review*, 1866, p. 544.

fingers are as good as three strokes, three strokes are as good as three clicks of the tongue, three clicks of the tongue are as good as the sound *three*, or *trois*, or *drei*, or *shalosh* in Hebrew, or *san* in Chinese. But all these are signs; and being signs, symbols, or embodiments of concepts, they fall under the general category of *logos* or language. 'As a matter of necessity,' Professor Mansel remarked, 'men must think by symbols; as a matter of fact, they do think by language.'[15]

Nothing, however, seems of any avail to convince our opponents that they cannot do what they imagine they have been doing all their lives, viz., thinking silently, or without words. Some of the Polynesian savages would seen to have a far truer insight into the nature of thought, for their expression for thinking is 'speaking in the stomach.' But modern philosophers imagine they are wiser than these primitive savages; and in order to put an end to all controversy, they have had recourse even to the test of experiment. I shall try to describe these experiments as well as I can, and if my description seems incredible, it is certainly not my fault. As far as I can follow those who have tried the experiment, they begin by shutting their eyes and ears, and holding their breath. They then sink into unconsciousness, and when all is dark and still, they try their new art of ventriloquism, thinking thoughts without words. They begin with a very simple case. They want to conjure up the thought of a.... I must not say what, for it is to be a nameless thing, it is gulped down and ordered to vanish. However, in confidence, I may whisper that they want to conjure up the thought of a – *dog*.

Now the word dog is determinately suppressed; hound, cur, and all the rest, too, are ordered away. Then begins the work. 'Rise up, thou quadruped with ears and wagging tail!' But alas! the charm is already broken! Quadruped, ears, tail, wagging, all are words which cannot be admitted.

Silence is restored, and a new effort begins. This time there is to be nothing about quadruped, or animal, or hairy brute; the inner consciousness sinks lower, and at last there rises a being, to be developed gradually and insensibly into a dog. But, alas! 'being,' too, is a word, and as soon as it is whispered, all the potential dogs vanish into nothing.

[15] *North British Review*, 1850.

A last appeal, however, remains. No animal, no being, nothing is to be talked of; complete silence is restored; no breath is drawn. There is something coming near, the ghost appears, when suddenly he is greeted by the recognising self with Bow-wow! bow-wow! Then, at last, the effort is given up as hopeless, the eyes are opened, the ears unstopped, the breath is allowed to rise again, and as soon as the word dog is uttered, the ghost appears, the concept is there, we know what we mean, we think and say Dog. Let any one try to think without words, and, if he is honest, he will confess that the process which he goes through is somewhat like the one I have just tried to describe.

I believe that there would have been far less unwillingness to admit that conceptual thought is impossible without language, if people had not been frightened by the recollection of the old controversies between Nominalism and Realism. But the Science of Language has nothing to do with either Nominalism or Realism. It does not teach that concepts are nothing without words, and words nothing without concepts. If Condillac maintained that science is but a well-made language, he was right, but only because he assigned to language a much fuller meaning that it usually has. Again, when Horne Tooke said that the business of the mind extended no further than to receive impressions, that what are called its operations are merely the operations of language, he too was right, only that he used mind where we generally use sense, and language where we use λόγος or reason. I quoted on a former occasion[16] the words of Schelling and Hegel on the indivisibility of thought and language; I may add to-day the testimony of one who looked upon the philosophy of Schelling and Hegel as *verba præterquam nihil*, and who yet fully supports their view on this point.

'That language (verbal or other) is inseparable from thought, is rendered morally certain by the impossibility under which we all labour of forming universal symbols. The instant we advance beyond the perception of that which is present *now* and *here*, our knowledge can be only representative; as soon as we rise above the individual object, our representative sign must be arbitrary. The phantasms of imagination may have more or less resemblance to the objects of sense; but they bear that resemblance solely by virtue of being, like those objects

---

[16] *Lectures on the Science of Language*, II. p. 77.

themselves, individual. I may recall to mind, with more or less vividness, the features of an absent friend, as I may paint his portrait with more of less accuracy; but the likeness in neither case ceases to be the individual representation of an individual man. But my conception of a man in general can attain universality only by surrendering resemblance; it becomes the representative of all mankind only because it has no special likeness to any one man.'[17]

But this is not all. The Science of Language teaches us not only that there can be no concept without a word, but that every word of our language, (with the exception of purely interjectural and imitative words) is based on a concept.

Let us clear the ground a little before we proceed. We know,[18] first of all, that all words which express abstract ideas are borrowed from some material appearance. 'Right means straight; *wrong* means twisted. *Spirit* primarily means wind; *transgression*, the crossing of a line; *supercilious*, the raising of the eyebrow.'

We know that *anima* in Latin means the wind, the breath of living beings, life, and lastly soul. Sallust says, *Ingenii facinora, sicut anima, immortalia sunt*, the works of genius are immortal, like the soul. We may therefore say that in *anima*, the French *âme*, the original concept is breathing. But we have now to advance a step farther into that earlier stratum of language and thought where we want to find out, not only the original concept of *anima*, wind. Why was it, and how was it, that the wind was ever called *anima*? In fact, why has any word in Sanskrit, Greek and Latin, just that form and what we want to know if, as scholars, we speculate on the origin of language.

The answer which the Science of Language gives is this: Take any word you like in any language which has a past, and you will invariably find that it is based on a concept. The process of names-giving was, in fact, the first attempt at classification, very weak, very unscientific, no doubt, but for that very reason all the more interesting for watching the pre-historic growth of the human mind. Thus, in the old Aryan name for horse, Sansk, asva, equus, ἵππος, Old Saxon, *ehu*, we discover nothing like the neighing of a horse, but we discover the concept of

---

[17] *Letters, Lectures, and Reviews*, by H. L. Mansel, p. 8.
[18] See Emerson, *Complete Works*, Vol. II. p. 149.

quickness embodied in the root AK, to be sharp, to be quick, from which we have likewise the names for mental quickness, such as *acutus*. We therefore see here, not in theory, but by actual historical evidence, that the concept of quickness existed, *had been fully elaborated first*, and that through it the conceptual, as distinct from the purely intuitional knowledge of horse was realised. That name, the quick, might have been applied to many other animals too; but having been repeatedly applied to horses, it became for that very reason unfit for any other purpose. Serpents, for instance, are quick enough when they fall on their prey, but their name was formed from another concept, that of squeezing or throttling. They were called *ahi* in Sanskrit; ἔχις in Greek; *anguis* in Latin, all from a root AH, to squeeze; or *sarpa*, in Latin serpens, from a root SARP, to creep, to go.

The goose is called haṃsa-s in Sanskrit; gós (for gans) in Anglo-Saxon; 'ans-er (for ganser) in Latin. The root from which these words are derived was GHA, to open the mouth, to gape, modified to GHAN in χαίνω, and to GHANS. The Greek χήν, χηνός, comes from the same root in its simpler form GHAN. The goose was, therefore, originally conceived as the gaping, or hissing bird, and hence its name.

The wolf was called varka-s, from a root VARK, to tear, and the same word appears as the name of the wolf in Sanskrit as vrika-s; in Greek as Fλύκο-ς; in Latin as Lupus-s (vlupus); in Gothic as vulf-s.

The pig was called sus, ὕς; Old High-German, sū; Gothic, *svein*: all from a root SU, to beget; the sow being considered the most prolific of domestic animals. The Sanskrit sūkara-s, lit. the su-maker or grunter, is clearly a play of popular etymology.

By the same simple process, class after class of animals was separated from the crude mass of intuitional knowledge; birds, fishes, worms, trees and plants, stones and metals, were all distinguished by conceptual names, and man, too, received his proper name, either as the earth-born (homo), or as the dying creature (mortalis), or as the measurer and thinker (manus).

Birds were called in Sanskrit vi, plural, vayas; the Latin, avis; the Greek οἰ in οἰ-ωνός, lit. a large bird. The name meant probably at first no more than the movers, from the root VĪ, which also yielded vāyus-s, a name for the wind in Sanskrit and Zend;[19] but it soon answered the purpose of distinguishing the flying animals from all others. As other distinguishing qualities of birds came to be observed, they, too, found expression in language. Thus we have in Sanskrit pakshin, possessed of wings, from paksha, wing;[20] patrin, feathered, from patra-m, feather; patatrin, feathered, from patatra-m, feather; a*n*daga-s, egg-born or oviparous; khaga-s, sky-goer, &c. In Greek we have besides οἰωνός, ὄρνις, ὄρνιθος, it may be found from a root AR, to rise; πτηνόν, the flying animal. In Latin we find *volucris*, flying; *ales, alitis*, winged, &c.

For fish there is no name that could be claimed for the early Aryan period; and the names which occur in Sanskrit, Greek, and Latin, matsya, ἰχθύς, piscis, do not clearly reveal their predicative power.

The name for worm in Sanskrit is k*r*imi-s; in Lithuanian, *kirmi-s*, both of which can be derived from the root KRAM, to walk, to roam. The Latin vermis, and the Gothic vaurm-s, come probably from the same source, but the Greek ἕλμις must be derived from the root VAL, to twist.

In this manner, and in no other, our concepts and our names, our intellect and our language, were formed together. Some single feature was fixed upon as characteristic of an object, or of a class of objects, a root was there which expressed that feature, and by the addition of a pronominal base, a compound was formed, meaning originally whatever the roots expresses, substantiated in a certain place, predicated of a certain object. Thus the root *yudh*, to fight, comes to mean by the mere addition of a pronominal base, commonly called the termination of the nominative singular, the fight, the fighter, and the instrument of fighting. This ambiguity was afterwards removed by the introduction of so-called suffixes, by which a distinction was made between such words as *yudh-i*, the act of fighting; *yudh-ma*, a fighter; *(ā)yudh-a*, a weapon. In these words we say that *yudh* appears as the root; and how real that root is we can easily see by its frequent occurrence, not only as a root, but as a perfect word in the oldest Sanskrit, that of the Veda. We find there[21] the locative yudh-i, in the battle; the instrumen-

---

[19] See Justi, *Handbuch*, s.v. VI. Pictet's statement (1,509) that vī means in Zend fish also, is unfounded.
[20] Benfey compares pakshin with Goth. *fugl*. fowl.
[21] M. M. *Translation of Rig-Veda*, vol. I, p. 202.

tal yudh-ā, with a weapon; the locative plural, yut-su, among fighters; just as we find yu-yudh-e, he has fought, and ayuddha, he fought, &c. The difference between the nominal and verbal compounds is simply this, that the former express fighting-there, fighting-he, fighting-one, fighter: the latter fighting-I, fighting-thou, fighting-he.

Without entering further into the niceties of these grammatical compositions, I only wish to point out here, first, that the whole of our language, from the simplest word to the most complex paulo-post future, is conceptual; secondly, that language pre-supposes the formation of concepts; and thirdly, that all such concepts are embodied in roots. The two problems, therefore, that of the elaboration of concepts, and that of the elaboration of roots, become in reality one, and must be solved together, if they are to be solved at all.

Now, whatever difference of opinion there may be among the philosophers as to the real origin of concepts, there can be none as to the origin of roots. It is true these roots are frequently spoken of as something mysterious, like many other mysteries, would seem to be of our own making.

Let us see, first of all, what roots are not. Roots are not either interjections or imitations. Interjections such as pooh, and imitations such as bow-wow, are the very opposite of roots. *They are vague and varying in sound, and special in meaning; while roots are definite in sound, but general in meaning.* Interjections, however, and imitations are the only possible materials out of which human language could be framed; and the real problem, therefore, is this how, starting with interjections and imitations, can we ever arrive at roots?

Interjections and imitations deserve a much more careful study than they have hitherto received, even from those who imagine that our words can be derived straight from interjections and imitations.

Nothing seems at first sight so easy, yet nothing is in reality so difficult as to represent either the sounds by which our own feelings manifest themselves, or the sounds of nature, such as the notes of birds, the howling of the wind, the falling of a stone, by articulate sounds. From the very beginning the process must have given rise to an infinite variety of imitations, many of which it would be almost impossible to recognise or understand, without traditional or social helps. Even in our times and among civilised nations, with languages fixed by thousands of years of tradition, usage, literature, and grammar, the expressions for the most ordinary feelings vary considerably. The Frenchman, as an observant traveller has remarked, expresses surprise by Ah!, the Englishman by Oh!, the German by Ih! The Frenchman says, *Ah, c'est magnifique*; the Englishman, *Oh, that is capital*; the German, *Ih, das ist prächtig*. Nor do these interjections express exactly the same feeling; they all express surprise, no doubt, but the surprise peculiar to each of these three national characters. The surprise of the Frenchman is simple and open; in saying Ah! he is all agape, *il est ébahi*. The surprise of the Englishman is restrained and deep; in saying Oh! he swallows half of his admiration. The surprise of the German is high and sharp; in saying Ih! he almost chirps with delight.

In Chinese surprise is expressed by *hu* and *fu*, applause by *tsai*, misery by *i*, contempt by *ai*, pain by *uhu*.

Frequently it is as difficult to define the exact sound as the exact meaning of these interjections, so that in an Italian grammar no less than twenty significations are ascribed to the interjections *ah! ahi!* With a little more imagination quite as many and even more meanings might be detected in the English Ah!

Some scholars have brought themselves to imagine that there is some hidden connection between the letter N and the concept of negation. Yet, all that we have a right to say is that *no* may express negation, but not, that it must. As a matter of fact, there are languages in which *no* means *yes*.

This uncertainty becomes still more startling when we come to examine the way in which the sounds uttered by animals are imitated in different languages. I shall give a few specimens from Chinese. What would you guess to be the meaning of *kiao kiao?* It is meant for the cry of the cock; *kao kao* stands for the cry of the wild goose; *siao siao* is meant to represent the sound of rain and wind; *lin lin* of rolling carriages; *tsiang tsiang*, of chains; *kan kan*, of drums, and so on.

This subject is in reality endless; and the more we compare the representations of the cries of animals in different languages, the more shall we see that a comparative grammar of them is almost impossible.

I shall give you the imitations which occur in German of the cries of some animals, chiefly birds, but I doubt whether you will easily recognise them.

What is *zir zir*? It is meant for the thrush. What is *quak quak*? The duck, no doubt; but in other places the guttural has been changed into the labial (what scholars call labialism), and the sound uttered by the duck is rendered by *pak, pak.* Thus the cry of the owl is represented in German, not only by *uhú, uhú,* but likewise by *schu hu hu hu,* and by *pu pu*; in Latin by *tu tu*, in Greek, by κικκαβάυ; thus showing us, first of all, Dentalism, change of initial guttural into dental; then Labialism, change of guttural into labial; then Zetacism and assibilation, change of guttural or dental into sh; lastly, aphæresis of initial guttural, as in *uhu* for *kuhu*!

The frog in German says *quak* and *kik*, in Greek βρεκεκὲξ κοὰξ κοάξ.

Pink, in German, is the note of the finch.

Ga ga ga, Daddado, drussla, drussla, is meant for goose; in Chinese, the wild goose says *kao kao*; in Mongolian, *kór kór.*

The cock in German says *kikeriki*, in Chinese, as we saw, *kiao kiao*, in Mongolian, *dchor dchor.* The German hen, if not otherwise occupied, says *gack gack*; while laying eggs, she says *glu glu glu*; when calling her chicks, *tuck tuck tuck*; and yet, when she is called herself, she is addressed by *putt putt putt,* and her little chicks by *bi bi bi.*

The dog says *wau wau* and *bau bau*, sometimes *hu hu*, and *kliff klaff.* When very angry and growling he says *r*, which the Romans called the dog letter, the *litera canina.*

I am afraid there is no time for more; but I must just add one more German phonograph, that of the nightingale: it is, *Zucküt, zicküt, zicküt! Zidiwik, zidiwik, zidiwik! Zifizigo, zifizigo, zifizigo! tididon, zi zi! Tandaradei!* A great phonetic artist, not satisfied with these popular representations of the note of the nightingale, devoted many days and nights to a careful study of this subject, and the precious result at which he arrived was this:

Deilidurei faledirannurei lidundei faladaritturei!

It would be easy to produce similar words from other languages in order to show, first, how difficult and fanciful all imitations of inarticulate by means of articulate sounds must be; secondly, how, after all, every one of those imitations expresses and can express a single impression only. One might imagine the possibility of a language consisting altogether of such imitative sounds. The combination of two such imitative sounds, for instance, as *bow wow, pooh!* might form a sentence to convey the meaning the a certain dog was harmless, that he might bark but would not bite; but, as a matter of fact, no tribe even of the lowest savages has yet been discovered employing no more than such utterances.

The problem, therefore, which we have to solve, is this – How, if we start with such interjections and imitations, can we ever arrive at the real elements of language, the residue of all scientific analysis – I mean *the Roots*. If we can account for this transition of interjections and imitations into roots, we have done all that the most exacting sceptic can demand. Analysis of all given language leads us back to roots; experience gives us interjections and imitations as the only utterance. If the two can be united, the problem is solved.

Let us go back once more to the first beginning of conceptual knowledge, for it is here, if anywhere, that the key must be found. The simplest concept is the dual, when we count two things as one. This dual concept can be formed in two ways, either by combination or by abstraction.

If we have a word for *father* and a word for *mother*, then in order to express the concept of *parents*, we may combine the two. Thus, we actually find in Sanskrit, *pitar*, father, *mātar*, mother, *mātāpitarau*, mother and father, i.e. parents. The same in Chinese.[22] Father is *fú*, mother *mù*; *fú–mù*, parents. Again, a biped with feathers is *'kin* in Chinese; a quadruped with hair is *sheu*; animals in general are called *'kin-sheu*. Light is *'king*, heavy *ćúng*; *'king-ćúng* is used to express the concept of weight.

It is clear, however, that this process of combining single words could not be carried on *ad infinitum*: otherwise life might become too short for finishing one single sentence. We may call our parents father and mother, *fú–mù*, but how should we call our family?

Here, the faculty of abstraction comes to our help. A very simple case will show us how the work of thought and speech could be abbreviated. As long as people talk of sheep as sheep, and of cows as cows, they might very well indicate the former by *baa*, the latter by *moo*. But when, for the first time a want was felt of speaking of a flock, neither *baa* nor *moo* would do. As long as there were only sheep and cows, a combination of *baa* and *moo* might have answered, but when more animals were included, their separate sounds were those most to be

---

[22] Endlicher, *Chinesische Grammatik*, p. 133.

avoided, because they would have conveyed a meaning which was not intended.

So, again, it was easy enough to imitate the cries of the cuckoo and the cock, and the sounds *cuckoo* and *cock* might be used as the phonetic signs of these two birds. But if a phonetic sign was required for the singing of more birds, or it may be, of all possible birds, every imitation of a special note became not only useless but dangerous; and nothing but a compromise, nothing but a filing down of the sharp corners of those imitative sounds, would answer the new purpose.

This phonetic process of what I call the *Friction* or *Despecialisation* of imitative sounds runs exactly parallel with the process of generalisation of our impressions, and through this process alone are we able to understand how, after a long struggle, the uncertain phonetic imitations of special impressions became the definite phonetic representations of general concepts.

Thus, there must have been many imitations of the falling of stones, trees, leaves, rivers, rain, and hail, but in the end they were all combined in the simple root PAT, expressive of quick movement, whether in falling, flying, or running. By giving up all that could remind the hearer of any special sound of rushing objects, the root PAT became fitted as the sign of the general concept of quick movement, and from this concept and this root sprang afterwards a number of words in Sanskrit, Greek, Latin, and other Aryan languages. In Sanskrit we find patati, he flies, he soars, he falls; pata-s, flight; pataga-s, and patanga-s, a bird, also a grasshopper; patatra-m, a wing; pataka-s, a flag; pattra-m, a wing, a leaf of a flower, a leaf of paper, a letter; pattrin, a bird; pāta-s, falling, happening, accident, also fall, in the sense of sin, in which sense pātaka-m is more frequently used; possibly even pātāla, the Indian name for hell.

In Greek we find πέτομαι, I fly; πετηνός, winged; ὠκυπέτης, quickly flying or running; ποτή, flight; πτερόν and πτέρυξ, feather, wing, instead of π(ε)τερὸν, π(ε)τέρυξ; also ποταμός, river. Again πίπτω, I fall, instead of πιπ(έ)τω; πότμος, fall, accident, fate; πτῶσις, fall, case, used first in a philosophical, then in a grammatical sense. In Latin we find from the same root, *peto*, to fall on, to assail; to make for, to seek, to demand, with its many derivative applications; *im-petus*, onslaught;

præpes, quickly flying; also *penna*, feather, the old *pesna*, for *pet-na*.

The number of words derived from this root in modern languages seems endless. In English alone we have *petition, petulance, appetite, competition, repetition*, then *pen, pinnacle, feather*, and many more, all to be traced back, step by step, and letter by letter, to the old root PAT, and to no other root, not to any of the imitative sounds of falling, out of which PAT was selected, or out of which PAT by a higher degree of fitness struggled into life and fixity.

In one of my Lectures on the Science of Language, I examined in full detail the immense progeny of the root MAR, to grind, to break. This root itself must be looked upon as tuned down from innumerable imitations of the sounds of breaking, crushing, crunching, crashing, smashing, mashing, cracking, creaking, rattling and clattering, mawling and marring, till at last, after removing all that seemed too special, there remained the smooth and manageable Aryan root of MAR.

If we once clearly understand this natural, nay this necessary process of the mutual friction of imitative sounds, representing outwardly the process of generalisation of single intuitions and the origin of abstract concepts, we are prepared to find what we actually do find in the further development of roots. Some roots, being useful for special purposes, retained something of their sharper outline, and became popular on that very account; while others that had reached the highest point of generalisation, and were therefore used most frequently, supplanted parallel roots of a more special meaning.

Again, in this struggle for generalisation, many roots must have crossed each other, and the *summum genus* of going, moving, doing, sounding, must have been reached again and again from very different starting-points.

From this point of view nothing is easier to understand than that, though beginning with the same materials, families, villages, tribes and races, would, after a very short separation, if it took place during the Radical Period, have become of necessity mutually unintelligible. Not only different dialects, and different languages, but different families of languages with different roots for their supply, could thus have sprung from one common source; and to deny the possibility of a common origin of the Aryan and Semitic families of speech, from this point of view, would be simply absurd.

Another question which has frequently been asked, viz., whether what are commonly called secondary and tertiary roots were derived from primary roots, or whether they are remnants of earlier stages in the development of language, does not admit of an equally conclusive answer. If we meet with three such roots as sar, to go; sarp, to creep; sarg, to let go, we have a right to look upon the additional letters p and g as modificatory elements, and upon the roots formed by them, as derived and secondary. This is particularly the case when these additional letters are used systematically, as, for instance, in forming causative, desiderative, inchoative, and intensive roots.

But there are other cases, where we must admit parallel roots, representing to us independent attempts of fixing general concepts. If one root was possible, so were others, similar in sound and meaning, varieties, not by genealogical succession, but by collateral development, – a process which has of late been far too much neglected, not only in the Science of Language, but in many other branches of Natural Science.

After what I have now explained, it will, I hope, have become clear to those who may have listened here to my Lectures on the Science of Language, that what I formerly called *Roots*, or *Phonetic Types*, are indeed the ultimate facts in the analysis of language, but that, from a higher and philosophical point of view, they admit of a perfectly intelligible explanation. They represent the *nuclei* formed in the chaos of interjectional or imitative sounds; the fixed centres which become settled in the *vortex* of natural selection. The scholar begins and ends with these phonetic types; or, if he ignores them, and traces words back to the cries of animals, or the interjections of men, he does so at his own peril. The philosopher goes beyond, and he discovers in the line which separates rational from emotional language, – conceptual from intuitional knowledge, – he discovers in the roots of all languages, the true barrier between Man and Beast. I do not ask, like others, for a persuasive appeal from the throat of a nightingale, or for a gruff remonstrance from a gorilla, before I admit that they may be along the ancestors of the human race. I do not wait even, like Professor Schleicher, till I hear a pig say, 'I am a pig,' before I grant that the same blood may run through his veins and our own, and – what is far more important – that his thoughts, may run through the same conceptual channels as our own.

Show me only one single root in the language of animals, such as AK, to be sharp and quick; and from it two such derivatives as asva, the quick one – the horse – and *acutus*, sharp or quick witted; nay, show me one animal that has the power of forming roots, that can put one and one together, and realise the simplest dual concept; show me one animal that can think and say *Two*, and I should say that, as far as language is concerned, we cannot oppose Mr. Darwin's argument, and that man has, or at least may have been, developed from some lower animal. I do not deny that there is some force in Mr. Darwin's remark, that both man and monkey are born without language; but I consider that the real problem which this remark places before us is to find out why a man always learns to speak, a monkey never. If, instead of this, we say that, under favourable circumstances, an unknown kind of monkey may have learnt to speak, and thus, through his descendants, have become what he is now, viz. man, we deal in fairy-stories, but not in scientific research. Mr. Darwin says, 'Language is certainly not a true instinct, as every language has to be learnt.' Yes, every language has to be learnt, but language itself, never. It matters little whether we call language in this sense an instinct, a gift, a talent, a faculty, or the *proprium* of the species Man. Certain it is, that neither the power of language, nor the conditions under which alone language can exist, are to be discovered in any of the lower animals.

There is one class of philosophers who, in the interest, as they believe, of freedom and inquiry, lay great stress on admitting, if not the reality, at least the possibility or conceivableness of the development of man from a lower animal. What is conceivable, depends, however, quite as much on the conceiver as on the conceived. Nor do I see what, in our case, we should gain by saying, that the transition of a lower animal into man is conceivable, considering that the very opposite, too, viz., the non-transition of any lower animal into man is equally conceivable, and, in addition to this, at least as far as our experience goes, is real. Surely there is something in this word *real*; there is some weight to be attached in every argument to experience, as far as it goes. There are hundreds and thousands of things in nature where we see no reason why they should be what they are, and where we may easily imagine that they might be different from what they are. Why should not trees grow into the sky? why should not birds fly up to the moon? To say that they would die, is saying nothing, at least as far as evolutionist philosophers are concerned; for why should they alone not possess the power of adapting themselves to new environments?

But what should we gain by saying that all such things are conceivable? Would it not be far more useful to try to discover why there are such hard and fast lines in nature; why certain creatures never pass certain limits: why man, for instance, was enabled, or if you like, prompted and tempted, to generalise, to from a world of concepts or roots, to derive from these roots, names of new concepts, to elaborate, in fact, language, and then to make language the foundation of a culture, which, marvellously as it is in our century, is probably the seed only for a future growth, while no animal ever made even the first step in this direction?

To admit everything is possible, may be very excellent in theory, and, as logicians, we no doubt all admit that the sun may to-morrow rise in the west. But I doubt whether that neutral state of mind is the best adapted for real work, and for the advancement of real knowledge. The chemist who, for the time being, denies the possibility of a decomposition of what he calls elementary substances, and who declares a change of lifeless into living matter as inadmissible, is much more likely to cross the frontier, if it can be crossed, than he who from the beginning looks upon all these distinctions as mere vanishing lines.

If we do not simply play with words, if we take *conceivable* in that sense in which it has among professional students, viz., something which is in accordance with known facts, then we ought not to say that the elaboration of language by any animal is conceivable; but, on the contrary, it becomes our duty to warn the valiant disciples of Mr. Darwin that before they can claim a real victory, before they can call man the descendant of a mute animal, they must lay a regular siege to a fortress which is not to be frightened into submission by a few random shots; the fortress of language, which, as yet, stands untaken and unshaken on the very frontier between the animal kingdom and man.

I trust that, in the course of these Lectures, when arguing against the conclusions of the Darwinian school, I have never shown any want of respect for Mr. Darwin. The results at which I have arrived by a life-long study of language and thought are incompatible with the results to which a minute study of the human body has led Mr. Darwin. One of us must be wrong, and it therefore seems to me mere cowardice to shrink from an open combat. It is true 'that Mr. Darwin has not paid special attention to the problem of language and thought, and that all he says about it may be contained in some six or eight largely-printed small octavo pages.' But I submit that six or eight pages from Mr. Darwin may have more weight than a volume from many other writers. Anyhow, if Mr. Darwin is right, then language is not what I hold it to be; it is not the embodiment of conceptual thought, it is not developed from roots, it is not based on concepts. If, on the contrary, language is what I hold it to be, then man cannot be the descendant of some lower animal, because no animal except man possesses the faculty, or the faintest germs of the faculty, of abstracting and generalising, and therefore no animal, except man, could ever have developed what we mean by language.

Gentlemen, it matters very little who is right and who is wrong, but it matters a great deal what is right and what is wrong. By no one should I more gladly confess myself vanquished than by Mr. Darwin. I feel for him the most sincere admiration; nay, I have never concealed my strong sympathy with the general tendency of his speculations. His power of persuasion, no doubt, is great, but equally great is his honest love of truth; and when I find him again and again admitting that no intermediate links between the highest apes and man have yet been discovered, that the gap between ape and man, small as it is, can be filled with imaginary animals only, I ask myself how it is possible, in the absence of all tangible evidence, that our matter-of-fact philosophers should have listened to such arguments. Unless there were, in fact, some important germs of truth in his philosophy, I cannot think that Mr. Darwin could ever have carried us along with him so powerfully and almost irresistibly.

If Mr. Darwin were more anxious for victory than for truth, I have no doubt he would have handled the argument of language, too, in a very different spirit. He feels the difficulty of language, he fully admits it; but not seeing how much is presupposed by language – looking upon language as a means for the communication rather than for the formation of thought, he thinks it might be in man a development of germs that may be discovered in animals.

Now a clever pleader – of whom we have too many, even in the courts of science – might say, 'Why, does not the very theory you have propounded of the origin of roots prove that Mr. Darwin is right? Have you not shown that animals possess the materials of language in interjections; that they imitate the cries of other animals; that they communicate with each other, and give warning by shrill cries; that they know their own names, and understand the commands of their masters? Have you not "blessed us altogether," by showing how interjections and imitations can be filed down, lose their sharp corners, become general – become, in fact, roots? Surely, after this, Mr. Darwin will be justified more than ever in saying that the language of man is the result of mere development, and that there must have been one or several generations of men who had not yet generalised their intuitions, and not yet filed down their intuitions, and not yet filed down the sharp corners of their interjections.'

I have no doubt that such pleading would seem plausible in many a court, nay, to judge from the remarks that have been addressed to me both by word of mouth and by letter, I should not be surprised if several members of the jury I am now addressing were to lean to the side of the animals. Some young ladies have assured me that, if I only knew their dog, I should have spoken very differently; that no one who has not been loved by a dog can know what true love and faithfulness are. Some elderly ladies have told me that I knew nothing about cats, and that their cats possess quite as much cleverness, quite as much intellect – as they themselves. The very statement with which I concluded, and by which I wished to bring the whole question into the narrowest compass, when I said that no animal could form the lowest generalisation, could count two, or think and say Two, has been met by the pigeons at Venice. They, at all events, I was told, can count two; for every day, as soon as the clock of St. Mark's strikes two, neither sooner nor later, they assemble from all parts of Venice to be fed on the piazza. Surely, therefore, they can count two. This seemed indeed unanswerable. But fortunately my informant went on to say that the other clocks of Venice strike two first, and the pigeons pay no attention, but when St. Mark's strikes, they all come. What does that prove? It proves that they do not count two, but that their hungry stomach strikes two, and that it is the peculiar sound of the St. Mark's clock, even were it to strike twelve, that brings them together to their dinner.

Our own clock reminds me that it is time to finish. It was not easy to say all I wanted to say in the course of three Lectures, and I am deeply conscious that some of the points on which I touched but lightly ought to have been treated far more fully. I hope to do this on a future occasion, after I have had time to examine carefully the objections which these Lectures have elicited, and may still elicit. But I trust I have said enough to show you the Science of Language in a new light; and to make you see its paramount importance for a truly scientific study of Psychology, and for the solution of problems which hang like storm-clouds over our heads, and make our very soul to quiver.

THE ORIGIN OF LANGUAGE
Anonymous

Source: Westminster Review (1874), vol. 102

1. *Lectures on M. Darwin's Philosophy of Language.* By Professor MAX MUELLER. *Fraser's Magazine*, May, June, July, 1873.
2. *The Descent of Man.* Chapter II. By CHARLES DARWIN, M.A., F.R.S., &c.
3. *Chapters on Language.* By the Rev. FREDERICK W. FARRAR, D.D., F.R.S. Longmans, Green, and Co. 1873. New Edition.
4. *Language: its Origin and Development.* By T. HEWITT KEY, M.A., F.R.S. London: George Bell and Sons. 1874.

When an old French lady in the last century was asked to contribute towards the expense of an improved version of the Psalms, she indignantly wondered whether the applicants thought they could write better French than the king and prophet David. This old woman's saying has the advantage of expressing as a definite firmly-held opinion, what was probably in many other minds a vague sentiment half unconsciously indulged. It happens repeatedly that we allow our conduct and views to be influenced in this illogical manner, by tacitly accepted beliefs which we should never venture to put into set phrase. Especially in regard to human speech, there seems to have been a recurring tendency in nations to fancy that language means exclusively their own language, and that all other utterance is jargon. The spread of education and extended intercourse have made such a feeling now almost impossible, but a trace of it remains in an incapacity which is by no means rare, an incapacity of understanding that the genius of a foreign language may be totally different from the genius of our own. It requires some teaching to make us apprehend the difference of sense which may have grown up between kindred words in two closely connected languages. For example, a Frenchman, familiar with the use of the word *bête* in his own tongue, called his maid-servant 'beast' for some trivial piece of stupidity, unaware that he was translating a commonplace term of reproach into an atrocious insult. Mistakes of much more serious consequence and far more difficult to correct, have arisen when, not the sense of particular words has been in question, but the whole mental tone of a language and the literature contained therein. Controversies often spring up about the *obvious* sense of what has been written, and its *natural* meaning, while it escapes all the parties to the dispute that both these terms are relative terms, and that the interpretations which seem so very obvious to their eyes, may never even have occurred to the view of the original authors writing in distant lands, in distant ages, and under quite different mental conditions. If we were always to mean what we say, and say what we mean, language would still be far from adequate to inform our neighbours of our real thoughts, since in a majority of cases our neighbour would take the words in his sense of them rather than in ours. Thus when a lady sends word to a friend at the door that she is *indisposed*, the obvious and natural sense to some minds will be, that the lady is unwell; to others, that she is *indisposed* to receive that particular visitor. On the other hand, we should often do much injustice by binding others to the full value, so to speak, of what they utter. A man is anxious to catch a train, and still more anxious to receive his letters before leaving home. 'A plague,' he cried, 'on all loitering postmen!' yet the same man would perhaps sacrifice his correspondence for a year, rather than see one dilatory letter carrier perish by pestilence. The courteous dishonesties of social life will probably remain in vogue till men and women square their conduct much more thoroughly than at present with accepted standards, so as to justify by a real brotherhood the conventional affection and faithfulness pretended to in the phrases of ordinary correspondence. Gross impieties of language are happily less familiar to our own than to past generations. A military officer nowadays may reprove a trooper for swearing without accompanying the rebuke, as sometimes formerly happened, with the most violent oaths and curses. But that such an inconsistency should ever have been possible shows how faulty a representative language may be of what is really intended. No one can easily suppose that men of character and position really indulged the feelings towards God and man implied in the expressions at one time commonly used on the most trivial occasions, and so characteristic of ourselves that an old author could speak of the march of ten thousand English Goddams as a synonym for the progress of that number of English soldiers. Physicians tell us how difficult it is to get a prescribed treatment exactly carried out by ill-educated and untrained nurses, because of the false interpretations which such persons put upon words. Not what the physician said, but what they think he *must* have meant is the guide they are pleased to follow. Consciously or unconsciously we almost all treat language, whether sacred or profane, much in the same way. Certain theories as to what is right and true are taken for granted, and words describing ascertained facts or making authoritative declarations, if they will not fit the theories, must be forced to do so. Language moreover long retains expressions which have had their origin in opinions since modified, or in exploded and almost forgotten errors. It is a mere common-place to remark that the firmament no longer means a firm and solid crystal dome, and that we speak of lunatics without any reference to the influence of the moon upon their madness. We still talk of a kind heart, and have scarcely ceased to talk of the bowels of compassion, although modern physiology would reject the idea that the emotions of affection and sympathy are seated either in the heart or the bowels. A man will own to having drunk a glass of spirits without admitting or even knowing Lord Bacon's dictum that 'all bodies have spirits, and pneumatical parts within them.' Let us be ever so truthful in inclination and ever so learned as to the origin of words, we should never be able to get at an absolutely truthful mode of speech. The further we traced a word back, the less we should like the look of it. We should feel ourselves hampered in every direction. Not only would eloquence begin to seem a hateful tissue of lies or a silly set of misapprehensions, but in writing a simple letter we should be stopped at the outset. We could not conscientiously say 'Sir,' 'that is,' 'Senior,' or 'Elder,' without knowing our correspondent's age to be fairly advanced, or, at any rate greater than our own. We could not date the letter October, well knowing that month not to be the eighth, as its name implies, but the tenth in the year. We might avoid mentioning the day of the week by its heathenish name of Monday, as though it were a day consecrated to the moon; but the number of the year would involve us in much tribulation, unless we appended a short article on chronology to show that the vulgar era is probably wrong by four years, and that we are therefore justified in writing 1878 rather than 1874.

Very little inquiry into the nature and use of language shows that, although an invaluable instrument of thought, it is on many accounts a very imperfect one. The same estimate holds good of it as a medium of intercourse; it is invaluable, but imperfect. Often it justifies the old sarcasm of the diplomatist that its use is to conceal one's meaning, so that over and over again men argue at cross-purposes because the words which they use in common are not symbols of the same thoughts to each. The poverty of language hampers us. Its riches are a snare and entanglement. Sometimes we have ideas without words to express them; at others we fancy a problem has been explained when it has only been set forth with a difference of phraseology.

Language is so cumbrous, especially in scientific nomenclature, that few men can readily command the names of objects with which they would wish to be familiar, unless by special and serious efforts directed to particular branches of that kind of learning. Minds of ordinary education are soon bewildered and disgusted with subjects where such words as zygapophyses, parallelopipeds, cheirotheria, potamogetonaceæ, collembola, and dinitro-brombenzene are necessary *for simplicity's sake*. While too the aid of language in the association of ideas is essential to the progress of poetry and the progress of science alike, it often involves the pioneer, the discoverer, the man who gets a new hold upon truth, in this dilemma – that he must either use words round which all sorts of erroneous ideas are still clustering, or invent others which will sound to the multitude as repulsive jargon. In the attempt to convey, in popular language, new, unexpected, and therefore unpopular information, he will sometimes be told that the very words he is using ought to have taught him better. Between the first flash of a new hypothesis across the scientific imagination and a theory firmly and conclusively established is a wide interval. The point where 'it may be' merges into 'it is' can scarcely be defined. It will vary with different temperaments. The sanguine will speak at once with a prophet's decisive tone of what is still only an inchoate probability, while the cautious will scarcely forego a modest peradventure even when the debate is closed. The consequence is that the one will be accused by opponents of absolute untruthfulness, and the other twitted with conjugating the potential mood, with having no confidence in his own opinions, and on such grounds the world at large will often be invited to dismiss, without a hearing, the results of the most elaborate and prolonged inquiry.

Stubborn as language appears to be under some aspects, under others we cannot help marvelling at its wonderful elasticity. Thus the lawyer claims to be able to drive a coach and six through an Act of Parliament. Knowing very well what its framers intended to prescribe, he stretches the language to bear an opposite interpretation. Hostile religious parties find support for their various views in the same formularies, so that, for instance, men of the greatest piety, antiquarians, scholars, lawyers, merchants, find it impossible to decide by common consent which is the north side of a rectangular table having its edges parallel to the walls of a rectangular building standing due east and west. Gulliver in the kingdom of Lilliput very likely heard the question disputed, with heat and vehemence, by the philosophers of that ingenious realm. At the first blush one would be inclined to maintain that every rectangle has four sides; but how abashed one would be, after staking a fortune on the assertion, to find that it was quite untenable, and that no rectangular figure but a square or a rhombus has four sides – in all others two of what we thought were sides being nothing but ends. Words of authority – of which at one time a man says they can bear but one meaning – all of a sudden, under some new light, assume an entirely different aspect. Without giving here any opinion as to the time, whether early or late, when death was introduced into the world, we may take an instructive example from that question. A writer of evident intelligence, who had become acquainted with some of the facts of geology, thus expresses himself: 'I was accustomed,' he says, 'to entertain the idea of death having passed generally upon the whole creation, at the fall of man. But when I heard of the discoveries of geologists, I was led to examine into the foundation of this opinion. I referred to Scripture; but upon examination I found no passage which supports such a notion.'[1] Yet we well know that the notion is built upon Scripture; and doubtless this writer himself, along with millions of other men, both in the past and present, held it upon that very authority; for he goes on to say: 'Not find-

---

[1] See Pye-Smith, 'Scripture and Geology,' Supplementary Note A.

ing it declared in Scripture, I began to consider what reason there might be for supposing it; and I was led to the conclusion that there was none.' We are not now concerned with the accuracy of this person's opinions, either first or last, but only with the contrast between them. He had long held that a particular inference was warranted by the language of a certain record. The record remains the same; its credibility and truthfulness remain seated as firmly as ever in his mind; yet he suddenly, and with a clear conscience, gives up the inference as having no warrant either in the record or anywhere else. We must admit that it is an imperfection, or, to use the mildest term, an inconvenience in language that that this should be possible. Not only do intolerable controversies and heartburnings arise from it, because the new light never strikes all men at the same moment, but it insidiously fosters immorality. What one man does with a clear conscience, another will do out of conceit or cowardice, or from other selfish motives. Men, whose minds have been thoroughly penetrated by the new light, will profess to retain the old view, or give out that there is much to be said on either part, as if sense and nonsense were of equal authority. Were it not for this capacity in language of stretching, so that we can use forms of speech with one intention in them for our own mind, and another for those who hear us, we could never tamper as we do with truth. It is quite a mistake to suppose that a man is respected for speaking the truth, except in social and mercantile affairs where direct and obvious self-interest makes the veracity of our neighbours a matter of pressing moment. If he tells us what he really thinks, and we do not happen to agree with him, we say he is preaching falsehood. As a rule, we consider not the truth of facts and opinions, but what we suppose to be their tendency. You will hear whole branches of knowledge described as dangerous and unsettling. A man who simply sets forth the proved conclusions of an unpopular subject, will be called a 'very dangerous man.' 'Fancy his saying such things to a carpenter,' you will hear, or, 'Fancy his saying such things to a child.' 'Why, what want of tact!' one will say; and another will answer, 'Well, I never heard of these things when I was young, and I'm too old for them now.' Hence, what with the danger of novelty to the young and foolish, and the incapacity for its reception in the old and ignorant, the wonder is that truth, every particle of which must, at one time or another, have been new to mankind, has ever made any progress in the world at all.

The town-clerk of Ephesus told his fellow citizens that all the world knew that the city of the Ephesians was a worshipper of the great goddess Diana, and of the image which fell down from Jupiter. The still popular view of language would undoubtedly accord with the Ephesian feeling about the image which fell down from Jupiter in deeming it simply a miraculous gift, needing, therefore, no further explanation of its origin, but requiring its honour to be vindicated by more or less of anger and resentment shown towards any who should call that origin in question. In one sense all things are miraculous, and all things we enjoy, with language among them, are miraculous gifts; but when a hen lays an egg, and gradually a chicken is formed within the shell, and in time comes forth and feeds itself, gathers feathers and wings about its curious little body, grows up into a cock and begins to crow, we are agreed not to call that course of events miraculous. In the same sense of the word we shall now presume to contend that the origin of language is not miraculous, and all that we have been saying about its poverty, its cumbrous character, its deceitfulness, and the chains with which it entangles the intellect, has been by way of apology for introducing an opinion so contrary to the common view.

Of plants and animals we say that one species differs from another species when the members of the two will not breed together. If we may say of two forms of language that they are specifically different when a man from his knowledge of the one is not able to understand the other, it will be lawful for us to maintain that we can trace our own English language back to a time when it is no longer, or rather has not yet become, our own English language. The main steps are well known which lead us back through the names of great authors and celebrated works – the translation of the Bible, and Shakespeare, and Spenser, and 'Dan Chaucer's well of English undefiled,' and the vision of Piers Plowman, and the Saxon Chronicle, to the Old Saxon and Old Frisian, which are certainly not intelligible from a simple knowledge of modern English. We know too that the process of change is still going on. Words fall into disuse; new words are coined; a change in pronunciation comes into fashion; words are clipped in one district and drawled in another; foreign idioms are introduced; foreign words imported, but so disguised under a new accent as to seem equally alien to the tongue which borrows and the tongue which lends. In short, it will be admitted without difficulty, whatever we may think of language in the abstract, that the various forms of it at present in the world have been shaped in the mental factories of mankind. By ingenious analysis words are traced back to their roots; a single syllable is found to be, as it were, the parent of a large group of words extending through numerous languages; it may be compounded with other roots to modify its meaning and to adapt it to the different parts of speech; it may lose almost all, or all, resemblance to its original self by what are called phonetic changes, as when a man pronounces a 'w' for an 'r,' or 'th' for an 's,' and says, 'Weally, what a thocking thtory!' But besides all this, it frequently comes to convey an entirely different meaning from that with which it first started. To account for this we have only to remember that wherever the primary roots themselves may have come from, at any rate starting from them language has been formed by human beings, and not by them with any definite concert and plan, but in the haphazard style of ordinary intercourse, all having a chance of a share in its production, as well the unskilled as the well-trained labourer. It need not, therefore, always be the reflection of very consistent thinking, and while in some instances the derivatives will depart by almost insensible gradations from the original intention of the root, in others there will be odd jumps of thought and freaks of fancy manifested, just as in common converse you may be discussing Dartmoor mutton, and some one will suddenly tell you that talking of sheep reminds him of a good thing in the 'Essays of Elia,' the only link of association to the topic of mutton being that the 'Essays of Elia' were written by Charles Lamb. The Latin word which gives us our English *lenient* means to soften, and from it comes the word lentus, which has the two opposite meanings of *ready* and *unready*. You can easily understand that what is softened may become pliant, what is plaint does not easily break, a thing not easily broken is tough, and toughness carried to a certain point makes things hard to bend, or just the reverse of pliant. Pliancy and toughness applied to morals and the intellect easily suggest the opposite characteristics of the yielding and the stubborn, the ready and the unready. Every schoolboy is taught with the first smattering of classics that the word which means school in English means leisure and idleness in

Greek, and not a few of them prefer the Greek acceptation of the term.

The deservedly popular works of Professor Max Müller may be referred to as repositories of facts and proofs sufficiently conclusive that all the languages of the world with which we have any satisfactory acquaintance have sprung from roots. The botanical metaphor employed is fairly convenient, since to the ordinary student of language it is sufficient to trace back words to the simple forms from which whole groups have been derived, as it is sufficient for the ordinary gardener to know from what roots the produce with which he is specially concerned has been developed. How the earth came to possess such roots is in each of these cases another, and a most interesting, but distinct question, or at any rate one which for certain purposes may be treated as distinct.

An important volume has just been published by Professor Key, on the 'Origin and Development of Language.' Such a title implies that both the questions of which we have been speaking have been handled by the author. It is true that for five hundred pages about the development, there are only five-and-twenty about the origin of speech; but from so eminent a scholar it is valuable to have even this brief exposition of his view – a view that cannot be impeached as the result of juvenile giddiness, ready to accept any plausible novelty, since we learn from the preface that Mr. Key is in his seventy-sixth year, and can judge from the rest of the work that his well-trained powers are still unimpaired. Much of the book appears to have been quite recently written (see p. 214); but the principles of philology with which the chief part of it is concerned, were given to the world tentatively some years ago in a pamphlet entitled 'Quæritur,' and in other essays. These principles are now supported by a wide induction. It would not be to our present purpose to enter into remote points of philological controversy, but everything which helps to explain what has seemed to be unmeaning and lawless in language leads on to a recognition of linguistic science as possible, besides being itself a step in scientific progress. Certainly after having been told in Latin Primers that the name of a town at which a man was said to have lived or died or eaten his dinner was to be put not always in the same case, but in a case varying according to the number and declension of the noun, it was a great satisfaction to discover that this monstrosity of a rule was erroneous, and that the case required was always the same, though like other cases it had various forms.[2] The same sort of satisfaction is excited by Professor Keys' chapter on Grammatical Figures. It is only too common an absurdity against which he warns the student – the disposition, namely, to regard the Greek names by which these figures are known as philosophical explanations. Prosthesis, Epenthesis, Paragoge, Metathesis, have a formidable appearance; and when a young philologer meets with a prefix to a word, or a transposition of letters for which he cannot account, he will think it an important addition to his knowledge to learn that the one is due to Prosthesis, the other to Metathesis; or, as he might be told in equivalent words, that the prefix is due to the figure Prefixing or Affixing, and the transposition of letters to an interchange of places between them. The first three of the figures just mentioned Professor Key would 'cancel as being utterly without a title,' on the ground that they have to do with the lengthening of words, while 'the one law which governs the changes in form of words is that general law which characterizes the action of man on every side, the desire to abbreviate labour; and hence we may safely refuse to admit the claims of those figures which pretend to extend words in form without any addition to the idea conveyed, whether such extension be claimed for the commencement, the middle, or the close of a word.' Here is a reasonable and satisfactory principle, although, as Professor Key almost immediately afterwards admits, it does not quite run to the length of wholly cancelling the figure Prosthesis; for, as he observes, 'when a foreign word which begins with two consonants is presented to the ears of a race not accustomed to the combination, there is, undoubtedly, a tendency to prefix a short vowel,' of which he gives some instances; and he might no doubt have added from a schoolmaster's experience the change by beginners in Greek of such a word as *xenos* into *exenos*, with no reference whatever to its derivation or original form. Here the prefixing of the initial *e* before the *x* or *ks* may very well be designated Prosthesis, if only we remember that it is not *due* to that figure, but to some defect of power, whether natural or from want of training, in the organs of the speaker.

---

[2] Max Müller, 'Lectures on the Science of Language,' p. 228: Fourth Edition.

From such involuntary changes it may be understood how, in spite of any longings and efforts for a universal language, the confusion of tongues must almost inevitably continue. Widespreading languages like widely-extended empires have an inherent tendency to break up, which can only be counteracted by greater facilities for oral intercourse than the world at present commands. But though men's organs of speech like their powers of reason vary to some extent, so that ere now a man has lost his life because they said unto him, 'Say now, Shibboleth, and he said Sibboleth; for he could not frame to pronounce it right;' still the organs of speech do not vary indefinitely. Hence it is that we can pass, in analysing languages, from the domain of caprice and accident to guiding principles, such as the subjection of letter-changes to fixed laws, or laws that are seldom violated. Thus we have the law commonly known as Grimm's law, but to the first notice of which, Professor Key, on the evidence of Bopp, asserts the claim of the Danish scholar Erasmus Rask. According to this, in the passage from Latin to English, for instance, thin consonants or tenues pass into aspirates, aspirates into thick or mediæ, mediæ into tenues, so that *p* in pater, becomes *f* in father, *f* in frater, *b* in brother, *b* in labium, *p* in lip.

The results that legitimately follow from philological laws are sometimes so surprising as to make the unwary imagine all things lawful in philology, so that given a word 'the letters of which, if tossed in a bag and then thrown out, might by a happy accident take the form'[3] of another word, such a lottery will be accepted as proof that one is derived from the other, or both from a common stem. As Professor Key, however, is very little likely to err from want of caution, it is interesting to find him accepting the opinion of Ewald and Lepsius, 'that the Hebrew names for the numerals 'six' and 'seven' are in themselves so far good evidence for a distant connexion between the Semitic and Indo-European languages,' and closing his volume with an argument which leads to the following conclusion: 'I trust, then, that the affinity of Finn, Lapp, and their cognates with the Indo-European stock will now be allowed by philologers; and if so, the whole family of so-called Tatar languages must go with them; and even a connexion of Chinese with our European stock is not to be summarily rejected.'[4] As

[3] 'Language: its Origin and Development,' p. 104.
[4] 'Language, its Origin and Development,' p. 516, 529.

an illustration, which may be understood at a glance, of the unity of the Indo-European stock itself, we take, from his lists of numerals, the words meaning 'seven' and 'ten.' They are: – Sanskrit, saptan, daçan; Zend, haptan, daçan; Greek, ἑπτα, δεκα; Latin, septem, decem; Lithuanian, septyni-, deszimt; Old Slavic, sedmi, desiati; Gothic, sibun, taihun; Old German, sibun, zehan; German, sieben, zeh(e)n; Norse, sjö, tiu; Old Erse, secht, deich; Old Welsh, seith, dec; Breton, seiz, dek.[5] The connexion between such forms is easily accepted. More consideration will be required for the following lists, containing the words for 'son' and 'daughter,' especially when we are given to understand that there is a virtual identity, not only in all the words for 'son' and in all those for 'daughter,' but between the words 'son' and 'daughter' also. The lists, then, are as follow: – Sanskrit, sunu-, duhitar; Greek, ὑ-ιο-, θυγατερ-; Latin, filio-, filia-; Slavic, syn, doch; Lithuanian, sunu-, dukter-; Gothic, sunu, dauhtar; Old German, sunu-, tohtar; Old Norse, son-r, dôttir-; French, fils, fille; Spanish, hijo, hija[6]. To make the union of all these forms credible we must follow Professor Key's suggestions, which will quickly supply a trace of order amidst the apparent confusion. First of all, the modern Greek has θυγος in place of θυγατερ and ὑγιος as a variety of ὑιος. 'Sanskritists deduce their *duhitar*, 'daughter,' from a verb, *doh* '*draw*' *(milk), some making the term* = '*milkeress*,' *so to say, in the sense of* '*dairy-maid*'; Lassen, I think with more reason, 'suckling.' Θυγ of θυγατηρ θυγος must of course be one with the Sanscrit *doh*; and I believe it also to be one with the Latin *sug-* and the Latin *duc-*,' Then as regards the limitation of meaning from 'drawing' generally to 'drawing milk' compare the French *traire* (to milk) from *trahere*, and the Greek ἑλκειν μαστον, as also such a phrase as Ovid's 'materna rigescere sentit ubera, nec sequitur *ducentem* lacteus humor.' As between θυγατηρ and filius, how a Greek θ passes into a Latin *f* may

---

[5] Ibid., p. 517. The plausible explanation of the Indo-European names for 'ten,' as coming from dva-, 2, and kvan-, 5, is questioned by Mr. Ferrar, in his Comparative Grammar, p. 307, note, on the ground that there are no traces of the two *v*'s. Mr. Key (p. 282) takes the root-syllable to be *dec*, the same as that of dico (deico), δεικνυμι δακτυλος, digitus, and so to mean originally the fingers. He ingeniously compares the German zehen, toes, zehen, ten. Mr. Ferrar (l.c.) regards the likeness between the Shemitic and Indo-European names for 'six' and 'seven' as merely accidental. See, too, Dr. Farrar, 'Chapters on Language,' p. 199, note.
[6] Ibid., p. 518.

be seen is such words as θηρ, fera; how *g* passes into *l* and vice versâ may be seen in the equivalents μογις, μολις, and in the Spanish *muger*, *ageno* corresponding to *mulier* and *alienus*. While *hijo* comes near to ὑιος and ὑγιος on the one hand, its connexion on the other hand with *filius*, through the Old Spanish *fijo*, cannot be disputed. 'There remains our own term *son*, German, *Sohn*, a word widely spread, as it occurs in the form *sunus* in Sanskrit, Lithuanian, and Gothic; and in the two former, as also in the Old Russian, *soun-s*, the first vowel is long, as it also is in the German *Sohn*. It may therefore well be that the word is compressed from a fuller, *sugnus* or *sucnus*, and so be a derivative from such a verb as *sugo*. The immediate relation of a child to her mother is best exhibited as her "suckling." '[7]

Though on many points of detail Mr. Key is at issue with the German school of philologers, and seems to hold his own very successfully against them, it will be seen from what has been quoted that he does not very widely differ from their general view or methods of reasoning. His may be said to be not so much a different view as an enlarged one, while his reasonings are cautionary and corrective rather than a condemnation of theirs.

On the origin of language as distinct from its development he accepts, without hesitation or reserve, the theory discussed some years ago in these columns, and then represented as sure of that final victory against all odds which it is no doubt slowly winning.[8]

Before, however, bringing forward Professor Key's opinion on this topic, we will turn to Professor Max Müller's Lectures of last year, especially and not incidentally devoted to the subject. In these lectures he sharply distinguishes between emotional language, which, he says, 'is certainly shared in common by man and animals,'[9] and rational language, the whole of which can be traced back to roots, every root being the sign of a general concept; or, in other words, expressive of some general idea. In drawing this distinction, the learned and eloquent professor aims at establishing the following thesis, that rational language is such a barrier between man and all

[7] 'Language: its Origin and Development,' pp. 373–375.
[8] *Westminster Review*, No. lix., July, 1866.
[9] *Fraser's Magazine*, June, 1873, p. 675.

other animals, that the theory of man's evolution from any lower form of life breaks down before it. This opinion, and the arguments he uses in its favour, we propose to examine.

One thing we may observe at the outset – he does not suggest and cannot for a moment be suspected of believing, that the earliest members of the human race were taught the roots of language by any miraculous interposition. This is probably not an uncommon view, and it may be called the parrot theory of the origin of language, implying, as it does, that articulate sounds were first supplied to men as we supply them to parrots. This, however, is not Professor Max Müller's view. While confessing, as every one must, that to account for the origin of those roots, to which analysis of all given language leads us back, is a difficult problem, he adds that 'experience gives us interjections and imitations as the only conceivable beginning of human utterance;' that is, as it seems to us, he directly affiliates the language which he calls rational to the language which he calls emotional, and of which he had already admitted that 'it is certainly shared in common by man and animals.' He shows, indeed, an uneasy consciousness that such a conclusion may naturally be drawn from his argument, by the following passage at the close of it. His words are these:–

> 'Now a clever pleader – of whom we have too many, even in the courts of science – might say. Why, does not the very theory you have propounded of the origin of roots prove that Mr. Darwin is right? Have you not shown that animals possess the materials of language in interjections; that they imitate the cries of other animals; that they communicate with each other, and give warning by shrill cries; that they know their own names, and understand the commands of their masters? Have you not 'blessed us altogether' by showing how interjections and imitations can be filed down, lose their sharp corners, become general – become, in fact, roots? Surely, after this, Mr. Darwin will be justified more than ever in saying that the language of men is the result of mere development, and that there must have been one or several generations of men who had not yet generalized their intuitions, and not yet filed down the sharp corners of their interjections.'[10]

[10] *Fraser's Magazine*, July, 1873, p. 19.

We shall have by-and-by to consider why the 'clever pleader' who puts the case so forcibly against himself, is still persuaded that this way of putting it is more plausible than truthful.

When the lectures from which we have just been quoting appeared, the 'Chapters on Language,' published in 1865, by the eloquent and learned Head Master of Marlborough College, were out of print. Dr. Farrar has long been known as a bold opponent of Professor Max Müller, and the 'Lectures' have been speedily followed by a new edition of the 'Chapters.' This reissue, on many grounds most desirable, may have been further prompted by the commendation given to the work in Mr. Darwin's 'Descent of Man.'[11] Dr. Farrar will be very generally accepted as an enlightened champion of orthodoxy. It will therefore be worth while to quote his opinion on language as a human discovery. He supports his opinion by numerous arguments, for which his books may be usefully consulted: –

'Those theologians,' he says, 'who by the liberal intrusion of unrecorded and purely imaginary miracles into every lacuna of their air-built theories, do their best to render science impossible, have earned thereby the merited suspicion of scientific men. Nevertheless, all *but* the most obstinate and the most prejudiced even of theologians ought to admit that if man *could* have invented language, we may safely conclude that he *did*; for the wasteful prodigality of direct interposition and miraculous power which plays the chief part in the idle and anti-scriptural exegesis of many churchmen, finds no place in the divine economy of God's dealings displayed to us either in nature, in history, or in the inspired Word itself. This single consideration ought to be sufficient for every mind philosophically trained.'[12]

It is rather curious that Dr. Farrar, no less than Professor Max Müller, appears to be strongly opposed to the theory of

---

[11] We have referred at the head of this paper to one chapter of Mr. Darwin's work – namely, that on the 'Comparison of the Mental Powers of Man and the Lower Animals;' not for comment or criticism, nor only because it is to this chapter especially that Professor Max Müller addresses his reply, but because it seems to us a brief and admirable summary of all that human science has yet attained to in regard to the origin of language. Very important details and reasoning will be found in Chapters V. and VI., on 'Emotional and Imitative Language,' of Mr. E. B. Tylor's 'Primitive Culture.'

[12] 'Chapters on Language,' p. 4.

evolution as applied to mankind. Witness the following passage from his sermon on 'The Voice of Conscience,' a sermon, like all his writings, full of poetic fervour. Thus he speaks: –

> 'If any rejoice to fling aside the old and inspiring conviction that man, 'so noble in reason, so infinite in faculty, in form and moving so express and admirable, in action so like an angel, in apprehension so like a god,' originated because God made him out of the dust of the earth, and breathed into his nostrils the breath of life, and to take in exchange for it the humiliating and wholly undemonstrable hypothesis that he came into being by some accident of development, I know not how, from some film of protoplasm, I know not where – still man *is*, and the facts of his inner being remain unchanged. Such beliefs, if they can be called beliefs, have indeed spread with a rapidity out of all proportion to the cogency of the arguments by which they are supposed to have been established. The great thinker who originated the theory, and whose name it is impossible to mention without admiration and respect, has distinctly declared himself against an atheistic materialism; and it has been left for his violent and reckless followers to maintain, to the outrage of all sense and of all religion, that man sprang from a single primordial moneres, which was self-generated and self-evolved, and that therefore the belief in a Creator is unscientific and exploded. Enough of such: but even in England it has been thought a necessary sequence of this belief in evolution to argue that man, thus developed, proceeded to develop a moral sense out of social instincts, fortified by hereditary transmission, and it is probably that very many even of my younger hearers have read that celebrated book on the Descent of Man, which professes – to quote the author's own words – to "approach the conscience exclusively from the side of natural history." '[13]

A little further on Dr. Farrar continues: 'Since it is common, in these times, to try and represent the clergy as wilfully shutting their eyes to all recent investigation, I only allude to these forms of scientific assertion and negation to show that what is called the silence of ignorance may sometimes be the silence of repudiation, sometimes even the reticence of scorn.' Surely,

---

[13] 'The Silence and the Voices of God.' Sermon II.

after characterizing an hypothesis as humiliating and wholly undemonstrable, and those who accept it as violent and reckless, it is rather Hibernian to say that you repudiate the whole affair in silence and dumb contempt. That a man of Dr. Farrar's calibre should apply the term 'humiliating' to a scientific hypothesis as if it could even remotely affect the question of its truth; or as if it ought to affect any mind whatever in accepting or rejecting it, is most extraordinary; whether we consider that the central fact of Christianity is intimately concerned with the deepest humiliation, or that the facts of natural science can no more be affected by our sentiments about them than iceberg. How little, too, the rhapsody from Shakespeare has to do with the matter may be seen by a moment's reflection. In form and moving we suit, perhaps, our own standard of taste; to the eagle, the shark, the lion and the fawn, we must appear feeble, awkward and slow, almost fettered to our patch of earth, unless when aided by machinery dangerous, cumbersome, and attended by noise and smoke, and other inconveniences. Of the action of angels we know nothing; that our faculties are not infinite we know very well. To say that man in apprehension is like a god is very unscriptural – unless we mean, like the silly, quarrelsome, impure gods of the heathen, gods which are no gods, but only disreputable likenesses of disreputable men. To serve a turn we may admit that man is noble in reason; but if we are writing a satire on the vanity of human wishes, or a sermon on the follies of the age, or declaiming against rationalists, this noble reason will hear itself abused as violent, reckless, petty, contemptible, retrograde, degraded, with many more 'jibes and flouts and sneers' of similar character.

One is tempted to ask who it is that describes the single primordial moneres from which some evolutionists believe man to have sprung as self-generated and self-evolved, except in a special scientific and non-theological sense of the words. An organism generated or evolved from inorganic matter, is not self-generated or self-evolved; any more than an organism generated from another organism like itself, or evolved from one unlike, is self-generated or self-evolved.[14] Haeckel's supposition, whatever we may think of his phrase for expressing it, of an animal organism 'becoming' by natural process from

[14] For Professor Max Müller's criticism on Haeckel's opinion, see *Fraser's Magazine*, July, 1873, p. 3.

inorganic matter is no more *atheistic* in itself than the *supposition* that lightnings flash among the clouds, and hail descends from the sky by natural process, although in the olden time it was Zeus that thundered, and Jehovah that rained down hailstones from heaven. As to the evolution of man and the evolution of conscience, we cannot resist confronting Dr. Farrar with his own words, that if man *could* have invented language, we may safely conclude that he *did*. In the same way, if man's body and his mental and moral powers *could* have been developed or evolved, we may safely conclude that they *were*. That they *can* be we know, because they *are* in the endless repetition of the stages through which the individual man passes between the fetus and the adult state. We ought, therefore, on Dr. Farrar's own showing, gratefully to accept the theory of evolution, even as applied to conscience, as rescuing us from a belief in 'the wasteful prodigality of interposition and miraculous power which finds no place in the Divine economy.'

At any rate, we have in Dr. Farrar a scholar and theologian of eminence strongly opposed to any hypotheses or conclusions which seem to favour an atheistic materialism; and yet at the same time one who stoutly maintains that language is a human invention. He even appends a note of admiration or astonishment when he declares that, 'some modern writers, essentially aggressive, and essentially retrogressive – doctors of that school which learns nothing and forgets nothing, and whom eighteen centuries have only pushed back behind the earliest Fathers in tolerance and liberality – can only see in the certainty of a language discovered by mankind a materialiste and deistic hypothesis.'[15] While pressing his point with great force of expression and clearness of argument, that language is undoubtedly a human discovery, he ridicules, as a piece of 'futile and baseless arrogance,' the objection that before the discovery man must have borne the undignified and degraded position of being, through long and feeble periods of animalism and ignorance, a dumb creature. 'Disbelieving,' he says, 'on the scientific ground of the fixity of type, the Darwinian hypothesis, we should yet consider it disgraceful and humiliating to try to shake it by an *ad captandum* argument, or a claptrap platform appeal to the unfathomable ignorance and unlimited

[15] 'Chapters on Language,' p. 8.

arrogance of a prejudiced assembly. We should blush to meet it with an anathema or a sneer; and in doing so we should be very far from the ludicrous and complacent assumption that we were on the side of the angels.'[16] In the sermon, it will be remembered, it was the Darwinian hypothesis itself that was humiliating; here it is the unreasoning condemnation of it that earns that epithet. The preacher seems closely to agree with the platform orator in the assumption, which is at least complacent, whether ludicrous or not, of thinking man 'in action so like an angel.' But in estimating the merit of such an appeal to the feelings against the Simian origin of mankind, we ought not, perhaps, to forget that the pulpit was the pulpit of Cambridge University, while Mr. Disraeli was only adressing the ignorance and arrogance of an Oxford mob.

Considering that Dr. Farrar, on many and apparently solid grounds, is satisfied that 'science banishes amongst myths and chimeras the fancy of a primitive man, burning with youth and beauty; to show us upon icy shores I know not what abject being more hideous than the Australian, more savage than the Patagonian, a fierce animal struggling against the animals with which he disputes his miserable existence,'[17] there is a taste, a slight savour of that dogmatism which he elsewhere censures in Professor Max Müller, in his subsequent declaration, that, 'undoubtedly the idea of speech existed in the human intelligence, as a part of our moral and mental constitution when man first appeared upon the surface of the earth.'[18] If man was not man till he had the idea of speech, and if there was no human intelligence prior to that form or degree of intelligience which had the idea of speech existing in it, then the statement is a truism: if it means more than this, it begs the question. One who, like Dr. Farrar, 'can contemplate the human race as originally created in a low and barbarous condition,' who does not refuse to see in his far-off ancestors a 'miserable population, maintaining an inglorious struggle with the powers of nature, wrestling with naked bodies against the forest animals, and forced to dispute their cave-dwellings with the hyæna and the wolf;' one who sees nothing 'irreverent or absurd' in the hypothesis, though he disbelieves it, 'that myriads of centuries

---

[16] Ibid., p. 44.
[17] Ibid., p. 43.
[18] Ibid., p. 51.

ago, there may have been a near genetic connexion between the highest of the animals and the lowest of the human race,' may well be content with the positions he has really won, without claiming ground which his inquiries and argument certainly do not cover. 'Thus far shalt thou come and no further,' is a cry too often addressed to science even by its most devoted and successful students. So, one philosopher will carry language back to 'roots,' but forbid inquiry as to the origin of these roots themselves; another will solve that mystery, and display to us human beings 'with the germs of language and the primitive idea of it:' but lower than that he will not permit us to delve. He can imagine and allow a creature angel-like in mien and movement, god-like in reasoning power and moral state, to be at least possibly descended from an ape; but those who dare track the possible ancestral monkey back to a primordial moneres are fools and atheists; they cannot be allowed to protest that the wisdom of God is just as much glorified by the *results*, whether we trace back an Elijah and an Æschylus, or any other king among men, gradually to shapeless protoplasm, or abruptly to lifeless dust. If even a man believes matter to be eternal, does it make him an atheist, seeing that all hold the Supreme Being unchangeable, whence it follows that to the Divine mind all things that are both ever have been, and ever will be, what they are? Before many years are over the doctrine of the evolution of all organic life from lifeless inorganic material may come to be proclaimed by eloquent and orthodox theologians as agreeing with the express statement of the Book of Genesis, that 'The Lord God formed man of the dust of the ground.' We shall then be told that those who maintain the old view of the direct creation of living beings, 'distinctly contradict the very book to which, in their desire to usurp the keys of all knowledge, they groundlessly appeal as a scientific authority,' and that to assert the *creation* of animals as opposed to their *evolution*, 'is, after the manner of certain ignorant divines, to force upon us as an article of faith, that which is nothing more than an arbitrary and anti-philosophic hypothesis.'[19] Just as the kindly and well-intentioned barbarians of Melita, when they saw the viper fasten upon Paul's hand, said among themselves, 'No doubt this man is a murderer, whom, though he hath escaped the sea, yet vengeance suffereth not to

[19] 'Chapters on Language,' p. 6.

live;' but, after they had looked a great while and saw no harm come to him, changed their minds and said that he was a god; even so, when some slightly venomous epithet, such as 'infidel,' or 'atheistic,' is fastened upon a new scientific theory, the multitude expect it to collapse, and presently fall dead; but after looking a great while, and seeing no harm come to it, they change their minds and say that it is divine.

A writer in these columns, to whom we have already referred, pointed out, as we think, with great force and truth, that the origin of language ought not to be assigned to a twofold source, interjections *and* imitative cries, since the interjection itself must be due in the first instance to imitation. The new edition of Dr. Farrar's work being only a reprint, he has not had the opportunity of giving his opinion upon this simplification of the view which he has himself so ably urged and illustrated. Had he taken it into consideration, it could have scarcely failed to open his eyes to the more than probability that man, without even interjections, with nothing vocal except mere animal cries, in the state in which he must have been upon this theory before the evolution of language, will have been something less than man. Once admit that something less than man could become, and has become man, and all controversy of man's evolution from this, that, or the other stage of degradation, humiliation, savagery, animalism, or protoplasm, will speedily die out, or be relegated to that cold but serene region of inquiry in which wishes and emotions, and 'prejudicate opinions' have no sway. The riddle so repeatedly quoted from Wilhelm v. Humboldt's writings, that 'man is only man through language, but to invent language he must already have been man,' is not solved by the answer that language, properly speaking, was never invented but slowly developed, without the additional remark that neither was man, properly speaking, ever invented, but like language, slowly developed, so that at one stage of the process there will have been a half-human creature with a half articulate language; at another stage a savage, with few abstract ideas, and few, if not fewer, words to express them, with no general term for existence, no logic, no grammar; and only after many ages of lisping and stammering, and specializing and despecializing, and picturing, and writing, and printing, is a philosopher sure, whenever he is addressing human beings, of addressing *rational* animals.

Professor Key fully and explicitly accepts the mimetic theory.

'I conclude,' he says, 'with the expression of a strong opinion that original language is mimetic – in other words, consisted solely in the imitation of natural sounds; nor am I deterred from this conclusion by what I readily admit, that in a very large number of cases we are still unable to explain the rationale of the selection. Meanwhile I look in vain for any other tenable theory' (p. 22). We cannot help thinking that it would have been graceful in Professor Key to have noticed Dr. Farrar's eloquent writings in support of the theory to which he thus gives his decided adhesion. For any such notice we have looked in vain. There is, moreover, a slight querulousness of tone in more than one passage, in reference to other writers, which would have been as well avoided by a scholar in Mr. Key's acknowledged and assured position. For instance, after repeating, from his writings of forty years ago, the opinion 'that the fifth syllable in the Sapphic stanza ought for the most part to have a strong accent,' and a protest 'against the misleading influence of the anti-Jacobin verses in pseudo-Sapphic form, entitled the "Knife-Grinder," ' it was scarcely worth while to find occasion for the following statement: – 'The same doctrine and the same illustration appeared in the first edition of the 'Varronianus' (p. 275 note), without any reference to either of my articles.' The explanation in a foot note scarcely mends the matter; it is this:–

'I purposely insert this evidence of the plagiarism of Dr. Donaldson in a trifling matter, that I may express my contempt for the silly statement of a Reviewer, that it is 'shocking' to make such a reference to one who is no more. As I publicly exposed his doings during his lifetime, so now, too, I reject the doctrine *de mortuis nil nisi bonum*, for what is better morality, *nil nisi verum*.'

But surely one cannot want better morality than for a man to abstain from attacking an antagonist who is no longer in a position to defend himself. Besides, whatever Dr. Donaldson's merits or demerits may have been, and no doubt he had some of both, the stream of controversy, in which in his day he was at least a lively swimmer, has now passed on beyond him. For the praise of men he is no longer a competitor; by their dispraise we can scarcely suppose him to be affected, so that jealousy and righteous indignation alike would seem to be misspent in making him their mark. It may be well and useful to point out where he has slipped in philology or brought forward a grammatical form without authority; but a charge of trivial plagiarism had far better be allowed to slumber. It is notorious that thinkers in all departments at times come independently to the same conclusions, couching them in almost the same phraseology, supporting them by the same illustrations. A student who reads much and thinks much may be excused if he sometimes forgets what part of the stores of his mind is due to the first process and what to the second. Mr. Key may believe that this would apply to the theft of his opinion about the accent in Sapphics, or to the theft of his illustration, each taken simply, but that it cannot excuse the appropriation of both together. This, however, is not so certain, since the very familiarity of an illustration may create an impression that the idea which it illustrates is equally familiar, and has in fact all along been our own. Some writers, among whom we may single out Mr. E. B. Tylor as a very favourable example, have so suggestive a style, that before they reveal their discoveries their readers have made them for themselves; just as we read that among the Athenians wit well matched between speaker and audience often made the hearers fancy themselves the authors beforehand of what the orator's ingenuity propounded. There are, it may be admitted, unscrupulous writers whose plagiarisms deserve exposure, but the exposure to be useful should be in the lifetime of the plagiarist, and should not include trifles.

Turning now again to Professor Max Müller's lectures, one must confess that he seems entirely to concede the whole point in controversy between himself and Dr. Farrar, for though he still holds that his '*roots* or *phonetic types* are indeed the ultimate facts in the analysis of language,' he admits 'that, from a higher and philosophical point of view, they admit of a perfectly intelligible explanation,' since, as he says, 'experience gives us interjections and imitations as the only conceivable beginning of human utterance.' This is rather like saying that the Land's End is indeed the last portion of English territory looking westward, though, from a higher and geographical point of view, we know that the Scilly Isles, which are also English territory, lie beyond it. But while accepting as possible, as probable, as almost certain, the evolution of language from interjections and imitative cries through what he calls a process of *friction* or *despecialization*, Professor Max Müller is as anxious as ever to combat the possibility of man's evolution from 'an animal.' He appeals to what he designates as 'one palpable fact,' viz., 'that whatever animals may do or not do, *no animal has ever spoken.*'[20] He maintains as an axiom that thought without language is impossible[21] and declares that 'no animal except man possesses the faculty, or the faintest germs of the faculty, of abstracting and generalizing, and that therefore no animal, except man, could ever have developed what we mean by language.'[22] On the historical ground that no animal ever *has* spoken, he raises, it will be perceived, a strong presumption that no animal ever *will* speak. On the philosophical ground that language without thought is as impossible as thought without language, he seems to carry that presumption to demonstration, if a creature can never use language until it can reason, and can never reason until it has the use of language.

But surely all this is begging the very question in dispute; for if the theory of evolution be true as applied to mankind and men are descended, it matters little through how many generations, from animals which were dumb, as some human beings are even now, it will no longer be true that *no animal has ever spoken.* According to the theory under discussion there must have come a time when some of these animals learned to make a general application of some of their interjections and imitative cries; and this they must have done either with thought or without it. If the language was antecedent to the thought, then language without thought is possible; if the thought was antecendent to the language, then thought without language is possible; if neither could have the precedence, it simply follows that the thought and the expression of it must have occurred to the mind of the animal simultaneously. Mr. Darwin says, 'Man not only uses inarticulate cries, gestures, and expressions, but has invented articulate language;' and then adds, with his usual mixture of caution and insight – 'if, indeed, the word *invented* can be applied to a process completed by innumerable steps, half-consciously made.' This reflection, extended to thought and reason, releases us from any dilemma as to the alternative priority of words and con-

---

[20] *Fraser's Magazine*, June, 1873, p. 674.
[21] Ibid., May, 1873, p. 528.
[22] *Fraser's Magazine*, July, 1873, p. 23.

cepts. Professor Max Müller, too, affirms that 'in the usual sense of that word language was never invented,' apparently imagining that he is establishing a position in support of his own views. His opinion on the impassable gulf which separates the human from the animal intellect, that no number of steps could ever lead from the one to the other, may best be seen by an illustration of his own devising. He asks, 'What do we mean when we say we know a thing?' He then introduces a child for the first time in its life seeing an elephant, staring at, feeling, and measuring it, but concludes that we should never say, the first time the child sees an elephant, that he knows it. When, however, the child sees the same elephant, or another elephant, a second time, and *recognises* the animal as the same, or nearly the same which he saw before, then, for the first time, we say that the child knows the elephant.

Still 'this is knowledge in its lowest and crudest form.' 'It is properly speaking *remembering* only, and not yet *cognition*. The animal intellect, according to the ordinary interpretation, would go as far as this, but no farther.' We are then invited to take, not exactly a child, but a boy who for the first time sees an elephant. This clever boy, it seems, though he does not know the elephant, knows that what he sees for the first time is an *animal*. 'What does that mean? It means that the boy possesses the concept of a living and breathing being, different from man, and that he recognises this general concept in the elephant before him.' But why should we not take not exactly a boy, but a dog, who for the first time sees an elephant. Assuredly the dog, though he does not know the elephant, will know that what he sees for the first time is an animal, and then we may ask, what does that mean? and answer, as the Professor answers, *mutatis mutandis*, concluding, as he concludes, 'Now an animal, as such, has no actual existence. A boy (or a dog) may have seen dogs, cats, and mice, but never an animal in general. The concept of animal is therefore of man's (or dog's) own making, and its only object is to enable man (or dog) to know?' But, without appealing to any quadruped, we think that the Professor explicitly admits and affirms the very thing which he is striving to prove impossible, for he admits as an unquestioned truth, 'that language, in the usual sense of the word, is not the only organ of conceptual thought;' that, 'besides the phonetic symbols of language there are other less perfect symbols of thought;' that 'we can form the concept of "*three*," without any spoken word, by simply holding up three fingers,' that 'this is how people who possessed no organs of speech would speak; this is how the deaf and dumb *do* speak.' It is almost startling, after having been told on the previous page, in emphatic italics, that '*there is no thought without words, as little as there are words without thought;*' and, while respectfully regarding the fortress of language as a fortress still 'untaken and unshaken on the very frontier between the animal kingdom and man,' nevertheless to have to read, that 'three fingers are as good as three strokes; three strokes are as good as three clicks of the tongue, three clicks of the tongue are as good as the sound *three*, or *trois*, or *drei*, or *shalosh* in Hebrew, or *san* in Chinese. But all these are signs, and being signs, symbols, or embodiments of concepts, they fall under the general category of *logos* or language?[23]

Such signs and symbols animals have at their command, and undoubtedly use, whether for showing an acquaintance with arithmetic, we need not discuss, but certainly for communications which imply the possession of conceptual or discursive thought. The nocturnal intruder, the ill-dressed applicant, are recognised by the dog, and the creature not only says to itself, but by gait, by action, by voice, all perfectly intelligible, declares to its human friends and companions, that men are at hand, but not men of the right sort, nor present in the right time or in the right place. The Professor seems to have been almost overwhelmed by ladies, young and old, with anecdotes of intellectual cats and dogs, but for the subject he is handling too many cannot be accumulated, if only they are truthful. We know a dog which has been taught to sit up and beg by waving its two fore-paws conjointly up and down. Eager and impetuous expectancy it expresses most ludicrously by rapidity of the movement. The slow and intermittent motion, as hope of success dwindles to despair, is proportionately pathetic. The eyes at the same time appear to exchange imperious glances for looks of supplication. Food and exercise are two of the principal requirements of canine existence; it is about these, therefore, that the dog oftenest *speaks* to those on whom he is dependent for their satisfaction. Accordingly, the dog to which we have been referring, uses its greatest urgency of appeal when a chance of a walk presents itself. It will also be

[23] *Fraser's Magazine*, July, 1873, p. 13.

quiet through the earlier portion of dinner, till its favourite course comes on, although the number of courses which precede it is not a constant one. Whether for walking or feeding, it pleads most persistently with those who are in general most ready to oblige it, whilst with others it will make a short effort and then desist. Another dog, accustomed as so many are, to beg at mealtime, could be dismissed by a gesture of opening the arms to signify that we had no more to give it. This gesture we employed, in the first instance almost unconsciously, but the dog, both on that occasion and many subsequent ones seemed fully to comprehend its meaning, if we may judge by its at once quitting our side to seek indulgence elsewhere.

Professor Max Müller quotes an instance of a pike, which was separated from some small fishes in the same aquarium by a pane of glass. After hurting himself severely in several ineffectual attempts to seize these fishes, the pike gave up the attempt, and when some months later, the pane of glass was removed, continued to respect his original companions, though he swallowed any strange fish that was thrown in with natural voracity. Then comes the inference, translated with approval from a paper by Professor Möbius, 'the training of this pike was not therefore based on judgment; it consisted only in the establishment of a certain direction of will in consequence of uniformly recurrent sensuous impressions.' The view of the familiar fishes 'provoked in him, no doubt, the natural desire to swallow them, but it evoked at the same time the recollection of the pain which he had suffered on their account, and the sad impression that it was impossible to reach the prey which he so much desired.' The same sensuous impression, proceeding from the same fishes and overpowering his voracious instinct, was always 'the beginning of the same series of psychic acts. He could not help repeating this series, like a machine, but like a machine with a soul, which has this advantage over mechanical machines, that it can adapt its work to unforeseen circumstances, while a mechanical machine cannot. The pane of glass was to the organism of the pike one of these unforeseen circumstances'.

This philosophy, if new as applied to fishes, is not altogether new in itself, which, after ascribing to the pike a certain direction of *will*, declares that, willy nilly, he *could not help* repeating a series of psychic acts. But what is this machine with a soul that can adapt itself to unforeseen circumstances, when the unforeseen circumstance is a pane of glass, yet cannot adapt itself when the unforeseen circumstance is the removal of the pane? It may have been an error of judgment on the pike's part not to eat the familiar fish when the barrier was removed, but surely we may say that he associated with the attempt to devour them the *ideas* of danger and distress, and *judged* it safer not to make the attempt. He feels the natural desire to swallow them, he remembers the pain formerly suffered through trying to gratify his desire, and abstains. How does this result differ from that which we aim at in the treatment of the dangerous classes, the pikes of human society? We seek in them to establish a 'certain direction of the will, in consequence of uniformly recurrent sensuous impressions.' The misfortune is that we cannot make the impressions recur with sufficient uniformity. The idle boy learns his lesson to avoid the rod. The same sensuous impression, overpowering his natural love of ease, is always in his soul the beginning of the same series of psychic acts. He cannot help repeating this series like a machine, but like a machine with a soul, which has the advantage of being able to adapt its work to unforeseen circumstances, such as his master's ascertained and protracted absence, and then he finds that he *can* help repeating the series, just as sometimes a fracas breaks out in 'a happy family' or a tame lion scalps the lion-tamer.

The pike, with a persistency worthy of Robert Bruce, continued its onsets against the transparent barrier, though with diminishing frequency, for three months, before what we must call its judgment was convinced that, even for pikes, 'there is no armour against fate;' that some *super-piscal* power was interfering for the protection of its natural prey. It is rather too much to ask us to believe that the pike was restrained by 'the sad impression that it was impossible to reach the prey which he so much desired,' at the very time when he was swimming freely among these fishes, before whom he 'always halted at a respectful distance of about an inch.' The whole analysis of the pike's education might be fitted to the analysis of human education in the sphere of morals and personal prudence, so that of the loftiest actions done in obedience to the dictates of conscience, we should have to say that they were 'not based on judgment,' but due only to 'the establishment of a certain direction of will in consequence of uniformly recurrent sensuous impressions.' It is an old doctrine in regard to human character that by training and habit our wills do become so set in one direction that morally we lose the power of choice and *cannot help* acting in the manner which has become habitual to us. That a pike should be like a man in this respect will be no great matter for surprise to an evolutionist; his only wonder will be that such a conclusion should be approved and welcomed by an opponent of evolution. For, if it shows, which we question, 'how much can be achieved by purely intuitional knowledge, possessed in common by men and animals,' without the help of conceptual knowledge, it shows still more forcibly how narrow an interval separates the education and moral development of a fish from that of a human being.

After admitting that the deaf and dumb can acquire some kind of conceptual thought and language, though, of course, their language cannot possibly include *phonetic* types, Professor Max Müller gives a facetious description of abortive attempts to think silently, to conjure up without words the thought, for instance, of a *dog*. Banish all synonyms, and begin, 'Rise up, then, quadruped, with ears and wagging tail.' Alas! words, words; we must begin again. 'The inner consciousness sinks lower, and at last there rises a being to be developed gradually and insensibly into a dog.' But 'being,' too, is a word. We must try again in breathless silence. This time we are greeted with the Professor's favourite 'bow-wow,' itself a word, and the attempt is relinquished as hopeless. He scarcely seems, in this obviously imaginary description, to have remembered the power which the association of ideas exercises over the human mind, owing to which we may be unable to separate an idea from the verbal symbol of it, when once the two have been connected together, while, if we *were* able to effect such a separation, it would obviously be out of the question to convey to other minds a notion of our success by words. 'We do not complain,' the Professor says, 'that we cannot move without legs. Why, then, should we consider it humiliating that we cannot think without words?' Certainly, as a matter of sentiment, there is nothing humiliating in the use either of legs or of language; but, as a matter of fact, men do manage to move who have lost their legs; men do manage to think even when they are dumb; and numbers of other animals move, although they have no legs, by means of other contrivances. So that if we may trust the simile, there may be other contrivances besides language to make thought possible. What else, indeed, can be the meaning of St. Paul's expression, when he speaks of 'groanings which cannot be uttered;' and of poets, when they tell of thoughts too deep for words? Are there no general ideas involved in the emotions thus alluded to? How is it with infants? How is it with us in maturer age at times when we are just awaking from sleep, or awaking from the confusion of some surprise, and go through the process known as collecting our thoughts; or again, when the memory is half-treacherous, and we are conscious of remembering, and are yet unable to convey the idea in language? Who is not conscious that he often says much more than he means, and often much less than he means? What is the feeling that we cannot find words to express what is in our minds if there be no thought without language? Professor Max Müller himself speaks of the work as occasionally still being accomplished, of coining a new word for a new thought, though how such coining is possible, or why it is necessary, if you cannot have the thought without the word, he does not explain. He tells us, on what he deems good authority, 'that deaf and dumb persons, if left entirely to themselves, have no concepts except such as can be expressed by less perfect symbols; and that it is only by being taught that they acquire some kind of conceptual thought and language.' The sentence appears to be self-contradictory, for if they have, when left to themselves, such concepts as can be expressed by less perfect symbols, they have a kind of conceptual thought and language independently of teaching. That it is a very imperfect kind, compared with that which they may acquire by instruction, will not be denied. Rather, it will be insisted on as indicating the possible or conceivable gradations in the development of man from a lower animal. When stress is laid on the possibility or conceivableness of such a development, it shows a curious misapprehension to answer that 'the very opposite, the non-transition of any lower animal into man, is equally conceivable.'[24] No one ever denied it, while hundreds have declaimed against the theory of evolution, both as inconceivable in itself, and a piece of inconceivable folly on the part of its propounders. To say that, moreover, the non-transition, at least, as far as our experience goes, is real, seems altogether

[24] *Fraser's Magazine*, July, 1873, p. 22.

beside the point, since the non-creation of any animal whatever, *at least, as far as our experience goes*, is equally real.

Professor Max Müller believes that language was made by men at a period beyond the reach of tradition, but still at a period which must have had an historical reality. He enforces his view by a geological comparison. 'As,' he says, 'during enormous periods of time the earth was absorbed in producing the abundant carboniferous vegetation, which still supplies us with the means of warmth, light, and life, there must have been a period during which the human mind had no other work but that of linguistic vegetation, the produce of which still supplies the stores of our grammars and dictionaries.'[25]

Geologists will scarcely agree with him that the earth was ever absorbed, if that means exclusively occupied, in producing carboniferous vegetation; but, letting that pass, we may fairly inquire what were the seeds from which the linguistic vegetation sprung, and it almost looks as if we should be driven back upon the answer which 'the clever pleader' gave us, that rational language was gradually developed from emotional language – that it grew out of those ejaculations and imitative cries which man shares in common with other animals.

In one passage Professor Max Müller tells us that if Mr. Darwin is right, then the great German philosopher, Kant, and all who follow him, will simply be out of court. It may seem, then, something too positive on his part when, in another passage, he speaks of Kant's great work, 'The Criticism of Pure Reason,' as 'a work which, in the onward stream of philosophic thought, has stood, and will stand for ever, like the rocks of Niagara.' Here, again, the geologist will tell him that the rocks of Niagara will certainly not stand for ever, unless the laws of friction and of aqueous and atmospheric action in general are to be altered in their favour. But supposing the philosophy of Kant to be an eternal verity, lasting, therefore, when the rocks of Niagara have been worn to powder, a great part of Darwin's theory might still be maintained, the Professor himself being the judge, for he says,—

> 'Were we to accept the theory of evolution which traces the human mind back to the inner life of a mollusc, we should even then be able to remain Kantians, in so far as it would

[25] *Fraser's Magazine*, May, 1873, p. 528.

be, even then, the category of causality that works in the mollusc, and makes it extend its tentacles towards the crumb of bread which has touched it, and has evoked in it a reflex action, a grasping after the prey. In this lowest form of animal life, therefore, the category of causality, if we may use such a term, would show itself simply as conscious, or, at all events, as no longer involuntary, re-action; in human life, it shows itself in the first glance of recognition that lights up the infant's vacant stare.'[26]

To ordinary minds to speak of the category of causality working in a mollusc, or working in a man, will seem equally unintelligible modes of expression; but whatever these may mean, since reflex actions can be excited in animals, and fragments of animals, without the will or knowledge of the patient, we cannot infer simply from the existence of such movements that the reaction is either conscious or voluntary. We have similar phenomena in vegetable irritability, well-known especially in the tribe of sensitive plants, without, it may safely be said, either consciousness or will. There may even be animals, such as sponges, in which all the actions necessary to their life and sustenance are carried on without voluntary effort, and with a scarcely appreciable glimmer of consciousness. Here, then, at the outset, among the lowest members of the animal kingdom, we have the whole controversy at once before us. If reflex actions could never develop into voluntary and conscious actions, but must have been so by the work of original creation, or not at all, then, indeed, the theory of development, without further parley, is out of court. Between the unconscious and the conscious the interval is surely as great as that between an animal which jabbers and an animal which talks.

Some may be well pleased to take the issue in this form, feeling confident that we shall never be able to discover what the feelings of a sponge are, or whether its ancestors were absolutely without any. No doubt to many minds the sentiment of the French proverb will occur, 'c'est le premier pas qui coûte,' but in reality each onward step is as difficult as the first, the development of higher powers of consciousness from the lower as difficult as the development of the lower from none

[26] *Fraser's Magazine*, May, 1873, p. 540.

at all. Yet it can scarcely be profound philosophy to say that these onward steps can never be taken because we do not understand how they can. How often must it be repeated that the theory of development seeks to explain what has actually come to pass in the world's history, not why it has come to pass in that way rather than another! It is not a whit more reasonable to speak of it as a theory of creation without Creator, than it would be for a man, who knows that he has passed through various embryonic and unconscious stages to the ripeness of perfect manhood, to say that he had attained to that state without having had any parents. Such a reasoner might, so far as we can see, prove that he had never been a baby at all by precisely the same line of argument which is used to prove that man cannot have descended from a mute animal. Substitute *infants* for *animals* in the language of Professor Max Müller, and observe what the alteration will make him say: 'The rules of positive philosophy,' he will tell you, 'forbid us to assert anything about their instincts or intellectual faculties. We may allow ourselves to be guided by our own fancies or by analogy, and we may guess and assert very plausibly many things about the inner life of *infants*; but however strong our own belief may be, the whole subject is transcendant, *i.e.*, beyond the reach of positive knowledge;' only we can 'appeal to one palpable fact, viz., that whatever infants may do or not do, no *infant* has ever spoken,' from which line of argument it seems we are to infer that no infant has ever developed into a man.

Again, language, such as we speak, is founded on reason, reason meaning for philosophical purposes the faculty of forming and handling general concepts; and as that power manifests itself outwardly by articulate language only, we, as positive philosophers, have a right to say that *infants* being devoid of the only tangible sign of reason which we know, viz., language, may by us be treated as irrational beings, irrational ... 'in the sense of devoid of the power of forming and handling general concepts.'

But we all know that the apparently unconscious embryo *does* pass by certain gradations into the apparently conscious infant, and the apparently irrational infant into the reasoning man. Professor Max Müller finds fault with the expression 'insensible graduation.' He says it 'is self contradictory,' that, 'translated into English it means graduation without graduation, degrees without degrees, or something which is at the same time perceptible and imperceptible.' 'Exact science,' he affirms, 'has nothing to do with insensible graduation.' 'The admission,' he maintains, 'of this insensible graduation would eliminate, not only the difference between ape and man, but likewise between black and white, hot and cold, a high and a low note in music; in fact it would do away,' he says, 'with the possibility of all exact and definite knowledge.'

But what, we may ask, is the worth of exact and definite knowledge unless it be true? We speak of the deepest black and the purest white and of many intermediate shades of grey, but it is easy at least to conceive that there may be innumerable gradations besides those to which we give names, which our senses with all available aids are not fine enough to distinguish; and these we should call insensible gradations.[27] Indeed, as it seems to us, one would naturally use the above illustrations of black and white, hot and cold, high and low, to show how real differences of great importance may be gradually established by stages so small that, as far as human perception is concerned, we may have, not, as often in argument, a distinction without a difference, but a difference without, for us, the possibility of distinction. A white garment may gradually become black, and frozen water slowly pass to a temperature at boiling point, and in this way the difference may be eliminated between black and white, hot and cold, just as the difference between ape and man may have been eliminated by the process of development. But in truth it is a faulty mode of expression to speak of the difference as eliminated in either case, for no one pretends that ape and man are actually alike, any more than they would pretend that ice and steam are of the same temperature, when arguing that one may be developed from the other. When the eloquent Professor maintains that, in a supposed series of beings intermediate between ape and man, the point where the animal ends and man begins could be determined with absolute precision, in that it would be coincident with the first formation of a general idea embodied in a general term, he can scarcely perceive the full force of his own obser-

---

[27] Compare 'Language: its Origin and Development,' p. 28. 'Of necessity the symbols for vowel-sounds must be limited, but this must not be allowed to hide from us the fact that the sounds themselves are simply infinite, the passage from the one to the other of the few which have a special notation being by *imperceptible gradations*.'

vation. He must, one would think, mean that at this point there would be a specific difference between the animal possessing a general term for a general concept and the animal without such a term. He must, we say, mean this, for the whole controversy turns on the question whether two such animals could stand to one another in the relationship of parent and child. But if he means this, what is there to prevent some one else from affirming that the possession or absence of a musical ear constitutes another specific difference, and that either persons who can distinguish the tune of 'God save the Queen' are something more than human, or that those who cannot are something less? No savage ever wrote an opera or an oratorio, but it would be extremely arbitrary to maintain on that account that the men who write them are a different species from the Fuegians and the Andamaners. The whole art and science of music itself has attained its present perfection through insensible gradations from beginnings which, if the figures of ancient instruments and the usages of the modern savage may be trusted, would have been regarded by Handel and Mozart as little better than atrocious noise and discord. The point, moreover, at which the Professor separates the animal from man he defines as *coincident* with the outburst of a general idea. This is worthy of notice, because not only would the coincidence separate father and son into two distinct species, but it might just as well separate one and the same individual into two species, not otherwise than would be the case if a man by learning to read ceased to be a man and became a demigod. In fact, the coincidence in question lands us in this dilemma, that, either the human infant has general ideas without general terms to express them, which the learned Professor denies to be possible, or else, the human infant, as long as it is an infant is not human but only an animal, separated with absolute precision, by wanting the *proprium* of rational language, from the species man.

The acquisition of rational language has no doubt given to the human mind a gigantic superiority over that of every other animal, but this very superiority has been one of gradual acquisition, aided immensely by other acquisitions which come more or less within the known period of history. Such are the arts of writing and printing, the applications of steam and electricity, nay, even algebra and road-making, since all of these have contributed to make the exceptional sagacity of individual men the common property of the whole race and its enduring heritage.

The question is often asked why, if man was originally a mute animal, other creatures should so long have remained dumb, especially as dogs, apes, and elephants, have the beginnings of reason attributed to them no less than the supposed speechless ancestry of mankind. In answer to this it must be remembered that, compared with man's whole career upon the earth, the time during which he has possessed articulate speech may be but a short period, and that the other animals may be at a less relative distance behind us than we are apt to suppose. Twenty thousand years hence, when dogs have learned to speak, but not yet learned to print, the orthodox philosophers of the day will contend that the fortress of printing 'stands untaken and unshaken on the very frontier between the animal kingdom and man,' and 'still appeal to one palpable fact, that whatever animals may do or not do, no animal has ever' *printed*.

In a deficiency of the power of generalizing, savage languages, as Dr. Farrar well shows (p. 177), from numerous authors, have that very peculiarity on which Professor Max Müller relies so much in regard to the mental faculties of the lower animals. Between the tribe which first acquired some feeble form of human language, and the anthropoid tribes nearest to it, there is no reason to suppose any great difference to have existed at the outset. But such difference as there was would be rapidly increased in two ways: in the first place, the human being would improve and turn to various uses his new faculty, while the Simian, not having the faculty to being with, would make no advance. In the second place the human tribe, with its improved means of combination, would be almost sure to stamp out its immediate inferiors, as being its most powerful rivals in the struggle for life. It would be in its power, it would be in its interest, to do so. Can the result be doubted at an early stage of civilization, seeing that in our own day the less cultured races of mankind are continually falling before the Anglo-Saxon overflow, and thus making the distance between men and animals ever wider and wider? Practically language has been a weapon of war, an instrument for gaining the mastery. How little anxious men will have been in past days to impart it to other animals may be understood from what has happened in the parallel and analogous case of reading. Though a man incapable of reading is only half a man compared with his fellows who have that capacity, still it is only with serious misgivings and the greatest reluctance that the governing classes of our own country have been induced to concede education in this respect in any secure and substantial form to the classes beneath them. To substitute an instructed mind for a machine-like pair of hands was thought dangerous to the exigences of farm-labour and domestic service, and many religious and kindly persons, fully if unconsciously believing in the divine right of the upper ten thousand, would gladly find some expedient, if they could, by which the children of the poor might be taught how to read the Bible and Catechism, without learning how to read any other literature which can only make them 'uppish,' 'above their places,' discontented with the state of life to which they have been called, and thorns in the sides of their 'betters,' instead of obedient machines, to work and work on without comment and without reproach, till they and their masters alike—

'Must in the ground be equal laid
With the poor crooked scythe and spade.'

Dr. Farrar closes his very interesting chapter on Interjections to which, aided by association of ideas, he attributes the beginnings of language, with an allusion to the subject we have been discussing. After declaring that the divine secret of language lay completely revealed in the use of two or three despised 'interjections,' he appends the following note:—

'The objection, "Why, then, did not animals also discover language?" rises so often from the grave where it was long since buried and appears to be endowed with such inextinguishable vitality, that we must *again* repeat that it was not the *mere* possession of these vocal cries that enabled man to invent a language, but that, the Innate Idea of language being already in his mind by virtue of his divinely created organism, the possession of these natural sounds taught him how, and supplied him the materials wherewith, to develop the Idea into perfect speech.'

It is a pity to confuse a scientific argument by the use of expressions either theological or simply rhetorical, and in either case inadmissible for the purpose in hand. If language were an express revelation, according to the old opinion which Dr.

Farrar emphatically rejects, it would be appropriate to speak of it as *a divine secret*; but being, as he admits, a human discovery, it is as little of a divine secret as printing or painting. His explanation, too, why man alone has developed speech is not a reason at all, but a theological opinion. Man, and animals below man, are alike organisms divinely created, alike in possession of vocal cries. To affirm that man alone developed speech because man alone had the innate idea of it implanted in his mind, is to provoke the question. How do you know that what you are saying is true? It does not seem especially reverential to the Author of the Universe, that we should only fit in His agency, like that of a theatrical *deus ex machinâ*, in those odd corners, and on those occasions where and when we find ourselves unable to solve a scientific enigma. The old theory of mountain ranges was that they were so shaped when the foundations of the earth were laid by the Creative hand. The natural processes are now known of aqueous deposition, the massing together of organic remains, slow and gradual, or rapid but intermittent, upheavals, with concurrent and atmospheric disintegration and waste. No one, therefore, any longer speaks in a scientific treatise of the divine secret of mountain formations; and we venture to think that the most pious among educated persons would be disgusted with a geologist, who, being asked to explain why some parts of the earth had been elevated into ranges of hills, while others remained level plains, should answer that the rise of a hill was due to the innate principle of elevation, residing in its constituent materials by virtue of their divinely created formation. Yet this innate principle of elevation would be as easy to assert and as difficult to disprove as Dr. Farrar's innate idea of language. As scientific explanations they have this slight drawback to their value, that they explain nothing. Between this divinely implanted innate idea of language, prior to any actual form of speech, and Professor Max Müller's phonetic types existing, 'as Plato would say, by nature, though with Plato we would add, that when we say by nature, we mean by the hand of God,' there seems but little to choose on the score of consistency, since both authors alike reject the miraculous origin of language.

Language may now be claimed as congenital to man – born with him; but it is only congenital as a beard and moustache are congenital. Had the faculty been a special endowment, abruptly bestowed, instead of being, as we contend, the result of gradual development, there is no reason why an infant should not have received the power to speak as soon as it is born, just as a chicken begins to pick up food as soon as it emerges from the shell. How much odious squalling of babies would be saved! How much needless pain would be spared if the babies could communicate their sorrows and disgusts in some more intelligible manner than by cries and yells! But the theory of development makes it easy to understand the present state of affairs. For language, as an acquisition, would have reached its grand climacteric, not first in the minds and mouths of animals very young or newly born, but in those of the adult and mature. Then, like many other variations, it would have a tendency to be inherited at a corresponding age, and, in course of time, at successively earlier periods of life. This theory, be it remembered, of inheritance at corresponding ages, and then at ages earlier and earlier, is not invented here and now for the sake of the present argument. It was invented to account for ascertained facts in the development of crustaceans; and it must be admitted as at least a remarkable coincidence when the same theory will equally account for certain phases in the life-history of a shrimp, and for the fact that infants cannot speak, while both boys and men are able to do so. Some, very likely, will be ready to ask, why should not infants, too, have acquired this useful faculty of speech by natural selection; as Professor Max Müller asks, why, on the principle of evolution, should not trees grow into the sky, and why should not birds fly up to the moon; and endeavours to anticipate all excuses by the further question, why should they alone not possess the power of adapting themselves to new environments? Questions of this sort almost drive one to despair, not of being able to maintain the disputed theory, but of making people apprehend its elements. By a tree growing up into the sky must be meant a tree growing up at least beyond the reach of our atmosphere, that is to say, a tree about thirty or forty miles high. Now, since according to evolutionist philosophers, it has taken all the millions of years which, as not only they, but many others maintain, have elapsed since life began upon the earth, to develop a tree like the *Wellingtonia gigantea*, of some 450 feet at its greatest height, is it reasonable to pretend that according to their views there might just as well be trees forty miles high? It is on the theory of abrupt creation, and not on that of evolution, that you might expect these trees growing into the sky, and birds flying up to the moon, or anything else you are pleased to fancy. That the time may come when children will be born with the faculty of speech developed, enabling them to learn at once a rational language, is easily conceivable. Other mental characteristics are sometimes developed, as the word *precocious* indicates, at a far earlier period of life than that to which they seem properly to belong. The self-restraint of the young Jewish princes in their luxurious Babylonish captivity, the genius for command of the youthful Alexander, the sagacity of William Pitt, who was Chancellor of the Exchequer at twenty-three, are instances in point. The accidental circumstance that none of these men left children inheriting the early ripeness of great qualities, is sufficient to remind us how slow the process of evolution must be; so slow that men are tempted to fancy it goes not on at all, but that the state of the world is ever in one stay, just as they are tempted to fancy that the rocks of Niagara will stand for ever, because they do not notice, year by year, or day by day, the slight successive diminutions of their bulk.

To confirm the distinction drawn between rational and emotional language, reference is made to the phenomena of a certain disease of a particular part of the brain – a disease known as *aphasia*, which, physicians say, 'may induce partial or complete defect of intellectual language, and not cause corresponding defect of emotional or interjectional language.' Now Professor Ferrier, following up the researches of Hitzig and Fritsch, has recently been experimenting on the brains of various animals, and on that of the monkey among others, and 'the part,' he tells us, 'that appeared to be connected with the opening of the mouth and the movement of the tongue was homologous with the part affected in man in cases of *aphasia*.' This must surely be admitted again as at least a very curious coincidence, easily explicable, indeed, on the evolution theory, but not easily on any other. A certain intimate connexion between the organs of speech and a particular portion of the brain appears to be essential to man's use of rational language. In the course of evolution, therefore, such a connexion would need to be established before rational language could be acquired; and this very intermediate stage, where the connexion exists, although the further acquisition of speech has not yet been attained, is now presented to us in the monkey, a creature of all animals, beyond contradiction, in general appearance and physical conditions, most closely similar to ourselves.

A writer, who is far from being a Darwinian, tells us that among baboons—

'The leaders have a mode of communicating their orders to their subordinates, and they again to those placed under them, in a curiously varied language of intonations. Short and sharp barks, prolonged howls, sudden screams, quick jabberings, and even gestures of limbs and persons, are all used with singular rapidity, and repeated from one to the other. There was a system of military telegraphing, by means of attitudes and sounds, which was invented some time ago, and which really might have been copied from the baboons, so much do their natural tactics resemble the artificial inventions of mankind.'

It is hard to see why language such as is here described, used for the purposes described, should be presumed incapable of development into the rational language of human beings. The author quoted, a well-known and very entertaining writer on natural history, deplores that such details should be used in favour of what he evidently considers a very objectionable theory, yet he cannot forbear to give his readers the following story as coming within the possibilities of Simian intelligence. An Oriental had a baboon which he taught to watch his dinner during the process of cooking. Man has been defined as the only cooking animal, but the faithful creature soon learned to take a personal interest in this peculiarly human occupation. On one occasion a fowl was boiling in the pot. Curiosity prompted the removal of the lid. The pleasant odour that came forth suggested one little taste; and taste followed taste, till by almost insensible gradations the fowl was picked quite clean. Then followed the stings of conscience, and dread of what would befall when the master came back for his dinner. Here was an exigency to tax the wit and resource of a Syrus or a Scapin! But a brilliant plan of campaign occurred to the baboon, a plan dependent partly on his own personal conformation and partly on the circumstances of the region in which he found himself. For the first, nature had provided him with a bright red patch of colour, so that, by dint of rolling himself in the dust and adopting a certain posture, he wore the appearance of a stone with some raw meat on the top. For the second, in that locality numerous birds of prey are soon drawn together at the least scent of cooking. The savour of boiled chicken still gave fragrance to the air. The kites assembled after their wont, and, not making nice distinctions between flesh and fowl, stooped down to clutch, as they thought, that nice raw steak. But before they could achieve their object, the owner of that piece of flesh in good earnest clutched one of them, thrust it screaming into the pot, feathers and claws, and beak and all, shut down the lid, and then, to use Mr. Wood's own words, 'resumed its post of sentry with the placid ease that belongs to a conscience void of offence.'

All this, however, would, as it seems, make no difference to Professor Max Müller. He would still treat the baboon as an irrational being – 'irrational,' as he says, 'not in the sense of devoid of observation, shrewdness, calculation, presence of mind, reasoning in the sense of weighing, or even genius, but simply in the sense of devoid of the power of forming and handling general concepts.' Though why he denies this power to the baboon, and grants it to the deaf and dumb among mankind – why he should maintain in one essay that articulate language is 'the only tangible sign of reason which we know,' and admit in another that 'language, in the usual sense of the word, is not the only organ of conceptual thought' – does not appear to be explained, and is probably not capable of any valid explanation.

Let us not, however, lead any one to mistake the attitude in which so distinguished a writer stands towards this and every other scientific inquiry. The question, he declares, is not whether the Darwinian opinion is monstrous, 'but simply and solely whether it is true.' When human beings in general take that standpoint in matters intellectual, and the corresponding stand-point in morality, so as no longer to square their opinions and actions with what for the moment seems agreeable and safe, but in all things to think and act in accordance with what they best know of truth and justice, with the uttermost disregard of consequences such as are often now deemed paramount to govern conviction and to guide the ways of life; when, as a race, men have learned that false thinking and base action, besides leading on the one to the other and each to each, are sure to be fraught with far more evil consequence than unswerving candour and magnanimity; when that time comes, though it can come but slowly, yet when it comes, the race of mankind, without therefore ceasing to be the race of mankind, will have made as grand a step in the process of development as that which separates the ingenuity of the most knavish ape from the logic and sweet-voiced eloquence of Greece and Rome, and Germany and England.

PROFESSOR WHITNEY ON THE ORIGIN OF LANGUAGE
George H. Darwin

Source: Contemporary Review, vol. 24, November 1874

It is remarkable that in the same month of July 1874 we find an anonymous writer in England saying:

'Few recent intellectual phenomena are more astounding than the ignorance of these elementary yet fundamental distinctions and principles (*i.e.*, as to the essence of language) exhibited by conspicuous advocates of the monistic hypothesis. Mr. Darwin, for example, does not exhibit the faintest indication of having grasped them.'[1]

Whilst in the United States the distinguished philologist, Professor W. D. Whitney, observes that:

'Mr. Darwin himself shows a remarkable moderation and soundness of judgment in his treatment of the element of language.... Very little exception is to be taken by a linguistic scholar to any of his statements. Though no master, such as Müller is, of the facts of many languages, his general view of speech in its anthropological relations, his sense of what it is to man, and how, is far truer than that of the scholar who has attempted by the evidence of language to overthrow his whole theory.'[2]

Truly no man is a prophet in his own country!

Professor Whitney is the first philologist of note, who has professedly taken on himself to combat the views of Professor Max Müller; and as the opinions of the latter most properly command a vast deal of respect in England, we think it will be a good service to direct the attention of English readers to

---

[1] *Quarterly Review*. 'Primitive Man: Tylor and Lubbock,' p. 45.
[2] *North American Review*. 'Darwinism and Language.'

this powerful attack, and as we think, successful refutation of the somewhat dogmatic views of our Oxford linguist.

The Professor's article is a review of Schleicher's book, 'Uber die Bedeutung der Sprache für die Naturgeschichte des Menschen,'[3] and of Max Müller's well-known lectures on 'Mr. Darwin's Philosophy of Language'; but in fact the article deals almost entirely with the latter, Schleicher being dismissed with a single paragraph.

Turning to Müller the Professor happily observes: – 'It is never entirely easy to reduce to a skeleton of logical statement a discussion as carried on by Müller, because he is careless of logical sequence and connection, preferring to pour himself out, as it were, over his subject, in a gush of genial assertion and interesting illustration.' In taking up the cudgels, Müller is clearly impelled 'by an over-mastering fear lest man should lose' 'his proud position in the creation,' if his animal descent is proved. He maintains the extraordinary position that if an insensible gradation could be established between ape and man, their minds would be *identical*, and that by a similar argument the distinction between black and white, hot and cold, a high and low note might be eliminated: he overlooks, too, 'the undoubted and undisputed fact that species do actually vary in nature.' The same line of proof would show that the stature of a man and boy were *identical*, because the boy passes through every gradation in attaining the one stature from the other. No one could maintain such a position, who grasped the doctrines of continuity, and of the differential calculus. Professor Whitney justly points out, that in biology the gradations are not infinitesimal, but are such as are observed in nature to exist between parent and offspring. According to what is called the 'Darwinian theory,' organisms are in fact *precisely* the result of a multiple integration of a complex function of a very great number of variables; many of such variables being bound together by relationships amongst themselves: an example of one such relationship being afforded by the law, which has been called 'correlation of growth.'

Professor Whitney says:

'As a linguist (Professor Müller) claims to have found in language an endowment which has no analogies, and no

[3] Translated into English by Dr. Bikkers, under the title 'Darwinism tested by the Science of Language.'

preparations in even the beings nearest to man, and of which, therefore, no process of transmutation could furnish an explanation. Here is the pivot on which his whole argument rests and revolves.'

And he urges that Müller does not argue his 'case with moderation and acuteness, on strict scientific grounds and by scientific methods,' in setting up language as *the* specific difference between man and animals. Many other writers in fact have adduced other differences as *the* correct ones; thus that he

> 'Alone is capable of progressive improvement; that he alone makes use of tools or fire, domesticates other animals, possesses property, or employs language; that no other animal is self-conscious, comprehends itself, has the power of abstraction, or possesses general ideas; that man alone has a sense of beauty, is liable to caprice, has the feeling of gratitude, mystery, &c., believes on God, or is endowed with a conscience.'[4]

Many of these asserted distinctions are successfully combated in 'The Descent of Man.'

Although Müller asserts that animals receive their knowledge through the senses only, and that no animal possesses 'the faintest germs of the faculty, of abstracting and generalising,' he elsewhere says that 'if there is a *terra incognita* which excludes all positive knowledge, it is the mind of animals;' the whole subject is transcendent. It seems strange that the same person should be involved in such profound ignorance, and yet have so complete a knowledge of the limits of the animal mind. Professor Whitney, however, justly points out that the minds of our fellow-men are a *terra incognita*, in exactly the same sense as are those of animals:

> 'Who, for example, can be sure that, if he had a friend's sensorium in his brain instead of his own, he would get precisely the same sensation of colour as at present from the green grass and the blue sky?' . . . 'We believe that the horse sees green, and tastes water, and feels pain, as confidently, and on nearly the same grounds, as we believe that our neighbour does the same.'

---

[4] 'Descent of Man.' Vol. i. p. 49.

It is true that with man we have an additional source of evidence in language, but it can hardly be asserted that this is the only one.

With reference to the denial of conceptual knowledge to animals, Mr. Darwin says:—[5]

'But when a dog sees another dog at a distance it is often clear that he perceives that it is a dog in the abstract; for when he gets nearer, his whole manner suddenly changes, if the other dog is a friend. A recent writer remarks that in all such cases it is a pure assumption to assert, that the mental act is not essentially of the same nature in the animal as in the man. If either refers what he perceives with his senses to a mental concept, then so do both. Vide Mr. Hookham, letter to Professor M. Müller, "*Birmingham News,*" May, 1873.'

To most persons it will be sufficient to know, with Prof. Whitney, that—

'An animal like a dog perfectly knows what a man is, never confounds it with any other creature, knows what to fear and hope from it, in order to hold, with a confidence that is proof against all authority, the doctrine that an animal lower than myself possesses such germs of the faculty of generalizing as are distinct only in degree from those which I possess.'

The allusion to authority in this passage refers to the attempt of Müller to crush his adversaries, by a reference to Kant, Hume, Berkeley, and Locke. But fortunately we live in an age, which (except for temporary relapses) does not pay any very great attention to the pious founder, and which tries to judge for itself.

On examining the extract from Locke made by Müller, Prof. Whitney finds that the power of forming general ideas is denied to animals, simply on the ground that they do not talk, and observes that, 'The fallacy lurking here is the assumption that, if general ideas were formed, they could not help finding expression in words; and that I can see no good ground for.' Prof. Müller, however, adheres to and restates Locke's position in his own words; and reason is defined by him, as the *power* of forming and handling general concepts.

Prof. Whitney then says;

---

[5] 'Descent of Man.' (New edition to be published shortly, p. 83.)

Reason 'is that power over general concepts which we possess, and which is so much higher than anything possessed by brutes, that it is properly called by a different name. Again, "handling" general concepts is an ambiguous and unscientific phrase, and involves, perhaps, more power than "forming" them; we might fairly enough say that the effective management of ideas is possible only by means of a system of signs, which the brute confessedly has not. But to put the formation of general concepts at the very top, and the power of weighing probabilities and calculating results, even genius itself, far below, is to turn the natural order of things topsy-turvy.... Nor, once more, is articulate language, or language of any kind, the only intelligible manifestation of reason. There is rational conduct as well as rational speech, and it is quite as effective as speech.... Müller himself acknowledges... that, "though the faculty of language may be congenital, all languages are traditional." Unless, then, reason is a matter of tradition rather than a natural gift, a man may fail to have had any language handed down to him, and so many fail to give what Müller regards as the only possible evidence of reason, and yet may be rational.'

In thorough consistency with himself, Müller would appear to hold that the born deaf and dumb have no concepts, 'except such as can be expressed by less perfect symbols.' If, however, they can form *any* concepts, they can, as Prof. Whitney urges, reason.

It is curious to observe that the Quarterly Reviewer, who is just as much bent as Prof. Max Müller on the dualistic hypothesis of man's origin, takes up the deaf and dumb man also.[6] He however, maintains that—

'The intellectual activity of their minds is indeed evidenced by the peculiar construction of their sentences. Mr. Taylor tell us (p. 25), "Their usual construction is not 'black horse' but 'horse black;' not 'bring a black hat,' but 'hat black bring." ' ... There can be no doubt that a society of dumb men would soon elaborate a gesture language of great complexity.'

---

[6] 'Primitive Man,' July, 1874, p. 46.

It seems, then, that the Reviewer is as much opposed to Müller as are the evolutionists; and on this point at least he seems to have sound sense on his side.

Müller asks, 'Are concepts possible, or, at least, are concepts ever realised, without some form or outward body?' and answer the query by saying that 'if the science of language has proved anything, it has proved that conceptual or discursive thought can be carried on in words only.' He maintains that thought and language are as necessary to the existence of each other, as the peel to an orange. To this Prof. Whitney observes, that concepts may be formed and yet not put before the consciousness of the conceiver, so that he 'realises' what he is doing; complex thoughts are doubtless impossible without symbols, just as are the higher mathematics. Yet we know that dogs doubt and hesitate, and finally determine to act without any external determining circumstance.

Whitney very happily illustrates the independence of thought from language, by calling up our state of mind when casting about, 'often in the most open manner, for new designations,' for new forms of knowledge, or when 'drawing distinctions, and pointing conclusions which words are then stretched or narrowed to cover.' 'If Müller had brought before him some wholly new animal he would find that he could shut his eyes and call up the image of it readily enough without any accompanying name.'

It is a proof that we realised and conceived the idea of the texture and nature of a musical sound before we had a word for it, that we have had to borrow the expressive word 'timbre' from the French.

Prof. Whitney says, however, that he is convinced that Müller does not quite understand 'the theory of the antecedency of the idea to the word, in the minds of those who hold that theory.' He cannot bear anything which seems to derogate from the dignity of language. Whitney fancies that Müller may only mean to deny 'that men elaborate a great store of ideas, and then, by an afterthought, proceed to invent names' for them; and that he may mean that when a sign has been sought and found for a concept, it is used 'as a necessary standing-ground from which to rise another step.' And he illustrates this possible interpretation, by showing how much Müller has of late changed his position with respect to the 'bow-wow' and 'pooh-pooh' theories of language; for even he now says, 'interjections and imitations are the only possible materials out of which human language could be formed.' Although he still guards himself from being confused with the ordinary pooh-poohists, by holding that words come from roots, and roots from interjections and imitations, whilst *they* do not interpose the roots on the evolutional road!

Professor Whitney says that human nature is the sum of certain endowments above and beyond those of animals. To human nature concrete speech does not belong, but only the capacities and tendencies for its development. Its development has been slow, as in other branches of human activity; but every race has worked out *some* system of verbal signs, just as every race uses some tools. These results constitute the civilization of the race. The name of 'reason' is due to the capacities, and not to the results themselves. The most important capacities for language have been memory, distinct conception, abstraction, reflection, and the review of our own mental processes; and, of not less importance, the power of adapting means to ends. The end of language is intercommunication.

> 'It is where speech cuts loose from its narrow and inextensive instinctive basis, and becomes, instead of a cry to relieve the speaker's own feelings, an utterance to bring a thought before another that its unlimited growth becomes possible and that its history begins; here it makes that transition from emotional to rational, upon which Müller with good reason lays so much stress.'

The capacities, he continues, are not wanting in some of the lower animals, though their degree is so much lower than ours. Animals understand much that we try to signify to them; and it is in the largeness of our 'power of connecting definite sounds with definite ideas,'[7] that lies our pre-eminence.

Professor Whitney thinks that we shall never discover the steps between 'the wholly instinctive expression of the animals' and 'the wholly conventional expression of man.'

> 'The wishes and expectations of those (for there are such) who still look to find a connecting series are founded on a misapprehension, and are futile; their fear to find that nature has made a *saltus* in passing from the one to the other is

---

[7] 'Descent of Man.'

equally in vain. There is neither *saltus* nor gradual transition in the case; no transition, because the two are essentially different; no *saltus* because human speech is an historical development out of infinitesmal beginnings, which may have been of less extent even than the instinctive speech of many a brute. If we had the missing links supplied we should not find the more and more anthropoid beings possessing a larger and larger stock of definite articulations to which they by instinct attached definite ideas; there are no such elements in human language, present or traceable in the past; and as we approach man, the detailed instincts leading to definite acts or products diminish rather than increase; we should find those beings showing more and more plainly the essentially human power of adapting means to ends, both by reflection and unconscious action, in communication and expression, as in other departments of activity.'

Professor Whitney agrees with Mr. Darwin in thinking that man does not owe his existence, *as man*, to language, but that language has enabled him to reach a higher level of manhood. And à propos to Mr. Darwin's opinion on this point, the *Quarterly Reviewer*, before alluded to, charges him[8] with contradicting himself in the *Descent of Man*, thus:—

'In one place (vol. i., p. 54) he attributes the faculty of speech in man to his having acquired a higher intellectual nature, while in another place (vol. ii., p. 391) he ascribes man's intellectual nature to his having acquired the faculty of speech.'

In all justice, however, the latter reference should have been given to pp. 390 and 391, and then we find as follows:—
Vol. i. p. 54—

'It is not the mere power of articulation that distinguishes man from other animals, for as every one knows parrots can talk; but it is his large power of connecting definite sounds with definite ideas; and this obviously depends on the development of the mental faculties.'

And Vol. ii. p. 390—

'A great stride in the development of the intellect will have

[8] P. 45.

followed as soon as, through a previous considerable advance, the half-art and half-instinct of language came into use; for the continued use of language will have reacted on the brain, and produced an inherited effect; and this again will have reacted on the improvement of language. P. 391 – The large size of the brain in man ... may be attributed in chief part ... to the early use of some simple form of language ...'

The asserted contradiction then lies in a skilful reading of the sentence on p. 391 *apart* from its context on p. 390.

With all deference to the great weight of Professor Whitney's opinion, I venture to think that he makes a dangerous assertion when he says that we shall never know anything of the transitional forms through which language has passed. It is ever a doubtful policy to assert that science is incapable of anything. Does Professor Whitney mean that it is impossible to track the Aryan languages higher than their roots, or to discover the imitational and interjectional sources of those roots? The attempt to do so has already been made, but with what degree of success I must leave professed philologists to judge. Count Liancourt and Mr. Pincott have just published a work on the 'Primitive Laws of Language.'[9]

I will give a short sketch of their method, in the hope that competent judges may be induced to consider their views.

Our authors state their objections to the 'bow-wow,' to 'pooh-pooh,' and 'ding-dong' theories of language, but then proceed to expound their own theory of its origin; their views, however, *exactly* accord with what I, at least, have always thought I understood by the ordinarily received onomatopœic theory. The idea which, I believe, is new in their work is the reduction of the received roots of language (of which they state there are 1800 in Sanskrit) down to a very small number of still more primitive roots, and of these they give the onomatopœic origin. Whether or not they push this analysis to a fanciful extent, I will not pretend to say. The method will be best illustrated by some of their examples. They trace the words 'and,' 'other,' 'or,' 'either,' down to the Sanskrit 'antara' and

---

[9] 'Primitive and Universal Laws of Language.' By Count G. A. de Goddes-and Liancourt and F. Pincott. London: W. H. Allen. 1874. These authors, by the bye, seem to agree with Müller in the point attacked by Whitney, for they say that *'man spoke before he reasoned.'*

'itara.' The latter consists of two parts, 'i' and 'tara'; 'i' is the root 'to go' and 'tara' is derived from the verbal base 'trî,' 'to cross over.' We meet 'tara' again in the comparative 'better,' but it generally dwindles down to the mere letter r in comparatives. We meet trî again in trans:—

'The primitive meaning of trî is, however, "cross over;" it is a compound formed of .t., the remote definite = "there" + ri = "go," and is, therefore, equivalent to "go there," *i.e.*, "motion to that place." '

Similarly 'pri' is the origin of 'præ,' 'pro,' 'forth,' &c., and is derived from 'pă' the sound 'produced by a puff of breath,' which 'would aptly convey an idea like "forth," ' and 'ri,' to 'go.' 'Ri' they consider as a sort of intensified form of 'i'; the letter r being one natural way of reduplicating and intensifying a sound. By methods such as above indicated, they reduce all the roots down to a few 'onomatops,' – G the onomatop of 'throat,' 'swallow,' 'seize,' &c., – I = 'here,' denoting 'self,' 'unity,' 'motion towards the speaker' and 'motion in general' – L the onomatop of 'tongue,' 'lick,' 'smear,' 'bright,' &c. – P that of 'puff,' 'forward,' &c. – another P that of 'suck,' 'drink,' nourish' – T the onomatop of definition, that which is exterior to self, 'other,' 'there,' 'beyond,' &c. This indication suffices to sketch the method pursued, and it will be interesting if some competent judge will criticize it.

Professor Whitney nothwithstanding, I cannot see that it is wholly useless to speculate on some of the influences, which must have had their bearings on the formation of language, – whether or not we fancy that we can still trace the remains of such influences in languages, as they exist at present.

According to Mr. Darwin's views, man owes his extraordinary power of modulating the voice, and producing diversity of sounds, in great part to sexual selection. Doubtless in very early times his apelike forefathers possessed vocal organs, with which they gave forth a limited number of significant cries, serving to convey various signals and emotions to their brethren; but Mr. Darwin's view is that the voice attained its present perfection by its constant use as a sexual charm (as in the case of the singing gibbons), and by the selection consequent on such use in courting. It is curious if man is indebted for language, not entirely to the vast utility of so perfect a means of intercommunication, but partly to the philoprogenitive nature of his ancestors!

Again, if this view is correct, music is antecedent to language. Mr. Spencer's view is exactly the other way, for he thinks that music owes its origin to the imitation of the various intonations, made use of in the verbal expression of the emotions; and these varied intonations he ascribed to purely physiological causes. Influenced by what Mr. Spencer would call the 'family bias,' I cannot but think that my father's view is the more probable, since it serves far better to explain the strong emotional effect of music, and since the voice is so largely used in many other departments of the animal kingdom as a love-charm.

I have heard it suggested that though animals give significant cries, yet that as they are never known to approach conventionality, but continue stereotyped, we do not here see any real approach to language; for that the whole essence of language lies in its conventionality. But I think that this objection can be scarcely justified, for when one holds a stick, and gives it to a dog to worry, he growls – but yet in a way so very distinct from that of real anger, that one can only interpret the growl as a sort of conventional mark of his anger. Again, it has been asserted that all the cries of animals are purely emotional; yet I know a terrier, who has, untaught, invented a peculiar low bark, like 'wuff!' which is never used except to mean 'open the door.' And the domestic cock has a well-known peculiar cry, only used to summon his wives to any food which he has found. The ease with which a conventionalised cry might be adopted by animals, is illustrated by the undoubted fact that the barking of dogs is a mode of giving tongue only learnt under domestication; for the dogs, which ran wild on the island of Juan Fernandez, had, after thirty-three years, quite lost the art, and some which were recaptured re-acquired it; and, further, individual wolves and jackals, kept in confinement, have learnt to bark like dogs.[10]

An animal giving various significant cries, and also practising singing, would hardly fail to make his cries yet more significant by imparting to them some of the intonations of his song, and this might easily give to such cries a much wider significance. It is said that savages when excited naturally speak in a sort

---

[10] Darwin: 'Animal and Plants under Domestication,' vol. i., p. 27.

of song, which would accord well with this view, though in no way contradictory of Mr. Spencer's.

It is clear, too, that in a much later stage of the development of language, when the metaphorical power, of which language exhibits such extraordinary diversity, had become somewhat developed, that the same quasi-word, or conventionalised cry or exclamation, might come to bear very widely different meanings according to his intonation; when however there came to be synonyms for the same object or idea, that word would be likely to survive the best, which differed from others, not merely in intonation, but in its consonants. This would at least be likely to hold good of languages still in a progressive condition. May not this possibly serve as an explanation of the fact that in such a fossilised language as Chinese, we find so great a variety of tones? Mr. Swinhoe told me that the same monosyllable had eight different meanings according to its intonation! How great is the weakness to a tongue springing from this source, may be realized by what Mr. Swinhoe also told me, viz.: that a Chinaman barely understands another, when spoken to unexpectedly, so that it is usual to preface any remark by 'look here,' or 'I wish to speak.'

To return to Professor Whitney, – I do not understand the grounds on which he denies that any transitional stage is possible in the formation of language. He does not imagine that a language, however incomplete, sprang forth fully caparisoned from a single generation of anthropoid apes. It is surely probable that many generations of quasi-men passed away, who used a small vocabulary of conventionalised cries; that these cries became more and more conventionalised, by departing more and more from the sounds of exclamations, from which they took their origin. Many roots would probably propagate themselves by fission, and give rise to new roots, gradually to become entirely separate from their onomatopœic originals. I should imagine that the imitative origin of quasi-words (serving alike as verbs, adjectives, and nouns) would in early times have served as a kind of *memoria technica* of their meanings. It is obvious that any system of verbal signs would have a much more retentive hold on the memory, when such signs had a relationship however feeble with the objects represented. An English child learns and remembers the word 'baa-lamb,' and calls a cow a 'moo-cow,' for long before he can keep the mere signs 'lamb' and 'cow' in his memory; and he frequently begins by calling dogs and cows 'bow-wows' and 'moos' and continues to use these words, even after he pronounces these syllables in a quite conventionalised manner. And will not something of the same kind surely have taken place in the infancy of the human race?

If the complete conventionalism and fossilisation of onomatopœic roots did not take place in a single generation, – and to me it seems impossible that it should have done so – then surely it is erroneous to say that there is no transitional stage of language possible; and it is not absolutely chimerical to hope that *some* of the steps in such transitions may yet be discoverable, though such speculations must necessarily remain highly doubtful, and the results can never be tabulated along with those more certain results, to which we are led in other branches of science.

Again, Professor Whitney says that—

'Hovel, cottage, and palace do not grow by insensible gradation out of bees' cells, or birds' nests, or beavers' huts, or any other animal structures; they began when man, a shelterless creature, with no building instincts, felt the discomforting influences of external nature, and saw how, by the appropriate use of materials lying within his reach, they could be avoided.'

But we know that some of the anthropoid apes build themselves a platform to rest on, a hardly ruder piece of architecture, than the shelter corrected by the Fuegians; such building is probably instinctive. Now, how can Professor Whitney know that an animal, endowed with high mental power, would not consciously extend such instinctive habits, and that the instinctiveness of the action would not gradually dwindle, and become displaced by a complete rationality? When the orang, mentioned by Mr. Darwin, used a mat to shelter his back from the sun, he probably did it rationally, while he would also probably build his platform instinctively. May we not look at the conscious use of the mat, as a proof that instinct and rationality blend into one another? It is true that we have but little evidence that an action performed wholly instinctively by one generation of animals, is ever performed partly rationally by the next, or that an act done instinctively in youth, is done rationally in later years, but we have no reason to deny its possibility, and it is even *à priori* probable. Although it has been asserted that instinct and reason vary inversely as one another, yet the best observers agree in maintaining that the very reverse is true, and that the more closely any supposed instinctive action of animals is watched, the more it is found blended with reason. Mr. L. H. Morgan, who has observed the habits of beavers probably more closely than any man alive, goes so far as to believe that their wonderful constructions are built entirely under the guidance of reason. And by experiments, Huber showed how immediately bees called in reason to help their cell-making instinct, when he placed them under new and anomalous conditions.

In conclusion, we recommend all who feel an interest in the subject to read Professor Whitney in the original, as his matter is already so much condensed, that any abstract, such as I have endeavoured to give, must do but feeble justice to it.

NATURE AND ORIGIN OF LANGUAGE
W. D. Whitney

Source: The Life and Growth of Language (1875), Chap. xiv

Language an acquisition, a part of culture. Its universality among men; limitation to man; difference between human and other means of expression. Communication the direct motive to the production of speech; this the conscious and determining element in all language-history. Natural cries as basis of the development; question as to their nature and range; postulation of instinctive articulate utterances uncalled for. Use of the voice as principal means of expression. Imitative element in the beginnings of speech; range and limits of onomatopœic expression. The doctrine of roots. Sufficiency of this view of the origin of language; the opposing miraculous theory. Capacity involved in language-making; difference in this respect between men and lower animals. Relation of language to development of man; rate and manner of its growth.

Our examination of the history of language, of its mode of transmission, preservation, and alteration, has shown us clearly enough what we are to hold respecting its nature. It is not a faculty, a capacity; it is not an immediate exertion of the thinking power; it is a mediate product and an instrumentality. To many, superficial or prejudiced, inquirers this seems an unsatisfactory, even a low, view; but it is because they confound together two very different senses of the word *language*. Man possesses, as one of his most marked and distinctive characteristics, a faculty or capacity of speech – or, more accurately, various faculties and capacities which lead inevitably to the production of speech: but the faculties are one thing, and their elaborated products are another and very different one. So man has a capacity for art, for the invention of instruments, for finding out and applying the resources of mathematics, for many other great and noble things; but no man is born an artist, an engineer, or a calculist, any more than he is born a speaker. In regard to these various exercises of our activities our condition is the same. In all alike, the race has been undergoing almost from the beginning a training of its capacities, step by step, each step being embodied in a product. The growth of art implies a period of rude shapings, and a rise to higher and higher production by improving on former models and processes. Mechanics still more clearly has the same history; it was by the use of ruder instruments, by the dexterity acquired in that use and the consequent suggestion of improvements, that men came finally to locomotives and power-looms. Mathematics began with the apprehension that one and one are two, and its development has been like that of the others. And every new individual of the race has to go through the same series of steps, from the same humble beginnings. Only, he takes them at lightning-speed, as compared with their first elaboration; because he is led onward by others over a beaten and smoothed track. The half-grown boy now is often a more advanced mathematician or mechanician than the wisest of the Greeks: not because his gifts are superior to theirs, but because he has only to receive and assimilate what they and their successors have wrought out for him. Though possessing the endowments of a Homer or a Demosthenes, no man can speak any language until he has learned it, as truly learned it as he learns the multiplication-table, or the demonstrations of Euclid.

Now these collected products of the exercise of man's developing powers, which are passed on from one generation to another, increasing and changing as they go, we call institutions, constituents of our culture. Something of them is possessed by every section of humanity. There is no member of any community, however barbarous, who is not raised vastly above what he would otherwise be by learning what his fellows have to teach him, acquiring their fragments of knowledge, however scanty, and their arts – including the art of speech. Doubtless the most degraded community has more to teach the most gifted individual than he would have learned, to the end of his life, by the use of his own faculties unaided; certainly this is so as regards speech. Every one acquires that which the accident of birth places within his reach, exercising his faculties upon that foundation, expanded and at the same time constrained by it, making to it his individual contribution, if he have one to make: just as truly in the case of language as of any other part. Language is in no way to be separated from the rest: it is in some respects very unlike them; but so are they unlike one another; if it be the one most fundamentally important, most highly characteristic, most obviously the product and expression of reason, that is only a difference of degree.

We regard every language, then, as an institution, one of those which, in each community, make up its culture. Like all the constituent elements of culture, it is various in every community, even in the different individuals composing each. There are communities in which it has come down within the strict limits of race; in others it has been, partly or wholly, taken from strange races; for, like the rest, it is capable of being transferred or shifted. Race-characteristics can only go down by blood; but race-acquisitions – language not less than religion, or science – can be borrowed and lent.

The universality of language, we may remark in passing, is thus due to nothing more profound or mysterious than that every division of the human race has been long enough in existence for its language-capacities to work themselves out to some manner of result. Precisely so, there is a universal possession by men of some body of instruments, to help the hands in providing for human needs. This universality does not at all prove that, if we could see coming into being a new race, by whatever means brought the existing race into being, we should find it within any definite assignable period possessed of instruments – or of speech.

But, as things are, every community of men has a common language, while none of the lower animals are possessed of such; their means of communication being of so different a character that it has no right to be called by the same name. No special obligation rests upon the linguist to explain this difference, any more than upon the historian of art or of mechanics to explain why the lower animals are neither artists nor machine-makers. It is enough for him a to point out that, the gifts of man being such as they are, he invariably comes to the possession of this as well as of the other elements of culture, while not one of the lower races has shown itself capable of originating a civilization, in any element, linguistic or other; their utmost capacity being that of being trained by the higher race to the exercise of activities which in their own keeping had remained undeveloped, of being taught various arts and acts, performed partly mechanically, partly with a certain hardly determinable degree of intelligence. But the subject is one upon which erroneous views are so prevalent that we can hardly help giving it a brief consideration.

The essential difference, which separates man's means of communication in kind as well as degree from that of the other animals, is that, while the latter is instinctive, the former is, in all its parts, arbitrary and conventional. That this is so, the whole course of our exposition has sufficiently shown. It is fully proved by the single circumstance that for each object, or act, or quality, there are as many names as there are languages in the world, each answering as good a purpose as any other, and capable of being substituted for another in the usage of any individual. There is not in a known language a single item which can be truly claimed to exist φύσει, 'by nature;' each stands in its accepted use Aέσει, 'by an act of attribution,' in which men's circumstances, habits, preferences, will, are the determining force. Even where the onomatopœic or imitative element is most conspicuous – as in *cuckoo* and *pewee*, in *crack* and *whiz* – there is no tie of necessity, but only of convenience: if there were a necessity, it would extend equally to other animals and other noises; and also to all tongues; while in fact these conceptions have elsewhere wholly other names. No man can become possessed of any existing language without learning it; no animal (that we know of) has any expression which he learns, which is not the direct gift of nature to him. We are not less generously treated in this latter respect than the animals; we have also our 'natural' expression, in grimace, gesture, and tone; and we make use of it: on the one hand, for communication where the usual conventional means is made of no avail – as between men of different tongue, or those who by deafness are cut off from the use of speech – and, on the other hand, for embellishing and explaining and enforcing our ordinary language: where it is of a power and value that no student of language can afford to overlook. In the domain of feeling and persuasion, in all that is intended to impress the personality of the communicator upon the recipient, it possesses the highest consequence. We say with literal truth that a look, a tone, a gesture, is often more eloquent than elaborate speech. Language is harmed for some uses by its conventionality. Words of sympathy or affection can be repeated parrot-like by one whose heartless tone takes all value from them; there is no persuasion in a discourse which is given as if from a mere animated speaking-machine. And herein comes clearly to light the true sphere of natural expression; it indicates feeling, and feeling only. From the cry and groan and laugh and smile up to the lightest variations of tone and feature which the skilled elocutionist uses, it is emotional, subjective. Not a title of evidence has ever been brought forward to show that there is such a thing as the natural expression of an intellectual conception, of a judgment, of a cognition. It is where expression quits its emotional natural basis, and turns to intellectual uses, that the history of language begins.

Nor is it less plain what inaugurates the conversion, and becomes the main determining element in the whole history of production of speech; it is the desire of communication. This turns the instinctive into the intentional. As itself becomes more distinct and conscious, it lifts expression of all kinds above its natural basis, and makes of it an instrumentality; capable, as such, of indefinite extension and improvement. He who (as many do) leaves this force out of account, cannot but make utter shipwreck of his whole linguistic philosophy. Where the impulse to communication is wanting, no speech comes into being. Here, again, the parallelism between language and the other departments of culture is close and instructive. The man growing up in solitude would initiate no culture. He would never come to a knowledge of any of the higher things of which he was capable. It needs not only the inward power, but also the outwards occasion, to make man what he is capable of becoming. This is characteristic of his whole historical attitude. Races and generations of men have passed away in barbarism and ignorance who were as capable of civilization as the mass of the present civilized communities: indeed, there are such actually passing away around us. It is in no wise to deny the grand endowments of human nature that we ascribe the acquisition of speech to an external inducement. We may illustrate the case by a comparison. A stone has lain motionless for ages on the verge of a precipice, and may lie there for ages longer; all the cosmic forces of gravity will not stir it. But a chance thrust from some passing animal jostles it from its equilibrium, and it goes crashing down. Which, shall we say, caused the fall? gravity, or the thrust? Each, in its way; the great force would not have wrought this particular effect but for the aid of the petty one; and there is nothing derogatory to the dignity of gravitation in admitting the fact. Just so in language: the great and wonderful powers of the human soul would never move in this particular direction but for the added push given by the desire of communication; when this leads the way, all the rest follows.

Our recognition of the determining force of this element is far from implying that communication is the sole end, or the highest end, of speech. We have sufficiently noticed, in the second chapter, the infinite value of expression to the operations of each individual mind and soul, and its fundamental value as an element in the progress of the race. But it is here as elsewhere; men strive after that which is nearest and most obvious to them, and attain thereby a vast deal more than they foresaw. In the devising and constructing of instruments, of all kinds, men have had directly in view only what may be called the lower uses of them, their immediate contributions to comfort and safety and sensuous enjoyment; but the result has been a calling-out of many of the higher powers which could find appropriate exercise in no other way, a reduction of Nature to service in a manner that allows a part of the race to engage in the more elevated and elevating occupations; and a discovery of truths in bewildering abundance. A yet closer parallel is afforded by the closely kindred art of writing, which adds to and enhances all the advantages belonging to the art of speech, and is as indispensable to the highest culture as is speech to the lower; but, like speech, it came into being by a process in which the only conscious motive was communication; all its superior uses followed in the train of that, and were unthought of until experience disclosed them; indeed, they are even yet unthought of by the greater part of those who derive advantage from them. And this last is true, to a degree which we must not fail to observe, of spoken language also: its higher uses are not conscious ones. Not one in a hundred, or a thousand, of those who speak realizes that he 'uses language;' but there is no one who does not know well enough that he can talk. That is to say, language, to the general apprehension of its users, is simply a means of receiving from others and giving to them: what it is to the individual soul, what it is to the race, few have reach of vision to see. And least of all is such penetration to be credited to primitive man: he, especially, needs some motive right before his eyes, and of which he can feel every moment the impelling force; and the desire to communicate with his fellows is that motive, the sole and the wholly sufficient one. He had no thoughts swelling in his soul and demanding utterance; he has no foreboding of high capacities which only need education to make him a little lower than the angels; he feels nothing but the nearest and most urgent needs. If language broke out from within, driven by the wants of the soul, it ought to come forth fastest and most fully in the solitary' since he, cut off from other means of improvement, is thrown back upon this as his only resource: but the solitary man is as speechless as the lower animals.

There might be ground for questioning this conclusion as to the decisive value of the impulse to communication in the initiation of language-history, if the after-course of that history showed entire independence of it. That is no acceptable scientific explanation which calls in a special force at the beginning, like a *deus ex machina*, to accomplish what we cannot see to be otherwise feasible, and then to retire and act no more. But communication is the leading determinative force throughout. This it is for which and by which we make our first acquisitions; this leads us, when circumstances change, to lay our old acquisitions aside and make new; this determines the unity of a language, and puts a restraint upon its dialectic variation this is, both consciously and unconsciously, recognized by every individual as the regulator: we speak so as to be intelligible to others; we hear and learn that we may understand them; we do not speak simply as we ourselves choose, letting others understand us if they can and will.

If this be so, then we have virtually solved, so far as it admits of solution, the problem of the origin of language; we have ascertained what was the original basis, and what the character of its development. The basis was the natural cries of human beings, expressive of their feelings, and capable of being understood as such by their fellows. That is to say, the basis so far as audible speech is concerned; for it is not to be maintained that this was the only, or even the principal, means of primitive expression. Gesture and grimace are every whit as natural and as immediately intelligible; and in the undeveloped condition of expression every available means will unquestionably have been resorted to, perhaps with a long predominance of the visible over the audible. But it cannot be that the use of the voice for expression should not have been suggested and initiated by Nature's own endowments in this direction.

Here, however, comes in a question respecting which even the most recent opinions, and among those who in general accept the view of language here taken, are divided. How wide was this basis, and of what and how definite character? Did it consist of articulate sounds instinctively attached to certain conceptions? Was there a limited natural vocabulary of actual words or roots, of the same kind with later language, and needing only to be extended into the latter? There are those who would answer these questions in the affirmative, and who hold, therefore, that the fruitful way to investigate concretely the problem of the origin of language is to study the means of expression of the lower animals, especially of those which stand nearest to man, in order to find there something analogous with the roots of our speech. But this view has its basis in the clinging impression, which many of those who reason and write about language cannot possibly get rid of, that there is somehow a real internal connection between at least a part of our words and the ideas which these represent – if one could only find out what it is. If we recognize the truths that all existing human speech is in every part and particle conventional, that all of which there is record in the past was of the same character, and that there is an utter absense of evidence going to show that any uttered sound, any combination of articulations, comes or ever came into existence as the natural sign of an intellectual conception – we shall be led to look with extreme disfavor upon any suggestion of this kind. Beyond all question, it is wholly uncalled for by necessity: the tones significant of feeling, of which no one can deny the existence because they are still an important part of our expression, are fully capable of becoming the effective initiators of language. Spoken language began, we may say, when a cry of pain, formerly wrung out by real suffering, and seen to be understood and sympathized with, was repeated in imitation, no longer as a mere instinctive utterance, but for the purpose of intimating to another, 'I am (was, shall be) suffering;' when an angry growl, formerly the direct expression of passion, was reproduced to signify disapprobation and threatening; and the like. This was enough to serve as foundation for all that should be built upon it.

It is further to be considered, in judging this point, that, as we approach man, the general capacities increase, but the specific instincts, the already formed and as it were educated capacities, decrease. It is among the insects that we find those wonderful arts which seem like the perfected results of training of a limited intellect; it is among birds that we find specific modes of nest-building and a highly art-like, almost artistic, song. Man is capable of acquiring everything, but he begins in the actual possession of next to nothing. Except suckling, he can hardly be said to be born with an instinct. His long helpless infancy, while the chicken and the calf run about and help themselves from the very day of their birth, is characteristic of Nature's whole mode of treatment of him. There is no plausibility in the suggestion that he should have begun social life with a naturally implanted capital of the means of social communication – and any more in the form of words than in that of gestures. It is a blunder of our educated habit to regard the voice as the specific instrument of expression; it is only one of several instruments. We might just as hopefully look among the higher animals for the particular and definite beginnings out of which our clothes, our buildings, our instruments, are a development. In these departments of human production, we see clearly enough what the natural beginning should have been. No animal save man is known to make any attempt at dressing; but if any did, it would amount to nothing; for there are tribes of men that go utterly, or almost utterly, naked: and no one, probably, would think of suggesting that the rudiments of dress are not a turning to account, for perceived purposes of comfort or decency, just such materials as Nature placed in man's way. The earliest shelters were of the same sort: it would be of high interest to find the animals nearest to man showing that kind of capacity which he possesses, of putting to use freely, simply as directed by circumstances, the varied resources of Nature; but probably the idea has never come into any one's head that man, as an animal uneducated, would be found building a particular style of shelter (as the beaver its dam, the oriole its hanging nest, the wasp its cells), out of which have grown by a process showing nowhere a *saltus* or *lacuna*, the huts and palaces and temples of the more educated races. And the same thing is true of instruments: clubs and stones we allow to have been the first, only because Nature offers such most conveniently within reach of the beings who were gifted

300 *The Origin of Language*

with mind enough to see how they could be made available for perceived needs.

Now it is only an unclear or a false view of the nature of speech that prevents any form seeing that its case is entirely analogous with these others, and that to postulate, and then seek for traces of, a primitive basis for language in the form of specific articulate signs for ideas is an uncalled-for, even a necessarily vain and futile, proceeding. It is, indeed, a matter of high interest, and promising of valuable instruction, to investigate as closely as possible the means of communication of the lower animals, so as to determine its character and scope; but the point calling for special attention is, how far the natural tones and utterances and postures and movements are used secondarily and mediately, for the purpose of signifying something, in rudimentary correspondence with what we have seen to be the inferable beginnings of human language-making. We need not be surprised to find, in more than one quarter, such methods of communication in use, only limited, and, for lack of the right kind and degree of capacity in their users, incapable of development; and these would be the real analogues of speech, and would bridge the *saltus* of which some are so afraid. If the Darwinian theory is true, and man a development out of some lower animal, it is at any rate conceded that the last and nearest transition-forms have perished, perhaps exterminated by him in the struggle for existence, as his special rivals, during his prehistoric ages of wildness; if they could be restored, we should find the transition-forms toward our speech to be, not at all a minor provision of natural articulate signs, but an inferior system of conventional signs, in tone, gesture, and grimace.

As between the three natural means of expression just mentioned, and constantly had in view by us in this discussion, it is simply by a kind of process of natural selection and survival of the fittest that the voice has gained the upper hand, and come to be so much the most prominent that we give the name of *language* ('tonguiness') to all expression. There is no mysterious connection between the thinking apparatus and the articulating apparatus, whereby the action that forms a thought sets the tongue swinging to utter it. Apart from the emotional (and non-articulate) natural cries and tones, the muscles of the larynx and mouth are no nearer to the soul than those of voluntary motion, by which, among other things, gestures are produced. Besides the lack of all evidence in language, rightly understood, to indicate such connection, it is sufficiently disproved, in a positive way, by the absence of vocal expression in the deaf, whose thinking and articulating apparatus is all in normal order, but who, by the numbing of the single nerve of audition, are removed from the disturbing infection of conventional speech; it ought to be many times more instructive to watch the 'natural utterances' of a person thus affected than to study the jabberings of monkeys. The analogy between gesture and speech here is in the highest degree instructive. The hands and arms are muscular instruments under control of the same mind which produces conceptions and judgments. Among their manifold capacities, they are able to make gestures, of infinite variety, all of which are reported by the vibrations of the luminiferous ether to a certain apprehending organ, the eye, both of the maker and of others. There is a natural basis of instinctive gesture, which to the human intellect is capable of suggesting a method of intimation of intended meaning, developable into a complete system of expression; and it is so developed for the use of those who by lack of power to hear are cut off from the superior advantages of the other means of expression. In the same manner, the larynx and the parts which lie between it and the outer world are muscular organs, movable by the same will which moves the arms and hands. The parts have other offices to perform besides that of shaping tone; and the tone which it is the sole office of the vocal chords to generate is for other purposes as well as that of utterance: yet, along with other things, they can produce an indefinite variety of modified vibrations, reported through the sympathetic vibrations of the air to another apprehending organ, the ear, both of the producer and of others; and the sounds so reported are capable of combination into groups practically infinite in number. There is a natural basis of tonic expression; and on this and by its suggestion human intelligence has worked out a great number of diverse systems of expression, used, one or other of them, by all ordinarily endowed men.

There is nothing here to require the admission of a peculiar connection between thought and articulate utterance. In a certain sense, it is true, the voice may fairly be said to have been given us for the purpose of speech; but it is only as the hands have been given us to write with; our speaking organs do also our tasting, breathing, eating. So iron has been given us to make rails with for fast traveling: that is to say, among the various substances provided in the world for man's various uses, iron is the one best suited to this use; its qualities had only to be discovered by men, in the course of their experiences of Nature, and, when the time for the use came, the perception of its adaptedness, and the application, necessarily followed. In the course of man's experience, it has come to light that the voice is, on the whole, the most available means of communication, for reasons which are not hard to understand: it acts with least expenditure of effort; it leaves the hands, much more variously efficient and hard-worked members, at leisure for other work at the same time; and it most easily compels attention from any direction. Only the smallest part of its capacities are laid under contribution for the uses of speech; of the indefinite number of distinguishable sounds which it can produce, only a fraction, of twelve to fifty, are put to use in any one language; and there is nothing in the selection to characterize a race, or to be used (except in the same historical way as language in general) for ethnological distinction: from among the many possibles, these have chanced to be taken; mainly the sounds easiest to make, and broadly distinguished from one another.

Under these determining considerations, vocal utterance has become everywhere the leading means of expression, and has so multiplied its resources that tone, and still more gesture, has assumed the subordinate office of aiding the effectiveness of what is uttered. And the lower the intellectual condition of the speaker and the spoken-to, the more indispensable is the addition of tone and gesture. It belongs to the highest development of speech that the word written and read should have something like the same power as the word spoken and heard; that the personality of the writer, even his frame of mind, should be felt, and should move the sympathetic feeling of the reader. And yet, it should also be noted here that, as we saw in the twelfth chapter, there are languages (e.g. Chinese) in which tone and inflection come to be used, in a secondary and conventional way, to eke out the too scanty resources of intellectual designation.

If we thus accept the impulse to communicate as the governing principle of speech-development, and the voice as the agent whose action we have especially to trace, it will not be difficult to establish other points in the earliest history. Whatever offered itself as the most feasible means of arriving at mutual understanding would be soonest turned to account. We have regarded the reproduction, with intent to signify something, of the natural tones and cries, as the positively earliest speech; but this would so immediately and certainly come to be combined with imitative or onomatopoetic utterances, that the distinction in time between the two is rather theoretical than actual. Indeed, the reproduction itself is in a certain way onomatopoetic: it imitates, so to speak, the cries of the human animal, in order to intimate secondarily what those cries in their primary use signified directly. Just as soon, at any rate, as an inkling of the value of communication was gained, and the process began to be performed a little more consciously, the range of imitation would be extended. This is a direct corollary to the principles laid down above. Mutual intelligence being aimed at, and audible utterance the means employed, audible sounds will be the matter most readily represented and conveyed; just as something else would come easiest to one who used a different means. To repeat once more the old and well-worn, but telling, illustration: if we had the conception of a dog to signify, and the instrumentality were pictorial, we should draw the outline figure of a dog; if the means were gesture, we should imitate some characteristic visible act of the animal – for example, its bite, or the wagging of its tail; if it were voice, we should say 'bow-wow.' This is the simple explanation of the importance which is and must be attributed to the onomatopoetic principle in the early stages of language-making. We have no need of appealing to any special tendency toward imitation. Man is, to be sure, an imitative animal, as we may fairly say; but not in an instinctive or mechanical way; he is imitative because he has the capacity to notice and appreciate what he sees, in other animals or in nature, and to reproduce it in imitative show, if anything is to be gained thereby – whether amusement, or artistic pleasure, or communication. He is an imitator just as he is an artist; the latter is only the higher development of the former.

The scope of the imitative principle is by no means restricted to the sounds which occur in nature, although these are the most obvious and easiest subjects of significative reproduction. What it is, may be seen in part from the range of onomatopoetic words in known languages. There is a figurative use of imitation, where-by rapid, slow, abrupt, repetitive motions are capable of being signified by combinations of sounds which make something such an impression on the mind through the ear as the motions in question do through the eye. And we can well conceive that, while this was the chief efficient suggestion of expression, men's minds may have been sharpened to catch and incorporate analogies which now escape our notice, because, having a plentiful provision of expression from other sources, we no longer have our attention keenly directed to them. Our judgments on such points as this can only be partially trusted, and must be tested with extreme caution, because we are all of us now the creatures of educated habit, and cannot look at things as men uneducated and with no formed habits would do. We can safely investigate and combine and speculate in this direction, if we keep fully in mind the governing principle that mutual intelligence is the end, and that whatever conduces to mutual intelligence, and that alone, is the acceptable means. We shall thus be saved from running off into, or toward, that most absurd doctrine, the absolute natural significance of articulate sounds, and the successful intimation of complex ideas by a process of piecing these elements together.

There are one or two further points connected with this theory of the imitative origin of language which call for a few words of explanation. In the first place, it does not rest on a discovery of the signs of onomatopœia as predominant in the early traceable stages of language. Those stages are still too far from the beginning to furnish any such discovery. The intent was to find means of mutual intelligence; and when this was won, the way it came was a matter of small consequence, and might be left to be covered up. This has been, as we abundantly saw above, a governing tendency in the growth of speech down to the present time. Speakers know not and care not whence their words came; they know simply what they mean; even the wisest of us can trace the history of only a small part of his vocabulary, and only a little way. The very earliest dialects are as exclusively conventional as the latest; the savage has no keener sense of etymological connection than the man of higher civilization. Nothing has done so much to discredit the imitative theory with sound and sober linguistic scholars as the way in which some pass beyond the bounds of true science in their attempts to trace our living vocabularies to mimetic originals. The theory does, indeed, rest in part on the undeniable presence of a considerable onomatopœic element in later speech, and on the fact that new material is actually won in this way through the whole history of language; onomatopœia is thus raised to the rank of a *vera causa*, attested by familiar fact; and nothing that is not so attested – for example, the assumed immediate intellectual significance of articulate combinations – has the right to stand as a *causa* at all; but it rests also in part, and in the main part, on the necessities of the case, as inferred from the whole traceable history of speech and its relation to thought, its use and its value. Here is just the other support which it needs: no account of the origin of language is scientific which does not join directly on to the later history of language without a break, being of one piece with that history.

But, in the second place, it may at first sight seem to some that there is a break in the history: for why do we not still go on to make words abundantly by onomatopœia? A moment's thought will show the baselessness of this objection. The office of onomatopœia was the provision, by the easiest attainable method, of the means of mutual intelligence; in proportion, then, as it became easier to make the same provision by another method, the differentiation and new application of signs already existing, the primitive method went into comparative disuse – as it has ever since continued, though never absolutely unused.

Once more, our theory furnishes the satisfactory solution of a difficulty which has had influence with some minds. Why should the germs of speech be what we have called roots, elements indicative of such abstract things as acts and qualities? surely concrete objects are soonest and most easily apprehended by the mind. Without stopping to dispute on more philosophical grounds this last assertion, claiming instead that we apprehend only the concreted qualities and acts of objects, it will be more to the point with those who feel the difficulty to note that the process of speech is one of signifying, and that only the separate qualities of objects, at any rate, are capable of being signified. To revert to our former example: there may be a state of mind in which there should exist a confused concrete impression of a dog, just sufficient to make it possible to recognize another as agreeing with one already seen, but without any distinct sense of its various attributes. But so long as that is the case, no production of a sign is possible: it is only when one has so clear a conception of its form that he can signify it by a rude outline picture, or of its characteristic acts that he can reproduce the bite, or wag, or bark, in imitation of them, that he is ready for an act of language-making of which the dog shall be the subject. And so with every other case; the first acts of comparing and abstracting must precede, and the first signs must follow; even as we have before seen that it is through the whole history of speech: the conception first, then the nomenclative act. And *bow-wow* is a type, a normal example, of the whole genus 'root.' It is a sign, a hint, that calls before the properly prepared mind a certain conception, or set of related conceptions: the animal itself, the act, the time and other circumstances of hearing it, and what followed. It does not mean any one of these things exclusively; it comprehends them all. It is not a verb, for that adds the idea of pedication; nor is it a name: it may be put to use in either of these two senses. What it comes nearest in itself to meaning is 'the action of barking' – just that form of abstraction into which we now most naturally and properly cast the sense of a 'root.' And so with both the other suggested signs. Only, the outline figure has a decidedly more concrete character than either of the others, and is in a certain way their antithesis. It is a curious fact, and one tellingly illustrative of how the character of the sign depends on the instrumentality by which it is made, that hieroglyphic systems of representation of thought (which are in their origin independent systems, parallel with speech, though they are wont finally to come into servitude to speech) begin with the signs for concrete objects, and arrive from these, and secondarily, at the designation of acts and qualities. In Chinese, a combination of the hieroglyphs of sun and moon makes the character for 'light' and 'shine;' in speech, on the contrary, both luminaries are apt to be named from their shining (see above, p. 83). In Egyptian, a picture of a pair of legs in motion means 'walk;' while, with us, the *foot* is so named as being the 'walker.'

That by the methods thus described it was possible to make a provision of signs capable of development, by processes not different from those traceable in the historic period of language, into such vocabularies as we find actually existing, it does not seem as if any one could reasonably deny. If this is true, and if the methods are not only not inconsistent, but even in complete harmony, with the whole traceable course of human action on language, then we have found an acceptable solution of that part of the problem we are seeking to solve which is at present within our reach. A scientific solution requires that we take man as he is, with no other gifts than those we see him to possess, but also with all those that constitute his endowment as man, and examine whether and how he would possess himself of the beginnings of speech, analogous with those which our historical analysis shows to have been the germs of the after-development, but beyond which historical research will not carry us. As he would, if need were, make the acquisition now, so may he, or must he, have made it of old. This is not a part of the historical science of language, but a corollary to it, a subject for the anthropologist who is also a linguistic scholar, who knows what language is to man, and how. He is not prepared to deal with it who is merely master of the facts of many languages.

Of course, a language thus produced would be a rude and rudimentary means of expression. But that constitutes, in the mind of the modern anthropologist, no bar to the acceptance of the theory. If we deny to primitive man the possession of the other elements of civilization, and hold him to have gradually developed them out of scanty beginnings made by himself, then there is no reason why we should not hold the same view in respect to language, which is only such an element. Even in existing languages the differences of degree are great, as in existing states of culture in general. An infinity of things can be said in English which cannot be said in Fijian or Hottentot; a vast deal, doubtless, can be said in Fijian or Hottentot which could not be said in the first human languages. For what can be done in the way of distinct, even cultivated and elaborate, expression, by only a few hundred formless roots, we have a brilliant, almost a startling, example in the Chinese. Of how sentences can be made of roots alone, with the relations left to be supplied by the intelligently apprehending mind, the same tongue is a sufficient illustration. The Greek, or German, or English, can elaborate a thought in a period half a page long, determining by proper connectives the relation of each of its clauses to the central idea, and also, in widely varying degree and method, that of the members of each clause to one another. This is a capacity which belongs only to languages of high cultivation, working on a richly inflective basis. Many another tongue can form only simple clauses, possessing no more intricate apparatus of connection than 'ands' and 'buts,' though having form enough in its words to construct a clause of defined parts. Yet others lack this definition of parts; they strike only at the leading ideas, presenting them in such order that the hearer supplies the missing relations out of his general comprehension of what must be the intended meaning. And it is but another step backward to the primitive root-condition of speech, where an utterance or two had to do the duty of a whole clause. Men thus began, not with parts of speech which they afterward learned to piece together into sentences, but with comprehensive utterances in which the parts of speech lay as yet undeveloped, sentences in the germ; a single word signifying a whole statement, as even yet sometimes with us: only then from poverty, as now from economy. To demand that 'sentences,' in the present sense of that term, with subject and predicate, with adjuncts and modifiers, should have been the first speech, is precisely analogous with demanding that the first human abodes should have contained at least two stories and a cellar; or that the earliest garments should not have lacked buttons and braces; or that the first instruments should have had handles, and been put together with screws. These conditions, in the last three cases, are at once recognized as possible only to a miraculous endowment of humanity, a gifting of man, at his birth, not with capacities alone, but also with their elaborated results, with the fruits of education; and the assumption in regard to language is really precisely the same, a proper part of a miraculous theory of the origin of speech, but of no other.

The word 'miraculous,' rather than 'divine,' is here used to characterize the theory in question, because it is the only truly descriptive one. One may hold the views advocated in this chapter without any detriment to his belief in the divine origin of language; since he may be persuaded that the capacities and tendencies which lead man universally and inevitably to the acquisition of speech were implanted in him by the Creator for that end, and only work themselves out to a foreseen and intended result. If language itself were a gift, a faculty, a capacity, it might admit of being regarded as the subject of direct bestowal; being only a result, a historical result, to assert that it sprang into developed being along with man is to assert a miracle; the doctrine has no right to make its appearance except in company with a general miraculous account of the beginnings of human existence. That view of the nature of language which linguistic science establishes takes entirely away the foundation on which the doctrine of divine origin, in its form as once held, reposed.

The human capacity to which the production of language is most directly due is, as has been seen, the power of intelligently, and not by blind instinct alone, adapting means to ends. This is by no means a unitary capacity; on the contrary, it is a highly composite and intricate one. But it does not belong to the linguistic student to unravel and explain, any more than to the student of the history of civilization in its other departments; it falls, rather, to the student of the human mind and its powers, to the psychologist. So also with all the mental capacities involved in language, the psychic forces which underlie that practical faculty, and which, being by it brought to conscious action, are drawn out and trained and developed. The psychologist has a work of highest interest and importance to do, in analyzing and exhibiting this ultimate groundwork, on which have grown up the great institutions that make man what he is: language, society, the arts of life, machinery, art, and so on; and in tracing the history of education of the human powers in connection with them; and his aid and criticism must be everywhere of great value to their student. And this is most of all the case with regard to language; for language is in an especial manner the incorporation and revelation of the acts of the soul. Out of this relation has grown the error of those who look upon linguistic science as a branch of psychology, would force it into a psychologic mould and conduct it by psychologic methods: an error which is so refuted by the whole view we have taken of language and its history, that we do not need to spend any more words upon it here. Language is merely that product and instrumentality of the inner powers which exhibits them most directly and most fully in their various modes of action; by which, so far as the case admits, our inner consciousness is externized, turned up to the light for ourselves and others to see and study.

Out of the same close relation grows another and a far grosser error, that of actually identifying speech with thought and reason. This, too, we may take as sufficiently refuted by our whole argument; nothing but the most imperfect comprehension of language can account for a blunder so radical. The word, *reason*, to be sure, is used so loosely, in such a variety of senses, that an unclear thinker and illogical arguer can comparatively easily become confused by it: but no one who attempts to enlighten his fellow-men on this class of subjects is excusable for such inability to grasp their most fundamental principles. Language is, upon the whole, the most conspicuous of the manifestations of man's higher endowments, and the one of widest and deepest influence on every other; and the superiority of man's endowments is vaguely known as reason – and that is the whole ground of the assertion of identity. There are many faculties which go to the production of speech; and they have other modes of manifestation besides speech. And we have only to take the most normally endowed human being and cut off artificially the avenue of a single class of sensuous impressions, those of hearing, and he will never have any speech. If speech, then, is reason, reason will have to be defined as a function of the auditory nerve.

Whether, among the powers that contribute to the production of language, there is one, or more than one, not belonging in any degree to a single animal below man, is a point which must be left to the psychologist to decide. It may fairly be claimed, however, that none such has yet been demonstrated; and also, that none such is necessary: a simple difference of degree in the capacities common to both is amply sufficient to account for the possession and the lack, on the one side and the other. A heightened power of comparison, of the general perception of resemblances and differences; an accompanying higher power of abstraction, or of viewing the resemblances and differences as attributes, characteristic of the objects compared; and, above all else, a heightened command of consciousness, a power of looking upon one's self also as acting and feeling, of studying one's own mental movements – these, it is believed, are the directions in which the decisive superiority is to be looked for. It is the height of injustice to maintain that there is not an approach, and a very marked approach, made by some of the lower animals to the capacity of language. In the ratio of what we call their 'intelligence,' they are able distinctly and fruitfully to associate conceptions with signs – signs, namely, which we make for them, and by which we guide and govern them. But, as an actual fact, their capacity, though rising thus far, stops short of the native production of such a sign, even of its acquisition from the higher race and its independent use among themselves. There is a long interval, incapable of being crossed by the lower animals, between their endowments and ours; and he is a coward who, out of fear for the preservation of man's supremacy, attempts to stretch it out, or to set up barriers upon it.

There is yet another important corollary from our established view of language as a constituent element of human civilization. Its production had nothing to do, as a cause, with the development of man out of any other and lower race. Its province was to raise man from a savage state to the plane which he was capable of reaching. The only development in which it was concerned is the historical development of man's faculties. Except, of course, that minor and limited change which falls within the sphere of ordinary heredity. The descendant of a cultivated race is more cultivable than the descendant of a wild one. The capacity of a yet higher cultivation grows with the slow increase of cultivation; and if a people is suddenly brought in contact with a civilization too far in advance of it, it is rather deteriorated and wasted than elevated. The power of brain, the capacity of thought, is enhanced by speech; but no such differences are produced as separate one animal species from another. All men speak, each race in accordance with its gift and culture; but all together are only one species. To the zoologist, man was what he is now when the first beginnings of speech were made; it is to the historian that he was infinitely different. 'Man could not become man except by language; but in order to possess language, he needed already to be man,' is one of those Orphic sayings which, if taken for what they are meant to be, poetic expressions whose apparently paradoxical character shall compel attention and suggest thought and inquiry, are admirable enough. To make them the foundation or test of scientific views is simply ridiculous; it is as if one were to say: 'A pig is not a pig without being fattened; but in order to be fattened he must first be a pig.' The trick of the aphorism in question lies in its play upon the double sense of the word *man*; properly interpreted, it becomes an acceptable expression of our own view: 'Man could not rise from what he was by nature to what he was able and intended to become, and ought to become, except by the aid of speech; but he could never have produced speech had he not been at the outset gifted with just those powers of which we still see him in possession, and which make him man.'

We have already noted the linguist's inability at present to form even any valuable conjectures as to the precise point in the history of man at which the germs of speech should have appeared, and the time which they should have occupied in the successive steps of their development. Men's views are greatly at variance as to this, and with no prospect of reconciliation at present, because there is no criterion by which they can be tested. That the process was a slow one, all our knowledge of the history of later speech gives us reason to believe. As to the precise degree of slowness, that is an unessential point, which we may well enough leave for future knowledge to settle – if it can. What we have to guard especially against is the tendency to look upon language-making as a task in which men engage, to which they direct their attention, which absorbs a part of their nervous energy, so that they are thereby prevented from working as effectively in other directions of effort. Language-making is a mere incident of social life and of cultural growth; its every act is suggested or called forth by an occasion which is by comparison the engrossing thing, to which the nomenclative set is wholly subordinate. It is as great an error to hold that at some period men are engaged in making and laying up expressions for their own future use and that of their descendants, as that, at another period, men are packing away conceptions and judgments for which their successors shall find expression. Each period provides just what it has occasion for; nothing more. A generation or period may, indeed, by a successful incorporation in speech of an exceptionally fertile distinction, start a train of development which shall lead to immense consequences in the future, and lay a foundation on which a great deal shall admit of being built: such, for example (as we thought to see above), was the early Indo-European establishment of a special predicative form, a verb. This is truly analogous with those fortunate inventions or discoveries (like that of treating iron, of domesticating useful animals) which appear now and then to have given a happy turn to the history of a race, initiating an upward career of growth which would have seemed *á priori* equally within the reach of any other race. Such occurrences we are in the habit of calling accidental; and properly enough, if we are careful to understand by this only that they are the product of forces and circumstances so numerous and so indeterminable that we cannot estimate them, and could not have predicted their result. But, slower or more rapid, the production of language is a continuous process; it varies in rate and kind with the circumstances and habits of the speaking community; but it never ceases; there was never a time when it was more truly going on than at present.

What term we shall apply to the process and its result is a matter of very inferior consequence. Invention, fabrication, devisal, production, generation – all these are terms which have their favorers and also their violent opposers. Provided we understand what the thing in reality is, we need care little about the phraseology used in characterizing it. Each word may be not unfitly compared to an invention; it has its own place, mode, and circumstances of devisal, its preparation in the previous habits of speech, its influence in determining the after-progress of speech-development; but every language in the gross is an institution, on which scores or hundreds of generations and unnumbered thousands of individual workers have labored.

THE SIMIAN TONGUE
R. L. Garner

Source: New Review, vols. 4–6, June, November and February 1891–2

I

IN coming before the world with a new theory, I am aware that it may have to undergo many repairs, and be modified by many new ideas. On entering the world of science, it begins its 'struggle for life,' and under the law of 'the survival of the fittest' its fate must be decided. I am aware that it is heresy to doubt the dogmas of science as well as of some religious sects; but sustained by proofs too strong to be ignored, I am willing to incur the ridicule of the wise and the sneer of bigots, and assert that 'articulate speech' prevails among the lower primates, and that their speech contains the rudiments from which the tongues of mankind could easily develop; and to me it seems quite possible to find proofs to show that such is the origin of human speech.

I have long believed that each sound uttered by an animal had a meaning which any other animal of the same kind would interpret at once. Animals soon learn to interpret certain words of man and to obey them, but never try to repeat them. When they reply to man, it is always in their own peculiar speech. I have often watched the conduct of a dog as he would speak, until I could interpret a meaning to his combined act and speech. I observe the same thing in other species with the same results; and it occurred to me that if I could correctly imitate these sounds I might learn to interpret them more fully and prove to myself whether it was really a uniform speech or not.

Some seven years ago, in the Cincinnati Zoological Garden, I was deeply impressed by the conduct of a number of monkeys caged with a savage rib-nosed mandril, which they seemed to fear very much. The cage was divided by a wall through which was a small doorway leading from the inner to an outer compartment, in which was a tall upright, supporting a platform at its top. Every movement of this mandril seemed to be closely watched by the monkeys that could see him, and instantly reported to those in the other compartment. The conduct of these monkeys so confirmed my belief and inspired me with new hopes and new zeal that I believed 'the key to the secret chamber' was within my grasp. I regarded the task of learning the monkey tongue as very much the same as learning that of a strange race of mankind; more difficult in the degree of its inferiority, but less in volume. Year by year, as new ideas were revealed to me, new barriers arose, and I began to realise how great a task was mine. One difficulty was to *utter* the sounds I heard; another was to recall them; and yet another was to translate them. Impelled by an eternal hope, and not discouraged by poor success, I continued my studies as best I could, in the gardens of New York, Philadelphia, Cincinnati, and Chicago, and with such specimens as I could find with the travelling menagerie museum, or hand organ, or aboard some ship, or kept as a pet in some family. They have all aided in teaching me the little I know of their native tongues. But at last came a revelation! I new idea dawned upon me; and after wrestling half a night with it I felt assured of ultimate success. I went to Washington, and called upon Dr. Frank Baker, Director of the National Zoological Garden and proposed the novel experiment of acting as interpreter between, two monkeys. Of course he laughed, but not in derision or in doubt, for scientific men are always credulous and believe all they are told. I then explained to him how it was possible, and he quite agreed with me. We set the time and prepared for the work. The plan was quite simple. We separated two monkeys which had been caged together, and placed them in separate rooms. I then arranged a phonograph near the cage of the female, and caused her to utter a few sounds, which were recorded on the cylinder. The machine was then placed near the cage containing the male, and the record repeated to him and his conduct closely studied. The surprise and perplexity of the male were evident.

He traced the sounds to the horn from which they came, and failing to find his mate he thrust his hand and arm into the horn quite up to his shoulder, withdrew it, and peeped into the horn again and again. He would then retreat and again cautiously approach the horn, which he examined with evident interest. The expressions of his face were indeed a study. Having satisfied myself that he recognised the sounds as those of his mate, I next proceeded to record some of his efforts, but my success was not fully up to my hopes. Yet I had secured from him enough to win the attention of his mate, and elicit from her some signs of recognition. And thus, for the first time in the history of philology, the simian tongue was reduced to record. My belief was now confirmed, and the faith of others strengthened. I noted some of the defects in my experiment, and provided against them for the future. Some weeks later, in the Chicago Zoological Garden, I made some splendid phonographic records; and thence I went to the Cincinnati Garden, where I secured, among others, a fine, distinct record of the two chimpanzees, all of which I brought home with me for study. I placed them on the machine and repeated them over and over, until I became quite familiar with the sounds and improved myself very much in my efforts to utter them. I returned to Cincinnati and Chicago some weeks later, and tried my skill as a linguist with a degree of success far beyond my wildest hopes.

Having described to some friends who were with me the word I would use, I stood for a while with my side turned to the cage containing a capuchin monkey (*cebus capucinus*). I uttered the word or sound which I had translated 'milk.' My first effort caught his ear and caused him to turn and look at me. On repeating it some three or four times he answered me very distinctly with the same word I had used, and then turned to a small pan kept in the cage for him to drink from. I repeated the word again, and he placed the pan near the front of the cage and came quite up to the bars and uttered the word. I had not shown him any milk or anything of the kind. But the man in charge then brought me some milk, which I gave to him, and he drank it with great zest; then looked at me, held up the pan, and repeated the sound some three or four times. I gave him more milk, and thus continued till I was quite sure he used the same sound each time he wanted milk.

I next described to the friends who were with me a word which was very hard to render well, but I translated it 'to eat.' I now held a banana in front of the cage and he at once gave the word I had described. Repeated tests showed to me that he used the same word for apple, carrot, bread, and banana, hence I concluded that it meant 'food,' or 'hunger,' as also 'to eat.' After this I began on a word which I had interpreted 'pain,' or 'sick,' and with such result as made me feel quite sure I was not far from right. My next word was 'weather,' or 'storm,' and while the idea may seem far-fetched, I felt fairly well sustained by my tests. For many other words I had a vague idea of a meaning, and still believe that I can verify them in the end. These are only a few of many trials I have made to solve the problem of the simian tongue, and while I have only gone a step, as it were, I believe that I have found a clue to the great secret of speech, and pointed out the way which leads to its solution.

I went next to the Cincinnati Garden. When the visitors had left the monkey-house I approached the cage of a capuchin monkey, and found him crouched in the rear of his cage. I spoke to him in his own tongue, using the word which I had called 'milk.' He rose, answered me with the same word, and came at once to the front of the cage. He looked at me as if in doubt, and I repeated the word; he did the same, and turned at once to a small pan in the cage, which he picked up and placed near the door at the side, and returned to me and uttered the word again. I asked the keeper for milk, which he did not have, however, but brought me some water. The efforts of my little simian friend to secure the glass were very earnest, and the pleading manner and tone assured me of his extreme thirst. I allowed him to dip his hand into the glass and he would suck his fingers and reach again. I kept the glass from reach of his hand, and he would repeat the sound and beg for more. I was thus convinced that the word I had translated 'milk' must also mean 'water,' and from this and other tests, I at last determined that it meant also 'drink' and probably 'thirst.' I have never seen a capuchin monkey that did not use these two words. The sounds are very soft and not unlike a flute; very difficult to imitate and quite impossible to write. They are purely vocal, except faint traces of 'h' or 'wh' as in the word 'who'; a very feeble w'; and here and there a slight gutteral 'ch.'

To imitate the word which I interpret 'food,' fix the mouth as if to whistle: draw the tongue far back into the mouth, and try to utter the word 'who' by blowing. The pitch of sound is a trifle higher than the cooing of a pigeon, and not wholly unlike it. The phonics appear to me to be 'wh-u-w,' with the consonant elements so faint as to be almost imaginary. In music the tone is F sharp, thus

and this seems to be the vocal pitch of the entire species, though they have a wide range of voice. The sound which I have translated 'drink' or 'thirst' is nearly uttered by relaxing and parting the lips, and placing the tongue as it is found in ending the German word 'ich,' and in this position try to utter 'ch-e-u-w,' making the 'ch' like 'k,' blending the 'e' and 'u' like 'slurred' notes in music, and suppressing the 'w' as in the first case. The consonant elements can barely be detected, and the tone is about an octave higher than the word used for 'food.' Another sound I suspected was a 'menace' or 'cry of alarm,' but I was unable to utter it, except with the phonograph; but during February I had access to a fine specimen of the capuchin, in Charleston, S.C. On my first visit to him I found him very gentle, and we at once became good friends. He ate from my hands and seemed to regard me very kindly. The next day, while feeding him, I uttered the peculiar sound of 'alarm,' whereupon he sprang at once to a perch in the top of his cage, and as I continued the sound he seemed almost frantic with fright. I could not tempt him by any means to come down. I then retired some twenty feet from the cage, and his master (of whom he is very fond) induced him to come down from the perch, and while he was fondling him I gave the alarm from where I stood. He jumped again to his perch and nothing would induce him to leave it while I remained in sight. The next day, on my approach, he fled to his perch and I could not induce him on any terms to return. It is now some time since I began my visits, and I have never, since his first fright, induced him to accept anything from me, and only with great patience can I get him to leave his perch at all, although I have not repeated this peculiar sound since my third visit, nor can I again elicit a reply from him when I say his word for 'food' or 'drink.'

This sound may be fairly imitated by placing the back of the hand very gently to the mouth, and kissing it, drawing in the air, and producing a shrill, whistling sound, prolonged and slightly circumflexed.

Its pitch is the highest F sharp on the piano. It is not whistled, however, by a monkey, but is made with the vocal organs. While this is the highest vocal pitch of a capuchin, there are other sounds much more difficult to imitate or describe. It must be remembered than an attempt to *spell* a sound which is almost an absolute vowel, can at best convey only a very imperfect idea of the true sounds or the manner of uttering them.

I have access also to another specimen of the same variety, with which I am experimenting, but I have never tried the 'alarm' on him as I do not wish to lose his friendship. He uses all the words I know in his language, and speaks them well.

My work has been confined chiefly to the capuchin monkey, because he seems to have one of the best defined languages of any of his genus, besides being less vicious and more willing to treat one civilly. So far as I have seen, the capuchin is the Caucasian of the monkey race. The chimpanzee has a strong but monotonous voice, confined to a small range of sounds, but affords a fine study while in the act of talking. I have not gone far enough with him as yet to give much detail of his language. There are only three in America now, and they talk but little and are hard to record. I have recorded but one sound made by a sooty monkey; three by a mandril; five by the white-face sapajou; and a few of less value. But from the best proof I have found I have arrived, as I believe, at some strange facts, which I shall here state.

1. The simian tongue has about eight or nine sounds, which may be changed by modulation into three or four times that number.

2. They seem to be half-way between a whistle and a pure vocal sound, and have a range of four octaves, and so far as I have tried they all chord with F sharp on a piano.

3. The sound used most is very much like 'u'-'oo,' in 'shoot.' The next one something like 'e' in 'be.' So far I find no a, i, or o.

4. Faint traces of consonant sounds can be found in words of low pitch, but they are few and quite feeble; but I have had cause to believe that they develop in a small degree by a change of environment.

5. The present state of their speech has been reached by development from a lower form.

6. Each race or kind has its own peculiar tongue, slightly

shaded into dialects, and the radical or cardinal sounds do not have the same meanings in all tongues.

7. The words are monosyllabic, ambiguous and collective, having no negative terms except resentment.

8. The phonic character of their speech is very much the same as that of children in their early efforts to talk, except as regards the pitch.

9. Their language seems to obey the same laws of change and growth as human speech.

10. When caged together one monkey will learn to understand the language of another kind, but does not try to speak it. His replies are in his own vernacular.

11. They use their lips in talking in very much the same way that men do; but seldom speak when alone or when not necessary.

12. I think their speech, compared to their physical, mental, and social state, is in about the same relative condition as that of man by the same standard.

13. The more fixed and pronounced the social and gregarious instincts are in any species, the higher the type of its speech.

14. Simians reason from cause to effect, and their reasoning differs from that of man *in degree, but not in kind.*

To reason, they *must think*, and if it be true that *man cannot think without words*, it must be true of monkeys: hence, they must formulate those thoughts into words, and words are the natural exponents of thoughts.

15. Words are the audible, and signs the visible, expression of thought, and any voluntary sound made by the vocal organs with a constant meaning is a word.

16. The state of their language seems to correspond with their power to think, and to express their thoughts.

If we compare the tongues of civilised races with those of the savage tribes of Africa which are confined to a few score of words, we gain some idea of the growth of language within the limits of our own genus. The few wants and simple modes of life in such a state account for this paucity of words; and this small range of sounds gives but little scope for vocal development, and hence their difficulty in learning to speak the tongues of civilised men. This is, doubtless, the reason why the negroes of the United States, after a sojourn of two hundred years with the white race, are unable to utter the sounds of 'th,' 'thr,' and other double consonants; the former of which they pronounce 'd' if breathing, and 't' if aspirate; the latter like 'trw.' The sound of 'v' they usually pronounce 'b,' while 'r' resembles 'w' or 'rw' when initial, and as a final is usually entirely suppressed. They have a marked tendency to omit auxiliaries and final sounds, and in all departures from the higher types of speech tend back to ancestral forms. I believe, if we could apply the rule of perspectives and throw our vanishing point far back beyond the chasm that separates man from his simian prototype, that we should find one unbroken outline, tangent to every circle of life from man to protozoa, in language mind, and matter.

The sage of science finds the fossil rays of light still shining in the chamber of sleeping epochs, and by their aid he reads the legends on the guide-posts of time; but the echoes of time are lost and its lips are dumb; hence our search for the first voice of speech must come within the brief era of man; but if his prototype survives, does not his parent speech survive? If the races of mankind may be the progeny of the simian stock, may not their languages by the progeny of the simian tongue?

II

The world of science has received with so much kind and candid interest the brief account of my attempts to unlock the portals of speech which lead us from the realm of human thought into the secret precincts of Simian emotions, that I feel it a duty to comply with the urgent wish of so many, and give the anxious friends of progress some conclusions deduced from recent experiments in my novel field of research. I proceed, however, on a line which takes for granted that my reader has read my former article on this same subject.

Later experiments have somewhat modified the details of my theory, but as a whole have added much strength to my belief in the certainty of my cause.

Since writing the sounds used by the capuchin monkeys, as well as I could represent them by the letters of our alphabet, I have had no reason to alter the literal formula by which they are expressed; but I have found that the word which I had construed to mean *food*, and sometimes perhaps to mean *drink*, has a still wider sense. It is difficult to formulate, in human speech, anything equivalent to it, since our human mode of speech has been so changed by accretions and by our higher modes of thought that we cannot grasp the thought from such a slight suggestion, and our habits of redundancy make us incapable of their modes of speech. It impresses me that the sound formerly described as meaning food is used in some way as a kind of 'shibboleth.' It is possible that this may arise from the Simian idea of food as the chief source of all happiness, and that the satisfaction which it gives is the supreme thought of his life, and in this manner he associates that sound with every kindness and pacific office; but from a lack of opportunities I have not been able to ascertain to what extent these are associated ideas with him.

I have described in my former paper the fright which I gave to a monkey named Jokes, in Charleston, and at the time of writing that article I had not been able to renew friendly relations with him. After a lapse of some ten or twelve days from the time I had frightened him, I resorted to harsher means of bringing him to terms: I began to threaten him with a rod. At first he would resent it, but when he failed to frighten me by his threats and assaults, he soon yielded and came down from the perch in his cage, although greatly frightened. He would place the side of his head on the floor, put out his tongue, and utter a very plaintive sound, having a slight interrogative inflection. At first this novel demeanour quite defied interpretation; but during the same period I was visiting a young monkey of the same kind called Jack: we were quite good friends for comparative strangers, and he allowed me many liberties with him, which the family to whom he belonged assured me he denied to others. On one of my frequent visits he displayed his temper and made an attack upon me because I refused to let go a saucer from which I was feeding him some milk. I jerked him up by the chain and slapped him sharply for this, whereupon he instantly laid the side of his head on the floor, put out his tongue, and made just such a sound as Jokes had made several times before, under the stress of great fear. It occurred to me that must be a sign of surrender or submission. And many subsequent tests have confirmed this opinion.

But my daily visits to Jokes had not won him back after a lapse of more than two months, and on my approach he would manifest great fear and go through with this strange act of humiliation. I observed that he had a great dislike for a certain negro boy on the place, who teased and vexed him very much, so I had the boy come up near the cage, and Jokes would fairly rave with anger. So great was his dislike for this boy that he seemed to forget all other things about him in his efforts to get to him. I would feign to beat the boy with a stick, and this gave Jokes great delight. I would hold the boy so near the cage as to allow the monkey to scratch and claw his clothes, and this would fill his whole Simian soul with joy. I would then release the boy and drive him away with sticks and wads of paper, to the evident pleasure of the monkey. I repeated these things many times, and we became the very best of friends again. After each encounter he would come up to the bars, touch my hand with his tongue, chatter and play with my fingers, and show all signs of friendship. He always warns me of the approach of anyone, and his conduct towards them is very largely controlled by my own. He never fails to greet me with the sound described in my former paper. The sound is a compound, as I have shown by reversing the cylinder of the graphophone, and repeating it backward. This will be referred to farther on.

I may here relate that on one occasion a boy was teasing Jokes with a stick, when I approached the cage and put my hand in, and allowed him to caress it; in the meanwhile the boy would reach his hand into the cage under my arm and catch Jokes' tail or toe, which seemed at first to surprise him greatly, but in a trice he detected the author and flew at him with great violence, and every time the boy would reach his hand into or towards the cage the monkey would spring at him and try to catch his hand. In his haste and anger he once grabbed my hand in mistake; but he discovered it so quickly that I had scarcely realised the situation myself before I found him crouched down and his head on the floor, his tongue out, uttering that peculiar sound (which I cannot reduce to letters), in the most suppliant manner, and he continued to do so until he had been assured of peace. When he assaults anyone else he always returns to me and touches my hand with his tongue, which seems to be a kind of sign of a covenant.

Another little monkey of this species which I visited a few times was called Jennie. Her master had warned me in advance that she was not kindly disposed to strangers and I should watch her, that she might not do me any harm. At my request he had her chained in a small side yard and forbade any of the family entering it. I approached her little ladyship with the usual salutation, which she seemed to recognise at once, and I sat down by her and began to feed her from my hands. She seemed to regard me as a friend, but of a different species. She eyed me with evident interest and some suspicion, but when I would utter that sound for *food* she would respond promptly. While we were indulging in a kind of mutual investigation of affairs a negro girl, who lived with the family and frequently fed Jennie, being overcome by her curiosity, came into the yard and came up within a few feet of us. I at once decided that I would offer her as a sacrifice on the altar of science, so I arose and placed her between myself and the monkey and began to sound the 'alarm' or 'menace' with great vigour. Jennie flew into a perfect fit of fright. I continued to sound it, and at the same time to attack the girl with a great display of violence, thus causing the monkey to believe that the girl had made the alarm. I then drove the girl away from the yard with a great flourish of paper wads and pea-nut shells, and returned to the little monkey to pacify her. She became quite calm and seemed to think I was her hero, but for days she would not allow the girl to feed or approach her. This quite confirmed my opinion as to the meaning of this peculiar piercing sound.

A few weeks later I went to Cincinnati to visit my chimpanzee friends again, and I found immediately that they gave evidence of understanding one of the words which I used on approaching them. This word I had learned from the record of their speech which I had made last year. I have not had the opportunities to experiment with them which would justify my giving a very full account of any of their traits of speech, only to say this, that I am quite sure from my studies of their vocal character in the graphophone, and by listening to them in their cages, if I could be more intimately associated with them I could soon master their language; but they are kept in a large cage, entirely enclosed in a house of glass, the outer doors of which are kept closed to avoid any change of temperature which might tell on their health, and the keeper is so apprehensive of some ill befalling them that he keeps them for ever under his eye. I succeeded in getting their attention as I tried to utter a sound of theirs, and I could get the female to come to me every time I would use it. I cannot fully describe it here, although it comes within the compass of human speech, and is not very difficult to utter. It is not quite, but nearly, represented by *h-ou-wh*, very slightly nasal, and, so far, the only trace of a nasal intonation in the vocal products of any of the lower animals which I have ever detected. They have more words than a capuchin monkey, and all the words they speak, so far as I have ever been able to hear, can be reproduced by human vocal organs. My recent visit to them has quite satisfied me that I can make myself understood by them; and while it is premature as yet to mention it, I am now trying to arrange for a trip to interior Africa to visit the *troglodytes* in their native wilds, and if my plans (which are all practicable) can be arranged, I agree to give to the world a revelation which will rattle the dry bones of philology in a wholly new light. Mr. Edison has kindly agreed, if I can make certain arrangements, that he will aid me in the phonograph feature – the only thing which makes these studies possible – and I promise to perform some feats which will be worthy of public attention.

A short time since I made a phonograph record of the great Anubis baboon in the Philadelphia garden. I did not expect to find in him a highly developed language, but my purpose was to compare it with other Simian sounds, to see if I could not establish a series of steps in the quality of vocal sounds which would coincide with other certain characters, and determine whether there was not some unit of linguistic measure by which we might arrive at some standard in any given type. In other words, to see if the vocal powers were in homology in their development with other characters; and I am gratified to find by a series of comparisons that, in my opinion, each cranial model has a certain vocal type which is as much a conformation as are the cerebral hemispheres; that the vocal powers are measured by the gnathic index; that mind and voice are commensurate; and that as the craniofacial angle widens the voice loses in quality and flexibility. I find in man the highest type of vocalisation, and just as we descend in the cranial scale the vocal type degrades into sounds less flexible, less musical, and less capable. These facts apply only in mammals; in birds, insects, &c., there may be quite a different standard of development.

Unlike human speech, the Simian idea is expressed in a single word of one sound, or syllable. For example, the one sound described before, which sounds like *wh-oo-w* as nearly as I can put it into letters, not only means *food*, but anything which is connected with food, all the inflections of the noun *food*, all inflection of the verb *to eat*, the adjective *hungry*, the noun *hunger*, the results obtained from the act, &c., such as to express satisfaction, that it is good, and so on. These ideas are expressed in one radical sound, or root. Sometimes a monkey repeats this one sound as rapidly as to cause the casual observer to mistake them for a series of words. This is easily detected in the phonograph, because we can repeat the sounds at our pleasure and compare any two parts of the record.

I have found it necessary to coin a new word to describe the character of their speech, and as each idea seems to be couched in a single word of one syllable and nearly, indeed, of one letter, I have called it a *monophone*, which is suggestive of its peculiar character. I have experimented with a few green monkeys, but not with very startling results, and it is one of the most trying things in life to get a monkey to talk into a phonograph. He will talk as much as a country squire until you want him to put himself to record in the phonograph, and then he grows as dumb as a milestone, and looks as if he was under penance for having lived.

I have tried many novel experiments with the phonograph in analysing sounds, and they have caused me to halt before I can accept some of the dogmas of philology. I find by reversing the cylinder on the graphophone that sounds are perfectly analysed. I find that the sound *oo*, as in shoot, is the dominant phonic in the speech of both man and ape. I find consonants are generally elided or converted into some other form, and pure vocals, as they are called, are converted into words of three syllables, all of which will be described in the near future.

My desire to induce other workers to enter the field which I have only just discovered, and aid in the task which I have just begun, induces me to state my conclusions in a brief form, that each one of itself may furnish a text, as it were, for the critic and student.

I very naturally expect this subject to elicit the unkind comments of the unlearned, and be derided by many who think they know things that they really do not know. But I trust that men of ability and of integrity will not disdain it as unworthy of their time.

The following will express in a crude way my conclusions:—

1. The Simian words are ambiguous *monotones*.

2. Speech is materialised thought, and thoughts are factors of consciousness.

3. Signs were the first form of speech, and sounds are evolved from them.

4. All animals are capable of expressing as much as they can think.

5. All mammals are capable of emotions, and all emotions capable of expression.

6. All voluntary sounds are the products of thought, and if they convey a meaning to another they perform the functions of human speech.

7. Consciousness is the differentiation of thoughts, thoughts formulate mental words, and they develop into sounds as exponents.

8. Voluntary sounds are the manifestation of thought as matter is of force.

9. Vocal power is commensurate with use, and this by the needs of the mind.

10. The vocal unit is commensurate with the unit of methodic cerebration.

11. The arc of vocalisation will subtend the craniofacial angle.

12. Words are the body of which thoughts are the soul.

III

A short time ago I made arrangements with the superintendent of the Zoological Garden at Central Park, N.Y., to make some experiments with the phonograph and the monkeys contained in that excellent collection of animals. From the vast interest manifested on the part of the reading public, and the scientific world in general, I feel called upon to give a description of some of these experiments, and show to them how I am progressing in the solution of the Simian tongue. Early in the morning I retired to the monkey house, and, for the first time, approached a cage containing four brown Capuchin monkeys, two white-faced Sapajous or Ringtails, one Cudge monkey, and a small Spider monkey, none of which I had ever seen or conversed with before. On approaching the cage I saluted them with the word which I have translated from the Capuchin tongue to mean 'food,' and also, as described in a former article of mine, as being used in a much wider sense, possibly as a kind of 'Shibboleth,' or peace-making term, among them. On delivering this word to them, almost immediately one of them responded to it and came to the front of the cage, on repeating it two or three times more the remaining three came to the front, and on thrusting my fingers through the bars of the cage they took hold of them and began playing with them with great familiarity and apparent pleasure. They seemed to recognise the sound at once, and also to realise that it had been delivered to them by myself. Whether they regarded me as a great ape or monkey, or some other kind of an animal speaking their tongue, or not I am unable to say. Up to this time I had shown them no food, or drink, or anything of the kind; but soon thereafter I secured some apples and carrots and gave them small bits of them in response to their continual request, using this particular sound until I had satisfied those present that they really understood the word that I had used, and that it was properly translated food. This was not only gratifying to me, but doubly so in view of the fact that I satisfied those present who had come to witness these experiments that I was correct in my solution of this word. Then, placing my phonograph in order, I made a record of the sound, and turning the instrument upon a cage containing one small Rhesus monkey, together with two or three other varieties, I recorded a word of the Rhesus monkey which I had believed to correspond in meaning, though quite different in sense, to the Capuchin word for food. I then turned the cylinder and repeated it to some monkeys of the same variety in another cage. Then, on presenting some small bits of apple and carrot, I induced the monkeys in the other cage to use the same sound, which they continually did and appeared to me to be asking for food. The cage contained some eighteen or twenty monkeys, and I took a very accurate record of them, almost in chorus. This was just before and during the breakfast hour; I was satisfied that I had discovered the sound in the Rhesus dialect which meant food, though it was used in a somewhat more restricted sense than the word which I have described as meaning food (and also with a wider meaning) in the Capuchin dialect.

On the same evening there arrived in Central Park a shipment of monkeys brought there from Europe. They were seven in number. At my request they were placed in the upper part of the old Armoury building, entirely out of communication with any other monkeys. They had never seen or heard any of the monkeys in Central Park.

Early on the following morning I repaired to the room in which the monkeys had been placed. In company with me were the superintendent of the Zoological Garden and two or three other gentlemen who had been permitted to come to witness the experiments. I requested them not to offer the monkeys anything to eat, or display anything of the kind, or by any means to attempt to induce them to talk, until I could arrange my phonograph to deliver to them the cylinder which I had recorded on the preceding day. Having arranged my phonograph I repeated this record that I had made in the monkey house. Up to this time there had not been a word spoken or a sound emitted by any of the new arrivals; but immediately upon the reproduction of the record taken in the monkey house they began to respond, using the same sounds, and gave every evidence of understanding the meaning of the sounds delivered through the horn. It is exceedingly difficult to represent this sound by any formula. But as nearly as I can express it in letters it is approximated by the letters nqu-u-w, being the long u, equivalent to double o in the word shoot. One of the most difficult things in the study of the language of the Simian is to find either verbal or literal expressions that will adequately convey the idea of either the meaning of the word or its sound, because in the Simian tongue one word often represents an entire sentence, and this one word is generally composed of sounds which are not usually represented by alphabetic characters; hence the great difficulty. The needs or demands in this particular language have never heretofore caused an alphabet to be invented, although it is possible to invent letters to represent their sounds as it was to invent letters to represent the sounds of the human voice. But as there has never been any use for them before, there have never been any letters invented to represent the Simian sounds. Their peculiar mode of thought gives rise to their peculiar mode of expression, and there are no expressions in the human speech that are equivalent to the simple *monophones* (as I denominated them) in the Simian tongue. I next proceeded to take a record of the new arrivals. They were all of the same species, being Rhesus monkeys. There were three mothers and four babes, one of the babes being an orphan, the mother having died on her passage across the ocean. Of these I succeeded in getting two very excellent records – one of the orphan babe and the other of one in an adjoining compartment. He was exceedingly talkative, very noisy, but quite intelligent for his age. These monkeys do not generally talk or make a noise, except when they really desire to communicate some idea by their sounds. I do not think that they are given to habitually chattering in a meaningless or senseless way, but my opinion is that their chattering is always accompanied with definite ideas and a desire to convey them to others. After having made records of these two young monkeys, I carried the cylinders to the monkeys' house, where I reproduced them on the phonograph, in the presence of the Rhesus monkeys confined there, and found that they gave evidence of understanding; although the great number of them prevented its having the effect that it otherwise would have had, because it was impossible for them to distinguish whether these sounds were made by some of their own number, or some new monkey that had been introduced into the house. The consequence is I did not get their attention in such a marked degree as I have in many other instances. And as I succeeded in getting the attention of the new arrivals, having them to themselves, where they were not interrupted by the continuous babble of the monkey house, I feel thoroughly satisfied that the new word which I have discovered in the Rhesus dialect is indeed the word for food, as used among these monkeys. And I confidently feel that one more step in the direction of the mastery of the Simian tongue has been taken. And I believe this translation to be practically correct and tenable. Remember that these records were taken under very great difficulties, and yet I regard the experiments as being very conclusive. The great difficulty of taking the records, or rather of reproducing them with the desired effect in the presence of so many monkeys, of course can only be appreciated after one has tried these experiments. But where one monkey is alone very much better results can be reached, since in that event you can attract his attention and keep it fixed on what you are trying to do; whereas a number of them occupying the same cage or even the same house are in such close proximity to one another that their chattering and continual talking attract the attention of the monkey upon which you are trying to operate, and thus in a measure defeat your purpose. However, I am thoroughly satisfied with my experiments and their results on my last visit to Central Park.

After an absence of some days I returned to the park, and, entering the monkey house, approached the cage which contained my little brown Capuchin friend. There were a good many visitors in the house at the time, but on the instant of my entering the door my little Simian friend recognised me and immediately set up quite a howl, begging me to come to him. I went to the cage, giving him my hand to play with: he gave every evidence of great pleasure at my visit. There was another little monkey of the same species in the same cage with him, who had shown some disposition to become friendly with me, and on former visits had manifested some interest in me. On this occasion he came playfully to the bars of the cage and desired to share the pleasure of my visit with his Simian brother, but this was denied him by the first monkey (whose name was McGinty), who pounced upon him immediately and drove him away, as he also did the other monkeys in the cage, monopolising my entire society himself. He refused under any conditions to allow any other inmates of the cage to receive any of my caresses, or any of the food that I had for them. I have made a good many observations among the Spider monkeys, but they are not very intelligent, and possess only a very limited number of sounds. Their vocal powers are very inferior, and their sounds exceedingly ambiguous. They are well disposed and docile, but their language is almost as far inferior to that of the brown Capuchin as the brown Capuchin's appears to be below the Chimpanzee's, and as the Chimpanzee's appears to be below the lowest order of human speech.

For the past month I have been making records in the Zoological Garden at Washington at such times and with such subjects as I could find.

In the collection in that Garden is still to be found old 'Prince,' the original grey Macacus from which I made the first record in the phonograph that I ever made. I regard his language, however, as very far inferior to that of the brown Capuchin which, as I believed a year ago, was superior to that of any other monkey. In the Garden here I also found some four or five Capuchins, some of them very good specimens, all except one being quite young. The brightest one in the collection is a little brown monkey, whose name is 'Pedro,' he is exceedingly clever and communicative. On my first visit to him a month ago I found him caged with several others. In the same cage was a small Spider monkey who was very fond of playing with little Pedro, and who had a habit of catching him by the tail and dragging him around on the floor. This, Pedro seemed to dislike very heartily. He complained very frequently and very loudly, but to no purpose. The other monkeys seemed to impose upon him, depriving him of his food and all other liberties that a bright little monkey ought to have had in a free country like this. And when I first visited the cage I took his part against the other monkeys, and we soon became friends. He would catch hold of my fingers through the meshes of the cage and chatter and show every mark of appreciation. We soon became quite good friends. A little later I had him placed in a cage to himself, where I have been able to handle him with comparative ease. I have made a splendid phonographic record of his speech. I got him to hold his mouth right up to the tube and talk quite loud. Each succeeding experiment gives me more and more assurance of the ultimate success of my studies. And when I see how many truly scientific people and great scholars and naturalists are firm believers in my theory, I can well afford to ignore the shallow wags who try to say something funny about it. Were it not for such moral support, however, one might feel discouraged at the great tax on time and patience which is necessary to learn even one word of this most singular language. The discovery of the Rhesus word for food has accelerated my efforts and intensified my hopes; and, while it has required many months of labour to learn this one new word, I feel amply rewarded for my pains. I hope very soon to be able to add one more to the list, in which event it will be duly announced. I shall soon furnish a full description of my work here at Washington.